NEW PROCLAMAT

Year C, 2004

Easter through Pentecost

Neil Elliott

Richard P. Carlson

Jeanne Stevenson-Moessner

Lucy Lind Hogan

Harold W. Rast, editor

FORTRESS PRESS

Minneapolis

NEW PROCLAMATION
Year C, 2004
Easter through Pentecost

The Library of Congress has catalogued this series as follows.
New proclamation year A, 2001–2002 : Advent through Holy Week / Francis J. Moloney . . . [et al.].
      p. cm.
  Includes bibliographical references.
  ISBN 0-8006-4245-7 (alk. paper)
      1. Church year. I. Moloney, Francis J.
  BV30 .N48 2001
  251'.6—dc21
                                                  2001023746

New Proclamation, Year C, 2004, Easter through Pentecost
ISBN 0-8006-4250-3

Manufactured in Canada
07   06   05   04   03   1   2   3   4   5   6   7   8   9   10

NEW PROCLAMATION

CONTENTS

THE SEASON OF PENTECOST
JEANNE STEVENSON-MOESSNER

THE SEASON OF PENTECOST
LUCY LIND HOGAN

PREFACE

New Proclamation continues the time-honored Fortress Press tradition of offering a lectionary preaching resource that provides first-rate biblical exegetical aids for a variety of lectionary traditions.

Thoroughly ecumenical and built around the three-year lectionary cycle, *New Proclamation* focuses on the biblical texts, based on the conviction that those who acquire a deeper understanding of the pericopes in both their historical and liturgical contexts will be motivated to preach engaging and effective sermons. For this reason, the most capable North American biblical scholars and homileticians are invited to contribute to *New Proclamation*.

We have asked the contributors to follow a similar pattern in their presentations but have allowed them to alter and improve that pattern in ways they think might be more helpful to the user. For example, one of the authors in a previous volume began each discussion of the Sunday lections with the Gospel rather than the First Reading, since it is assumed that most users preach on the Gospel reading for the day. In other instances, some authors have chosen to combine the interpretation and response to the texts into one section rather than separating them into two distinct sections.

In general, *New Proclamation* is planned and designed to be user-friendly in the following ways:

- *New Proclamation* is published in two volumes per year, designed for convenience. The present volume covers the lections for the second half of the church year, Easter through Pentecost, which culminates in Christ the King Sunday.
- The two-volume format offers a larger, workbook-style page with a lay-flat binding and space for making notes.

- Each season of the church year is prefaced by an introduction that provides insights into the background and spiritual significance of the period.
- The application of biblical texts to contemporary situations is an important concern of each contributor. Exegetical work is concise, and thoughts on how the texts address today's world and our personal situations have a prominent role.
- Although the psalms ("Responsive Reading") are infrequently used as preaching texts, brief comments on each assigned psalm are included so that the preacher can incorporate reflections also on these in the sermon. The psalms, for the most part, represent the congregation's response to the first reading and are not intended as another reading.
- Boxed quotations in the margins help signal important themes in the texts for the day.
- The material for Year C is here dated specifically for the year 2004 for easier coordination with other dated lectionary materials.
- These materials can be adapted for uses other than for corporate worship on the day indicated. They are well suited for adult discussion groups or personal meditation and reflection.

It is important to keep in mind that the Gospel is the formative principle of the lectionary and that most sermons are based on it. From the First Sunday of Advent to Trinity Sunday of each year, the Old Testament reading is closely related to the Gospel reading for the day. However, from the first Sunday after Trinity Sunday to the end of the year (Christ the King), provision has been made for two patterns of reading the Old Testament in the RCL: (1) paired readings in which the Old Testament and Gospel readings are closely related, and (2) semi-continuous Old Testament readings that are not necessarily related to the Gospel.

We are grateful to our contributors—Neil Elliott, Richard P. Carlson, Jeanne Stevenson-Moessner, and Lucy Lind Hogan—for their insights and for their commitment to effective Christian preaching. We hope that you find in this volume ideas, stimulation, and encouragement for your ministry of proclamation.

HAROLD W. RAST

THE SEASON OF EASTER

NEIL ELLIOTT

"Alleluia. Christ is risen!"
"The Lord is risen indeed. Alleluia!"

With these phrases, the church joyfully proclaims our risen Lord. The simplicity of the exchange condenses the rich, complex, and powerful hope that is the vital heart of Christian life and practice. Jesus' resurrection is not merely one particularly important doctrine among others, nor is it simply the occasion of especially poignant sentiment for Christians. We proclaim that in this event we see the future of all human living. We confess that Christ's resurrection reveals the power of God to shape our common destiny, in starkest contrast to the designs and machinations of this world's ruling powers (1 Cor. 2:7-10).

In other words, Easter is the source and inspiration of our common hope, not merely the object of our belief. We rightly celebrate the resurrection by calling attention beyond it. As Jürgen Moltmann has written, Easter is meaningful "only if its framework is the history which the resurrection itself throws open: the history of the liberation of human beings and nature from the power of death."[1] If we seek to memorialize that resurrection as an event of the increasingly distant past, we obscure its very nature as a sign—for Christians, *the* sign—of God's ever-creative, life-giving power in our world.

EASTER IS THE SOURCE AND INSPIRATION OF OUR COMMON HOPE, NOT MERELY THE OBJECT OF OUR BELIEF.

Easter poses particular challenges to all who plan and preside over a community's worship. On one hand, it is natural to want to follow the austerities of Lent and the solemnity of Holy Week with extraordinary exuberance: with extravagances of light and color, sound, scent, and movement. The danger, of course, is that our efforts to be more festive than usual may simply call attention to themselves by way of contrast with what preceded them. Ritual observance works best when it draws us into contact with the reality it seeks to proclaim; but it fails if it draws attention to itself.

The ancient maxim *lex orandi, lex credendi* (the law of prayer is the law of belief, or, more simply, we believe what we pray) is nowhere as relevant as it is with regard to the celebration of Easter. If in our worship we act out a sort of theatrical relief that Jesus is "not still dead," we run the risk of reducing Easter to a sort of "happy ending" to what we think is the tragedy of Good Friday. But the reality we proclaim is much greater than a sort of theological Groundhog Day! Easter marks for us the awesome beginning of God's new and just creation. It is *that* hope that we rightly proclaim and celebrate.

On the other hand, it may be hard for us to perceive God's new creation amid the grinding misery, futility, and injustice of our world. Meanwhile, the routines of the Easter "shopping season" surround us with mind-dulling banality and an emotionally desolate sentimentality. How strongly our environment encourages us to regard this feast, and this season, as nothing more than a time to put on a brave face in the midst of an unchanging world, to muster a little more cheeriness in conversation, whether or not we feel cheerful! If we carry these assumptions into worship, even unconsciously, we may convey to others that all any of us can do is to make the best of the desperate situation that is human life. Easter, however, is about hope.

In reaction to what they regard as a too-literal understanding of the resurrection, one that focuses too narrowly on the physical resuscitation of Jesus, some interpreters have argued for what they call a "metaphorical" understanding of Easter. John Dominic Crossan writes that "Christian faith experiences the *continuation* of divine empowerment through Jesus . . . after his death and burial." According to Crossan, this same faith was already "there beforehand among Jesus' first followers." The community that would ultimately produce the sayings source "Q" spoke not of resurrection "but of unbroken and abiding presence," the presence in Jesus of the Wisdom of God.[2] Similarly, Marcus Borg writes that Luke's account of an encounter with the risen Christ on the road to Emmaus (Luke 24) is "a metaphorical narrative with rich resonances of meaning," the heart of which is the claim that "the risen Christ journeys with us," and that we, like the first followers, can continue "to experience Jesus as a living reality after his death." That is, the heart of Easter faith is the "religious experience" of the presence of God, which meant, for the first disciples, "experiences of the same presence they had known in Jesus during his historical lifetime."[3]

The liability in this "metaphorical" understanding of the resurrection is that it risks reducing the horizon of Easter to the limits of my own "religious experience." In it, I hear the subtle suggestion that "resurrection" has to do only with my own inner perceptions; that it says fundamentally nothing about the larger world, which may go on with business as usual. My own understanding of Easter is shaped much more decisively by the proclamation of the apostle Paul, who regarded this world as simultaneously "subjected to futility" and awaiting a glorious liberation from decay, destruction, and the power of death (Rom. 8:18-21). For Paul, what we might call our "inner experience" is a matter of "groaning inwardly while we wait for adoption, the redemption of our bodies"; it is a matter of enduring "hope" (Rom. 8:22-25). Jesus himself did more than teach his disciples to accept and appreciate his presence with them; he taught them to hope, pray, and work for more—for the coming of the reign of God—just as we do so today (Matt. 6:9-13).[4]

The hope to which Christ's resurrection calls us is greater than the consolation we have known in any moment of spiritual intensity, however sublime. Easter is not a consolation prize for the wretched, the meek assurance that God is somehow present to us as we endure a world of suffering. Rather, it is the preeminent Christian sign that God wills another world, a world freed from the powers of sin and death. Our liturgical action needs to show forth that reality and draw us toward and into it.

Reading the Gospel Texts

If *hope for God's future* is at the heart of Easter,[5] then the Christian preacher faces a very particular challenge in Gospel texts that focus attention on an Event (or, as they narrate it, a series of events) *in the past.* Christian liturgy always unites the remembrance of Jesus' past with the expectation for God's future. How important it is, then, to seek a standpoint within the Gospel texts from which we may look outward and beyond them, to the horizon of hope which they project.

I presume two key observations from biblical scholarship in the pages that follow. First, the Easter accounts given in the four canonical Gospels and in Paul (in 1 Corinthians 15) differ so widely from one another as to be irreconcilable.[6] Basic questions find different answers in our sources: Who saw Jesus first? Did Jesus appear to his disciples first in Galilee or in Jerusalem? Did women see the risen Jesus or simply hear that he had been raised; did they respond in faith or with fear? Did the early appearances take place at the empty tomb or not? A word of caution, then, to preachers: any attempt to give an authoritative account of "what really happened" on Easter Sunday may end up preoccupied with hypothetical reconstructions of events—ones that may beg more questions than they answer!—more than with proclaiming the resurrection. Further, those differences are most readily explained as expressions of each Gospel writer's overriding theological concerns. The text choices we make—or rather, the choices our lectionaries have made for us!—will place us squarely within the theological perspective of one or another Evangelist.

The second observation has to do with the earliest form—and, more importantly, the earliest intent—of the Easter proclamation. As Ernst Käsemann wrote in discussing the earliest *kerygma* before Paul, "the raising of Jesus from the dead counted from the outset as an enthronement and the Easter appearances were conceived of as being manifestations of the one who was already exalted."[7] We know that decades before the Gospels were composed, believers shared visions of the risen Jesus. We also know that some, at least, of these visions were *heavenly encounters with an already exalted Jesus*: so Paul, with considerable irony, describes his own heavenly vision in 2 Cor. 12:1-4, to which we may compare Stephen's vision in Acts 7:54-60 and John's vision in Rev. 1:9-20. Only later did the feet-on-the-ground accounts that we read in the Gospels come to predominate, apparently for apologetic reasons, as an emerging orthodox Christian church struggled against overly spiritualized interpretations of the resurrection.[8] This means, again, that the preacher's effort to recover the full eschatological horizon of Easter may often require looking up from, and out from, the closer perspective of the Gospel texts.

THE RESURRECTION OF OUR LORD / EASTER DAY (EARLY SERVICE)

APRIL 11, 2004

The Episcopal *Book of Common Prayer* (BCP) offers the option of an early service—for example, a "sunrise" service—distinct from the principal service of Easter morning. That service, like the Easter Vigil itself (*Book of Common Prayer*, 285-95), uses Matt. 28:1-10, a passage that begins with dawn on Easter morning, and is thus especially appropriate for an early service.

FIRST READING

Use one of the Old Testament readings from the Vigil.

RESPONSIVE READING
PSALM 114 (BCP)

This psalm praises God for the powerful deliverance of Israel from Egypt; its use on Easter morning evokes the larger Paschal context of the day. It is appropriately paired with the reading of the account of the deliverance at the Reed Sea in Exod. 14:10—15:1 (one of the texts that may be chosen for the Great Vigil). The psalm evokes other mythic themes: the retreat of "the sea" (an ancient symbolization of chaos), the disruptive power of God's appearing (mountains skip, the earth trembles).

SECOND READING
ROMANS 6:3-11 (BCP)

Paul's baptismal exhortation has a special place among the Easter readings, being the first reading listed for the Great Vigil that is not optional. Here Paul—alone among the New Testament authors—describes baptism as a dying with Christ and being raised to "newness of life" with him.

The chorus of an old hymn declares, "You ask me how I know he lives; he lives within my heart!" A more Pauline expression might be: "We know Christ lives because we live in him." More than any other early Christian author, Paul makes brilliantly clear that the message of God's triumph—the *euangelion*—is not just a story about what happened to Jesus: it announces a new age for all who are in Christ, a "new creation" (2 Cor. 5:17).

Paul appears to be concerned in this letter to prevent misunderstandings of Christian baptism among the Roman Christians. Baptism marks our entering into a relationship of peace with God. It even constitutes a "boast," not based on any merits we possess but in our *hope* of sharing the glory of God (5:1-5). Now Paul declares that our "dying" and "rising" with Christ in baptism mean nothing less than a transfer from one "lordship" or "dominion," that of sin, to another, the lordship of God, whom we serve as "instruments of righteousness" (6:13).

THE GOSPEL

MATTHEW 28:1-10 (BCP)

The reading reports that Mary Magdalene and "the other Mary" (certainly the mother of James and Joseph named in 27:56 and 27:61) were the first witnesses to the empty tomb and, indeed—in contrast to the other Synoptic Gospels—to the risen Jesus himself.

Matthew provides "special effects" to increase the drama of the narrative. These include an earthquake and the descent of an angel from heaven to roll back the stone (28:2; in Mark and Luke the women discover the stone "rolled away" and are addressed by "a young man" or "two men"). Recall that in narrating the crucifixion, Matthew also offered not only "darkness over all the land" and the tearing of the temple veil (27:45, 51, with parallels in Mark and Luke), but also another earthquake (27:51-52) and the spontaneous resurrection of saints who erupted from their tombs and entered Jerusalem to appear "to many" (27:53). In that earlier scene, those astonishing events were enough to persuade the Roman guards that Jesus "was the Son of God!" (27:54). Here, the earthquake and the angel's appearance serve only to terrify the soldiers guarding the tomb (28:4). The angel reassures the women and urges them to go and announce Jesus' resurrection to his disciples, who will meet him in Galilee (28:7). While Matthew shares that command with Mark (16:7), Matthew reports that the women immediately comply "with fear and great joy"; Mark, infamously, ends the Gospel with the disturbing report that the women fled the tomb and "said nothing to anyone, for they were afraid" (16:8). Only Matthew will narrate the appearance of Jesus to his disciples on a mountaintop in Galilee (the commissioning scene in 28:16-20).

To those familiar with the full repertoire of Gospel accounts, Matthew's report of Jesus meeting the women (vv. 9-10) seems puzzling. Jesus' command to go and inform the disciples seems redundant after the angel's command in v. 7. The report of the encounter is terse. The women say nothing to Jesus. Now we are not even told that they go to do what they have been commanded: Matthew will never report, as does Luke 24:9-11, that the women relay what they have seen and heard to the male disciples. Their only response is to prostrate themselves in worship (*prosekynēsan* in Greek), as will the disciples in Galilee (28:17).

That response is unique to Matthew: while other Gospels report that the disciples are astonished by the appearance of the risen Jesus, or that they rejoiced to see him, only Matthew specifies that they *worshiped* him. The contrast is even more striking when we observe that of the three Gospels that recount appearances of the risen Jesus to his disciples, only in Matthew are the disciples given nothing to say. While the effect is less personal, less intimate than in the other Gospels, it is also solemn. The disciples' task is simply to worship and to obey the risen Lord.

> THE WOMEN CAME TO THE TOMB PREPARED TO PROVIDE THE CUSTOMARY CARE FOR THE DEAD. THEY WERE NOT PREPARED—WHO IS?—TO ENTER A NEW WORLD IN WHICH THE DEAD DO NOT STAY DEAD AND THE POWER OF DEATH IS BROKEN.

Responding to the Texts

In these readings, the memory of Easter morning's astonishment converges powerfully with the newness of life in which we are called to walk. The women came to the tomb prepared to provide the customary care for the dead. They were not prepared—who is?—to enter a new world in which the dead do not stay dead and the power of death is broken.

Our baptism into Christ calls us to live in that world. The Baptismal Covenant in the BCP calls us to "renounce the evil powers of this world which corrupt and destroy the creatures of God" (p. 302). No task is more important for us than to discern the form those powers take today and marshal the resources the Spirit has given us together to resist them.

THE RESURRECTION OF OUR LORD / EASTER DAY (PRINCIPAL SERVICE)

APRIL 11, 2004

REVISED COMMON	EPISCOPAL (BCP)	ROMAN CATHOLIC
Acts 10:34-43	Acts 10:34-43	Acts 10:34a, 37-43
or Isa. 65:17-25	or Isa. 51:9-11	
Ps. 118:1-2, 14-24	Ps. 118:14-29	Ps. 118:1-2, 16-17, 22-23
	or 118:14-17, 22-24	
1 Cor. 15:19-26	Col. 3:1-4	Col. 3:1-4
or Acts 10:34-43	or Acts 10:34-43	or 1 Cor. 5:6b-8
John 20:1-18	Luke 24:1-10	John 20:1-9
or Luke 24:1-12		

We Christians live by story; indeed, we live *in* the story of God's redemptive work in our world and in our lives. At the center of our eucharistic worship is *anamnesis*, "remembering"—not just Jesus' words and actions at the Last Supper, but the whole of the "mighty acts of God," beginning at creation itself. We place ourselves in the midst of that story when we proclaim "the mystery of faith," confessing that "Christ has died, Christ is risen, Christ will come again."

We do more than simply recite events from the hallowed past. Our liturgical storytelling is something we do to situate ourselves in a universe claimed by God. Naturally enough, we tell stories of the discovery of Jesus' empty tomb and of his encounters with his disciples today. Yet we also begin to hear readings from the book of Acts, readings that show us the earliest disciples' response to Jesus' resurrection, the ways they shaped their common life around a startling, new, and empowering reality.

FIRST READING
ISAIAH 65:17-25 (RCL, alt.)

The so-called Third Isaiah, chapters 56–66, is not an identifiable person but a collection of oracles from the period following the return of exiles from Babylon to Judah. These oracles reveal the often bitter struggles of the Jerusalem community as returning exiles under Persian auspices, and how the now largely disfranchised "people of the land" struggled to realize the promises of the Second Isaiah (chapters 40–55). Throughout Third Isaiah a prophetic anguish sounds, decrying the injustice that continued in a nation only superficially reformed. The first verses of Isaiah 65 represent the LORD's bitter indictment of "a rebellious people" who persist in offensive ritual practices, and contrasting assurances of blessing to God's "servants" who will be satisfied with food and drink (65:13-16).

Verses 17-25 evoke a vision of "new heavens and a new earth" (compare Rev. 21:1). Elements from the earlier Isaiah tradition are woven in: a command to forget "the former things" (65:17, compare 43:18), the vision of wolf and lamb feeding together (65:25, compare 11:6-9). Strikingly, in the midst of exalted imagery appears the mundane promise: God's people will live in their own houses and eat the food they themselves have grown (65:21-22). This simple yet profound vision of *shalom*—the beauty of ordinary life, free from oppression and exploitation, where labor leads naturally to satisfaction—touches the heart's deepest aspirations.

This passage points to the greater purposes of God behind and beyond Easter: toward the fulfillment of human living and the liberation of human labor. It reminds those who celebrate God's power in the resurrection that the risen Jesus cannot be the sole center of attention, the "guest of honor" on this day; rather, he is the host who invites us to a much greater banquet at which human hunger will be satisfied.

ISAIAH 51:9-11 (BCP, alt)

This short reading is a rousing cry, calling on the LORD to "put on strength" and act. God is addressed in terms borrowed from ancient mythology that depicted creation as a cosmic combat against a sea monster: "Was it not you who cut Rahab in pieces, who pierced the dragon?" (51:9). Yet that imagery is now turned to evoke the Exodus as well: "Was it not you . . . who made the depths of the sea a way for the redeemed to cross over?" (51:10). Here again the lectionary choices strike deeper chords beneath and behind the Easter story, evoking a broader horizon: the triumph of God's power and purpose for all creation.

ACTS 10:34-43 (RCL, BCP);
ACTS 10:34a, 37-43 (RC)

The view that the *kerygma,* or apostolic preaching, had a specific structure and content very early on depends on several New Testament passages, including this one from Acts. The RCL and BCP offer, as an option for either the first or second reading, Peter's brief summary sermon to the Roman centurion Cornelius. The scene is a crucial one for Luke, who wants to demonstrate that the

Gentile church was from the beginning made up of faithful, righteous Gentiles like this "devout man who feared God" (10:2). Luke also presents the beginnings of Gentile Christianity as an innovation duly authorized by the chief of the apostles, Peter, responding to the initiative of the Holy Spirit (who falls upon everyone present before Peter is even finished speaking, 10:44!). Peter's solemn declaration that "God shows no partiality, but in every nation anyone who fears him and does what is right is acceptable to him" (10:34-35, NRSV) is the heart of Luke's theological vision. But Luke also wants it clear that this vision was shared by "the circumcised believers" from Jerusalem (10:45-46). No less an observant Jew than Peter himself—who has already three times refused to obey what *seems* to be the voice of God, coming to him in a perplexing vision and commanding him to eat nonkosher food (10:9-17)—is prepared to follow the Spirit's lead and welcome these righteous Gentiles. His action, Luke seems to suggest, is thoroughly "kosher." It also comes well *before* Paul first ventures to speak to Gentiles about Jesus (13:44-52), serving another of Luke's apologetic concerns—to defend Paul against charges of being a renegade Jew (compare 18:32; 21:21-22).[9]

While Peter's speech may reflect the pattern of much early Christian preaching, it also reveals Luke's interests, especially in setting the apostles forward as witnesses of the risen Christ: "God raised him on the third day and allowed him to appear, not to all the people but to us who were chosen by God as witnesses, and who ate and drank with him after he rose from the dead" (10:40-41). Here Luke reinforces the importance he assigned to the period between resurrection and ascension, when Jesus "gave instructions through the Holy Spirit to the apostles whom he had chosen," and "presented himself alive to them by many convincing proofs, appearing to them during forty days and speaking about the kingdom of God" (1:2-3).

JESUS' SOJOURN AMONG THE APOSTLES, SHARING IN MEALS WITH THEM, CONSTITUTED THEM—AND, THROUGH THEM, THE CHURCH—AS WITNESSES TO THE RESURRECTION.

At the turn of the second century, that insistence served to promote a form of Christian unity based on continuity with the apostolic tradition. Later, ironically, churches would divide over the question: Just what constitutes continuity with the apostles?

The answer this scene suggests is that Jesus' sojourn among the apostles, sharing in meals with them, constituted them—and, through them, the church—as witnesses to the resurrection. Our own sharing of bread and wine in Jesus' name, and our opening our common life in hospitality to others, may be signs of our own continuity with their apostolic witness. As the apostle Paul wrote, "as often as you eat this bread and drink the cup, you proclaim the Lord's death until he comes" (1 Cor. 11:26).

PSALM 118:1-2, 14-24 (RCL)
PSALM 118:14-29 or 118:14-17, 22-24 (BCP)
PSALM 118:1-2, 16-17, 22-23 (RC)

This psalm gives thanks to God for victory. In the "core" verses present in all three lectionaries, the speaker—very possibly the king—asserts that "I shall not die, but I shall live, and recount the deeds of the LORD" (v. 17). A christological reading of the verse may have brought it into use for Easter. Similarly, vv. 22-23, where the speaker proclaims that "the stone that the builders rejected has become the chief cornerstone," were taken up in earliest Christianity as a prophecy of the rejection of Jesus by others, and of God's surprising vindication of him (see Matt. 21:42; Mark 12:10-11; Luke 20:17; 1 Pet. 2:7).

SECOND READING
1 CORINTHIANS 5:6b-8 (RC, alt.)

Paul rebukes the Corinthians for their "arrogance" and "boasting" because some in the church were apparently undisturbed by the sexual misconduct of one member (5:1). We use an abbreviated form of his admonition in our eucharistic liturgy, at the breaking of the bread: "Christ our passover is sacrificed for us; therefore let us keep the feast." We thus leave out the central thrust of Paul's exhortation—that "malice and evil" have no place at the Lord's table. This day provides an opportunity to give that liturgical exchange greater depth of meaning.

1 CORINTHIANS 15:19-26 (RCL)

In another passage from 1 Corinthians, Paul confronts what he considers an inadequate understanding of Christ's resurrection in the church. Controversy swirls around the extent to which some of the Corinthians held a clear and articulate theology that Paul found offensive.[10] It is at least apparent that some of the more influential members of the church relied on a few theological "slogans" to justify their behavior.

From the present text we may infer that some among the Corinthians denied, not that Jesus was risen, but that he had risen *from the dead*. Recall that earlier in the letter Paul had rebuked their self-satisfaction: "Already you have all you want! Already you have become rich! Quite apart from us you have become kings!" (4:8). Do we, too, in our complacency mistake our privilege and comfort for

God-given gifts, all the while ignoring the needy around us and among us? To the extent that we do, Paul's warning suggests that we fail to understand what Easter is all about. The resurrection was not God's congratulation for a self-made man; it was the vindication of one whose obedience had meant submitting to humiliation and death.

COLOSSIANS 3:1-4 (BCP)

As in Romans 6, this passage speaks of the baptized having been "raised with Christ" (3:1). Nevertheless, the author recognizes that the baptized are not themselves "above, where Christ is, seated at the right hand of God," and that their "life is hidden with Christ in God," to be revealed at Christ's return. Colossians retains more of Paul's reserve regarding the future exaltation of believers than does, for example, Ephesians.

Other important Pauline themes are close at hand: the renunciation of wickedness, which merits the wrath of God but has now been left behind (3:5-7); a new life "in Christ" in which social distinctions no longer carry weight (3:11); and the importance of holy living and mutual regard in the community (3:12-17). (It isn't until 3:18 that the notorious theme of subordination within the patriarchal household, the so-called household code, makes its appearance—one of the features of the letter that has long cast its Pauline authorship into doubt!)

THE GOSPEL

JOHN 20:1-18 (RCL)
JOHN 20:1-9 (RC)

The RCL provides a choice of two Gospel readings, both narrating the discovery at dawn of Jesus' empty tomb: either by women (Luke 24) or by one woman, Mary Magdalene (John 20). The BCP assigns Luke 24 for the principal Sunday service; the Roman Catholic lectionary uses a shorter version of John 20.

The Fourth Gospel narrates, first, Mary Magdalene's discovery (alone) of the tomb with its great stone door "removed" (John 20:1); then, upon her report, Simon Peter and the beloved disciple racing to the tomb and Simon Peter's discovery of the linen garments within (20:2-10); then, Mary Magdalene's encounter with the risen Lord, whom she at first mistakes for a gardener (20:11-18). (The Roman Catholic lectionary does not include this last encounter, in which Mary becomes the first apostle of the resurrection.) The peculiarities of this narrative are notorious and could easily occupy a study group—or distract a congregation from the thrust of a preacher's sermon. Why, for example, is Mary Magdalene alone, only in this Gospel (compare Matt. 28:1-10 and Mark 16:1-8)? Why does John alone narrate the "race" between Simon Peter and the "disciple whom Jesus loved"? Who is "the beloved disciple"? What is the significance of the linen garments within the empty tomb? Why does one disciple believe, while the other does not? When did Mary return to the tomb; why didn't Simon Peter and the beloved disciple see the angels whom she encounters within the tomb? Why doesn't Mary recognize Jesus at first; after she recognizes him later, why can't she touch him? What does he mean, he is "not yet glorified"? What "glorification" takes place between this encounter and the next, in which he does encourage his disciples to touch him (20:19-23)?

These questions seem to defy rational explanation. What is more, these events have little coherence as a sequence. As John Ashton has noted, "to attempt to make sense of 20:1-23 as a continuous narrative . . . is to enter an Alice-in-Wonderland world where one event succeeds another with the crazy logic of a dream." Ashton wisely recommends treating each story as an independent vignette, having its own lesson—its own interpretation of Jesus' resurrection—for the reader;[11] and I will follow that advice.

Mary Comes to the Tomb (20:1-2)

Mary Magdalene has played no significant role in the preceding narrative of Jesus' life in the Fourth Gospel. She was first introduced at the crucifixion (19:25) but was not named in connection with Jesus' burial (19:38-42). Her prominence in this and the following scene suggests, nevertheless, that John expected his readers to recognize her, and may show that he, and they, depend on an already fairly developed Christian tradition that hailed her as first witness to the risen Christ. (Indeed, many scholars believe John relied directly on the other Gospels.) In contrast to the Synoptic accounts, John separates the discovery of the empty tomb at this point from the encounter with angels in 20:11-13. This allows him to represent Mary as an example of resurrection faith (see below).

Two Disciples Come to See the Empty Tomb (20:2-10)

Mary comes to Simon Peter and "the other disciple, the one whom Jesus loved," and tells them her (mis)interpretation of what she has seen: that Jesus' body has been stolen. The two race to the tomb.

While Luke also narrates Peter's running to the tomb and discovery of the linen grave cloths (24:12),[12] the unnamed "disciple whom Jesus loved" is a feature of the Fourth Gospel alone. He first appears at the Last Supper (13:23-25), close enough to Jesus to learn the identity of the betrayer at the table (again, only in John). He stands at the cross with Jesus' mother and is given charge to care for her (19:26-27). After this scene, he appears once more, at the Sea of Tiberias, recognizing the risen Jesus on the shore (21:7), and as the subject of conversation between Jesus and Peter (21:20-23). He is surely the one who stands as source and guarantor of the traditions in the Gospel (the one who "witnesses and has written these things," 21:24; compare 18:15-16). While he clearly has symbolic importance in the Gospel, he is nevertheless apparently a historical figure whose recent death has alarmed some in the Johannine community (thus 21:20-23).

Unfortunately, efforts to identify the "beloved disciple" more closely remain unconvincing; we cannot explain why a figure as prominent as any of the candidates suggested from the Synoptic Gospels would go unnamed here.[13] It is tempting, but finally frustrating, to try homiletically to make the most of supposed differences between the personalities of these two men.

This disciple seems to have been a figure far more important within the Johannine community than outside it, serving as a conveyor of traditions about Jesus. Whatever nascent Christian rivalries may have been encoded in the "competition" between this disciple and Simon Peter (compare 13:21-26 and 21:1-25) are inaccessible to us now. Neither is it clear what we should make of the neatly rolled grave cloths, except that they imply some leisure on the part of the risen Jesus (and would thus serve as a rebuttal to charges that the body had been stolen: compare Matt. 27:62-66; 28:11-15).

THE BELOVED DISCIPLE THUS BECOMES A PROTOTYPE OF THE FAITH OF THE JOHANNINE COMMUNITY, WHO MUST ALSO BELIEVE WITHOUT BEING ABLE TO SEE OR TOUCH JESUS NOW.

The center of this vignette is the beloved disciple's faith (in contrast with Simon Peter's apparent lack of comprehension): "he saw and believed" (20:8). What he "saw," of course, was the evidence of Jesus' absence, which has now been reported to the reader. The beloved disciple thus becomes a prototype of the faith of the Johannine community, who must also believe without being able to see or touch Jesus now. (Compare the story of Thomas, John 20:24-29, in next week's lection.)

These paragraphs thus present us with a curious challenge. It is clear enough that Mary and the "beloved disciple" are significant because of the way they are remembered in the Johannine community. They are presented as disciples who knew Jesus, saw him, touched him, spoke with him; and now they provide a living connection, a mediating link, between the risen Jesus and a community that can no longer know Jesus in those ways. For us, on the other hand, Mary and the beloved disciple cannot function in the same way. They, like the earthly Jesus, belong to a distant past: we do not "know" them as the Fourth Evangelist expected his readers would.

Perhaps our task is not to try to transport ourselves by an exertion of the imagination into contemporaneity with Jesus or Mary or the other disciple whom

Jesus loved. Perhaps our task is to remember and renew those living connections in our own day that tie us to the ancient faith in the risen Lord. Who are the people who have shown us Jesus?

Mary Encounters the Risen Jesus (20:11-18)

Mary has apparently returned to the tomb (but when? alone, or with others?). By separating the discovery of the opened tomb from the conversation with angels (who announce the resurrection in the Synoptics), John is able to heighten the drama of Mary's coming to resurrection faith. Here, unlike the Synoptics, the presence of angels in the tomb does nothing to break through Mary's grief and lack of understanding (20:13). Even Jesus' address to her does not cut through the fog until he calls her by name.

The initial failure to recognize the risen Jesus and the inability to lay hold of his body are themes familiar to us from Luke's account of the two on the road to Emmaus (24:13-35). Contrast the ease with which the women take hold of Jesus' feet and worship him in Matt. 28:9! It is simply impossible to reconcile all these divergent accounts (along with Paul's heated argument in 1 Corinthians 15) into a single understanding of Jesus' resurrected body. Even John's story is not internally consistent: Jesus tells Mary he is "not yet glorified," yet he has already pronounced his own "glorification" at the Last Supper (13:31, "now the Son of Man has been glorified"; 17:10, "I have been glorified"—in the disciples). Later that evening he apparently has no qualms bidding his (male?) disciples touch him (20:19-23). John Ashton asks rhetorically, "Did Jesus go up and spend an hour or two in heaven, only to redescend that very same evening for a visit to the disciples?"—highlighting the absurdity to which we are driven if we seek a smooth, consistent narrative here.[14]

Even more remarkable, Jesus' declaration to Mary clearly implies an interval between his resurrection (which thus becomes a strictly earthly event) and his exaltation to heaven. While this apparently tears asunder the unity of resurrection and exaltation in the earliest Christian *kerygma* (see above), it replicates the resurrection-ascension sequence that Luke presents and which he may have invented (Acts 1:1-11). In Luke, however, the forty-day interval between these two "stages" serves a clear theological agenda, forming the apostolic band, and them alone, as Jesus' eyewitnesses. No such purpose is served in John, where the empowering and incorporation of the disciples into Jesus are announced as accomplished already at the Last Supper.

What purpose, then, is served by Jesus' warning to Mary not to hold him? The temptation has often proved irresistible to find some inadequacy in Mary's motives. Surely Jesus rebukes her because she can't let him go; she doesn't understand that he cannot belong to her in the way she desires. But efforts to psychologize Mary as emotionally or even erotically obsessed with Jesus (as, for example, in the musical *Jesus Christ Superstar*) are dubious, at best, revealing more about our modern preoccupations and prejudices than about the beliefs of the Johannine community. There is not a hint of disappointment in Mary's response as she rushes to obey her Lord (v. 18). There is genuine affection and tenderness in the scene, however! Jesus is in haste: he is on his way to the Father and must speed Mary on her way to announce his exaltation to the disciples (v. 17). Perhaps we should perceive the force of the scene not in Jesus' refusal of Mary's touch but in the time he takes, despite his don't-slow-me-down urgency, for this tender exchange with Mary.

Note, further, that the progression from Mary's initial failure to understand ("they have taken the Lord," vv. 2, 13, 15), to her partial recognition ("Rabbouni!" Teacher! v. 16), to a full confession of Jesus' identity as the one sent from God ("I have seen the Lord," v. 18) parallels other characters in John's Gospel: the woman at the well in Samaria (4:7-42), the man born blind (9:1-41), Martha of Bethany (11:20-27). In all these stories the characters come to recognize Jesus' identity through a process of discovery over time, in some cases despite challenges or outright hostility. In each case, Jesus' word is a sufficient basis for faithful response. The Samaritan woman and her neighbors come to confess that "this is truly the Savior of the world" without Jesus having miraculously provided water. After he receives his sight, the man born blind is moved from initial ignorance regarding Jesus ("I do not know where he is") to provisional faith ("he is a prophet," "a man from God") to full faith ("Lord, I believe"), in part by the hostility of the Pharisees but also by Jesus' word, "the one speaking with you is he" (the Son of Man). And Martha professes her faith that Jesus is "the Messiah, the Son of God," before Lazarus is raised. Here, Mary Magdalene declares her faith ("I have seen the Lord") on the basis of Jesus' word that he is ascending to his Father—nothing more (20:17-18).

> THE POWER OF HIS APPEARANCE TO MARY IS IN NO SMALL PART IN THE TENDERNESS OF THE SCENE; HERE AS ELSEWHERE, THIS GOSPEL PROVIDES THE MOST INTIMATE OF OUR PORTRAITS OF JESUS.

In recent years, much has been made of Mary Magdalene as the "first witness of the resurrection" and the "first apostle," based (by necessity) on John's account. We should bear in mind that in the Fourth Gospel Mary is not the only character, nor is she the only woman, to hold this kind of significance. Others—like the unnamed Samaritan woman, or Martha of Bethany—were also able to recognize Jesus' identity as Lord, even before the events of Easter. In this Gospel, it is not clear what advantage the witnesses to the risen Jesus have over other disciples, who "believe though they have not seen" (20:29). The power of his appearance to Mary is in no small part in the tenderness of the scene; here as elsewhere, this Gospel provides the most intimate of our portraits of Jesus.

LUKE 24:1-12 (RCL, alt.)
LUKE 24:1-10 (BCP)

Luke's account of Easter morning brings "the women who had come with [Jesus] from Galilee" (23:55)—Mary Magdalene, Joanna, Mary the mother of James, and "others" (24:10)—to the tomb again, to anoint his body with spices after the Sabbath (23:56). The women enter the tomb and find it empty (as in Mark; women do not make this discovery in Matthew or John). They prostrate themselves at the appearance of two men in dazzling apparel, whose question is the heart of Luke's story: "Why do you seek the living among the dead?"

Because Luke has placed all the appearances of the risen Jesus in or around Jerusalem—an important pivot for his plot[15]—he cannot allow Jesus to meet his disciples in Galilee (as he does in Matt. 28:7, 10, 16-20; Mark 16:7). In Luke, all that has happened in Galilee, as the two men at the tomb remind the women, was Jesus' warning to his disciples that the Son of Man must suffer death and be raised (v. 6; compare 9:22). It is important for Luke that Jesus' death was predicted by Israel's scriptures: Jesus will rebuke the two on the road to Emmaus for not believ-ing "all that the prophets have spoken" about this necessity (vv. 25-27) and will "open the scriptures" to them (v. 32), as he will do later for the eleven disciples at table

> DO WE LIVE IN A WORLD IN WHICH GOD'S POWER TO RAISE THE DEAD IS ACTIVE?

(vv. 44-45). Only Luke reports that the male disciples did not believe the women's report (v. 11)—an unedifying note (perhaps this is the reason the BCP drops it!), but one that might originally have served an apologetic purpose for the early church.[16] Otherwise, Luke is interested in depicting women as examples of faith (though usually in "supporting" roles!) throughout Luke and Acts.[17]

While many people find it devotionally powerful to try to imagine themselves "back" into these stories as participants, it may be more important—even urgent—for us to discern what these stories can tell us about the world in which we live today. Do we live in a world in which God's power to raise the dead is active? Does the answer change the way we live our lives?

THE RESURRECTION OF OUR LORD / EASTER DAY (EVENING SERVICE)

APRIL 11, 2004

REVISED COMMON	EPISCOPAL (BCP)	ROMAN CATHOLIC
Isa. 25:6-9	Acts 5:29a, 30-32 or Dan. 12:1-3	*As for the principal service*
Psalm 114	Psalm 114 *or* 136 or 118:14-17, 22-24	*As for the principal service*
1 Cor. 5:6b-8	1 Cor. 5:6b-8 or Acts 5:29a, 30-32	*As for the principal service*
Luke 24:13-49	Luke 24:13-35	Luke 24:13-35

All three lectionaries appoint for this evening service the wonderful narrative, unique to Luke's Gospel, in which two disheartened followers of Jesus meet a stranger on the road to Emmaus and discover that he is their risen Lord. Since their discovery comes at the evening meal, the story is especially appropriate for an evening service, and especially for a Eucharist. The climax of Luke's story, in 24:30-31, shapes the prayer occasionally spoken at our Eucharists: "Be known to us in the breaking of the bread."

FIRST READING
ISAIAH 25:6-9 (RCL)

This amazing passage offers a vision of a bountiful future meal in the very presence of God. The breathtaking promises given here—that God will "wipe away the tears from all faces" and remove the disgrace of the people of God—are taken up again at the end of our Bibles (see Rev. 21:3-4). The liturgical movement's rediscovery in the twentieth century of a broader eschatological vision as the proper horizon of our eucharistic practice points us to texts like this one. Note that the vision is not only of communion with God, but of an end to the dominion of death over the nations of the earth. What an extraordinarily powerful vision to proclaim when people have gathered to celebrate a Eucharist in the name of the risen Lord!

DANIEL 12:1-3 (BCP, alt.)

Part of the cryptic prophecy of the end of the book of Daniel, these verses are the earliest clear reference to the resurrection of the dead in the Bible. "Michael, the great prince" and protector of Israel, appeared already in 11:13-14 as a heavenly champion of Israel, confronted by a heavenly adversary, the "prince of the kingdom of Persia." Here the origins of the belief in resurrection in the Jewish apocalypticism of the Hellenistic age are obvious. So is the character of resurrection, not as our individual fate after we die, but as the vindication of God's righteous who have died.

RESPONSIVE READING
PSALM 114 (RCL; BCP)

See the remarks for the early service option, above.

PSALM 136 (BCP, alt.)

The pattern of this psalm is a series of thanksgivings and what appears to be a congregational response, "his steadfast love endures forever." The psalm—or a portion of it—may be recited that way for worship. On the other hand, the repetitive pattern leads to affirming God's striking down the firstborn of Egypt (v. 10) or the deaths and dispossession of the kings arrayed against Israel (vv. 17-22) as "the steadfast love" of God, something to which some congregations may object!

PSALM 118:14-17, 22-24 (BCP, alt.)

See the remarks for the day's principal service, above.

SECOND READING
ACTS 5:29a, 30-32 (BCP, alt.)

At an early point in Luke's account of the early church—when the apostles were gaining tremendous popularity but were regarded with some apprehension (5:12-13)—Luke reports that the high priest and the Sadducees "arrested the apostles" and imprisoned them. That night an angel sets them free and sends them back into the temple to proclaim the gospel (5:17-21). Arrested a second time, the apostles are brought before the council (i.e., the Sanhedrin) and ordered to cease their activity.

Luke puts onto Peter's lips the stirring reply, "We must obey God rather than any human authority!" (5:29b). That this retort is omitted from the lection is due not to the inclination of the lectionary's crafters to avoid a potentially subversive message but to focus attention on the summarizing narrative that follows, without the distraction of having to recite all that went before. On the other hand, preachers may wish to describe the preceding events and read the whole text: after all, bearing witness to the resurrection can have dramatic consequences!

1 CORINTHIANS 5:6b-8 (BCP, alt.)

See the remarks for the day's principal service, above.

THE GOSPEL
LUKE 24:13-49 (RCL);
LUKE 24:13-35 (BCP, RC)

While Luke's story is well known and much loved, the haze of familiarity may blind us to important motifs that bear deeper examination. We're accustomed, for example, to calling this the "Road to Emmaus" story, but it is much more to Luke's point to call it "the road *away from Jerusalem*." After all, the two disciples, otherwise unknown to us (only one is even named here: Cleopas), are leaving Jerusalem in abject despair. The one in whom they had placed their hopes has been put to death.

We should not disparage those hopes as too "this-worldly" or narrowly ethnic or "Jewish." Neither does Luke suggest in any way that their faith in Jesus as "a prophet mighty in deed and word before God and all the people" (v. 19) is inadequate. Jesus *is* such a prophet in Luke. Similarly, the disciples' poignant cry, "we had hoped that he was the one to redeem Israel" (v. 21), picks up the words of prophecy uttered at the very beginning of Luke's Gospel (1:54-55; 1:68-79; 2:32). For Luke, Jesus *is* the one who will redeem Israel.

When Jesus later rebukes the two, it is not for harboring false hopes, but for being "slow of heart" to trust God to fulfill those hopes (24:25). Similarly, when Luke's story resumes at the beginning of the Acts of the Apostles, the larger band of disciples ask Jesus, "Lord, is this the time when you will restore the kingdom to Israel?" (1:6). Jesus' reply is not, "Give up that misguided expectation!" but rather

"Wait": "you will receive power when the Holy Spirit has come upon you" (1:8).

Luke's point is that these two disciples' hearts have given way not to false hope but to needless despair. They have taken the execution of Jesus at the hands of the "chief priests and leaders" of the Jerusalem régime as the final word on Jesus. But God has the final word in this story not only by raising Jesus from the dead but by empowering his disciples to go forward in his name (in the Acts of the Apostles).

Alone among the Gospels, Luke invests his narration of appearances of the risen Jesus with a concern for the interpretation of prophecy. Jesus rebukes the two on the road for failing to understand the "necessity" of the Messiah's death before his vindication by God (his "entry into glory," v. 26). That is, they have failed to "believe all that the prophets have declared!" Luke then reports that "beginning with Moses and all the prophets, he interpreted to them the things about himself in all the scriptures" (v. 27; compare vv. 44-45).

Luke never says just which scriptures Jesus supposedly discussed, or how he read them as referring to himself. Today we recognize that Jewish scripture in fact contains no explicit "prophecy" of the Messiah's death; scholars doubt even the possibility of that concept having been current in Judaism before Jesus. We may also recognize that Luke has attributed to Jesus himself the "messianic exegesis," practiced after his death by the early church as they found "prophecies" to Jesus' life, death, and resurrection in unlikely passages from the Jewish scriptures.[18] These "discovered" prophecies came to seem obvious to what we might call the perfect hindsight of the early church. But that they were not *universally* self-evident—to say the least!—is clear from such ancient texts as Justin Martyr's "Dialogue with Trypho" (Trypho was a Jewish exegete).[19]

Interestingly, while Luke *asserts* that Jesus himself introduced this kind of "exegesis" to his disciples, Luke does not supply specific texts or interpretations. Perhaps he recognized how vulnerable such messianic prooftexting was to being contested and decided not to load that burden onto his narrative.

I do not think preachers should take on the responsibility for defending the logic of the ancient church's exegesis or Luke's choice of attributing that practice to the risen Jesus' own instruction. Surely it is more important to draw the congregation into Luke's larger themes. The God who raised Jesus from the dead intends the redemption of the world, the *tikkun olam.*

THAT SAME GOD IS PRESENT TO US, AS INTIMATELY AS OVER THAT TABLE IN EMMAUS, WHEN WE BREAK BREAD TOGETHER IN JESUS' NAME.

That same God is present to us, as intimately as over that table in Emmaus, when we break bread together in Jesus' name.

The RCL lection continues as the two disciples return to Jerusalem and find the other disciples, who are themselves then visited by the risen Jesus. Compared with other Gospel accounts, this scene may seem rather uneventful. Jesus offers his wounded hands and feet as proof that he is not "a ghost," but the theme does not receive the attentiveness that the Fourth Gospel provides (in the person of Thomas, John 20:24-29). He pronounces "peace" to the disciples, but again the notice seems almost peremptory compared to the solemnity of the Fourth Gospel, where Jesus breathes Holy Spirit on them and authorizes them to "forgive" and "retain" sins (20:21-24). (Luke, of course, will give a much more dramatic account of the giving of the Spirit later in his story on Pentecost, Acts 2:1-4).

Two aspects of Luke's story bear mention. First, Luke insists the risen Lord is really the Jesus who was crucified. Now the disciples (unlike the two on the road to Emmaus) recognize him but fear they are seeing a ghost; Jesus offers his flesh and bones for inspection (24:39-40), and—as if to seal the argument—eats a piece of fish (24:42-43). This aspect of the scene seems calculated to counter the idea (which emerged, not only as skepticism from outsiders, but as an interpretation within early Christian communities as well: see 1 John 4:2) that the Easter accounts were really some sort of apparition. Jesus also repeats the lesson he delivered in Emmaus: "that everything written about me in the law of Moses, the prophets, and the psalms must be fulfilled" (24:44). Again, Luke does not elaborate on the disciples' minds being "opened to understand the scriptures," but it is clearly important to his purpose to show that faith in the crucified and risen Jesus as Messiah is in no way a departure from the hope of Israel's scriptures.

In these ways Luke's account of Jesus' appearance to the disciples tends to "lean" into the book of Acts. The encounter is not self-sufficient or self-contained. Luke explicitly takes up the threads of scriptural hope—the hope of Israel for a restored people and a renewed creation—and weaves the resurrection into them. The seam between the Gospel of Luke and the book of Acts holds these two books together as one piece and reaches out from the empty tomb and the upper room to the life of the church in the world and the bright horizon of God's purpose.

SECOND SUNDAY OF EASTER

APRIL 18, 2004

REVISED COMMON	EPISCOPAL (BCP)	ROMAN CATHOLIC
Acts 5:27-32	Acts 5:12a, 17-22, 25-29 or Job 42:1-6	Acts 5:12-16
Ps. 118:14-29 or Psalm 150	Psalm 111 or 118:19-24	Ps. 118:2-4, 13-15, 22-24
Rev. 1:4-8	Rev. 1:(1-8) 9-19 or Acts 5:12a, 17-22, 25-29	Rev. 1:9-11a, 12-13, 17-19
John 20:19-31	John 20:19-31	John 20:19-31

Choosing Texts through the Easter Season

Beginning today and throughout the rest of the season of Easter, only the BCP will offer passages from the Hebrew Bible for the first reading—and only as alternatives to readings from Acts. The RCL and the Roman Catholic lectionary offer first readings from Acts and rely on the Revelation to John for the second reading. For those using the RCL and the Catholic lectionary, the psalms assigned will be the only First Testament texts heard throughout these weeks; those following the BCP will have a single Hebrew alternative each Sunday.

Given the prominence the readings from Acts and the Revelation will have in all three lectionaries, preachers may wish to consider sermon series on Luke's account of the growth of the early church's witness to the risen Christ or on John's startling vision of a living and powerful Christ in heaven. Preachers using the BCP will have the option—and the challenge!—of integrating a Hebrew Bible text into their Easter preaching.

FIRST READING
JOB 42:1-6 (BCP, alt.)

Those who frequent Episcopal churches are likely to know the book of Job primarily as the source of scriptures used in funeral services. In the sweep of the three-year BCP lectionary cycle, Job is heard only six times—and three of these are the same Holy Saturday liturgy each year! This is a pity: the profound questions raised in the book about "why bad things happen to good people" have a perennial power and appeal.[20] But those questions do not receive any clear, unambiguous answer in the narrative—one reason, perhaps, why many preachers (and lectionary committees!) shy away from the book.

At the end of the story, after Job's vehement protests and demand that God answer him, God appears; but rather than provide an explanation, God confronts Job with challenging questions that serve to put Job "in his place." "Where were *you* when I laid the foundations of the earth?" (38:4). Job's faltering attempt to answer (40:3-5) is overwhelmed by another speech by God: "Will you even put me in the wrong? Will you condemn me that you may be justified? Have you an arm like God, and can you thunder with a voice like his?" (40:8-9).

At last Job relents—in the verses assigned for today. The role of his response within the broader narrative of the book is not self-evident.[21] Some have read these verses as Job's quite unsatisfying resignation in the face of overwhelming divine bullying. Others find here Job's quiet acceptance of a more modest, but ultimately viable understanding of God's role in the universe.[22] Taken out of the narrative context of the book and juxtaposed with Easter readings, Job's speech may sound notes of praise for God's mighty work that echo in Christ's resurrection: "I know that you can do all things. . . . Now my eyes see you." But the preacher who chooses to read this passage may be taking on the challenge of explaining how that resurrection is an answer to Job's questions.

THE RCL OFFERS THE PREACHER AN OPPORTUNITY TO REFLECT ON THE RELATIONSHIP BETWEEN FAITH IN THE RISEN JESUS AND DEFIANCE OF AUTHORITIES THAT SET THEMSELVES AGAINST GOD.

ACTS 5:27-32 (RCL)

The three lectionaries assign three different readings, in effect choosing three different scenes from the story in Acts 5. The text assigned in the RCL is the fuller version of the text assigned in the BCP for an evening service Easter day (see that discussion above). The difference between the two is that the RCL includes Peter's response to the accusing Sanhedrin, "We must obey God rather than human beings." The RCL thus offers the preacher an opportunity to reflect on the relationship between faith in the risen Jesus and defiance of authorities that set themselves against God.

ACTS 5:12a, 17-22, 25-29 (BCP, alt.)

Moving backward in Acts, the BCP lection narrates the first action of the high priest and Sanhedrin to suppress the apostles' witness by arresting them and throwing them into prison. An angel releases them during the night (a motif repeated later, with more dramatic effect, at 12:6-11 and 16:25-26), leading to the denouement of the story, in which the apostles are discovered back in the temple, teaching the people, the next day.

If we hear only the miraculous jailbreak, we may be distracted or seduced by the fabulous quality of the story. After all, witnesses to Jesus languish in prison today, without angelic rescue (I think of the late Philip Berrigan and his "Plow-shares" comrades); they face death (the Jesuit martyrs of El Salvador; the assassinated priest Jean-Marie Vincent in Haiti). But we may presume that Luke's readers also knew that Peter and Paul had faced death in Rome. Luke is not describing an easy life, relying on supernatural bailouts: he portrays the courageous and defiant spirits of men and women who knew their Lord to have been risen from the dead.

ACTS 5:12-16 (RC)

Moving even further back in the story, the Roman Catholic lection highlights the "signs and wonders" done through the apostles in the early post-Easter days in Jerusalem, attracting adherents, and respect, among "the people." The apostolic power to work miracles extends even to Peter's shadow (5:15). This picture of Peter—so different from that provided in Mark (where any reversal of the disciples' "hardness of heart" is never narrated) or John (where tensions between Peter and the "Beloved Disciple" set Peter in an unfavorable light)—has been especially important for Roman Catholic devotion. But this divinely empowered apostolic work brings a consequence: the opposition of the high priest and Sanhedrin (the text assigned in the BCP). Luke's weaving together of these incidents raises an important question for us: What are the costs of apostolic witness in our world?

RESPONSIVE READING
PSALM 111 (BCP)

A psalm of praise to the LORD for his "mighty deeds," especially as these bring redemption and the fulfillment of God's covenant (v. 9).

NEIL
ELLIOTT

PSALM 118:19-24 (BCP, alt.);
PSALM 118:2-4, 13-15, 22-24 (RC);
PSALM 118:14-29 (RCL)

Three lectionaries provide three different selections from this psalm, but all three include the astonished declaration that "the stone that the builders rejected has become the chief cornerstone" (vv. 22-24). The early church took up this verse as a prophecy regarding Jesus' death and resurrection (e.g., Matt. 21:42 and parallels; Acts 4:11; 1 Pet. 2:7). In the Gospels, the "builders" are read allegorically as the leaders of the Jewish people, who rejected Jesus' message (cf. Matt. 21:43; Mark 12:12). It may be difficult—but it is important—for Christians to hear the verses without that association.

PSALM 150 (RCL alt.)

A psalm of praise to the LORD for "his mighty deeds" (v. 2). Given the rich musical imagery of the psalm, a setting with instrumental accompaniment is especially appropriate.

SECOND READING

REVELATION 1:4-8 (RCL);
REVELATION 1:(1-8) 9-19 (BCP);
REVELATION 1:9-11a, 12-13, 17-19 (RC)

Interpreting the Revelation to John

Through the Sundays of Eastertide, the Roman Catholic and RCL present readings from the Revelation (or Apocalypse) to John. Only the BCP makes these optional (Hebrew Bible texts may be chosen along with readings from Acts instead). Today's lections are from the introduction to the Revelation and thus should draw particular attention if the preacher decides to devote time in the coming weeks to John's message.

Surely no book in the New Testament evokes such apprehension for many readers as does the Revelation to John. A significant measure of the blame for that state of affairs accrues to the dispensationalist tradition, which originally flourished in the United States during the Civil War and its aftermath and found a new purchase in the midst of cultural convulsions and geopolitical upheavals in the 1970s. Interpreters from Cyrus Scofield to Hal Lindsey to best-selling "Left Behind" novelists Tim LaHaye and David Jenkins have promised to unlock the "code" of Revelation and decipher its prophecies concerning the sequence of contemporary events leading up to the second coming of Christ, thus providing an effective "countdown to Armageddon." Whether or not a preacher is *au courant* with this literature, very likely some, at least, of one's congregants are, and may even find it compelling.[23]

The power of this "rapture" tradition lies in its unwavering resolve to take the Bible seriously as providing guidance for contemporary life. Against such earnestness, a preacher's efforts to set the Revelation firmly in its ancient Roman context may seem to some like a reluctance to listen for the biblical word for *today*. Furthermore, to the extent it is successful, such an attempt will bring people to the very edge of the fissure that separates us from the first century: that is, the awareness that we have not seen the glorious consummation of history that John so fervently awaited. The obvious next question is, *why not?* Was John wrong? Or are the proponents of an imminent "rapture" right?

Given these challenges, it is often tempting to avoid Revelation altogether and stick to preaching from the Gospel! But there are important reasons to take John's vision seriously (far more seriously, in fact, than even a short sermon series allows: why not consider a more extended study series?). I doubt that John intended to deliver to his contemporaries an "encoded" text that would remain inscrutable until inspired minds in the nineteenth and twentieth centuries broke its secret. Although the "rapturists" want to read it this way, Revelation simply was not meant as a series of bizarre, otherwise opaque images awaiting decipherment in terms of "real" events in the here and now. As Elisabeth Schüssler Fiorenza (among others) has shown, the scenes in the book are meant to function allusively, conveying through repetitive and overlapping images a sense of God's power and holiness—not to provide a strict sequence of events.[24] That is, the Revelation "works" the other way around from the usual approach that seeks contemporary referents for the book's bizarre symbols. John's symbolic language referred, plainly enough, to persons and events his first-century contemporaries would recognize; the burden of his message was *to reveal how God saw those persons and events*.

THE SCENES IN THE BOOK ARE MEANT TO FUNCTION ALLUSIVELY, CONVEYING THROUGH REPETITIVE AND OVERLAPPING IMAGES A SENSE OF GOD'S POWER AND HOLINESS—NOT TO PROVIDE A STRICT SEQUENCE OF EVENTS.

Over against the claim to world-straddling rule represented in Roman imperial cult and imagery, John proclaims an alternative world, one in which God, not Caesar, reigns. He invites his readers to anticipate that rule by resisting the seductive vision of reality on offer from the empire, and to give their allegiance alone to the God who raised Jesus from the dead.[25] The book is not, finally, about transmitting information; it is about honoring the true God, which is why John's

visions are routinely punctuated by the transporting worship of the hosts that surround God's throne. It is no accident that the most-used phrases in Revelation
occur in our prayers and hymns of praise.

But why read the Revelation *in Easter?* Because John, more than any other
author in the New Testament, offers a searing vision of the risen Christ as the all-
powerful heavenly Lord, not only the agent of God's vindication at the last day,
but powerfully active in speaking to the church, guiding and challenging and confronting it *now.* Only John provides such a vivid sense of the contemporary presence of the lordly Christ—an important corrective to the one-sided celebration
of the resurrection *as past event* into which we might otherwise drift.

The Texts

The RCL begins the lection with v. 4. Unusual titles are here given to Jesus:
"faithful," i.e., obedient, "witness"; "ruler of the kings of the earth." The "seven
spirits" standing before God's throne may well be the seven angels of the seven
churches, through whom Christ's message is transmitted to the churches (1:20;
2:1, 8, 12, 18; 3:1, 7, 14). The reference to Jesus having "freed us from our sins by
his blood" is not otherwise elaborated; John is less interested in a theology of
atonement than in the imminence of Christ's coming.

Jesus is also hailed as the one who "made us to be a kingdom, priests serving
his God"—language that has been important for the Protestant understanding of
a "priesthood of all believers." John does not elaborate; there is no comparison
with the Jewish priesthood (compare Hebrews!), nor any reference to believers
doing anything particularly "priestly," other than offering their worship to God.
But that is the point, of course: compared to the elaborate representations of
power invested in imperial priestly ceremonial, believers are called simply to
honor the power of God with their lives.

The BCP text includes, as an option, the introduction to the whole Apocalypse
(vv. 1-8), which includes the promise of blessing to those who "hear and keep"
what is written in it (v. 3). The extension through v. 19 (beyond the RCL lection)
mentions John's situation as an exile on Patmos for the sake of "the word of God
and the testimony of Jesus," clearly sounding in our ears the serious potential consequences of living out discipleship to Jesus ("the persecution and the kingdom
and the patient endurance"). This reading also offers John's encounter with the
risen Christ.

Remarkably, this stupendous vision is the *only* physical description of Jesus in
our Bibles, a fact that bears reflection. I have asked groups to draw their mental
image of Jesus, and usually see pictures of a young man with wavy, long brown
hair, an olive complexion, in a nondescript white robe and sandals—the picture
that Christian art (and Hollywood!) have passed on to us based on the Gospels.
No one in these groups has drawn the picture we hear in Revelation. It's worth

asking how our faith would be different if we "saw" John's fierce heavenly Jesus as vividly as we see the gentle Palestinian Jesus!

The Roman Catholic lection takes up the latter part of what is included in the BCP lection, including Jesus' appearance to John; but the Roman Catholic text omits much of this description—the hair like white wool, the flaming eyes, the thunderous voice, etc.—and moves straightaway to John's reaction (v. 17). By omitting the names of the seven cities in Asia, the Roman Catholic reading supports the sense that John's message is as relevant to our own time—but, of course, the burden for making that case rests with the preacher.

The Gospel
JOHN 20:19-31 (RCL, BCP, RC)

One week after Easter, we read the story of Jesus' appearance to Thomas, one week after he has presented himself to the other apostles. Alas, poor Thomas: his name has been irreversibly linked with the adjective "doubting," even though the Fourth Gospel offers not the least disparagement of his faith! Note that upon hearing the witness of the other apostles, he asks for nothing more than they have been granted: to see and touch the wounds of the crucified Jesus, and thus to know that he is in fact risen. Note also that (despite the way this scene has consistently been represented in Christian art) we are never told that Thomas *touched* those wounds, only that upon Jesus' invitation, he fell to his knees and acknowledged Jesus as "my Lord and my God."

Clearly, the focus of the scene is not on any inadequacy on Thomas's part, but on his stubborn—one might even say loyal—insistence on knowing that Jesus is truly risen. Jesus' blessing in v. 29, "Blessed are those who have not seen and yet have come to believe," is not a rebuke of Thomas, but a promise for the Gospel's readers. But that promise *depends* on Thomas's stubbornness; he thus performs an important role within the narrative. The Fourth Gospel does not require readers to believe the bare assertion that Jesus has been raised, but provides the corroborating testimony of the first disciples, of "the beloved disciple," and of Thomas that they saw and touched Jesus (compare 1 John 1:1: "We declare to you . . . what we have heard, what we have seen with our eyes, what we have looked at and touched with our hands").

> THE FOCUS OF THE SCENE IS NOT ON ANY INADEQUACY ON THOMAS'S PART, BUT ON HIS STUBBORN—ONE MIGHT EVEN SAY LOYAL—INSISTENCE ON KNOWING THAT JESUS IS TRULY RISEN.

All of us today stand in the place of those earliest readers who "have not seen, yet have believed." We do not depend *alone* on the witnesses of the apostolic age, however. The Fourth Gospel is clear that Jesus not only revealed himself to his disciples, but sent them out (i.e., made them "apostles"), breathed the Holy Spirit upon them, and commissioned them to forgive as God forgives (20:21-23). The apostolic witness is not only to what several men and women saw two thousand years ago: it is to a living community where the power of the Spirit and the forgiveness of sins are experienced and practiced today.

The bestowal of the Spirit in this scene will seem anticlimactic for those familiar with the dramatic Lukan Pentecost scene. This is not a *public* event; neither does John narrate a public offer of divine forgiveness comparable to Peter's in Acts 2. Indeed, when Jesus breathes the Spirit on the disciples, we can be forgiven for wondering what has happened to the richly textured portrayal of the "Paraclete" in the Last Discourse (John 14–16). None of the things we have been told the Spirit will do—teach, convict, empower, console—happen here. There is not a hint here that the Spirit might be spoken of in *personal* terms.

Here again, as so often in John, it seems the narrative time of Jesus' earthly presence with his disciples is not in the author's focus. All of the promises concerning the Spirit's life within and among the disciples concern a time "later" than Jesus but contemporary with the author's community: then, we may presume, the declaration of the world's sin and the proclamation of forgiveness are announced. The spare narrative may serve to highlight the Johannine theme that it is in the contemporary community—not in some distant past—that the Spirit's work is to be discovered!

THIRD SUNDAY OF EASTER

APRIL 25, 2004

REVISED COMMON	EPISCOPAL (BCP)	ROMAN CATHOLIC
Acts 9:1-6 (7-20)	Acts 9:1-19a or Jer. 32:36-41	Acts 5:27-32, 40b-41
Psalm 30	Psalm 33 or 33:1-11	Ps. 30:2, 4, 5-6, 11-12, 13
Rev. 5:11-14	Rev. 5:6-14 or Acts 9:1-19a	Rev. 5:11-14
John 21:1-19	John 21:1-14	John 21:1-19 or 21:1-14

Two weeks after Easter, most of the holiday chocolate has been eaten, and many stores have pulled their discounted Easter merchandise off the shelves and begun to stock Fourth of July goods. The energy and excitement that led up to Easter has been forgotten, and minds begin to turn to summer plans. What difference does the resurrection make, anyway?

Today's texts present powerful visions of change and upheaval in the lives of individuals, communities, and nations. The challenge of preaching these texts is to provide the context in which a congregation can discern what changes the God who raised Jesus from the dead seeks to make in our world and in our midst!

FIRST READING
JEREMIAH 32:36-41 (BCP, alt.)

This is an astonishing text even for Jeremiah. It would be all too easy to hear only God's assuring word concerning "an everlasting covenant" (v. 40), and to hear that—along with echoes of the "new covenant" promised in Jer. 30:31 (a passage appointed for the Great Vigil of Easter in the BCP)—as simple references to salvation through the death and resurrection of Jesus.

This is an oracle concerning Jerusalem, the city over which Jeremiah has pronounced impending doom as God's punishment for the nation's injustice. Now, suddenly, the message shifts. Judgment is described as the *prophet's* theme ("concerning this city of which *you* say, 'it is being given into the hand of the king of Babylon'"); the word of the LORD, however, declares regathering, reconciliation, and restoration. As with the great eighth-century prophets, Jeremiah is not simply a social critic blasting the injustice of his nation. He also proclaims the fierce, unyielding, always surprising love and faithfulness of God. How challenging would it be for us to discern that enduring love in the midst of the sort of massive loss that Jeremiah and his contemporaries endured?

ACTS 9:1-6 (7-20) (RCL); ACTS 9:1-19a (BCP, alt.)

One of the most stirring narratives of an encounter with the risen Lord is this account of Saul's vision on the road to Damascus. It is now a commonplace in scholarship that Luke has shaped this story to his own purposes (it is, after all, repeated at key turning points in his narrative: 22:4-16; 26:9-18), and that those purposes are different from those that inform Paul's own comments about God's son being "revealed" to him (Gal. 1:13-17). For example, Luke's account is clearly "earth-bound," not heavenly (compare 2 Cor. 12:1-4!), and an audition rather than a vision.[26]

Luke intends in this story not to describe a "conversion" of Saul from one faith to another (the anachronism of later Christianity)[27] but the commissioning of Saul as the servant of Christ to the Jewish synagogues of the diaspora and to the Gentiles who made their homes there. (Paul calls himself simply the "apostle to the Gentiles"; but Luke's narrative sees Paul's mission field as including "Gentiles and kings and . . . the people of Israel," 9:15.) A great deal of the book of Acts is dedicated to describing and defending Paul's apostolic work as directly authorized by the risen Jesus and not the innovation of a single rogue Pharisee. Reducing Paul to a helpless and vulnerable state as he receives his commission (9:8-9) makes the point dramatically.

But this is not just the story of the vision that inaugurated Paul's mission. It is also a story about the faith of the early disciples, who responded to the leading of the Spirit even when the way set before them seemed a dead end. Accustomed as we are to regarding Paul as the source of some of our most important beliefs and practices, we do well to remember that Paul was welcomed into the radical, risky hospitality of the early church and baptized into their common life.

ACTS 5:27-32, 40b-41 (RC)

See the discussion for the Second Sunday of Easter, above.

PSALM 30 (RCL);
PSALM 30:2, 4-6, 11-12, 13 (RC)

This psalm is a thanksgiving for God's healing and restoration. Because the psalmist speaks of God having "brought up my soul from Sheol" and having "restored me to life from among those gone down to the Pit" (30:3), the psalm was read by the early church as a sort of prophecy of Jesus' death and resurrection (although we know the Hebrew people imagined Sheol as the shadowy abode of the dead, without hope or exit; thus the protest in 30:8-10). We may also hear in the rejoicing of vv. 11-12 an echo of the early disciples' Easter joy.

PSALM 33 or 33:1-11 (BCP)

A song of praise, this psalm strikes powerful chords reminiscent of Second Isaiah: "The LORD brings the counsel of the nations to nothing; he frustrates the plans of the peoples" (v. 10). Similarly, the warning that "a king is not saved by his great army . . ." (vv. 16-17) brings home how vain and futile the designs of governments and empires appear before the purpose of God. Against a mundane "Realpolitik," reading this psalm in Eastertide points us toward another "realism"—that of God's life-giving power manifest in one whom the Roman power thought to destroy.

Second Reading
REVELATION 5:11-14 (RCL, RC);
REVELATION 5:6-14 (BCP)

In the eucharistic prayers in the *Book of Common Prayer,* we declare that we join our voices with the endless chorus of "angels and archangels and all the company of heaven." Beginning at Rev. 4:2, John the seer describes that praise in a breathtaking vision of the heavenly throne room of God. That we participate in *heavenly* worship is a solemn assurance

> THE BURDEN OF THE APOCALYPSE IS TO PROCLAIM THAT DESPITE ALL APPEARANCES, THE HEAVENLY LORD REALLY IS LORD.

in Eastern Orthodox Christianity; Western traditions are somehow more reticent about the idea of praying with angels.

John's point is more than awe and reverence—though it is surely important to him to emphasize to Christians struggling against the constant seductive pressures of imperial imagery and ritual that even in their modest gatherings they participate in a far more powerful (because it's more *real*) worship. In the verses leading up to this text, John has despaired, because even in heaven, "no one was found worthy to open the scroll" in the right hand of the one seated on the throne (5:1-4). The assurance that "the Lion of the tribe of Judah, the Root of David, has conquered, so that he can open the scroll and its seven seals" (5:5) evokes the worship that rings through today's passage.

In other words, in a world so clearly at the disposition of Caesar and the gods of Rome, John assures his readers that Another—put to death by Rome, though innocent and obedient to God—is alone worthy to exercise dominion over human history, *and is about to do so*. The burden of the Apocalypse is to proclaim that despite all appearances, the heavenly Lord really is *Lord*.

The Gospel
JOHN 21:1-19 (RCL, RC);
JOHN 21:1-14 (BCP; RC, alt.)

Running through many of today's readings is a tension between the promise of God's lordship over human life and the evident absence of that lordship in the world in which we live. Where is God? What difference has the resurrection made, after all? Haven't life—and death—gone on pretty much as usual?

Today's Gospel presents a remarkable scene in which the risen Lord encounters his disciples in the midst of just such doubts.

The Fourth Gospel gives no hint that the disciple Peter would be martyred in Rome; or that his name would be known and revered in cosmopolitan Corinth; or even that he would be regarded as one of the "pillars" in the Jerusalem church! To the contrary, we are told that in the wake of the astounding drama of Easter, Peter goes back to Galilee and resumes fishing!

It is tempting to seize upon this account as a key to the psychological passage through which the disciples must have moved, from the disaster of Golgotha, to some mixture of despondency and denial in Galilee, to the joy of reunion and the challenge of the decades after Easter. Alas, the accounts available to us do not yield so smooth a story line! Matthew, who places the reunion of the risen Jesus with his disciples in Galilee, at the Lord's command (28:10, 16-20), ends the story with Jesus' command to "go . . . and make disciples," without narrating the disciples' response. Mark ends his story without the disciples even being told to meet Jesus in Galilee (16:7). And Luke—who alone crafts a second volume around the endeavors of the apostolic band, and particularly Peter—centers that story in

Jerusalem, without any encounters in Galilee! In brief, we have no other corroboration for a "revival" or "rehabilitation" of despondent disciples in Galilee.

Indeed, it isn't easy to discern what relationship this scene has to the Gospel that precedes. Because of differences of vocabulary and theme, scholars have long regarded the whole of chapter 21 as a later addition to the Gospel. Further, its similarity to Luke 5:1-11 has led many to consider both accounts to derive from a post-Easter story that originally functioned to authorize the disciples for mission—not to corroborate the resurrection.[28]

Whether or not the story actually happened just as this chapter (alone!) tells it, its place here in the Fourth Gospel raises intriguing questions for readers and hearers. Although this scene is identified as "the third time that Jesus appeared to his disciples" (v. 14), a story in which the disciples simply *went back to fishing* after the resurrection, seems quite odd—implying that earlier appearances didn't make the sort of difference for the disciples that other Gospels suggest it did. Could this story—originally—have been one way of recounting the *first* encounter with the risen Jesus?

There is nothing in this apparently miraculous catch of fish that points toward metaphor, as the story in Luke 5 does ("from now on you will be catching people!" 5:10); the fish simply end up as breakfast. There is something quietly striking about that gathering around a charcoal fire, however. Men—especially men who have grown up amid the powerful pressures of American expectations regarding masculinity—may readily recognize the silence of these disciples, even as they receive food from Jesus' hands in a gesture of tremendous, unspoken intimacy ("they knew it was the Lord"). How can we bring the powerful emotions of that intimacy to awareness and speech?

CAN WE—ESPECIALLY THOSE OF US WHO MAY BE UNACCUSTOMED TO EXPRESSING STRONG OR INTIMATE FEELINGS EASILY—MOVE FROM THE QUIET REVERIE OF OUR PRAYERS TO SPEAK OUR LOVE OF CHRIST?

The challenge for Peter after breakfast is to profess his love for Jesus, three times (echoing Peter's three denials of Jesus: 18:15-18, 25-27). The scene presents a double challenge for us. Can we—especially those of us who may be unaccustomed to expressing strong or intimate feelings easily—move from the quiet reverie of our prayers to speak our love of Christ? And can we, like Peter, show that love in the way we care for others ("feed my sheep")?

Jesus' warning to Peter regarding "the kind of death by which he would glorify God" (21:18-19) was really meant as an admonition to the Johannine community, who may well have been traumatized by the martyrdom of Peter in Rome. (We may compare the obvious shock felt earlier by Christians in distant Thessalonica when—contrary to their own expectations—some of their number died before the appearance of Christ: 1 Thess. 4:13-18.) The verses that follow the reading indicate, quite similarly, that the Johannine church had to deal with a second unexpected death, that of "the disciple whom Jesus loved" (21:20-23).

"In the midst of life, we are in death," reads one of the anthems for the service of burial. John's Gospel proclaims the resurrection of Jesus and depicts the intimacy of the common meal in the early lakeshore mist, to a people who know only too well that life and death continue—to all appearances, much as they had before. In the midst of life and of death, we are asked to find ever new ways to say, "Lord, you know we love you."

FOURTH SUNDAY OF EASTER

MAY 2, 2004

REVISED COMMON	EPISCOPAL (BCP)	ROMAN CATHOLIC
Acts 9:36-43	Acts 13:15-16, 26-33, (34-39) or Num. 27:12-23	Acts 13:14, 43-52
Psalm 23	Psalm 100	Ps. 100:1-2, 3, 5
Rev. 7:9-17	Rev. 7:9-17 or Acts 13:15-16, 26-33, (34-39)	Rev. 7:9, 14b-17
John 10:22-30	John 10:22-30	John 10:27-30

Of Sheep and Shepherds

Pastoral images swirl and flash through today's readings. God's care for the psalmist is like a shepherd's attentive care for sheep, without which they may face grave dangers (Psalm 23). Jesus speaks of his own as sheep who hear his voice and respond, and whom he protects (John 10). Many worship services will include hymns and songs playing on these themes.

It's tempting to sentimentalize this imagery, especially for people who don't actually live around sheep or work with them. But sheep are not known for marked intelligence or good disposition, and they tend to smell. People who spend a lot of time around sheep often resent being compared to them: calling someone a "sheep" is rarely meant as a compliment. And woe to the "pastor"—literally, the shepherd—who tries to force the metaphor by implying that the people put into his or her care must be as docile as sheep!

Two aspects of ancient Israelite culture shape the biblical imagery of shepherding. First, Hebrew scriptures betray their origins in a "pastoral nomadic society," located by archaeologists and historians in the hill country of the Galilee, above the fertile plains cultivated by the Canaanites. The contrast between these two cultures is evident almost from the beginning of the Bible, where God prefers Abel's properly pastoral sacrifice (a sheep) to Cain's offering of vegetables (Gen. 4:2-5). Keeping flocks of sheep and goats was Israel's way of life, and it is an important insistence in scripture that Israel's first great king, the one "after God's own heart," began as a youth "keeping the sheep" for his father (1 Sam. 16:11).[29] To speak of God as shepherd in such a context is to evoke a stubbornly independent way of life, a readiness to move on to the next grazing land, at odds with the settled order of the great Canaanite cities.

David's characterization points up the second important aspect of the pastoral imagery in the Bible. Centuries before Jesus took up these metaphors, they had become a reliable trope in Israel's political rhetoric. Jeremiah rebuked the nation's rulers as "shepherds who destroy and scatter the sheep" (Jer. 23:1-2); Ezekiel assailed the "shepherds" who slaughtered and fed on the sheep, rather than feeding and protecting them (Ezekiel 34). Already the metaphor begins to show strain. Actual shepherds, after all, tend sheep and protect them from harm until it is time for the slaughter and a banquet of roast lamb! The metaphor's power lies in the high value a pastoral society placed on the common good. The good shepherd looks after and defends the community's interest in the sheep; so the prophets called on Israel's rulers to act for the best interest of the people rather than to enrich themselves.

> THE GOOD SHEPHERD LOOKS AFTER AND DEFENDS THE COMMUNITY'S INTEREST IN THE SHEEP; SO THE PROPHETS CALLED ON ISRAEL'S RULERS TO ACT FOR THE BEST INTEREST OF THE PEOPLE RATHER THAN TO ENRICH THEMSELVES.

FIRST READING
NUMBERS 27:12-23 (BCP, alt.)

At first sight this is a strange text, especially for the Easter season! The LORD allows Moses to look over into the land promised to Israel but warns that Moses will not enter that land "because you rebelled against my word in the wilderness of Zin" (in Num. 20:12-13). At Moses' request, God then commands him to commission Joshua to take authority over Israel as they enter the land.

The text's relevance for the day lies not only in the fact that Joshua is Jesus' namesake. (Joshua's name, literally "Yahweh is salvation," was one of the most common names in the first century, as attested by Hebrew and Greek texts alike.) Moses asks God to appoint someone to lead the people into Canaan "so the people may not be like sheep without a shepherd" (v. 17). This phrase introduces one theme of the Gospel reading, where Jesus cares for his own as a shepherd watches over the sheep. The text thus effectively presents Joshua as the type for which Jesus is the antitype, the true Shepherd who eclipses his predecessor.

The text highlights the miraculous raising from death of a woman of faith, renowned in her community for "good works and acts of charity" (v. 36). Luke shows a recurrent interest in worthy women, especially women of some independence (Tabitha may have been one of the widows, and thus relatively free from social constraints); compare Lydia, the Godfearer of Thyatira, who offered Paul and his companions the hospitality of her home (16:11-15). It is worth noting (especially during the Easter season) that Luke gives not a hint that this miraculous raising is like Jesus' resurrection. Rather, Luke shows that the apostles now do the same works, through the power of the Spirit of Jesus, that Jesus himself did (e.g., Luke 7:1-10, 11-17), and that he hailed as signs that "the one who is to come" has in fact appeared (Luke 7:18-23).

ACTS 13:15-16, 26-33, (34-39) (BCP);
ACTS 13:14, 43-52 (RC)

Luke presents the first of several synagogue sermons by Paul that play an important role in the plot of the book of Acts. Here he speaks to a synagogue in Pisidian Antioch; when a week later the whole city turns out to hear him, "the Jews" were filled with jealousy and opposed him. Paul rebukes the Jews for their rejection and declares that he is now "turning to the Gentiles" (13:46). In Acts 18 Paul faces similar opposition from "the Jews" in Corinth and announces that he "will go to the Gentiles" (18:6). Finally—in the book's very last scene—Paul receives a mixed response from a Jewish audience in Rome and again declares, this time with citation of Isa. 6:9-10, that though "this people" will not listen, God's salvation "has been sent to the Gentiles; they will listen" (28:17-28).

These three scenes have been the focus of tremendous scholarly attention and debate over the character and purpose of Luke-Acts. Some have read these passages as closing off the era of Jewish receptiveness to the message about Jesus and inaugurating the Gentile church that will replace Israel.[30]

More recent observers, however, note first that Luke always describes a *mixed* reaction within Israel: *some* Jews (or "many") respond positively to Paul's message (13:43; 14:1, Iconium; 17:4, Thessalonica; 17:11, Beroea; 18:8, Corinth; 28:4, Rome); the opposition comes from a disgruntled minority who hound and harass the apostles (13:50; 14:2-5, 19; 17:5-7, 13; 18:12; 20:3; 21:27-30; 23:12-15; 25:7)—until he reaches Rome (see 28:21-22). They also observe that even after Paul has "turned to the Gentiles" in one community, his message spreads and flourishes among a mixed group of Gentiles and Jews together (e.g., 13:52; 14:2), and that Paul promptly marches to the next city and enters the synagogue there

(14:2; 17:1-2, 10; 18:4; 28:17). In fact, the pattern consistently plays out the prophecies spoken at the beginning of Luke's Gospel, that through Jesus salvation would come as "a light for revelation to the Gentiles and for glory to your people Israel" (Luke 2:32)—but that he would also bring division in Israel (2:34).[31]

The two lectionaries address Acts 13 in very different ways. The Roman Catholic lectionary omits all of Paul's sermon and highlights the antagonism of "the Jews" and Paul's declaration that he is "turning to the Gentiles." It is important—especially in view of Roman Catholic teaching regarding Judaism and the Jewish people—to interpret this text so as to avoid and oppose any hint of Christian supersessionism.[32]

The BCP, on the other hand, includes most of Paul's sermon, which focuses on the treachery of "the residents of Jerusalem and their leaders" in killing Jesus; God's fulfilling the ancient promises to Israel by raising Jesus from the dead; and the offer of forgiveness to all who believe, neatly avoiding the mention of Jewish hostility entirely. Paul cites several biblical passages (Ps. 2:7; Isa. 55:3; Ps. 16:10) as prophecies of the resurrection. Although to modern eyes they hardly seem to have been such originally. Luke may provide valuable evidence here for the early "messianic" appropriation of scripture by believers in the risen Jesus.

RESPONSIVE READING
PSALM 23 (RCL)

Certainly the best-known of the psalms, this text describes God as the shepherd who satisfies the psalmist's needs and protects the psalmist from harm. The pastoral imagery dominates through v. 4 (where the shepherd's rod and staff, instruments of guidance and protection, are symbols of God's providential care). At v. 5 the imagery changes to that of the banquet table, and God is described as a host who honors and vindicates the psalmist in the presence of enemies, showering hospitality and favor (anointing with oil and pouring wine). The "house of the LORD" is the temple. Though this psalm conjures for many feelings of serenity and peace, it speaks as if of the calm at the eye of the storm: a peace found in the midst of ravening beasts, or enemies, or in "the valley of the shadow of death."

PSALM 100 (BCP);
PSALM 100:1-2, 3, 5 (RC)

"Old Hundredth" is likewise a well-known and beloved psalm of praise, the *Jubilate* of daily prayers in the BCP and venerable Christian tradition. Note here, too, the pastoral imagery: "we are [God's] people, and the sheep of his pasture" (v. 3). The heart of the metaphor is not God's power over us but divine attentiveness and care: the LORD "is good, his steadfast love endures forever, and his faithfulness to all generations" (v. 5).

SECOND READING

REVELATION 7:9-17 (RCL; BCP); REVELATION 7:9, 14b-17 (RC)

Religious violence against Christians in various nations around the world has attracted considerable media interest in the last few years. As deplorable as that violence is, whether or not it constitutes an alarming new phenomenon depends upon the definition of "religious persecution." By the end of the 1980s, after all, the Roman Catholic Church in Guatemala and El Salvador had documented massive and vicious brutality against tens of thousands of Christians in base communities, carried out by military and paramilitary forces in those countries; yet those well-documented deaths are normally not cited in discussions of "modern martyrs" or "persecuted Christians" today.[33] Do some deaths simply not register in our awareness?

While the precise identities of the 144,000 "servants of our God" in Rev. 7:1-8 have long preoccupied the imaginations of apocalyptically minded Christians, John's emphasis in today's reading is on a different group: the "great multitude that no one could count, from every nation, from all tribes and peoples and languages, standing before the throne and before the Lamb, robed in white" (v. 9). These, John learns, are those "who have come out of the great ordeal," whose robes have been washed white "in the blood of the Lamb" (v. 14). We are startled immediately by the image: how can *blood* wash garments *white?* But the greater shock

> CAN WE DARE TO IMAGINE THAT THE LAMB'S REIGN IS AS IMMINENT IN OUR OWN WORLD AS IT WAS IN JOHN'S?

for John's contemporaries would have been the startling realization that *a multitude beyond number* had suffered persecution and death at the hands of the very empire that presented itself as the guarantor of peace and security.

Efforts to calculate the size of the persecutions under Nero or Domitian (the leading candidates for "the great ordeal") are less to the point than recognizing that in John's eyes, the violence of Rome seems limitless. But the empire's countless victims are not forgotten; they come front and center in John's vision, to the very presence of God, where they are promised eternal relief from hunger and thirst, scorching heat and mourning.

The Revelation provides a dramatic reversal of the assumptions of imperial culture. It is not, finally, the force of imperial armies or the pressure of the imperial economy that shapes history. The verses that follow immediately on today's reading describe how the prayers of the righteous, the holy dead who surround God in heaven and the saints on earth, ascend to God and evoke the momentous turnings that usher in the reign of God upon earth. Can we dare to imagine that the Lamb's reign is as imminent in our own world as it was in John's?

THE GOSPEL
JOHN 10:22-30 (RCL; BCP);
JOHN 10:27-30 (RC)

A number of pastoral images coalesce in John 10, only to fracture, then realign in ever-shifting patterns. Jesus is the gatekeeper calling to the sheep, who know his voice (10:3); he is the gate (10:9); he is the good shepherd, in contrast to thieves and hired hands (10:10-13); the good shepherd, who knows his own and lays down his life for them (10:14-17). The last theme dominates today's reading.

The broader context of John 10 includes Jesus' healing of a man born blind in John 9, and the curious development of this man's faith in direct proportion to the mounting opposition of "the Pharisees" or "the Jews" *(hoi Ioudaioi)*. As so often in John, that story shifts from a focus on the miracle itself to a debate over who Jesus is: the "Son of Man," the Lord (9:35-38), or a sinner (9:16, 24)? In today's reading, a difference of opinion leads to division among those hearing Jesus' words: Is he possessed by a demon, or is he the Messiah?

Two distinctive aspects of the Fourth Gospel appear here. First, the "plot" revolves around the question of Jesus' identity, to the extent that each vignette in the series—whether miracle story, dialogue, or controversy (as here)—becomes background for Jesus' extended monologue about himself, his heavenly origin (and destination), and his relation to the Father. Here, in dramatic contrast to the Synoptic Gospels, Jesus clearly announces himself as Messiah (v. 25), and more: he is one with God the Father (v. 30)! Furthermore, throughout the Gospel, Jesus' identity is immediately recognized by those to whom it has been given by God (see, e.g., 1:29-51), yet it remains opaque to those to whom it has not been given. So here Jesus declares that he has *already* proclaimed his identity as Messiah, but that the *Ioudaioi* "do not believe." When he announces, "The Father and I are one," the response (in the verses following today's text) is immediate: as the NRSV translates, "The Jews took up stones again to stone him" (v. 31).

HERE, IN DRAMATIC CONTRAST TO THE SYNOPTIC GOSPELS, JESUS CLEARLY ANNOUNCES HIMSELF AS MESSIAH (V. 25), AND MORE: HE IS ONE WITH GOD THE FATHER (V. 30)!

The apparent irrationality of "the Jews" is troubling enough that the lectionaries omit it. Yet this double effect of the presence of Jesus as the Word incarnate in the world is at the very heart of the Fourth Gospel, and of today's reading in particular. The sort of christological arguments that give structure to the Gospel of Matthew are absent in John: thus when the Pharisees charged that "we do not know where [Jesus] comes from" (9:29), the answer is not given in terms of messianic prooftexts—"from Bethlehem," "from Egypt" (see Matt. 2:1-6, 13-15)—but in terms of self-evident truth (to some): he comes "from God." Only the willfully blind would fail to see (John 9:30-34).

In today's reading, Jesus' words about shepherd and sheep perform the same function. They assure the disciples that they do indeed know Jesus, just as immediately, as reflexively, as naturally as sheep know the voice of their shepherd (v. 27). If outsiders continue to press for answers, it is only because they "do not belong to my sheep" (v. 26).

This aspect of the Gospel led John Calvin to speak of "double predestination."[34] It is also one reason some people find John's Gospel especially troubling: if I have doubts or questions, if I seek to understand my faith rationally, is it because I do not have the immediate, self-authenticating faith given to all who are "born from above" (John 3:3)? How important it is, then, for preachers to emphasize that this Gospel's presentation of what faith is, and how one comes to hold it, is but one among several understandings in the New Testament. And how important to grasp the *historical* circumstances that shaped this presentation!

> JESUS' WORDS ASSURE THE DISCIPLES THAT THEY DO INDEED KNOW JESUS, JUST AS IMMEDIATELY, AS REFLEXIVELY, AS NATURALLY AS SHEEP KNOW THE VOICE OF THEIR SHEPHERD (V. 27).

Since the middle of the twentieth century, Christians have been deeply troubled by the way the Fourth Gospel can speak of "the Jews" *(hoi Ioudaioi)* as those apparently predestined *not* to understand or recognize Jesus; as those who "search the scriptures" yet without understanding (5:39), who oppose Jesus as children of the devil (8:44-47). Scholars hear in these chapters not just the story of Jesus but simultaneous echoes of the experience of the Johannine church. In particular, the note in John 9:22—that the blind man's parents "were afraid of the Jews; for the Jews had already agreed that anyone who confessed Jesus to be the Messiah would be put out of the synagogue"—seems to many to describe the context of the later Johannine community, whose faith in Jesus had met direct hostility from the Jewish synagogue, rather than of Jesus' own time.[35] Some historians have taken evidence that toward the end of the first century C.E., Palestinian synagogues formulated a "blessing" or prayer for Sabbath worship, condemning "apostates" to be uprooted, and "Nazarenes and the heretics"—that is, presumably, Christians—to perish and "be erased from the Book of Life," as pointing to the likely historical context from which the Fourth Gospel—and its animus against "the Jews"—sprang up.[36]

Despite the apparent explanatory power of this theory, several aspects of the interpretation on which it depends has been challenged. How early was the so-called benediction against heretics really formulated; how widely was it actually disseminated among Jewish congregations; how consistently was it enforced—if it ever was? Is such language—which construes late first-century Judaism as a tightly organized and well policed orthodoxy—even appropriate? Do John's repeated pejorative references to *hoi Ioudaioi* mean what we mean when we translate "the Jews"?[37] Or—as some ancient evidence indicates, and as a growing number of scholars argue today—might they refer to a fairly sectarian group *within* Israel, a "particularist and purity-oriented community in and around Jerusalem," but *not* equivalent to "the Jews" as we use the term?[38] Rather than seeing the recurrent tension between Jesus and "the Jews" in John as evidence of a later split between "Jews" and "Christians," some recent scholarship suggests we read John in light of two competing definitions of what it meant to be "Israel": a more comprehensive vision—that presented by the Fourth Gospel as Jesus' own—in which "salvation is from the *Ioudaioi*," but is for *all* Israelites, including Samaritans and Galileans; and that of the (sectarian) *Ioudaioi* themselves, for whom strict rules about association, endogamy, and ritual purity restricted salvation to a minority within Israel.[39]

I take this detour through a current scholarly debate in order to set Jesus' words in today's reading in a (possible) historical context that may bring them more vividly to light. Let us imagine that the early Johannine community constituted of a range of people who considered themselves "Israel," and who faced opposition and rejection from the sectarian religious and political establishment in control of the temple (the self-proclaimed *Ioudaioi*). And let us imagine that opposition included the fervent prayer—whether or not set in a specific form, whether or not ever promoted "officially"—that followers of Jesus be "uprooted" and removed from the "book of life." Then how powerfully would these men and women have heard Jesus' assurances that "I give them eternal life and they will never perish"; that "no one will snatch them out of my hand"; that "what my Father has given me is greater than all else, and no one can snatch it [or: them] out of the Father's hand" (John 10:28-29)!

As preachers, we must discern whether or not that assurance is where we should place the weight of our preaching. Do the people hearing us need to be assured of God's love? Undoubtedly. But do they—do we—also sometimes presume it, as something of a privilege we possess by virtue of our religious affiliation? Do we approach this Gospel secure in the assumption that *we* are the "sheep," and that *others* are the outsiders? John's Gospel uses language to construct a powerful social world in which insiders and outsiders are carefully distinguished.[40] In what ways do our practices—of preaching, of worship, of hospitality—shape our communities along lines that separate "insiders" and "outsiders"? Becoming more intentional about those practices may well begin with the way we shape today's sermon!

FIFTH SUNDAY OF EASTER

MAY 9, 2004

REVISED COMMON	EPISCOPAL (BCP)	ROMAN CATHOLIC
Acts 11:1-18	Acts 13:44-52	Acts 14:21-27
	or Lev. 19:1-2, 9-18	
Psalm 148	Psalm 145 or 145:1-9	Ps. 145:8-9, 10-11, 12-13
Rev. 21:1-6	Rev. 19:1, 4-9	Rev. 21:1-5a
	or Acts 13:44-52	
John 13:31-35	John 13:31-35	John 13:31-33a, 34-35

Love and Justice

"In the Christian faith," Reinhold Niebuhr wrote more than half a century ago, "the final law in which all other law is fulfilled is the law of love." Nevertheless, the deep-rooted self-interest that pervades our lives and our communities means that the selfless love we proclaim in Christ is never a "simple possibility" in history. "The ordinary affairs of the community, the structures of politics and economics, must be governed by the spirit of justice."[41]

Niebuhr protested that American Christianity had become "irrelevant to the problems of justice" because it persisted in presenting a sentimental notion of love "as a simple solution for every communal problem." Christians too often imagined love as a kind of "philanthropy," he argued, "given to those who make no claims against us, who do not challenge our goodness or disinterestedness." This understanding of love expressed only our "power and moral complacency." *Justice,* on the other hand, "requires the humble recognition that the claim that another makes against us may be legitimate." Niebuhr advocated and worked tirelessly for a "profounder" Christian understanding of love which would encourage people "to create systems of justice which will save society, and themselves, from their own selfishness."[42]

In today's Gospel Jesus commands his disciples to "love one another." But what does such love require of us? The day's readings offer the preacher ample opportunities to consider the prophet's question and God's answer: "What does the LORD require of you but to do justice, and to love kindness, and to walk humbly with your God?" (Mic. 6:8).

LEVITICUS 19:1-2, 9-18 (BCP, alt.)

The book of Leviticus has fallen into disfavor and neglect in wide swaths of the church today. Its rules for diet and community life, its attitudes and expectations regarding slavery and sexual roles, its detailed attention to ritual purity especially regarding service in the temple—just to mention a few prominent themes—all strike modern Western Christians as alien and disquieting. What can such a strange book say to us?

The passage offered as an alternative in the BCP is part of the so-called Holiness Code (chapters 17–26), a section of Leviticus that prescribes social practices that would make Israel a whole and holy people in the land (19:2). (Not surprisingly, the lectionary avoids the discussion in vv. 5-8 of how to offer and eat the "sacrifice of well being.")

The clear message of the text is that holiness and justice are inextricably bound up with one another. Being a "holy people" depends upon guaranteeing that a portion of the people's produce—their land, their grain, their grapes—shall be left for "the poor and the alien" (vv. 9-10). Deceit, fraud, and perjury are prohibited (vv. 11-12). Even holding a laborer's wages overnight is offensive to God (v. 13)!

> THE CLEAR MESSAGE OF THE TEXT IS THAT HOLINESS AND JUSTICE ARE INEXTRICABLY BOUND UP WITH ONE ANOTHER.

These verses strike sharp and dissonant chords in modern capitalist society where the acts prohibited by Leviticus, translated into our own economy, might be considered good, even necessary business practice. (Recall that for centuries the Christian church considered usury—the charging of interest on loans—a mortal sin!) We like to think of the notorious corporate scandals that make headlines—insider trading, "restating" profits, exorbitant compensation packages for CEOs who successfully "downsize" their companies—as unfortunate exceptions to the rule, aberrations from the fundamental soundness of modern global capitalism. We tend to forget that so clear-sighted a prophet as Martin Luther King Jr. called us decades ago to reevaluate the basic structure and norms of our economic system, for "an edifice which produces beggars needs restructuring."[43] Today's reading offers the opportunity to revive that often avoided conversation!

ACTS 11:1-18 (RCL)

On Easter Day, all three lectionaries offered a reading from Acts 10:34-43, Peter's sermon to the Roman officer Cornelius and his household. The larger context of that reading included Peter's baffling vision of a sheet filled with unclean animals (10:9-17). In this reading, Peter rehearses that vision in a defense before "the circumcised believers" who have criticized him for eating with the uncircumcised (vv. 2-3). The upshot of this speech is that opposition to Peter is silenced, and the "circumcised believers" are convinced that "God has given even to the Gentiles the repentance that leads to life" (v. 18).

Because this point is obviously so important to Luke, and because it would be easy for a preacher, under the constraint of time, to rely on facile but historically dubious generalizations about Jewish "exclusivism" and Christian "inclusion," two points should be borne in mind: (1) the Torah nowhere prohibits eating with "the uncircumcised" as such. In fact, the Mishnah—the benchmark of orthodox Jewish practice, dating from about 200 C.E.—devotes considerable space in the tractate *Avodah Zarah* to the precautions and procedures that allow Jews to eat with Gentiles without fear of engaging unwittingly in idolatry. Luke-Acts scrupulously presents such meals as involving only Godfearing Gentiles like Cornelius. (2) Peter's vision in Acts 10 is not presented as a message from God to disregard the clear commandments of Torah prohibiting the eating of unclean animals. Rather, the point is that Peter, so diligently observant a Jew that even what seems to be an ecstatic vision from heaven will not persuade him to transgress the Torah, readily recognizes that God welcomes *Gentiles*. In effect, Luke wants to argue that Peter's common meal practice, *not* the scrupulosity of the "circumcised believers," represents authentic Judaism.[44]

ACTS 13:44-52 (BCP)

See the discussion of the Roman Catholic lection for the Fourth Sunday of Easter, above.

ACTS 14:21-27 (RC)

At times, readers have found Luke's tone too buoyant, too triumphant, as the fledgling movement of Jesus' disciples enjoys a seemingly geometric growth. That is certainly the tone of the summary statements that punctuate the narrative (e.g., 2:43-47; 4:32-35; 5:12-16). While sociologists might regard dramatic expansion as the normal pattern for a new social group,[45] Acts clearly describes this growth as the awe-inspiring work of the Holy Spirit, work accompanied by "wonders and signs" (2:43).

Luke is well aware of the hardships faced by the early followers of Jesus, however, and skillfully weaves them together with reports of progress to create a heroic narrative. Arrests and threats from the temple leadership only embolden the apostles (4:5-22; 5:17-26); the "severe persecution" sparked by Stephen's martyrdom scatters the apostles, providing opportunity for the spread of "the word" (8:1-8). The spine of the later chapters of the book is the dramatic story of the archpersecutor-turned-apostle, Paul, racing against time (and an antagonistic "posse" of diaspora Jews) to bring the message of salvation to audiences in Asia Minor and Greece, then using his appearances before Roman magistrates to proclaim his gospel (chapters 21–28).

Today's reading offers a vignette of these plot motifs. Driven from Lystra by violent opposition (14:19-20), Paul and Barnabas retrace their steps through cities and provinces in what is today eastern Turkey, covering hundreds of miles, returning at last to Antioch (from which they were originally sent off: 13:1-4). They "pro-

> LUKE IS WELL AWARE OF THE HARDSHIPS FACED BY THE EARLY FOLLOWERS OF JESUS, HOWEVER, AND SKILLFULLY WEAVES THEM TOGETHER WITH REPORTS OF PROGRESS TO CREATE A HEROIC NARRATIVE.

claimed the good news," "strengthened the souls of the disciples" and "encouraged them to continue in the faith"—but note *how* they did this: by declaring, "It is through many persecutions that we must enter the kingdom of God" (v. 22). Thus Luke sums up the adversity they have faced in the preceding narrative and points forward to Paul's fate in particular.

Preachers should take care not to generalize this theme into a counsel of resignation, as if the Lukan Paul were saying only that all people inevitably face suffering, and we must accustom ourselves to it. He speaks here of *apostolic* suffering, the opposition that those who proclaim and live out the values of the reign of God will face in a world implacably hostile to that reign. To the possibility of *that* suffering the church's leaders (the elders, *presbyteroi,* 14:23) are invited through prayer and fasting; and for that reason especially they are "entrusted . . . to the Lord."

RESPONSIVE READING
PSALM 145 or 145:1-9 (BCP); PSALM 145:8-9, 10-11, 12-13 (RC)

A psalm of praise to God as king. The LORD is praised in general terms for "mighty acts" (vv. 4-7) and for being "gracious and merciful, slow to anger and abounding in steadfast love" (v. 8). In particular the psalm praises the LORD for upholding those who are falling and raising up those who are "bowed down" (v. 14). Those using the BCP lection from Leviticus (see above) may wish to touch on themes in this psalm (in its full reading) as well: how are we to understand the claim that God gives everyone "their food in due season," "satisfying the desire of every living thing"? How do our social or economic practices thwart the satisfaction of human need?

PSALM 148 (RCL)

This psalm of praise highlights God's act in creating the cosmos—sun and moon, shining stars, and (in the ancient Hebrew cosmology) the "waters above the heavens" (v. 4), from which rain and snow proceed. All these creatures are called upon to praise God. A musical version of St. Francis' hymn of praise (for example, "All Creatures of Our God and King") may be suitable accompaniment.

Second Reading

REVELATION 19:1, 4-9 (BCP)

The BCP here shows the propriety and restraint for which Episcopalians are often teased, even by other Episcopalians like myself! The exultant praise of a great multitude in heaven sounds very much like other prayers from Revelation that appear as Canticles in Morning Prayer ("A Song to the Lamb," Rev. 4:11; 5:9-10, 13; BCP, p. 93; "The Song of the Redeemed," Rev. 15:3-4; BCP, p. 94). Decorum seems to require that praise for God's judgment of "the great whore who corrupted the earth with her fornication" and God's vengeance for "the blood of his servants" (v. 2) be omitted.

The "great whore" is, of course, Roma, the resplendent deity who sat enthroned upon the "seven hills of Rome" (see 17:9). Her condemnation was announced (with coded explanation, for those with "a mind that has wisdom") in 17:1-18. Her "fornication" is John's assessment of the predatory economy through which Rome gained tremendous wealth through "globalized" commerce and traffic in human slaves (see 18:9, 11-13). The fall of Rome, the breaking of Roman power, is the ecstatic theme of the angel's proclamation in 18:21-24 and the occasion of the praise that swells from heaven in today's text.

It is too easy for us to hear John's message with Hollywood's vision of Rome in our minds: arrogant emperors in luxuriant finery, gold-armored troops marching about. But John offers a prophetic analysis of the everyday commercial routines that constituted Rome's "whoring"—and threatened to seduce the Christian communities of Asia Minor.[46] Do preachers—especially we who stand before proper Episcopal congregations!—have the courage to preach that vision?

REVELATION 21:1-6 (RCL);
REVELATION 21:1-5a (RC)

This is the last of the seven visions in the Apocalypse. This final vision focuses on the new heaven and the new earth, culminating in God's declaration: "See, I am making all things new." So once again we hear the voice of Yahweh who, in Isaiah 43, had spoken to the weary exiles, encouraging them to forget "former things" and "the things of old" and to trust in God's declaration that "I am about to do a new thing." Now John sees the "new Jerusalem . . . coming down out of heaven from God" (v. 2), symbolizing the merger of the old and the new.

Paul declared in 2 Cor. 5:17, "Everything old has passed away; see, everything has become new!" It is the resurrection of Jesus that makes all things new. This is the compelling vision of the Easter season. The future in the risen Christ beckons us to forget the old and look to the new in hope. We are thus drawn into God's future, discarding our preoccupations with the past and moving along to a new day in which we now know God in a totally new way.

The Gospel
JOHN 13:31-35 (RCL, BCP);
JOHN 13:31-33a, 34-35 (RC)

The Fourth Gospel offers a startlingly different version of the Last Supper from what we find in the Synoptics. Here no one except Judas, who is thus identified—only in this Gospel—as the betrayer (13:22-26), eats anything. Jesus says nothing regarding his body and blood becoming food and drink for the disciples, and indeed for the world: those themes, so familiar in the Last Supper scenes in the Synoptics, are transposed to the miraculous feeding in John 6, where they receive much deeper treatment. Jesus' washing of his disciples' feet and his command to do the same (in Latin, his *mandatum*, the basis of our "Maundy" Thursday observances), and Judas's abrupt departure, are also found only in John. These unique features set the tone for the long "Farewell Discourse" that follows in chapters 14–17, as the Johannine Jesus gathers his disciples into a spiritual intimacy with himself, with the Father, and with the Spirit as companion and advocate *(paraklētos)*. This intimacy threatens again and again to break out of the constraints of narrative time, drawing the reader into a contemporaneity with the disciples in their mutual fellowship with the Lord.[47] But of course this same contemporaneity is also the effect of our eucharistic practice, as we place ourselves again and again at that last meal, eat and drink "for the remembrance of" Jesus, and look forward in prayer for the coming of God's kingdom.

Jesus can declare that "the Son of Man *has been glorified*," and God glorified in him (13:31), though a few chapters later Jesus will ask the Father to glorify him (17:1-5). This "glorification" is obviously not an event but a truth available to the eye of faith: thus the disciples saw Jesus' "glory" revealed already at the wedding in Cana (2:11). It is an important theme in the Fourth Gospel that Jesus does not seek his own glory but is given glory by the Father because he does what the Father wills (8:50-54); nevertheless, his opponents, the *Ioudaioi*,[48] insist that glory be given to God, *not* to Jesus (9:24). Here Jesus looks forward to his death not as a scandal or a tragedy but as his necessary departure from his disciples—and yet another opportunity to give glory to God and receive glory for his obedience (compare 12:27-33).

The "new commandment" to "love one another" is not new at all (as the author of 1 John acknowledges, 2:7; compare Lev. 19:18, "you shall love your neighbor as yourself"). What is new is the example that Jesus provides, giving definite shape to his command: "just as I have loved you," that is, "to the end" (13:1), thus "love one another" (v. 33). The import of that command is clear in the interchange with Peter that follows (vv. 36-38, verses that are omitted because they inevitably draw the reader back to the events of Holy Week).

WE ARE COMMANDED TO BEAR WITNESS AS DISCIPLES OF JESUS BY LOVING ONE ANOTHER (V. 35), PARTICIPATING IN THE LIGHT OF GOD AMID THE DARKNESS OF THE WORLD.

It is this peculiar character of the Fourth Gospel's narrative—its tendency to blur the boundaries of space and time, allowing Jesus to speak at one moment in the past to his disciples and in the next in the present to the Gospel's readers—that makes this text "work" in the weeks after Easter. Within the constraints of narrative time, Jesus in this scene is looking *forward* to his death—which is to say, "backward" to Holy Week, for those hearing this text in the season of Easter. But the Johannine Jesus is never bound to one place or time. *We* who hear the gospel are the "little children" who cannot follow Jesus now but will follow later (v. 36; compare the use of the phrase in 1 John 2:1, 12, 28; 3:7, 18; 4:4; 5:21). And *we* are commanded to bear witness as disciples of Jesus by loving one another (v. 35), participating in the light of God amid the darkness of the world (see 1 John 2:7-9; 4:7-21).

SIXTH SUNDAY OF EASTER

MAY 16, 2004

REVISED COMMON	EPISCOPAL (BCP)	ROMAN CATHOLIC
Acts 16:9-15	Psalm 67	Acts 15:1-2, 22-29
Psalm 67	Acts 14:8-18	Ps. 67:2-3, 5, 6, 8
	or Joel 2:21-27	
Rev. 21:10, 22—22:5	Rev. 21:22—22:5	Rev. 21:10-14, 22-23
	or Acts 14:8-18	
John 14:23-29	John 14:23-29	John 14:23-29
or John 5:1-9		

Living with Judas's Question

"There are no atheists in foxholes." That old adage survives, despite its inaccuracy, because it reinforces what many of us want to believe. If we are religious, it's gratifying to think that under severe stress, anyone would turn to faith in God, as we do. If we're not religious, we can take the adage as implying that religious beliefs are a ready crutch for the anxious, nothing more. As a matter of fact, however, atheists come through adversities, even battlefield experiences, with their convictions intact.

The vulnerability of standing before the great mysteries of life and death without a sense of complete certainty can be unbearably difficult. As the triumphant alleluias of Easter fade into hazy memory, and as daily routines, concerns, and anxieties swirl up around us, it is hard to be at peace with the emptiness and silence that are so often our only experience of God. Yet as the Most Rev. Rowan Williams, new Archbishop of Canterbury, has written, theological integrity requires that we resist the "totalizing perspective" that is the constant seduction of religious language. All true theology must begin in a dispossession before God and proceed under the discipline of *apophasis*, "the acknowledgment of the inadequacy of any form, verbal, visual or gestural, to picture God definitively, to finish the business of religious speech."

> AS THE TRIUMPHANT ALLELUIAS OF EASTER FADE INTO HAZY MEMORY, AND AS DAILY ROUTINES, CONCERNS, AND ANXIETIES SWIRL UP AROUND US, IT IS HARD TO BE AT PEACE WITH THE EMPTINESS AND SILENCE THAT ARE SO OFTEN OUR ONLY EXPERIENCE OF GOD.

Authentic theology, then, must begin in the discipline of prayer.[49] For Morning Prayer each day, the Episcopal *Book of Common Prayer* offers a prayer of St. John Chrysostom, which asks of God "in this world knowledge of your truth, and in the world to come life everlasting." The prayer requires us to own our vulnerability before God: we can hold neither divine truth nor eternal life as our own possession, but must receive them from God's gracious hand.

What do Easter memories still mean for us as our lives move on? We know that question had a terrible urgency for the early communities who first confessed Jesus as risen Lord. Paul's first letter to the Thessalonians reveals the anxiety his audience felt as members of their church had "fallen asleep" in death—something for which Paul's preaching of Jesus' imminent return had apparently not prepared them (1 Thess. 4:13-18). Luke's Gospel repeatedly takes on a didactic tone, warning against the false expectation of Jesus' contemporaries that "the kingdom of God was to appear immediately" (Luke 11:11), or that the "master is delayed in coming" (12:45; Matt. 24:48). Matthew extolled the bridesmaids who carried enough oil for a long wait (Matt. 25:1-13), and the servant who made the best of the time during his master's absence (25:14-30). The last verses of the Fourth Gospel reflect the dismay and surprise of the Johannine community when the "beloved disciple" died (John 21:20-23). Describing the "crisis" that overtook communities of Jesus' followers as early as the 40s of the first century, Paula Fredriksen has written, "After Easter, the world could no longer be the same place, nor was it—yet it was." Belief in Jesus' resurrection, "coupled with the delay of the End, plunged the early Christian movement into a kind of eschatological twilight zone": the passing of time itself constituted a "major trauma for the Christian movement."[50]

How can Jesus be the risen Lord if the world goes on as it ever has? *When* will Jesus reveal himself to the world? Those questions focus both the expectation and disappointment the early Christian communities felt in the decades after Easter. But in the Fourth Gospel, Judas (not Iscariot) asks a different question—and one that seems to presume a peculiar answer to those I've just phrased: "Lord, how is it that you will reveal yourself to us, *and not to the world?*" (John 14:22).

Deeply held convictions make us vulnerable to embarrassment, to grief, and to loss. In today's readings, we catch glimpses of early believers in Jesus feeling that sort of vulnerability. Perhaps we also see them trying to protect themselves from loss by adapting their hopes into new, perhaps less fragile forms, or by seeking reassurance in the difference between "our" beliefs and the beliefs of others.

How do *we* protect ourselves from intimacy with God? How do we try to evade our own vulnerability before the God "to whom all hearts are open, all desires known, and from whom no secrets are hid"?

JOEL 2:21-27 (BCP, alt.)

An earlier passage in Joel, the prophet's call for national repentance to avert catastrophe (2:1-2, 12-17), was an alternative reading for Ash Wednesday (BCP, p. 264). Now the prophet proclaims reassurance because God offers relief from calamity, a parching drought (v. 23) and a swarm of locusts (v. 25; cf. 1:4). By the alleviation of this crisis, the people will know that the LORD, and no other, is truly their God (v. 27).

Earlier verses, not included in today's reading, make clear that it was "in response to his people," specifically to their repentance and return, that the LORD acted (2:19). Do we imagine that God actually responds to our repentance? Or do we more often expect God's deliverance and favor as simply what we deserve?

ACTS 14:8-18 (BCP)

Paul—that is, the Lukan Paul who speaks here—shows himself able to deliver a "philosophical" sermon that any self-respecting Stoic would approve. In place of the foolishness of worshiping images and sacrificing animals, Paul calls the crowds in Lystra to turn to "the living God" who created the world and providentially sends the rain and fertility of field through which people are fed and satisfied (vv. 15-17). In theme, this sermon anticipates Paul's address to the Stoic and Epicurean philosophers in Athens (17:22-31), except that the sermon in Athens will conclude with a reference to God having raised Jesus from the dead, an idea that some of the philosophers find ludicrous (13:32). Here in Lystra, in contrast, Paul faces not sophisticated pagan philosophers, but an unsophisticated crowd of rustics (they speak their own language, not good *koinē* Greek: v. 11). The crowd quickly assimilates the miracle Paul and Barnabas have performed to their local cult: the apostles are "gods . . . come down to us in human form!" (v. 11).

Here we can see Luke making an appeal for the sympathy of his target audience, educated readers from the diaspora synagogue (Jews, or Gentile "Godfearers"), for whom the pagan notion of worshiping *people* would be as ridiculous as worshiping the gods through images, but (in contrast to the Areopagus crowd in chapter 17) for whom belief in miracles or of the future resurrection of the dead is deeply held. (Later, when Paul stands before the Sanhedrin in Jerusalem, Luke's appeal will be much more direct: Paul will call out to his "brothers" the Pharisees that he is "on trial concerning the hope of the resurrection of the dead" [23:6]).[51]

We would love to know what effect Paul's sermon might have had; would some of the Lycaonians come to their senses and honor the true God proclaimed by him? (Even in Athens, some of the philosophers became believers, 17:33.) What of the man who is suddenly able to stand "on his own two feet" for the first time in his life? We hear nothing more of him (contrast how the Fourth Gospel pursues those who receive healing from Jesus, asking what they now make of their healer: John 5:10-15; 9:1-41). Instead, Luke interrupts the scene to reintroduce Jewish antagonists who have pursued Paul from Antioch and Iconium to Lystra (14:19) and seek to stone him to death. These opponents, always motivated by irrational jealousy or greed, are an important plot device for Luke, sometimes functioning simply to move Paul from one place to the next (see 9:23-25; 13:50; 14:2-7; 17:5-8, 13-14; 18:6, 12-17; 20:3, 19; 21:27-30).

Luke crafts a subtle narrative world in which his chosen readers can feel at home. For enlightened men and women who already believe in one invisible God who created all things, who scorn idolatry and look for the resurrection of the dead, the apostle Paul is an attractive and congenial figure. Only people motivated by the basest of motives could oppose him! This text advances Paul's cause at the expense of the Lycaonians, who function almost as comic foils. Luke knows, however, that more serious charges have been raised against his protagonist, and therefore he will present an extended defense of the apostle Paul in later chapters (Acts 21—28).

> THIS TEXT ALMOST INVITES HEARERS TO CONGRATULATE THEMSELVES FOR NOT BEING BUMPKINS LIKE THE LYCAONIANS.

This text almost invites hearers to congratulate themselves for not being bumpkins like the Lycaonians. It's a far greater challenge—but how important!—to ask how this story can confront the ways we "idolize" our own religious preferences rather than attending to the liberation God wants to do in our midst!

ACTS 15:1-2, 22-29 (RC)

Acts 15 gives an account of the so-called apostolic council in Jerusalem, to which Paul also refers (in Gal. 2:1-10). The assigned reading leaves out the report of the council's deliberation, including Peter's sermon (which recites events in chapter 10), and James's announcement of what seems to be the definitive verdict (note v. 19, "I have reached the decision"). The story certainly implies that James holds unparalleled power in the Jerusalem church, though his verdict is endorsed by "the apostles and the elders, with the consent of the whole church" (v. 22). It also bears out Paul's own statement that James was among the "pillars" in the Jerusalem church who embraced his mission among the Gentiles (Gal. 2:9-10).

The widespread notion that James led a "Judaizing" front antagonistic to Paul owes much to Paul's reference (in Gal. 2:12) to "certain people" who came to Antioch "from James," prompting Peter to withdraw from common meals with Gentiles (Gal. 2:11-14)—though this account does not say that James *sent* people to impose a Torah-inspired segregation at meals.[52] According to Luke, the community of believers in Jesus arrives at a consensus that (1) refuses to impose the requirement of circumcision on Gentiles; that is, they may participate in the community of believers *as Gentiles,* but (2) requires of these Gentiles a reasonable accommodation to Jewish sensibilities at common meals: the avoidance of meat sacrificed to idols, blood, and meat from animals that had been strangled (that is, not slaughtered according to Jewish practice: 15:29). The prohibition of fornication is added for good measure. In effect, Gentiles observing these rules would eat kosher meat or none at all.

It has long been a fashion in Christian preaching to contrast Paul's gospel of "freedom" from and indifference to the law, on the one hand, with a Jewish Christianity that failed to break out of its ethnic prejudice into the clear light of Pauline universalism, on the other. That rather self-congratulatory habit is increasingly seen as historically untenable[53] and offensive especially to Jews for whom it suggests that genuine faith in God and Torah observance are incompatible.[54] Some important recent scholarship suggests, instead, that the "certain individuals" who sought to impose circumcision (Acts 15:2) were introducing an innovation that deviated from the apostolic consensus; they could no longer believe in Jesus' imminent return, so they sought to "consolidate the community within Judaism."[55]

It is, of course, much easier to write off what Paul calls "the circumcision faction" (Gal. 2:12) as people very different from us—observant Jews!—than to acknowledge that they may simply have felt the delay of Jesus' return as a greater challenge than we do. Their response to the vulnerability they felt as time went inexorably by was to seek reassurance in the routines of their ancestral religions and seek to impose them on others. Are there ways we do the same? Do we find it easier to urge others to move toward us—to join our religious communities, to share our beliefs and practices—than to stand with *them,* asking attentively what God seeks to do in their lives?

ACTS 16:9-15 (RCL)

Paul's vision in Troas is meant to strike chords of historical and mythic memory. Here, according to Homer's *Iliad,* Greek and Trojan warriors clashed and perished outside the walls of ancient Troy, fighting for honor, and incidentally the possession of a beautiful woman. From here, according to Virgil's *Aeneid,* the courageous Aeneas escaped, carrying his family to eventual safety in Italy and becoming the ancestor of the illustrious caesars. Luke could scarcely afford to describe Paul's move from Asia Minor to Greece as a merely pragmatic decision. The Spirit of Jesus directs Paul toward Troas (v. 7) in a dream, and a mysterious man pleads with him to "come over to Macedonia and help us." By implication, the new community Paul serves stakes a claim here to be recognized as a historic new people.

The journey by sea brings Paul face to face with Lydia, a worker in purple. Whether or not fair Helen's match in beauty, Lydia is clearly a woman of means, able to run her own business, decide (for herself and "her household") to accept a new faith, and serve as host to the church (v. 15). Prominent women like Lydia would have served as the sort of "patron" that Paul acknowledges in Rom. 16:1 (the deacon Phoebe) or perhaps in 1 Cor. 1:11 (Chloe of Corinth), and they are important in Luke's narrative.

Responsive Reading

PSALM 67 (RCL, BCP);
PSALM 67:2-3, 5, 6, 8 (RC)

The psalmist offers praise to God in gratitude for God's mercy in causing the earth to "yield its increase" (v. 6)—a theme that echoes the reading from Joel. God's graciousness is also sought in equity and harmony among the nations and peoples (vv. 2-5).

Second Reading

REVELATION 21:10, 22—22:5 (RCL);
REVELATION 21:22—22:5 (BCP);
REVELATION 21:10-14, 22-23 (RC)

In the wake of the awe-inspiring destruction of "Babylon" (i.e., Rome) in chapters 17–18, arguably the climax of the book (although curiously neglected in all three lectionaries), John sees a vision of holy Jerusalem "coming down out of heaven" (21:10). The Roman Catholic reading includes John's description of the city's appearance.

We don't yet comprehend the power of John's vision if we content ourselves with deciphering the code name "Babylon." John's revelation *(apokalypsis)* reveals what cannot be perceived with the naked eye or with a mind saturated with the imagery and propaganda of imperial ideology. In every city square across the

Mediterranean world, the Roman Empire was celebrated and hymned as having ushered in the age of prosperity, peace, and honor; even Roman force and conquest served heaven's ends. To speak of the downfall of "Babylon" and the punishment of "the great whore" was to turn against overwhelming cultural currents that presented Rome's power and splendor as simple normalcy.

If preachers do nothing more than discuss the defects of the long-departed Roman civilization, they subvert the power of the Revelation. For John, the arrogance, the injustice, and the brutality of ancient Babylon were not the stuff of historical memory alone but of *contemporary* experience in his own society. If we cannot speak of the reality of Babylon in our own world, don't we reduce John's vision to a matter of weak academic relevance alone?

Neither do we do justice to his message if we speak of the "new heaven and new earth" simply as the description of a distant afterlife. John proclaims a dazzling reality about the here and now. He wants, not to convince his hearers to accept as plausible his vision of the world's end, but

> IF WE CANNOT SPEAK OF THE REALITY OF BABYLON IN OUR OWN WORLD, DON'T WE REDUCE JOHN'S VISION TO A MATTER OF WEAK ACADEMIC RELEVANCE ALONE?

to move them to place their trust and allegiance in the God who even now is "making all things new" (21:5). In today's text, the city without a temple (21:22) is the object of longing and devotion *now* for all those who know that "the home of God is among mortals" (21:3).

Can we speak convincingly of what it means to live, in the midst of death-dealing Babylon, as citizens of the heavenly Jerusalem, where death and mourning shall no longer hold sway? What does that citizenship feel like; what are its practices, the disciplines that sustain it?

THE GOSPEL
JOHN 5:1-9 (RCL, alt.)

This story of the healing of a lame man in the pool Beth-zatha anticipates the healing of a blind man whom Jesus commands to wash in the pool of Siloam (9:1-7). The prominence of the pools in these stories reflects the nearly universal connection between water and healing, but it also hints at the ritual purity neither man could enjoy. Curiously, in the latter story Jesus repudiates his disciples' suggestion that the man born blind suffered because of sin (9:2-3), but in the verses that follow today's text, Jesus implicitly accepts just such a notion when he commands the healed man to sin no more "so that nothing worse happens to you" (5:14). Rather than attempt to harmonize these accounts, the lectionary simply omits the troubling verses. In both stories, Jesus' healing on the

Sabbath arouses indignation and opposition from the *Ioudaioi* (on the term see the discussion for the Fourth Sunday after Easter, above), although again those verses come after the current reading.

The story is not obviously an Easter scene, except in the sense that throughout the Fourth Gospel the Johannine Jesus speaks and acts as *already* the risen Lord. The account contrasts the man's decades-long, yet pathetically ineffective strategy of waiting by the side of the pool for the water to be stirred up, with the immediate and complete healing he receives at Jesus' command. (Manuscript variants at v. 4 offer the astonishing explanation that an angel periodically troubles the water, offering a first-come, first-served possibility of healing—a rather cynical prospect, given the man's condition.) A preacher may want to explore the ways we can limit ourselves to ineffective but familiar routines and shut out the power of God to heal. What would it be like if we simply took Jesus at his word and found our feet beneath us?

JOHN 14:23-29 (RCL, BCP, RC)

If we turn to the Fourth Gospel with the ringing apocalyptic scenarios of the Synoptics in our ears, Jesus' interchange with Judas will astonish us. After all, the other evangelists take great pains to sustain faith in the imminent, universally evident return of Jesus ("as the lightning comes from the east and flashes as far as the west . . ." Matt. 24:27), by identifying the clear public signs that will precede it (Matt. 24:4-35; Mark 13:3-37; Luke 21:8-36). In the face of the relentless, grinding pressure of time and history, those Gospels insist that though no one can name the day or hour, there *will* come a day and hour when the Son of Man is revealed to the world. Judas asks a very different question of the Johannine Jesus, a question that seems to presume the opposite of what the Synoptics work so strenuously to affirm: "How is it that you will reveal yourself to us and *not* to the world?"

Here some interpreters have perceived the complete collapse of the eschatological tension that drives so much of early Christian thought (and was, in Ernst Käsemann's famous phrase, the "mother of Christian theology"). And even more remarkably, the Johannine Jesus accepts the terms of the question as he responds with characteristic serenity. He will reveal himself to his disciples by making his home with them, together with the Father (14:23) and the Advocate, the Holy Spirit (14:26). The lightning flash of Matthew's apocalyptic horizon now seems restricted to illumining the interior of the believer's soul. Surely we see here the evidence that the Johannine community had made considerable progress down the road toward the notorious "so-called Gnostic" Christianities of the second century![56]

However congenial such a move away from apocalyptic "realism" might be for some contemporary Christians in the West, it comes at a cost. As spiritual heirs of the great revival movements of the eighteenth and early nineteenth centuries, we are accustomed to describing faith as a largely interior affair; but to surrender faith in the public manifestation of Jesus is to evacuate the term "messiah" of much of its meaning. The Johannine solution struck in today's text also puts tremendous weight on the community, and on individuals within it, to manifest the presence of God within—by loving Jesus and keeping his word (14:23), and by loving one another (13:34)—as the public corroboration evidence of their faith claims. On the Gospel's own terms, if the community does not manifest exemplary love in its common life, how shall anyone—within the community or without—know that those claims are true?

On the other hand, it is possible to read the whole of the Last Discourse(s) in John as an extended reflection on what it means to settle in for a long wait. Again and again Jesus warns his disciples he is leaving, though only for "a short while," prompting them to wonder just what "a little while" might mean (16:16-24). In the anxiety of the disciples in the upper room, we can recognize the concern of the Johannine community (and our own?) as we grapple with the long-extended "public" absence of the risen Jesus. The message conveyed by the medium itself—

> ON THE GOSPEL'S OWN TERMS, IF THE COMMUNITY DOES NOT MANIFEST EXEMPLARY LOVE IN ITS COMMON LIFE, HOW SHALL ANYONE—WITHIN THE COMMUNITY OR WITHOUT—KNOW THAT THOSE CLAIMS ARE TRUE?

a farewell discourse in the intimacy of this small room—is that Jesus remains present, indwelling the community of believers, even as they experience his absence.

We cannot say how many of these early communities were troubled by the apparent delay of an imminent consummation. We should be impressed, nevertheless, how often their means for negotiating what may have been a tremendous crisis of faith was to emphasize ever more strongly the simple imperative of love: for God, for one another, and for their neighbors. As we work and weep and wait for the coming of God's reign, can any other command provide better focus for our lives?

THE ASCENSION OF OUR LORD

MAY 20, 2004

REVISED COMMON	EPISCOPAL (BCP)	ROMAN CATHOLIC
Acts 1:1-11	Acts 1:1-11 or 2 Kings 2:1-15	Acts 1:1-11
Psalm 47 or Psalm 93	Psalm 47 or 110:1-5	Ps. 47:2-3, 6-7, 8-9
Eph. 1:15-23	Eph. 1:15-23 or Acts 1:1-11	Eph. 1:17-23 or Heb. 9:24-28; 10:19-23
Luke 24:44-53	Luke 24:49-53 or Mark 16:9-15, 19-20	Luke 24:46-53

Preaching the Ascension

I observed earlier that the earliest confession of Jesus as risen Lord understood the resurrection itself as Jesus' exaltation to heaven and the Easter experiences as manifestations of the one who was already exalted (see my comments on "The Challenge of Proclaiming the Risen Lord," above).[57] Of course, that is not the way Luke tells it! Alone among the Gospels, Luke describes the appearances of the risen Lord taking place over a specific finite period of forty days (Acts 1:3, echoing the duration of the temptation in the desert, Luke 4:2).[58] In contrast to earlier tradition, that is, Luke has created a forty-day interval of *earthly* encounters in which a risen, *but not yet exalted* Jesus interacts with his disciples. One function of this interim period is to set apart the Eleven (the Twelve minus Judas) as eyewitnesses of Jesus: they are "his apostles whom he had chosen," distinguished both as the recipients of "many convincing proofs" and his instructions "through the Holy Spirit" (Acts 1:2-3). (Note that the selection of Matthias to replace Judas in Acts 1:15-26 stipulates that he, also, was in the company of the Eleven during the critical time, "beginning from the baptism of John until the day when [Jesus] was taken up from us" [1:22].)

The Eleven (or reconstituted Twelve) are thus uniquely authorized as "witnesses to the resurrection," the source of apostolic teaching and practice for later generations. Luke's narrative also implies that any subsequent reports of visions of the risen Jesus are mistaken or fraudulent. Note that Paul's encounter with the risen Christ, which happens well *after* the forty-day period between Easter and the ascension, is only an *audition*; Luke stipulates that he "could see nothing," other than the light, which blinded him (9:3; see also 22:6, 9; 26:13).

To celebrate the Feast of the Ascension, then, is to celebrate an event unique to Luke's narrative, and one that clearly serves Luke's theological and ecclesiastical agenda. We do well to ask which aspects of that agenda we want to proclaim and which of the questions we bring to the text may be extrinsic to Luke's purpose. Luke was apparently more concerned, for example, to assure readers of the authority of the apostles than to represent the characteristics of a risen (but not yet ascended) Jesus. To press for answers to questions about Jesus' resurrected body may not be the best use of this text (remember Paul's stinging reproach in 1 Cor. 15:35-36).

On the other hand, affirming the authority of the apostles can raise more questions than it answers. In what, exactly, does that authority consist, and who bears it? For Luke, *apostolic* authority derives from the duty to bear witness (Luke 24:48-49; Acts 1:8). It is often a matter of consensus, achieved through hard deliberations, and not a few surprises! When Christians today seek to shut down conversation by appeals to "apostolic authority," we might well wonder if they have read the book of Acts.

FIRST READING
2 KINGS 2:1-15 (BCP, alt.)

At a surface level, the obvious reason to read this passage today is that it concerns Elijah's "ascension"—his being taken up in a whirlwind into heaven. Primarily, of course, this is a "succession" narrative in which Elisha takes up the senior prophet's mantle and authority, not just to speak in the LORD's name but to work mighty acts with the LORD's power (2:13-14).

The interaction between the two prophets is peculiar. Elijah is evasive, trying repeatedly to "shake off" Elisha (presumably to pass on to heaven alone). The prophets at the shrines of Bethel and Jericho know that the LORD is about to take Elijah, so this is a drama in the wider community's life as well. Recall that in the Deuteronomistic narrative there are eras in Israel's history when the word of God is available only to a few (though Elijah erred in believing he alone is left loyal to the LORD: 1 Kings 19:14, 18). The crisis in succession is a crisis for the presence of the word among the people: so Amos spoke (8:11) of a

> THE CRISIS IN SUCCESSION IS A CRISIS FOR THE PRESENCE OF THE WORD AMONG THE PEOPLE: SO AMOS SPOKE (8:11) OF A FAMINE "OF HEARING THE WORDS OF THE LORD." DO WE FACE SUCH FAMINES IN OUR OWN INDIVIDUAL OR COMMUNITY LIVES?

famine "of hearing the words of the Lord." Do we face such famines in our own individual or community lives?

ACTS 1:1-11 (RCL, BCP, RC)

This, Luke's second account of the ascension scene, is not simply a recapitulation of the first (Luke 24, see below). Jesus' farewell words serve to introduce the plot for all that follows in the book of Acts: "You will be my witnesses in Jerusalem, in all Judea and Samaria, and to the ends of the earth" (1:8). This scene also includes the sudden presence of "two men in white robes" who rebuke the disciples for staring into the now empty skies. Within Luke's larger purpose this scene provides yet another warning against a too-fervent expectation of Jesus' imminent return (compare Luke 17:20-21; 19:11; 21:8-9). The rebuke assures that Jesus "*will* come in the same way as you saw him go into heaven" (Acts 1:11)— but it does no good to stand and wait; better for the apostles to get on with the work ahead!

RESPONSIVE READING

PSALM 47 (RCL, BCP); PSALM 47:2-3, 6-7, 8-9 (RC)

This psalm is widely regarded as having had a ceremonial context in ancient Israel, connected perhaps with the succession of a new king, or with a presentation of the ark of the covenant as the LORD's throne. The language of the LORD's dominance over the nations ("he subdues peoples under us, and nations under our feet. . . . God is king over the nations. . . . The princes of the peoples gather as the people of the God of Abraham") is exaggerated and may have been sung in expression of hope for future triumph.

PSALM 93 (RCL, alt.)

A psalm of praise to the enthroned LORD. The "floods" in vv. 3-4 represent forces of chaos that threaten life and are reminiscent of the antagonist "Prince Sea" in ancient Canaanite myth.

PSALM 110:1-5 (BCP, alt.)

This psalm, in which the LORD promises victory to the king ("my lord," v. 1), is best known to Christians because of its use in the New Testament, where it clearly is read as a prophecy of the Messiah (see Matt. 22:44, where it is put on Jesus' lips; Acts 2:34; 1 Cor. 15:25; Eph. 1:20; Heb. 1:3, 13). The king is also promised priestly prerogative, "according to the order of Melchizedek" (v. 4), without known lineage (see Gen. 14:18): perhaps, without restriction to the lineage of Aaron (or Zadok).

SECOND READING
EPHESIANS 1:15-23 (RCL, BCP);
EPHESIANS 1:17-23 (RC)

The whole of this passage is actually one long run-on sentence in Greek, revealing the peculiar style that leads many scholars to doubt that Ephesians came from Paul's hand. Equally surprising is the opening phrase, that the author has "heard of your faith in the Lord Jesus," rather than knowing it firsthand, as we would expect Paul to know the faith of the Ephesians among whom he sojourned for so long (according to Acts 19:1-41; note also that 1 and 2 Corinthians were written from Ephesus). The author prays that the hearers may receive wisdom and insight into the "great power" of God, made known in the resurrection and exaltation: "God put this power to work in Christ when he raised him from the dead and seated him at his right hand in the heavenly places" (1:20).

Just here, where the epistle touches on the theme of Jesus' exaltation and ascension to heaven, it sounds yet another note discordant with the unquestioned letters of Paul. God *has* "put all things under his feet and has made him the head over all things for the church" (1:22), something that Paul himself speaks of strictly in the future tense (e.g., 1 Cor. 15:24-28: Jesus "must reign *until* he has put all his enemies under his feet"). The strong eschatological tension that runs through Paul's letters appears to be collapsed here.

HEBREWS 9:24-28; 10:19-23 (RC, alt.)

In this reading the anonymous author of Hebrews puts yet another distinctive spin on the theme of heavenly exaltation, subordinating aspects of the apocalyptic context in which this language originally made sense (see, e.g., Dan. 7:9-14) to the author's thoroughgoing allegorical scheme. According to this scheme, every practical aspect of worship in the Jerusalem Temple is read as a "shadow" or a "sketch" (9:23) of heavenly realities, which are associated with Jesus. Thus, in today's text, Jesus' ascension into heaven is assimilated with the high priest's entry into the Holy of Holies on the Day of Atonement (Leviticus 16), or rather, becomes the reality of which the priest's actions are a "mere copy." Similarly, Jesus' death on the cross is not simply labeled a sacrifice for sin (so also Rom. 3:24-25), but is explained in terms of the Day of Atonement ritual. The high priest must enter the sanctuary each year to make sacrifice for the people's inadvertent sins; Jesus, on the other hand, has offered the perfect sacrifice "once for all" (9:26). If the high priest sprinkles blood on the mercy seat of the ark, Jesus sprinkles his own blood to cleanse the hearts of sinners (10:19-22).

Here the letter's exhortative center, with all its liabilities, begins to come to the surface. If Christ is our true high priest and his death has taken him "behind the veil" in heaven to the place where atonement is accomplished "once for all," then there is no further opportunity for atonement, no "second chance," if one falls away from this purified clean state. The point is made explicit in 10:26-31, verses not included in today's reading and seldom heard from the pulpit. "There no longer remains a sacrifice for sins" for those who persist in sins after forgiveness in Christ's blood (10:26); "how much worse the punishment" for these people than for the Hebrews gathered outside the Holy of Holies on Yom Kippur (10:29-31). Remarkably, many churches have embraced this writing's theology of heavenly atonement for sin, though few have pressed the author's urgent warning that there is "no second chance" with God.

> IN TODAY'S TEXT, JESUS' ASCENSION INTO HEAVEN IS ASSIMILATED WITH THE HIGH PRIEST'S ENTRY INTO THE HOLY OF HOLIES ON THE DAY OF ATONEMENT.

THE GOSPEL
LUKE 24:44-53 (RCL);
LUKE 24:46-53 (RC);
LUKE 24:49-53 (BCP)

Just where does this story begin? The disagreement among the lectionaries allows us to see that Luke does not regard the ascension as a distinct and self-contained event, but as the climax of a process that has been continuing since the road to Emmaus. The RCL and Roman Catholic lections allow us to see this most clearly: they begin with Jesus' words to the disciples, still gathered behind closed doors, by which he "opened their minds to understand the scriptures" (vv. 44-46). Luke provides a summary of that revelation but no details: "Thus it is written, that the Messiah is to suffer and to rise from the dead on the third day, and that repentance of sins is to be proclaimed in his name to all nations." If we ask *where* in Jewish scripture the idea of a suffering, dying, and ris-

> LUKE DOES NOT REGARD THE ASCENSION AS A DISTINCT AND SELF-CONTAINED EVENT, BUT AS THE CLIMAX OF A PROCESS THAT HAS BEEN CONTINUING SINCE THE ROAD TO EMMAUS.

ing messiah appears, we receive no answer beyond the naked affirmation (as also at 24:26-27; Acts 3:18). Later in the book of Acts, Luke will provide glimpses into the "messianic exegesis" his church practiced, embedded in the sermons the apostles deliver (see Acts 2:25-28, 31; 4:11, 25-26; 8:30-35). As fragile as this web of "prophecies" appears to us (pity the student who submits such exegesis in a graduate course today!), it is meant to support what is obviously an important affirmation for Luke—that Jesus died as the *messiah*, "according to the scriptures." The BCP lection omits this theme entirely.

The narrative in Luke 24 omits what the reiteration of this story in Acts 1 provides, namely, the forty-day interval of Jesus' teaching and fellowship with his disciples. On the other hand, it foreshadows important aspects of the story's continuation in Acts: that the disciples will be empowered by the Holy Spirit (v. 49, cf. Acts 2:1-12), and that (in marked contrast to the Gospels of Matthew and Mark) they will stay in Jerusalem, continuing to worship in the temple and join in the life of the Jewish community there (vv. 52-53). Precisely because this Jerusalem community is so important for Luke (alone), it is surprising how quickly they move from the spotlight once Paul makes his appearance (in Acts 9), only reappearing at important junctures in his career (chapters 15, 21). For a deeper appreciation of this early Jewish form of faith in Jesus, we must look to much later sources, like the *Church History* of the fourth-century writer Eusebius.

Different as they are, Luke's two ascension scenes (in Luke 24 and Acts 1) both underline the broader theme throughout the two-volume work: that the disciples' proper focus of attention is not Jesus' path into heaven, but the work Jesus seeks to accomplish through his church on earth.

MARK 16:9-15, 19-20 (BCP, alt.)

We know from the critical comparison of ancient manuscripts that the "longer ending of Mark" was probably not originally part of the Gospel. It also appears to be derivative, depending on other Gospel accounts which it rather woodenly summarizes (v. 9 = John 20:1-2, 11-19; Luke 8:2; v. 11 = Luke 24:11, 22-25 and 20:19-29; vv. 12-13 = Luke 24:12-35; v. 14 = Matt. 29:19; Luke 24:47; v. 19 = Acts 1:2; vv. 17-18, 20 effectively summarize the book of Acts). Again, characteristic Episcopal circumspection is evident in the lectionary's avoidance of references to snake handling, glossolalia, and the power to drink poison without harm (16:16-18).

Other variant endings are printed in the NRSV text and footnotes. They all betray some level of apprehension about the abrupt ending of the story that was apparently original, at 16:8. That is, this text seeks to overcome the perceived inadequacy of the ending at 16:8 by providing supplemental endings more familiar to readers of the other Gospels. While the relatively modern science of text criticism has taught many of us to question the value of these alternative endings, the early church canonized *writings,* not manuscripts, with the result that all these endings have equal claim to being "canonical." Rather than forcing a choice among them, the use of this alternative reading presents an opportunity to reflect on our perception that one ending is more appropriate than another. What do we think we "need" to hear to make the Gospel complete? What would it be like to live with the echoes of "terror and amazement" that presumably originally ended the Gospel (16:8)?

SEVENTH SUNDAY OF EASTER

MAY 23, 2004

REVISED COMMON	EPISCOPAL (BCP)	ROMAN CATHOLIC
Acts 16:16-34	Acts 16:16-34 or 1 Sam. 12:19-24	Acts 7:55-60
Psalm 97	Ps. 68:1-20 or Psalm 47	Ps. 97:1-2, 6-7, 9

Rev. 22:12-14,
  16-17, 20-21
	Rev. 22:12-14
	  or Acts 16:16-34
		Rev. 22:12-14, 16-17, 20

John 17:20-26	John 17:20-26	John 17:20-26

God's Kingship?

If we were to remove from our worship the language of God as "king" ruling over the earth, we would fall mute for large swaths of our liturgies. In the Lord's Prayer, we pray continually for the coming of the kingdom of God; yet what exactly does that mean? Can we really detect signs of God's reign in the world around us *now,* or does history teach us instead that the language we use in prayer can refer only to an almost impossibly distant reality?

Today's readings provide a kaleidoscope of answers from different voices in the history of Israel and the early church. Dominant throughout them all is a sense of God's claim upon creation, and of justice and peace as the content of that claim.

FIRST READING
1 SAMUEL 12:19-24 (BCP, alt.)

The "Deuteronomistic" writers who crafted the narrative stretching from Joshua through 2 Kings wished, above all, to teach Israel the hard lessons they perceived in the exile. The latter part of that epic provides a series of vignettes sufficient to illustrate the theological plot of the whole, which is stated clearly in the verses that precede this reading. The prophet Samuel rebukes the people for having clamored for a king when "the LORD your God was your king" (1 Sam. 12:12). Nevertheless, he warns, "if you will fear the LORD . . . and if both you and the king who reigns over you will follow the LORD your God, it will be well"; otherwise, "the hand of the LORD will be against you and your king" (12:14-15).

History was not so neat, of course. The Deuteronomists were eventually compelled to explain that the offense of an evil king like Manasseh could outweigh the good done by his successor Josiah, even though the latter, more than any of his predecessors, "turned to the LORD with all his heart, with all his soul, and with all his might" (2 Kings 23:25). Thus the LORD allowed Josiah to be struck down in battle because of *Manasseh's* sins (23:26-30).

Today's text makes clear that Israel's fate was not the result of the actions of individual kings alone. The whole history of Israel leading up to the exile was the consequence of God having granted the people their disloyal wish. Nevertheless, the prophet's warning is seasoned with the promise of God's unconditional loyalty: "The LORD will not cast away his people, for his great name's sake, because it has pleased the LORD to make you a people for himself" (12:22). Here we see the powerful hope at the heart of the Deuteronomistic theology: even in the wake of the nation's destruction, God's purpose for the *people* remains.

ISRAEL'S FATE WAS NOT THE RESULT OF THE ACTIONS OF INDIVIDUAL KINGS ALONE.

ACTS 16:16-34 (RCL, BCP)

Psalm 97 (RCL, see below) describes God as a powerful deliverer, a king who brings low the rulers of the earth and lifts up the innocent and righteous. We hear now of God liberating a woman in Roman Philippi from a double bondage: she is possessed by a "spirit of divination," and she is owned by men who exploit her condition to turn a profit by exhibiting her "gifts." Not surprisingly, her deliverance at the hands of Paul and Silas enrages her erstwhile owners, who have just lost their means of livelihood. They respond by hauling the apostles before the city magistrates and accusing them of being "Jews and . . . advocating customs that are not lawful for us as Romans to adopt or observe" (v. 21).

The irony here is as sharp as anything in Luke-Acts. The accusers represent Roman civilization as unable to tolerate the apostles' action—but apparently ready enough to accept the abuse and exploitation the woman has suffered! (Note that their accusation is ambiguous: the "customs" they find so offensive might refer to Jewish observances *or* to the act of deliverance from oppression. No doubt Luke would be pleased if his hearers saw direct connections between the two).

Paul and Silas are subjected to severe civic punishment. (Here and elsewhere Luke is perfectly willing to portray Roman law as unjust and cruel.) The story continues, however, with a miracle reminiscent of the theophany in Psalm 97, where deliverance and earthquake coincide. Luke continues to heap up irony:

Paul and Silas are more concerned with the worship and praise of God from their cells (v. 25) than with escape. The jailer, their captor, now shows that he is as much a victim of Roman law as they are, for he anticipates the ultimate punishment for his "failure" to keep his prisoners in chains (v. 27). He is as relieved to find them still present as he is astonished by their deliverance, and accepts baptism with his family (vv. 30-32).

The dramatic denouement of the story follows today's reading: Paul refuses to be released without a public apology by the magistrates—which they give (16:35-39)!

ACTS 7:55-60 (RC)

Luke narrates the death of the first "martyr"—literally, "witness"—among Jesus' followers. While we often use the term to refer to those who tell a court what they know or have seen, or to those who talk about their faith to others, Stephen shows that Christian witness is a matter of what one does and how one lives—and dies. Stephen prays that God "not hold this sin against" those putting him to death (v. 60), just as his Lord prayed (in Luke alone) that those who had crucified him be forgiven (Luke 23:34).

Though the lectionary focuses on the martyrdom, it is important to understand what has brought Stephen to this point in Luke's account. Stephen's speech (the whole of Acts 7) is the longest speech in the book of Acts—even longer than any given by Paul! He has been brought before the Sanhedrin on charges of "saying things against this holy place," i.e., the temple, "and the law," and of alleging that Jesus would bring both to an end (6:13-14). As usual, Luke reports these charges because he intends to show that they are false.

Stephen does not speak against the value or sanctity of the temple (for in that case his accusers would be right—to Luke's great disadvantage). His extensive review of Israelite history shows that God does not "need" the temple or even the land of Israel, to relate to human beings; his speech is strongly reminiscent of 2 Sam 7:5-16, where God responds to David that God has no need of a "house" in which to dwell, but will secure David's house, that is, his dynasty.

All of this gives Stephen's views a sort of biblical pedigree. However provocative Stephen's opinions, they do not justify the charges made against him. As if to seal his own fate, however, Stephen goes on to accuse his hearers—including the high priest of Israel—of being a "stiff-necked people, uncircumcised in hearts and ears," and of resembling their ancestors who killed the prophets (7:51-53; compare Luke 11:47-51). Finally, he claims to have a vision of the "son of man standing at the right hand of God," in the position of authority and power. Personal insult and the claim to have a direct connection with heaven are too much for the Sanhedrin, who throw legal procedure to the wind and lynch Stephen.

Luke wants his readers to understand, first, that God's ancient promises to Israel are being fulfilled in the community of Jesus' disciples, which began as a gathering of law-abiding Jews in the temple (the first Gentile converts have not yet appeared). Second, Luke seeks to show that opposition to that community is always only based in the jealousy and anger of hostile enemies.

As with so much of Luke's narrative, it is tempting to hear this passage with a complacent self-satisfaction. For most modern Christians, the Jerusalem Temple and the observance of Torah are self-evidently irrelevant to faith. As distant as we feel from his Jewish antagonists, we clearly recognize Stephen as one of us. But that means we do not feel the weight of the questions—about the future of Israel and of the Torah—that drive Luke's story!

Precisely as members of the Gentile church that Luke sought to defend as consistent with God's ancient purpose, we do well to ask whether our congregations bear the marks that Luke ascribes, however idealistically, to the earliest church. Are we open to the disturbing new realms of relationship into which the Spirit calls us? Are we ready to accept the responsibilities that justice and mercy require? Are we giving "witness" to Jesus through our actions and commitments, not just our words?

RESPONSIVE READING
PSALM 47 (BCP, alt.)

This psalm, so familiar from its opening lines, "Clap your hands, all you peoples; shout to God with loud songs of joy," is difficult to place in a historical context. This is simply because the situation it describes, in which God has "subdued" peoples and nations under Israel's feet (v. 3) and the princes of the peoples "gather as the people of the God of Abraham" (v. 9), was never literally true of Israel's history. Historians prefer to speak of the *ceremonial* context of the psalm, its use in an enthronement ritual involving the ark of the covenant (which was, from the time of David on, in some sense at the disposal of the king, see 2 Samuel 6). Our ceremonial use of the psalm in Christian worship challenges us to ask in what sense God is "king over the nations."

PSALM 68:1-20 (BCP)

This psalm calls upon God to scatter God's enemies (and, presumably, those of the people of God), so that the righteous may rejoice. The dramatic revelations of God in the exodus and at Sinai are evoked (vv. 7-8) but are now connected directly with God's enthronement upon Zion (vv. 15-18). The psalmist juxtaposes the defeat of hostile armies and kings with the identification of God as "father of orphans and protector of widows," the one who "gives the desolate a home to live in" and delivers the prisoners (vv. 5-6). This is a rich and exultant reading, and its last line—"to God, the Lord, belongs escape from death" (v. 20)—makes it especially appropriate for this last Sunday in Easter.

PSALM 97 (RCL);
PSALM 97:1-2, 6-7, 9 (RC)

God is praised as "king" and "lord of all the earth." The dramatic language of theophany—the disruptive appearance of God in power and majesty, in "clouds and thick darkness," fire, lightning, earthquake (vv. 2-4)—accompanies the affirmation that "righteousness and justice are the foundation" of God's throne (v. 2). (Those using the RCL may hear echoes of this theophany language in the reading from Acts, below.)

SECOND READING

REVELATION 22:12-14 (BCP);
REVELATION 22:12-14, 16-17, 20-21 (RCL);
REVELATION 22:12-14, 16-17, 20 (RC)

Through the weeks after Easter, all three lectionaries have provided readings from the Revelation to John. This sequence comes to an end today with a reading from the Revelation's conclusion. The Lord speaks as the first and last, who comes to bring judgment according to people's works (v. 12). A special blessing is pronounced on those who "wash their robes," a phrase used in 7:13-15 to describe those who have remained obedient to God through the "great ordeal." The reference to robes may be an allusion to the garments of baptism.

The continuation of the reading in the RCL and Roman Catholic lectionaries brings a sense of closure to the whole book as Jesus refers again to the "testimony for the churches" (see chapters 1–3). We hear a series of invitations. First, the Spirit and the "bride," i.e., the heavenly Jerusalem (21:2), invite Jesus to "come." The verse might be interpreted as directed to the hearers, but the second invitation, spoken by "everyone who hears," is addressed to Jesus, as is the

WHILE MANY OF THE BOOKS AND MOVIES ABOUT REVELATION THAT HAVE BECOME SO POPULAR IN RECENT YEARS FOCUS ON THE DREAD OF BEING "LEFT BEHIND" AND THE CONFUSION, THEN REMORSE, OF THOSE WHO HAVE BEEN ABANDONED IN THE "RAPTURE," JOHN'S AUTHENTIC MESSAGE CONCLUDES WITH AN INVITATION TO JOIN IN CELEBRATION AND THE SANCTIFIED SHARING OF FOOD IN JESUS' NAME.

apocalyptic cry in v. 20, "Come, Lord Jesus!" The final invitations are for all who are thirsty and wish to take "the water of life" (v. 17).

A comparison with 1 Corinthians, where the Lord's Supper is explicitly discussed (11:17-34) and the letter concludes with the cry *Marana tha!*—that is, "our Lord, come!" (16:22)—suggests that both writings were meant to be read in the community's assembly for worship, and thus conclude with a call to the Lord's Supper that invokes the presence of the Lord. That possibility should give us pause. While many of the books and movies about Revelation that have become so popular in recent years focus on the dread of being "left behind" and the confusion, then remorse, of those who have been abandoned in the "rapture," John's authentic message concludes with an invitation to join in celebration and the sanctified sharing of food in Jesus' name. John's apocalyptic voice calls us, not into our bunkers, but to a banquet!

The Gospel
JOHN 17:20-26 (RCL, BCP, RC)

The last Sunday after Easter brings us to the climactic conclusion of the "last discourses" in John's Gospel. Jesus' extended prayer in John 17 is sometimes called the "high-priestly prayer" because of its strongly doxological content (literally, it "pronounces glory" to God). The whole chapter confirms a characteristic of the Gospel that we have seen before, the tendency of Jesus to speak as risen Lord, communing intimately with the Father, even while (in terms of the narrative) he is still upon the earth (e.g., v. 11: "I am no longer in the world . . . but I am coming to you"; vv. 12-13, "while I was with them . . . but now I am coming to you"). As we have also seen, the overall effect of this motif is to make the hearer of the Gospel contemporary with the disciples in the upper room, but also to let the upper room "bleed" into the present, where the believer has communion with the risen Jesus. So, in today's reading Jesus prays "not only on behalf of these," the disciples present with him in the "narrative time" of the Gospel, but "also on behalf of those who will believe in me through their word," i.e., the hearers.

The Fourth Gospel is sometimes described as having a "low ecclesiology," because Jesus says nothing explicit here about church offices or procedures. But the Johannine Jesus declares that he has given his disciples "the glory that you have given me" (v. 22). It is within and among them that God the Father, God the Son, and God the Advocate are present in the world.

The Jesus who speaks here is not the same Jesus who agonizes in the Garden of Gethsemane in the Synoptics; indeed, the Johannine Jesus refuses to pray the prayer attributed to him in the other Gospels (12:27). At the end of this prayer he will take his disciples to that garden (18:1), but he offers no prayer of anguish there. He is not in the least reluctant to face arrest; "knowing all that was to happen to him," he urges the mob that comes to lay hold of him to get on with it (18:4-10). Only the Fourth Gospel remarks that Jesus thus protected his disciples, in fulfillment of his own word (18:9; compare 6:39; 10:28; and most importantly 17:12). If (as many scholars believe) the Fourth Gospel arose in a community that had faced opposition and condemnation from some wider and more powerful community of *Ioudaioi* (see the discussion for the Fourth Sunday of Easter, above), those assurances must have resounded with great power and comfort among the Johannine believers.

Jesus' prayer does much more than ask that his disciples "be one" (17:20) and abide in the Father and the Son (17:21). The mutual indwelling of Jesus with the disciples, his "friends" (15:14-15), powerfully likened to the relation of vine and branches (15:1-11), has been a central theme throughout the last discourse. The final "high-priestly" prayer in chapter 17 has sealed this relationship and emphasized its consequences for the life of the believers in the world. Their union with Jesus means that they "do not belong to the world," just as Jesus does not (17:16); for that same reason the world "has hated them" (17:14). They will need God's protection (17:11) from "the evil one" (17:15), which is a continuation of Jesus' own protection (17:12).

The world's hostility to Jesus, rooted in its hostility to the one who sent him, has resounded throughout the Gospel, and Jesus has warned the disciples to expect lethal violence directed against them as well (16:1-4). Just this feature of the Fourth Gospel has made it particularly attractive to sectarian communities who seek to emphasize their alienation from the dominant society around them. On the other hand, such language may sound strange to hearers who feel quite comfortable in "the world."

Because its language so powerfully polarizes the circle of intimacy with Jesus over against the hostility of "the world," this text calls preachers, *and* their congregations, to serious and self-critical spiritual discernment. What social and cultural currents course through our lives and the rhythms of our common worship, carrying us along with their force? What privileges of class, race, or nationality have we come to presume as God-given, rather than the constructions of our national and global social order ("the world")? The rise of critical voices from the postcolonial world raise hard questions for us who live in the comforts that centuries of empire have provided. When we think of ourselves as united with Christ and separated from others ("the world"), do we subtly imag-

> BECAUSE ITS LANGUAGE SO POWERFULLY POLARIZES THE CIRCLE OF INTIMACY WITH JESUS OVER AGAINST THE HOSTILITY OF "THE WORLD," THIS TEXT CALLS PREACHERS, AND THEIR CONGREGATIONS, TO SERIOUS AND SELF-CRITICAL SPIRITUAL DISCERNMENT.

ine that division along lines of power, wealth, and color of skin? Are we simply applying a Johannine veneer to habits of thought and perception that we learned elsewhere?

Jesus' prayer militates against those habits. The dichotomy of "believers" against "the world" is not absolute. Jesus has sent his own into the world (17:18); it is "through their word" that others, for whom Jesus prays, will come to believe in him (17:20). It is through their evident unity with the Son and the Father that "the world may believe that you have sent me" (17:21-24). Jesus' friends are to bear to the world God's love, a love that (like them) is present "in the world" but is not the product of that world. This prayer strikes a powerful chord as we antic-ipate next week's readings, which draw our attention to the pouring out of the Spirit in and for the world!

Notes

1. Jürgen Moltmann, "The Resurrection of Christ: Hope for the World," in Gavin D'Costa, ed., *Resurrection Reconsidered* (Oxford: Oneworld Publications, 1996), 73–86.

2. John Dominic Crossan, *Jesus: A Revolutionary Biography* (San Francisco: HarperSanFrancisco, 1994), 163.

3. Marcus Borg, "The Truth of Easter," in Borg and N. T. Wright, *The Meaning of Jesus: Two Visions* (San Francisco: HarperSanFrancisco, 1999), 134–35.

4. I appreciate Rowan Williams's protests against "a liberal theology which appeals to some isolable core of encounter, unmediated awareness of the transcen-dent, buried beneath the accidental forms of historical givenness, a trans-cultural, pre-linguistic, inter-religious phenomenon" (*On Christian Theology* [Oxford: Black-well, 2000], 131). It is simply not true that the God whom we proclaim is the same as the content of our religious experience, no matter how powerful that may be.

5. The question facing us in Christ's resurrection, Moltmann writes, is "the eschatological one—the question, that is, about the end of this world's history of suffering, and the world's new creation" (*Resurrection of Christ*, 77). Moltmann's earlier work is seminal for my reflections here, especially *Theology of Hope,* trans. James W. Leitch (New York: Harper & Row, 1967).

6. John Dominic Crossan declares the prospect of harmonizing the Easter accounts "flatly impossible": "It is quite remarkable that an almost hour-by-hour remembrance prevailed for the death and burial of Jesus but an almost total dis-crepancy prevailed for what was, I would presume, even more important, namely, the extraordinary return of Jesus from beyond the grave" (*The Historical Jesus: The Life of a Mediterranean Jewish Peasant* [San Francisco: HarperSanFrancisco, 1991], 395).

7. Ernst Käsemann, "The Saving Significance of Jesus' Death," in *Perspectives on Paul*, trans. Margaret Kohl (Philadelphia: Fortress Press, 1971), 55 (emphasis added).

8. This argument was made forcefully by James M. Robinson, "Jesus—From Easter to Valentinus (or to the Apostles' Creed)," *Journal of Biblical Literature* 101 (1982): 5–37. On the importance of 2 Corinthians 12, see Alan F. Segal, *Paul the Convert: The Apostolate and Apostasy of Saul the Pharisee* (New Haven: Yale University Press, 1990).

9. See Jacob Jervell, *The Unknown Paul: Essays on Luke-Acts and Early Christian History* (Minneapolis: Augsburg, 1984); also the essays in Joseph B. Tyson, ed., *Luke-Acts and the Jewish People: Eight Critical Perspectives* (Minneapolis: Augsburg, 1988).

10. Since the 1970s, scholarship has shifted from trying to reconstruct the "theology" (or "heresy") of the Corinthians to exploring social inequalities and tensions and the theological slogans they may have generated. See Gerd Theissen, *The Social Setting of Pauline Christianity: Essays on Corinth,* trans. John Schütz (Philadelphia: Fortress Press, 1978); Wayne A. Meeks, *The First Urban Christians* (New Haven: Yale University Press, 1983); and my own discussion in Neil Elliott, *Liberating Paul: The Justice of God and the Politics of the Apostle* (Maryknoll: Orbis, 1994), 204–14 and passim.

11. John Ashton, *Understanding the Fourth Gospel* (Oxford: Clarendon, 1991), 502–3.

12. The report of Peter's visit to the tomb (Luke 24:12) is missing in some Western manuscripts but has recently been defended as genuine (D. Moody Smith, *John among the Gospels: The Relationship in Twentieth-Century Research* [Minneapolis: Fortress Press, 1992], 155).

13. See Brendan Byrne's discussion, "Beloved Disciple," *Anchor Bible Dictionary,* ed. David Noel Freedman (New York: Doubleday, 1993), 1:658–61.

14. Ashton, *Fourth Gospel,* 503.

15. It is in Jerusalem that Jesus commands the disciples to wait until clothed "with power from on high" (Luke 24:49; see Acts 1:4), and to Jerusalem they return after the ascension (24:52); Jesus commands them to be his witnesses "in Jerusalem, in all Judea and Samaria, and to the ends of the earth" (Acts 1:8). On the importance of Jerusalem see Jacob Jervell, *Luke and the People of God: A New Look at Luke-Acts* (Minneapolis: Augsburg, 1972); Robert Tannehill, "Israel in Luke-Acts: A Tragic Story," *Journal of Biblical Literature* 104 (1985): 69–85.

16. Since Paul did not mention the empty tomb in 1 Corinthians 15, which predated all the Gospels, interpreters have suggested that the empty tomb account emerged separately and later from the appearance accounts, probably for apologetic reasons (as evident in Matt. 27:62-66; 28:11-15). The disbelief of the (male) disciples, like the silence of the women in Mark 16:8, may originally have served to explain to critics why the empty tomb stories had not been circulated earlier

(so Rudolf Bultmann, *The History of the Synoptic Tradition,* trans. John Marsh [New York: Harper & Row, 1963], 285).

17. See Jane Schaberg's cautions to "read more carefully" before declaring Luke a "special 'friend' of women": they are also portrayed as "models of subordinate service." "Luke," in *The Women's Bible Commentary,* ed. Carol Newsom and Sharon Ringe (Louisville: Westminster John Knox, 1992), 275–92. See also Gail O'Day, "Acts," in ibid., 305–12.

18. See Donald Juel, *Messianic Exegesis* (Philadelphia: Fortress Press, 1988). John Dominic Crossan describes this post-Easter interpretive practice by the earliest followers of Jesus as "prophecy historicized" rather than history remembered in *The Historical Jesus.*

19. For a discussion of Justin's *Dialogue* see Stephen G. Wilson, *Related Strangers: Jews and Christians 70–170 C.E.* (Minneapolis: Fortress Press, 1995), 258–84.

20. This is one reason Rabbi Harold Kushner's best-selling book, *Why Bad Things Happen to Good People* (New York: HarperCollins, 1981), gives prominent attention to Job.

21. Expectations of "simplicity, consistency, and linearity . . . are confuted by the whole tenor of the book." So Moshe Greenberg, "Job," in *The Literary Guide to the Bible,* ed. Robert Alter and Frank Kermode (Cambridge, Mass.: Belknap Press of Harvard University Press, 1987), 283.

22. For example, the last chapters of Kushner, *Why Bad Things Happen to Good People.*

23. An excellent resource that rewards repeated study is Wes Howard-Brook and Anthony Gwyther, *Unveiling Empire: Reading Revelation Then and Now* (Maryknoll: Orbis, 1999).

24. This case is ably argued by Elisabeth Schüssler Fiorenza, *The Book of Revelation: Justice and Judgment* (Philadelphia: Fortress Press, 1985).

25. While the connections between the Revelation and ancient Roman imperial cult are now widely recognized, Howard-Brook and Gwyther *(Unveiling Empire)* are particularly helpful in drawing connections to the dynamics of empire in our own day.

26. Two landmark works in the discussion are J. Christiaan Beker, *Paul the Apostle: The Triumph of God in Life and Thought* (Philadelphia: Fortress, 1980), 28–33 and passim; and Alan F. Segal, *Paul the Convert: The Apostolate and Apostasy of Saul the Pharisee* (New Haven: Yale University Press, 1990).

27. See Krister Stendahl, *Paul among Jews and Gentiles* (Philadelphia: Fortress, 1976).

28. This is one of the most widely accepted elements in Rudolf Bultmann's complex theory of the Fourth Gospel's composition (*The Gospel of John: A Commentary,* trans. George R. Beasley-Murray, R. W. N. Hoare, and J. K. Riches

[Philadelphia: Westminster, 1971]); see now John Ashton, *Understanding the Fourth Gospel* (Oxford: Clarendon, 1991), and D. Moody Smith, *John among the Gospels* (Minneapolis: Fortress, 1992). On the other hand, some argue that "realistic" touches—Peter's impulsiveness in throwing himself naked into the sea, v. 7; the detail that 153 fish were caught, v. 11—point to an actual reminiscence.

29. David's origins bespeak a sort of trustworthiness, that he is one of the people and is unswervingly loyal to them (see, for example, 1 Sam. 22:22-23); his great downfall is not his adultery with Bathsheba alone, but the callousness with which he orders his own troops into lethal danger in order to cover up his crime (2 Sam. 11:14-26).

30. Especially Hans Conzelmann, *The Theology of St. Luke*, trans. Geoffrey Buswell (Philadelphia: Fortress Press, 1961).

31. The controversy is well represented in the essays collected in Joseph Tyson, ed., *Luke-Acts and the Jews: Eight Critical Perspectives* (Minneapolis: Augsburg, 1988).

32. See *Nostra Aetate* (the Declaration on the Relation of the Church to Non-Christian Religions), and subsequent Guidelines, in *Vatican Council II: The Conciliar and Post-Conciliar Documents,* vol. 1, ed. Austin Flannery, O.P. (Grand Rapids: Eerdmans, 1975), 738–49.

33. That violence against Christian minorities in other countries merits far more media attention than paramilitary violence against progressive Christian groups in the 1980s ever did may reflect aspects of what Noam Chomsky and Edward S. Herman call "the political economy of the mass media": see their illuminating case study and analysis in *Manufacturing Consent: The Political Economy of the Mass Media* (New York: Pantheon, 1988).

34. John Calvin, *The Institutes of the Christian Religion,* trans. J. Allen (Philadelphia, 1936).

35. J. Louis Martyn's works have been formative for this discussion regarding "the Jews" in the Fourth Gospel: see *The Gospel of John in Christian History* (New York: Doubleday, 1978); *History and Theology in the Fourth Gospel,* rev. ed. (Nashville: Abingdon, 1979). Martyn coined the phrase "two-level drama" to describe the juxtaposition of Jesus' own time with the time of the later Johannine church in the Gospel narrative.

36. A "Palestinian Recension" of the so-called Eighteen Benedictions is presented in Emil Schürer, *The History of the Jewish People in the Age of Jesus Christ: A New English Edition*, vol. 2, rev. and ed. Geza Vermes, Fergus Millar, and Matthew Black (Edinburgh: T. & T. Clark, 1979), 460–63. The editors declare that the "framework" of the prayer "undoubtedly originated during the last three decades of the first century A.D."

37. See, for example, R. Kimelman, "Birkat ha-Minim and the Lack of Evidence for an Anti-Christian Jewish Prayer in Late Antiquity," in *Aspects of Judaism*

in the Greco-Roman Period, Jewish and Christian Self-Definition, ed. E. P. Sanders, A. I. Baumgarten, and A. Mendelson, vol. 2 (Philadelphia: Fortress Press, 1981), 226–44; 391–403.

38. Daniel Boyarin presents a valuable summary of the discussion and his own provocative hypothesis, namely, that we should distinguish "Jews" (as we use the term, including all members of the community "Israel") from *Ioudaioi* or *Yahudim,* the members of a "confessional community" organized in the wake of the exile and return around the Temple in Jerusalem. See his essay, "The *Ioudaioi* in John and the Prehistory of 'Judaism,'" in *Pauline Conversations in Context: Essays in Honor of Calvin J. Roetzel,* ed. Janice Capell Anderson, Philip Sellew, and Claudia Setzer, JSNTSup 221 (Sheffield: Sheffield Academic Press, 2002), 216–39. Also see two works on which Boyarin depends: Shemaryahu Talmon, "The Emergence of Jewish Sectarianism in the Early Second Temple Period," in *Ancient Israelite Religion: Essays in Honor of Frank Moore Cross,* ed. P. D. Miller, P. D. Hanson, and S. D. McBride (Philadelphia: Fortress Press, 1987), 587–616; and J. Blenkinsopp, *Ezra-Nehemiah: A Commentary* (Philadelphia: Westminster, 1988).

39. See Boyarin's discussion, *Pauline Conversations,* especially pp. 234–39.

40. See the classic presentation by Wayne A. Meeks, "The Man from Heaven in Johannine Sectarianism," *Journal of Biblical Literature* 91 (1972): 44–72.

41. Reinhold Niebuhr, "The Spirit of Justice," *Christianity and Society* (summer 1950); reprinted in *Love and Justice: Selections from the Shorter Writings of Reinhold Niebuhr,* ed. D. B. Robertson (Gloucester, Mass.: Peter Smith, 1976), 25.

42. Reinhold Niebuhr, "Justice and Love," *Christianity and Society* (fall 1950); reprinted in *Love and Justice,* 27–29.

43. Martin Luther King Jr., "Where Do We Go from Here?" presidential address to the Southern Christian Leadership Conference, August 16, 1967; in *I Have a Dream: Writings and Speeches That Changed the World,* ed. James M. Washington (San Francisco: HarperSanFrancisco, 1986), 176–77.

44. For a careful and spirited discussion of these issues, see Paula Fredriksen, *From Jesus to Christ: The Development of New Testament Images of Jesus* (New Haven: Yale University Press, 1988), 145–51; idem, "Judaism, the Circumcision of Gentiles, and Apocalyptic Hope: Another Look at Galatians 1 and 2," *Journal of Theological Studies* 42:2 (1991), 541–42.

45. See Rodney Stark, *The Rise of Christianity* (San Francisco: HarperSanFrancisco, 1997).

46. Howard-Brook and Gwyther, *Unveiling Empire,* 157–96.

47. On "narrative time" and other literary features of the Fourth Gospel, see R. Alan Culpepper, *Anatomy of the Fourth Gospel: A Study in Literary Design* (Philadelphia: Fortress Press, 1983).

48. On John's use of this term, see the discussion for the Fourth Sunday of Easter, above.

49. Rowan Williams, "Theological Integrity," in *On Christian Theology*, Challenges in Contemporary Theology (Oxford: Blackwell, 2000), 3–15.

50. Fredriksen, *From Jesus to Christ*, 167. Fredriksen offers a compelling account of the way the "dynamics of expectation and disappointment" shaped the traditions behind our New Testament.

51. Neither does Luke share what might be a modern reader's embarrassment over miracles performed through Peter's shadow (5:15) or handkerchiefs that had touched Paul's skin (19:11). On the nuances of Luke's view of "magic" and the miraculous, see Susan R. Garrett, *The Demise of the Devil: Magic and the Demonic in Luke's Writings* (Minneapolis: Fortress Press, 1989).

52. The literature on the "apostolic council" is vast, and virtually every major treatment of Paul's relation to the Jewish law must offer some discussion of it. Johannes Munck first raised serious questions about F. C. Baur's polarized view (see the next note) and argued that the biblical evidence reflected a fundamental agreement between Paul and the Jerusalem apostles: *Paul and the Salvation of Mankind* (Richmond: John Knox, 1959).

53. Though its philosophical underpinnings in Hegelian thought are now widely rejected, F. C. Baur's schematic understanding of early Christianity as a conflict between Jewish particularism and Pauline universalism "provided both the framework and presuppositions for the modern study of Paul's writings until the mid-1970s" (S. J. Hafemann, "Paul and His Interpreters," in *Dictionary of Paul and His Letters: A Compendium of Contemporary Biblical Scholarship,* ed. Gerald F. Hawthorne, Ralph P. Martin, and Daniel G. Reid [Downers Grove, Ill.: InterVarsity Press, 1993], 666). The 1970s inaugurated a "paradigm shift" in Pauline studies with the publication of Rosemary Radford Ruether's *Faith and Fratricide* (New York: Crossroad, 1974), Krister Stendahl's *Paul among Jews and Gentiles,* and E. P. Sanders's *Paul and Palestinian Judaism: A Comparison of Patterns of Religion* (Philadelphia: Fortress Press, 1977).

54. See the incisive comments of Mark Nanos, *The Mystery of Romans: The Jewish Context of Paul's Letter* (Minneapolis: Fortress Press, 1996), esp. 88–95.

55. Fredriksen, *From Jesus to Christ,* 165–70.

56. Rudolf Bultmann presented a systematic interpretation of the Fourth Gospel (or rather, the most expansive stratum in the archaeological deposit that the Gospel now is) as the work of a proto-Gnostic believer who had "demythologized" the Christology of his sources: *The Gospel according to John,* trans. G. Beasley-Murray (Oxford: Blackwell, 1971); see also the work of Bultmann's student, Ernst Käsemann, *The Testament of Jesus according to John 17* (Philadelphia: Fortress Press, 1968).

57. Ernst Käsemann, "The Saving Significance of Jesus' Death," in *Perspectives on Paul,* 55 (emphasis added).

58. Only Matthew seems to narrate the moment of resurrection itself, if this is how we should understand the sudden shattering earthquake in 28:2. Matthew offers a final scene (at 28:16-20) with Jesus and his disciples on a mountaintop, resembling Luke's ascension scene, except that Matthew's scene takes place on a mountain in Galilee, while Luke's is in Bethany, outside Jerusalem; further, Matthew never explicitly mentions an ascension.

THE SEASON OF PENTECOST

RICHARD P. CARLSON

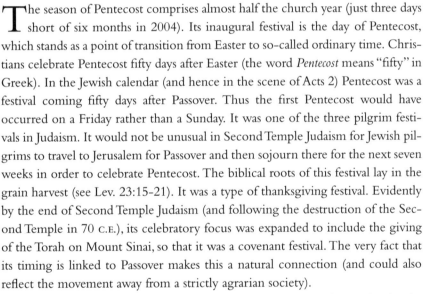

The season of Pentecost comprises almost half the church year (just three days short of six months in 2004). Its inaugural festival is the day of Pentecost, which stands as a point of transition from Easter to so-called ordinary time. Christians celebrate Pentecost fifty days after Easter (the word *Pentecost* means "fifty" in Greek). In the Jewish calendar (and hence in the scene of Acts 2) Pentecost was a festival coming fifty days after Passover. Thus the first Pentecost would have occurred on a Friday rather than a Sunday. It was one of the three pilgrim festivals in Judaism. It would not be unusual in Second Temple Judaism for Jewish pilgrims to travel to Jerusalem for Passover and then sojourn there for the next seven weeks in order to celebrate Pentecost. The biblical roots of this festival lay in the grain harvest (see Lev. 23:15-21). It was a type of thanksgiving festival. Evidently by the end of Second Temple Judaism (and following the destruction of the Second Temple in 70 C.E.), its celebratory focus was expanded to include the giving of the Torah on Mount Sinai, so that it was a covenant festival. The very fact that its timing is linked to Passover makes this a natural connection (and could also reflect the movement away from a strictly agrarian society).

In its New Testament context the day of Pentecost is not understood to be the founding or the birthday of the church. At the end of Luke's Gospel and at the beginning of Acts (recall that the same author wrote both volumes), there is already a community gathered around the risen Jesus; a community enjoying meal fellowship, experiencing instruction from scripture, and engaged in prayer and praise (cf. Luke 24:28-53; Acts 1:1-14, 15-26). The church existed prior to Pentecost Friday. Pentecost is a day of fulfillment and inauguration. The risen Christ had promised the community that it would receive the power of the Holy Spirit in order to inaugurate their mission of bringing to others the news of Jesus' death and resurrection according to scripture (Luke 24:45-49; Acts 1:4-8). The Greek of the introduction to the Pentecost story vividly captures this, although it is missed in English translations. The Greek of Acts 2:1 would be best rendered, "When the day of Pentecost was fulfilled." It is a day which fulfills not only what Jesus had promised about the coming of the Spirit but also what scripture had promised in Joel 2:28-32. As Acts 2:4 literally notes, it is also a day of inauguration ("they began to speak in other languages"). Thus in fulfillment of divine promises and according to divine plans, Pentecost is the inauguration of the Spirit-empowered mission of bringing the name of the Lord Jesus Christ into the world. Mission—not an organization—is being boldly birthed on Pentecost. It is an inclusive mission in two profound ways. First, it is inclusive because every member of the community is empowered by the Spirit for witness. The "all" of Acts 2:1, 4 refers not just to the apostles but to the entire community (cf. Acts 1:14-15). That is why the Joel prophecy is so important, since it promises the creation of a nation of prophets including females and males, young and old, masters and servants (2:16-21). Second, it is inclusive because the proclamation of Jesus Christ is being extended to members of all nations under heaven (2:5). Jesus envisioned a mission that began in Jerusalem and spread like waves flowing ever outward (Luke 24:47; Acts 1:8). The inclusive mission that is being inaugurated in Acts 2 will

PENTECOST IS NOT A UNIQUE, ONE-TIME, NEVER-TO-BE-REPEATED OCCURRENCE IN THE LIFE OF THE CHURCH.

eventually include unlikely witness such as Saul (Acts 9) and will reach out beyond the boundaries of Judaism to include Gentiles (Acts 10). Pentecost is not a unique, one-time, never-to-be-repeated occurrence in the life of the church. In fulfillment of divine promises and plans, it inaugurates the tidal wave of mission that will repeatedly flow out and wash over countless generations in countless locations. To be Christian is to be included in the Pentecost mission.

As noted, the Sundays following Pentecost are marked as "ordinary time." Yet Acts 2 also helps us to understand of what ordinary time consists. According to 2:41-47, the inaugural events of Pentecost resulted in a community engaged in proclamation, baptism, meal fellowship, worship, prayer, praise, fellowship, social ministry, study, stewardship, and outreach. This is the post-Pentecost mission reality of Christian life in "ordinary time" whether it be in the first century or the twenty-first century. Thus the texts for the Sundays of the season of Pentecost help us understand, enact, and experience these very facets of Christian life. The lessons are geared for us to discover anew what it means to live in a right covenant relationship with Jesus Christ as individuals and as community. In that regard there is nothing ordinary about these scriptural passages, for they are God's word challenging, enlightening, scolding, cajoling, comforting, and guiding us to live our covenant relationship in ways that reflect the reality of the relationship itself. Just as the Holy Spirit is the key to the events of Pentecost, the Spirit is the key to these texts becoming not just words to live by but God's word of life, forgiveness, mission, and salvation.

RICHARD P.
CARLSON

THE DAY OF PENTECOST

May 30, 2004

Revised Common	Episcopal (BCP)	Roman Catholic
Acts 2:1-21	Acts 2:1-11	Acts 2:1-11
or Gen. 11:1-9	or Joel 2:28-32	
Ps. 104:24-34, 35b	Ps. 104:25-37	Ps. 104:1, 24, 29-31, 34
	or 104:25-32	
	or 33:12-15, 18-22	
Rom. 8:14-17	1 Cor. 12:4-13	1 Cor. 12:3b-7, 12-13
or Acts 2:1-21	or Acts 2:1-11	or Rom. 8:8-17
John 14:8-17, (25-27)	John 20:19-23	John 20:19-23
	or John 14:8-17	or John 14:15-16, 23b-26

First Reading

ACTS 2:1-21 (rcl);
ACTS 2:1-11 (bcp, rc)

It is not unusual to hear Pentecost described as the birthday of the church. That is not, however, the vision of Pentecost presented in Acts 2. An inclusive community marked by word and sacrament has already been gathered around the risen Jesus (cf. Luke 24:28-35, 36-51; Acts 1:1-5, 12-26), and so what comes into being on Pentecost is not the church but rather the mission of the church in the world. Just as Luke's Gospel opened with the promise of the Spirit coming upon Mary to do the impossible (a virgin would conceive; 1:34-35), so Acts opens with the promise of the Spirit coming upon the community to the impossible (make the post-ascension community a nation of witnessing prophets; Acts 1:5-8; cf. Luke 24:45-49).

In the Pentecost story we are told how that impossible mission is inaugurated. Pentecost was a type of thanksgiving festival in which Jews from across the known world gathered in Jerusalem. It occurred fifty days after Passover. Hence the scene in Acts 2 takes place on a Friday morning, not on a Sunday morning. The notation in v. 1 that all were gathered together indicates that the inclusive community noted in 1:12-14 (including Mary) are the recipients of the Spirit and not just the twelve apostles. The appearance of the Spirit has the marks of a theophany (wind and fire, vv. 2-3). Note that the gift of tongues (v. 4) on Pentecost is not *glossolalia* but *xenolalia*. Glossolalia is the gift to speak in nonhuman languages of prayer or praise (cf. 1 Corinthians 12–14). Xenolalia is the gift to speak in foreign, human languages. In Pentecost the Spirit empowers each member of the community to speak in a variety of human languages so that a vast array of people are able to hear about God's saving activity (vv. 5-11). This is not chaos but clear communication. It is not an ecstatic one-time experience intended for a select few but the beginning of the church's inclusive mission in the world. The Spirit is not interested in empowering a select, elite group to bring a hidden message to a handful of people. Rather, the Spirit empowers an inclusive mission carried out by an inclusive com-

> IN PENTECOST THE SPIRIT EMPOWERS EACH MEMBER OF THE COMMUNITY TO SPEAK IN A VARIETY OF HUMAN LANGUAGES SO THAT A VAST ARRAY OF PEOPLE ARE ABLE TO HEAR ABOUT GOD'S SAVING ACTIVITY.

munity. What is birthed on Pentecost, then, is not a church but a church in mission under the power and guidance of the Spirit whose goal is summed up in the final line from the Joel prophecy: whoever calls on the name of the Lord shall be saved (Joel 2:32; Acts 2:21). Peter's entire sermon in vv. 14-36 has one goal: to make known that the Lord is none other than the crucified and risen Jesus Christ in whom divine salvation is now freely and inclusively poured out (vv. 36-41). This is what Pentecost is truly about.

What we celebrate at Pentecost is not how God established a church but how God, through the Spirit, continues to empower every single member of the community to bring the name of the Lord Jesus Christ into the world so that all may call upon the name of the Lord and be saved. Pentecost is the miracle of inclusive mission that continues anew each day through the Spirit's empowerment of each member of the community of Christ.

GENESIS 11:1-9 (RCL, alt.)

The tower of Babel story stands as the negative prequel to Pentecost. God had wanted humanity to be spread across the earth as stewards of God's creation (1:28; 10:32), but here people klatch together to secure their own unity, importance, and identity by building a city with a tower that would give them access to the divine dwelling place (v. 4). Their building project is not merely about bricks and mortar but about the creature once again attempting to be on the same level as the Creator (thus recalling 3:5). God assumes the role of divine building inspector and quickly realizes the implications of their building project. If their self-serving plans are not thwarted, once again God will be faced with an autonomous, divine-status-seeking humanity that is incapable of carrying out

God's designs for it and all creation. Thus God's punishment is to confuse human- ity's language so that they cannot hear each others speech (v. 7; cf. Acts 2:6-14, 22, 37 for the divine reversal of this action). The Lord also enforces the divine scattering principle so that what was commanded at creation (1:28) again comes to pass (vv. 8-9). It is important to note that God is not against human progress or the advancement of civilization. Rather, God is punishing a society's attempt to transcend its role and identity as creature. God is punishing a society whose end is its own fame. God is punishing a society that willfully neglects its stewardship for creation.

Pentecost reverses Babel in that now God empowers communication in mul- tiple languages to announce God's saving words in Christ and so to gather together an inclusive community in Christ's name from across the world.

JOEL 2:28-32 (BCP, alt.)

This is the original prophecy from Joel that forms the basis for Peter's Pentecost sermon in Acts 2:16-21. For a discussion of the passage in its Old Tes- tament context see Proper 25.

RESPONSIVE READING

PSALM 104:24-34, 35b (RCL);
PSALM 104:25-37 or 104:25-32 (BCP);
PSALM 104:1, 24, 29-31, 34 (RC)

As a whole, Psalm 104 is a grand pronouncement of God as the creator and sustainer of all reality. As a responsive reading for Pentecost Sunday, vv. 29-30 of this psalm are central, especially in the use of the Hebrew word for breath/spirit in each verse as they recall that life is created through God's breath or spirit (Gen. 1:2; 2:7). Because the psalmist is celebrating what God originally did at creation as well as what God continues to do for creation, there is a natural connection to God's activity of sustaining the church and the world through the outpouring of the Spirit on Pentecost. In this way, the events unleashed on Pentecost through the outpouring of God's Spirit are among the manifold works for which we, like the psalmist, give praise.

PSALM 33:12-15, 18-22 (BCP, alt.)

Psalm 33 is a wonderful example of how the Old Testament holds together two significant theological concepts: God's complete sovereignty and the pervasiveness of God's steadfast love. The psalmist proclaims that from the beginning, God is enthroned as sovereign Lord over all creation, nations, and peoples. Yet God is not simply watching creation from a distance, but out of divine love God remains actively involved to guide people and nations in the ways of righteousness and justice. Thus divine compassion is a vital component of divine sovereignty. This is also born out in the reality of Pentecost as the Spirit is poured out on all the members of the community so that the proclamation of God's mighty acts in the death and resurrection of Jesus Christ would flow out to all peoples (note that in Psalm 33 the word "all" appears five times, and in Acts 2 it is used thirteen times). By the end of the day of Pentecost, there is a new song of rejoicing because the steadfast love of the Lord fills the earth once again.

Second Reading
ROMANS 8:14-17 (RCL);
ROMANS 8:8-17 (RC, alt.)

In this section of Romans 8, Paul is explaining our Christian reality in terms of indebtedness and inheritance. Just prior to this, Paul has established the fundamental contrast between the Spirit and the flesh as they determine human reality and conduct. Flesh, here, does not refer to our physical existence but represents a theo-

> PAUL IS EXPLAINING OUR CHRISTIAN REALITY IN TERMS OF INDEBTEDNESS AND INHERITANCE.

logical depiction of our fallen existence wherein sin is inducing us to live self-centered, self-serving lives (vv. 5-8). Christians do no longer live in the realm of the flesh but in the realm of the Spirit (v. 9). Hence we are indebted to God and not to the flesh. We do not let the flesh set the standards for our conduct but put that former manner of conduct to death (vv. 12-13). Our indebtedness includes being led by the Spirit, which is also a mark of our inheritance as God's children (v. 14). In addition to guiding our conduct and bringing about our adoption, the Spirit also empowers us to address the transcendent Creator of the universe in the tender, intimate term "Abba" as a living testimony of our status as God's children (vv. 15-16). Such honored status means we are co-heirs of Christ (v. 17). That is, our inheritance includes participating in the sufferings of Christ in the present and participating in Christ's glorification in the future. For Paul, then, how we are to live (our indebtedness) is a reflection of what we are (our inheritance). The Spirit makes us God's children, guides our conduct and prayers as God's children, and promises us a glorious future with Christ.

1 CORINTHIANS 12:4-13 (BCP);
1 CORINTHIANS 12:3b-7, 12-13 (RC)

Spirituality was as big a topic in the mid-first-century church at Corinth as it is in churches at the dawn of the twenty-first century. The problem in Corinth, however, was that their understandings of spirituality were fracturing the God-given unity of the body of Christ. Some in Corinth were endowed with gifts of the Spirit such as speaking in tongues (glossolalia) or interpreting tongues. These spiritual gifts were more highly esteemed than other gifts and those who possessed them seemed spiritually superior to other Christians. Some Corinthians felt they did not have the Holy Spirit because they did not experience such dramatic outpourings of the Spirit. In 1 Cor. 12:1-13 Paul is helping the Corinthians understand spiritual gifts. His opening claim in v. 3 helps the Corinthians understand that the first and foremost work of the Spirit is to create faith so that one may confess that Jesus is Lord. It is impossible to have faith in Christ apart from the work of the Spirit. Paul then goes on to explain the diversity of spiritual gifts while emphasizing their divine unity. Spiritual gifts are diverse and empower diverse forms of ministry, but in each case it is the same Spirit that works them for the ministry of the same Lord (vv. 4-6). It is this fundamental divine unity that gives meaning, power, shape, and scope to spiritual diversity. Every single Christian is endowed with spiritual gifts (vv. 7a, 8-10). There is no such thing as a nonspiritual Christian. Similarly, the diverse gifts given to diverse members of the community all have the same goal: the mutual benefit and building up of the community (v. 7b). For Paul, spirituality is not a certain feeling or understanding or experience that is produced by an individual. Spirituality is the Spirit's reality at work in every Christian in diverse ways to create core Christian unity and energize the community for service and ministry.

THE GOSPEL
JOHN 14:8-17(25-27) (RCL);
JOHN 14:8-17 (BCP, alt.);
JOHN 14:15-16, 23b-26 (RC, alt.);
JOHN 20:19-23 (BCP, RC)

Interpreting the Text

In John's Gospel, Jesus is the Word who is sent into the world to embody the divine reality (1:14; 3:16). The Spirit is sent to birth that divine reality in the lives of those whom the Word has called and gathered (3:5-8). Following Jesus' glorification in his death, the Spirit is given to his followers (6:63; 7:39; 19:30) so that they truly live, worship, and participate in the divine reality in ways that are otherwise impossible to the world (3:5; 4:23-24; 7:39; 14:17, 26; 15:26; 16:13). In order to present the multidimensional, life-giving activity of the Spirit, John's Gospel employs the rich descriptive title "Paraclete" *(parakletos)* four times in the Farewell Discourse (14:16, 26; 15:26; 16:7). This title depicts the Spirit as God's witness, spokesperson, advocate, and counselor. The Gospel lections for Pentecost Sunday from John 14 or John 20 present "before/after" pictures of the effect that the Spirit's coming has on the disciples and their insight, faith, and mission activity in the world.

The reading from John 14 opens with a seemingly stupid request from Philip in v. 8, "Lord, show us the Father, and we will be satisfied." Philip is a disciple who has remained with Jesus from the beginning, seeing all that Jesus has done and hearing that which Jesus has proclaimed about himself, his intimate relationship with God, and his mission (1:35-51; 6:1-15; 12:20-36). If anyone should perceive how God has been at work in and through Jesus and how Jesus manifests God's reality, it should be Philip. Yet this is precisely the "before" snapshot. Before the coming of the Spirit, even the disciples who have remained with Jesus from the start are unable fully to see, comprehend, or be satisfied with the reality of the incarnation and the mission of Jesus. Jesus' words in 14:9-11 cannot truly penetrate into a person's life until the Spirit comes to teach and bring forth insightful remembrance (vv. 17, 25-26). Thus the Spirit does not give new revelations or additional insider information to the disciples but helps them fully comprehend what they have already heard, seen, and experienced. Jesus has already shown God to his disciples and even to the world because Jesus is God's self-revelation. The fundamental mutuality that exists between Jesus and God means that in seeing one, you see the reality of the other; in hearing one, you hear the disclosure of the other's will; in believing in one, you believe in the other. So the call to faith in these verses is a call to believe in the mutual presence and activity of God in Jesus and Jesus in God. This penetrating insight of faith, however, comes only with the sending of the Spirit into the lives of the disciples (vv. 16-20).

In addition to bringing forth insight and understanding, the Spirit also empowers the disciples for mission activity that will entail doing what Jesus does even to the point of doing greater works (v. 12). The first claim of v. 12, that Christians do what Jesus does, is not too surprising. Christians are not called on to do their own thing but are commanded by Jesus to manifest the divine love Jesus embodies and to serve others as Jesus has served (cf. 13:3-20, 34-35; 14:15, 21-24; 15:10-17). The second claim of v. 12, however, is indeed surprising, even shocking. How can Christians possibly do works that exceed what Jesus has done since Jesus is the incarnate Word who manifests God's very reality? For John, "greater" has three facets: time, geography, and quantity. Even after Jesus' return to God, the disciples will continue doing what Jesus has done so that there is no time limit to the disciples' work. As long as there are believers, the work of Jesus will be carried out. Similarly, Jesus' activity was confined to Galilee, Samaria, and Judea while the mission activity of Jesus' disciples will spread throughout the world. Finally, Jesus did a limited number of signs in John's story but that which Jesus' disciples do will be beyond quantification. Thus "greater" does not refer to bigger or more important works but shows how Jesus' works are multiplied and spread in countless contexts in countless ways in countless human lives by generation after generation of believers empowered by the Spirit for work in Jesus' name. This vision of expansive mission also serves as the interpretive framework for vv. 13-14. Jesus is not the divine sugar-daddy promising to give us whatever we ask. Jesus continues to be active in the world and for the community after his return to God in and through the community that bears his name. What Christians ask in Jesus' name is to be congruent with what Jesus asked of God because of the mutual participatory reality believers share with Jesus. Hence Christian asking is something taught to them by the Spirit who gives advice, counsel, and insight (vv. 16-17).

The Johannine Pentecost scene occurring on the evening of Jesus' resurrection and return to God (20:19-23) enacts that which Jesus had foretold throughout the Farewell Discourse. The scene opens with the disciples fearfully gathered behind locked doors. Jesus, however, is not barred by such human barriers but comes into their midst bringing the peace he had foretold (20:19; 14:27; 16:32-33). He shows to them the reality of his crucifixion so that the disciples' fear is transformed into joy (20:20; cf. 16:21-22) and confession (note the use of the title "Lord" in 20:20, 25). Jesus breathes the Spirit onto them (20:22, recalling especially Ezek. 37:9-10) thus fulfilling his promise of sending the Paraclete (14:16-17, 26; 15:26-27; 16:7-15) to empower them for the ongoing salvific mission involving the forgiveness or retention of sins (i.e., receiving or rejecting the revelatory truth and life that is Jesus; cf. 1:11-13; 3:16-21; 9:39-41; 15:22-24; 16:8-9; 20:23). By breathing the Spirit's reality into their lives, Jesus has kept his promises to the disciples, equipped them for the mission on which he is now sending them (an extension of the divine mission for which he was first sent), and linked their lives fully into his through the indwelling of the Spirit.

Responding to the Text

These two Johannine texts present an important threefold understanding of spirituality. First and foremost, John would have us spell this word with a capital "S," since it involves the reality of the Holy Spirit in our individual and corporate lives. In John's theological geography, Jesus has returned to God to dwell in the divine reality from which the Word first came. That does not mean, however, that his presence is removed. The Spirit brings the presence of the crucified, resurrected, ascended Christ fully into our lives and experiences. To be a Christian is to be in intimate, ongoing relationship with Christ via the presence of the Spirit who gives us birth from above so that while we dwell in this world, we dwell in Christ's incarnate reality (cf. 3:1-8; 14:16-17, 25-28; 15:26-27; 16:5-11). Second, if one would ask, "Is the Spirit's job description to teach or to announce or to guide or to convict or to empower or to bear witness or to advise?" John's Gospel would answer with a robust "Yes!" The work of the Spirit is multidimensional as it continues to embody Christ's reality and empower Christ's mission in the world. Third, the Spirit's activity thus promotes Christ's activity in and through us. Thus John's Gospel does not see spirituality as individualist or passive. Because of the Spirit's reality in our lives, mission hap-

> MOST CHRISTIANS ARE VERY FAMILIAR WITH JOHN 3:16, BUT HOW FAMILIAR ARE THEY WITH THE VISION FOR SPIRIT-EMPOWERED MISSION IN JOHN 20:21?

pens. Jesus happens. Forgiveness of sins and conviction of sin happens. There is an indispensable link between John 3:16 and John 20:21 through the presence and activity of the Spirit so that what Jesus has done is multiplied and expanded ever anew by the spirituality of the community bearing Jesus' name into the world (14:12-17). Most Christians are very familiar with John 3:16, but how familiar are they with the vision for Spirit-empowered mission in John 20:21?

HOLY TRINITY SUNDAY / FIRST SUNDAY AFTER PENTECOST

JUNE 6, 2004

REVISED COMMON	EPISCOPAL (BCP)	ROMAN CATHOLIC
Prov. 8:1-4, 22-31	Isa. 6:1-8	Prov. 8:22-31
Psalm 8	Psalm 29	Ps. 8:4-9
	or Canticles 2 or 13	
Rom. 5:1-5	Rev. 4:1-11	Rom. 5:1-5
John 16:12-15	John 16:(5-11), 12-15	John 16:12-15

FIRST READING

PROVERBS 8:1–4, 22–31 (RCL);
PROVERBS 8:22–31 (RC)

Proverbs 8 is not an ode to wisdom but an invitational declaration in which wisdom details who she is and what she has to offer to all who heed her summons. People do not quest after wisdom or the answers to life's difficult questions. Rather, wisdom quests after people in all the public spaces of the city (vv. 2-3). Wisdom's insights guide the cult, the court, the commerce, and the judicial components of civic life. Wisdom seeks to teach the key to all aspects of life and wants all to be her students (v. 4).

The lectionary leap from 8:4 to 8:22 is rather abrupt and passes over the declaration of the indispensable importance and benefits wisdom. What does connect v. 4 with vv. 22-25 is the imagery of offspring. Wisdom's call is to the offspring of humans (v. 4b), and wisdom herself is God's offspring (vv. 22, 24-25). Before God begins on creation, God begins with wisdom. From the get-go, wisdom is there because God established wisdom's preeminent position. This enables wisdom to teach the creative, foundational realities of existence (vv. 27-31).

In its original context, this text speaks nothing about God's being or the concept of the Trinity. Instead, it was seeking to declare that there is a unifying order to the universe and to daily life that is God's wisdom. As God wisely designed, ordered, and created everything, so God has wisely designed, ordered, and created the right way for us to go about life. Divine wisdom is the way and means of God's ongoing intimate involvement and ordering of life in the present. In early Christian theology, that which had been ascribed to wisdom becomes ascribed (and expanded) to Jesus Christ as the ultimate expression of God. In the Gospel lessons from John, the Spirit becomes a vital point of connection in the relationship between God, Jesus, and humanity.

ISAIAH 6:1–8 (BCP)

This text is not so much the call of Isaiah but his commissioning. It begins with Isaiah finding himself in a place where he clearly does not belong and ends with him being commissioned for an unspecified divine mission. Isaiah sees someone he has no business seeing: the Lord sitting upon the divine throne, i.e., upon the Ark of the Covenant. Flanking the enthroned Lord are seraphim, six-winged serpent-like creatures having a glowing appearance. Though they are members of the divine entourage, even they know they are in God's presence, for they use two of their wings to cover their eyes (so as not to see God's face) and two wings to cover their genitals (so as to hide their nakedness for God). As members of the divine court, they announce God's holy and glorious reality (v. 3). This acknowledgment of God's complete divinity causes the temple to be filled with smoke and its very foundations to shake. Isaiah clearly knows he is out of his league. His creaturely and sinful reality causes him to lament that he is doomed. Whereas one of the seraphim stressed God's complete holiness, Isaiah recognizes his complete unworthiness as one having unclean lips. Whereas the seraphim cover their eyes because they dare not see the Lord, Isaiah stands gawking at the true King of all reality. Yet the seraphim do not swoop down to peck out his eyes or strike him dead in an effort to guard God's majesty. Instead one swoops down and touches Isaiah's mouth with a holy coal, announcing to Isaiah that his guilt is removed and his sin forgiven. Now Isaiah belongs in this scene. He overhears a question the Lord asks of the divine entourage, "Whom shall I send, and who will go for us?" God is seeking advice more than asking for volunteers, but Isaiah volunteers anyway, saying, "Here I am! Send me!" The one who was made clean in order to stand in the midst of God's throne room is not content to remain there. He boldly offers himself as divine envoy without knowing the specifics of the mission.

> WE HAVE BEEN GIVEN CLEAN LIPS TO OFFER HOLY PRAISE TO GOD THE FATHER, GOD THE SON, GOD THE HOLY SPIRIT. WE ARE ALSO COMMISSIONED TO GO AND TELL THE REALITY OF THIS MYSTERY TO OTHERS SO THAT WHICH WE WORSHIP IS ALSO THAT TO WHICH WE BEAR WITNESS IN OUR GOING.

On Trinity Sunday we celebrate the mystery, majesty, and magnificence that are our triune God. To be allowed to do so is pure gift. We have been given clean lips to offer holy praise to God the Father, God the Son, God the Holy Spirit. We are also commissioned to go and tell the reality of this mystery to others so that which we worship is also that to which we bear witness in our going.

RESPONSIVE READING

PSALM 8 (RCL);
PSALM 8:4-9 (RC)

This psalm is one of scripture's most significant acclamations of the role and place humanity plays in the grand scope of things. Humanity has been given a royal status in creation not to the determent of God but because of God (vv. 4-7). We are not co-creators or even co-regents with God. Humanity does not rule instead of God as royal managers over God's creation. God retains the ownership papers over creation and over us. Neither creation nor humanity is worthless, disposable, or exploitable pieces of matter. Both stem from God's hand, and both celebrate the majesty of God's name to which Christians bear witness.

PSALM 29 (BCP)

Trinity Sunday spotlights the awesome and awe-inspiring mystery that is the one God in three persons. Psalm 29 praises and extols the mystery that is God in full majesty and sovereignty. This can be seen in the fact that the divine name "Yahweh" is used eighteen times in the psalm's eleven verses, that "glory" appears four times, and that the phrase "the voice of the LORD" repeats itself seven times. On the one hand, God's awesome nature and position cause heavenly beings to bow in worship, the mightiest trees to snap, and nations to quake. On the other hand, that same awesome nature and position that is God sustains us and bestows peace upon us. The majestic voice of the Lord does not squash us but nurtures us so that when we speak the name of the triune God we say, "Glory!"

SECOND READING

ROMANS 5:1-5 (RCL, RC)

In these verses, Paul helps us understand present Christian existence on the road from justification to glory. Drawing on previous assertions in the letter, v. 1 announces that Christians were justified (i.e., brought into a right, living relationship with God) through the death of Jesus Christ (3:21-25; 4:25—5:1a) and our subsequent belief/trust in that divine action as announced by the gospel proclamation (1:16-17; 4:1-5, 17-24). Thus through our Lord Jesus Christ, we have peace with God (v. 1b). This means we have access to the reality of grace that is our ground of confidence for an even greater future: the very glory of God (v. 2). Previously in the letter Paul had sought to dismantle any grounds of confidence (i.e., boasting) before God based on human achievement or credentials (cf. 2:17, 23; 3:27; 4:2). In a dramatic reversal, Paul declares that we now have such grounds based on God's achievements in Christ, whose ultimate goal is that we would participate in God's own glorious being, which will be bestowed upon us at the resurrection. Another aspect of our ground for confidence is tribulation, which produces perseverance, which, in turn, produces a tested character, which, in turn, brings us right back to hope (vv. 3-4). Paul lived in a day when tribulation and affliction were marks of divine displeasure. Paul, however, claims that this is the way of life for Christians and that such difficulties help reinforce our hope that in the end God will complete the work of salvation begun in the act of justification. Thus in the present we have peace with God but are not exempt from life's hardships or the enmity of others. There is

IN THE PRESENT WE HAVE PEACE WITH GOD BUT ARE NOT EXEMPT FROM LIFE'S HARDSHIPS OR THE ENMITY OF OTHERS.

no shame or disappointment in staking our lives on God's ultimate goals, because even now God's love has been poured into our hearts through the presence and activity of the Holy Spirit (v. 5). When the going gets tough, Christians neither keep a stiff upper lip nor rely on their own resources. Instead, Christians live in the wellspring of divine love that is at the center of our existence, which is being drawn toward a future, glorious existence. Our past, present, and future flow out of the reality and activity of God, Jesus Christ, and the Holy Spirit.

REVELATION 4:1-11 (BCP)

This is a scene of mystery and awe as the author of Revelation is taken up to the divine throne room from which God exercises sovereignty over all reality. It draws much of its imagery from Ezek. 1:4-28. When read in conjunction with the seven letters of Revelation 2–3, it reminds the readers that in the midst of cosmic turmoil, trials, and tribulations, God is ruling the cosmos and the heavenly pantheon in attendance never ceases praising God and celebrating God's eternal rule. Hence our human worship of the sovereign ruler of the cosmos is not an option whenever we have nothing better to do for an hour on a Sunday morning. To worship God is to participate in the reality of heaven itself. Worship renews our commitment to live in loyalty and praise to God even in the midst of life's difficulties, setbacks, and hardships. Christian worship, which at times might seem mundane or routine, actually means experiencing a little bit of heaven here on earth because the reality of heaven is perpetual worship.

THE GOSPEL

JOHN 16:12-15 (RCL, RC);
JOHN 16:(5-11), 12-15 (BCP)

Interpreting the Text

This brief four-verse text is the shortest Gospel lection in the Year C lectionary. It is part of the Johannine Farewell Discourse (chapters 13–17) in which Jesus is preparing the community for life, fellowship, and mission in the time following his return to the Father. What the community cannot fully fathom on the eve on Jesus' death will be made clearer to them when he sends the Spirit to them. In vv. 7-11 the disciples heard about the Spirit's role vis-à-vis the world (i.e., the realm of unbelief, darkness, and rejection). The Spirit will expose that realm for what it is, one of sin and rejection, bringing forth God's judgment on the world and its satanic overlord. In vv. 12-15, the disciples are told of the more positive role the Spirit will have within and for the community of faith. First of all, the Spirit will help them understand what they need to understand in a timely manner (v. 12). What they are incapable of comprehending at one given point, the Spirit will help them comprehend at a new point. Thus the Spirit's role is not to give a new divine revelation but to help make the ongoing divine revelation in Jesus Christ comprehensible in new times and for new situations. Second, the Spirit is defined as the Spirit of truth *(aletheias)* who will lead the way *(hodegesei)* for the community to live in the truth (v. 13). This recalls Jesus' self-designation in 14:6 that he is the way *(hodos)* and the truth *(aletheia)* and the life through whom one comes to God. Here, however, the direction and access are switched. Instead of focusing on humanity approaching God via Jesus, we are told that God approaches us through the Spirit who will speak the true, divine message of the Word incarnate. The Christian community can handle divine truth because the Spirit dwells within the community and guides it along the way of truth. Thus as Jesus spoke what he had heard from God (cf. 7:16-17; 8:26, 40; 12:49-50), so too does the Spirit declare to the community the same divine message (vv. 13-15). In that way, the Spirit will glorify Jesus (v. 14) because the Spirit's message spotlights God's saving activity in Jesus and makes it known anew in and for the life of the community. Third, the Spirit will declare to the community the things that are to come (v. 13). In its Johannine context, this does not mean that the Spirit has the job of predicting the future. Part of the function of the Farewell Discourse is to inform the community of that which is to come. Thus to declare "the things to come" means that the Spirit will help the community interpret what they are to experience in the future in light of what Jesus has proclaimed to them about his life, death, resurrection, and return to God, their ongoing relationship with Jesus, and their mission in the world. So while Jesus, on the eve of his death, has commanded the community to love as he has loved them (13:33-35; 15:12-17), the Spirit's job will be to help the community embody such love in the post-resurrection reality and circumstances that are to come.

Responding to the Text

That which John's Gospel declares about the Spirit in the Farewell Discourse helped form the seedbed for the development of Trinitarian theology in subsequent centuries. John's focus here, however, is not on the metaphysical or ontological reality of the Trinity. Rather, he is focusing on the Spirit's role for the life and mission of the community. Even the title "Paraclete," which he gives to the Spirit (16:7; also 14:16, 26; 15:26) is a title describing the role of the Spirit as one who advocates, guides, and gives comfort and counsel. John's entire Gospel revolves around Jesus as the eternal and ultimate self-revelation of God. Who God is and what God is about is revealed in and by Jesus. The Spirit's role is to continue that divine revelation and to manifest that divine presence in a post-resurrection age. Hence John does not stress the distinctiveness of the Father, the Son, and the Spirit but focuses on the ongoing complementary reality and function of the Father, the Son, and Spirit in the world and in the community created by and gathered around the Word made flesh.

The Spirit continues the presence and activity of God in Jesus Christ in both the world and the community. The Spirit holds the world accountable to God, its Lord and creator, even if the world refuses to acknowledge God's lordship. The Spirit brings Christ's presence into the community and helps guide the community in Christ's way so that the community can faithfully and fruitfully live out its Christ-given mission in the world. From John's perspective, the Spirit does not bring new truth or new revelations to the community but helps the community to understand God's revelation in Jesus

> FROM JOHN'S PERSPECTIVE, THE SPIRIT DOES NOT BRING NEW TRUTH OR NEW REVELATIONS TO THE COMMUNITY BUT HELPS THE COMMUNITY TO UNDERSTAND GOD'S REVELATION IN JESUS CHRIST IN NEW WAYS FOR NEW SITUATIONS AND NEW CIRCUMSTANCES.

Christ in new ways for new situations and new circumstances. Thus when the church shaped its understanding of the Trinity in the expression of the Nicene Creed, it did not do so as a result of a new or different revelation from God. Rather through the work of the Spirit, the community gave distinct expression to what God has revealed about God's own self in and through Jesus Christ. For John it simply does not matter whether the community of Christ lives in the first century, the fourth century, the sixteenth century, the twenty-first century, or the thirty-eighth century. Jesus Christ is God's ultimate manifestation. Through the presence and activity of the Spirit, Jesus Christ continuously dwells with the community, and the community continuously discerns what it means to abide in Christ and to manifest Christ to the world. Thus timing is everything. The Spirit brings Christ to our times and guides us to make God's ultimate revelation in Christ relevant for our times.

SECOND SUNDAY AFTER PENTECOST

BODY AND BLOOD OF CHRIST / PROPER 6
JUNE 13, 2004

REVISED COMMON	EPISCOPAL (BCP)	ROMAN CATHOLIC
2 Sam. 11:26—12:10, 13-15 or 1 Kings 21:1-10, (11-14), 15-21a	2 Sam. 11:26—12:10, 13-15	Gen. 14:18-20
Psalm 32 or 5:1-8	Psalm 32 or 32:1-8	Ps. 110:1-4
Gal. 2:15-21	Gal. 2:11-21	1 Cor. 11:23-26
Luke 7:36—8:3	Luke 7:36-50	Luke 9:11b-17

The lections for the Roman Catholic celebration of Corpus Christi have their own theme and focus. Thus they will be considered separately below.

FIRST READING
GENESIS 14:18-20 (RC)

Genesis 14 is a story about an international crisis in the Middle Eastern region when five vassal kings rebel against their overlord, Chedorlaomer, who rules in Elam (the southern part of modern day Iran). Chedorlaomer puts down the revolt and takes booty from Sodom and Gomorrah, since those kings were part of the uprising (14:5-11). While all of this would have been important to the ancient media, it only becomes important in the biblical narrative because Lot, Abraham's nephew, is also taken away along with his goods (14:12). Whereas Chedorlaomer led an alliance of four kings to subdue five kings, Abraham leads a paltry force of 318 (14:14). Might itself will not determine who controls the land of destiny. Abraham catches up to the royal alliance in Dan, wins a nighttime victory, secures Lots release, and brings back all the booty taken by Chedorlaomer's alliance (14:15-16). On his return, he is met by Melchizedek, the king of Salem (Jerusalem?) who is also a priest (v. 18). He welcomes Abraham, blesses him and his God, and acknowledges that military victory has not come about by military might or superiority but by the hand of the Most High God, the maker of heaven and earth (vv. 19-20). Abraham, in turn, acknowledges the priestly stature and blessing of Melchizedek by presenting him with a tithe of the recaptured booty.

Melchizedek, the royal priest, is right on target when he announces that the one in charge of the region is the one who created the cosmos, the one who will deliver Abraham and his family.

RESPONSIVE READING
PSALM 110:1-4 (RC)

Psalm 110 is a royal psalm extolling the lofty royal position in which God has placed the king who rules from Zion over all who oppose the king and the LORD (110:1-2). From earliest times, Christians have given a messianic interpretation to the psalm to celebrate Jesus' identity as Messiah (e.g., Mark 12:35-37) or his position as sovereign Lord of the cosmos (e.g., Acts 2:34-35; Heb. 1:13). When linked with the other lessons for Corpus Christi Sunday, v. 4 of the psalm takes on additional thrust in that Jesus, the royal Lord of the universe, is also the priestly host of the divine banquet in which the food offered his people for life is nothing less than his own self and life.

SECOND READING
1 CORINTHIANS 11:23-26 (RC)

In the second half of 1 Corinthians 11, Paul deals with abuses of fellowship that are occurring when the community gathers to celebrate its sacred meal. When the community gathered for worship in a home of a wealthier Christian, they did not check their social and economic perspectives at the front door but carried them into worship. Hence those of the highest social status were eating with the host in the dining area (which could have held from nine to fourteen people) while the poorer members ate together in the more open spaces of the house. Because some poorer members had to work (days off were not common and certainly not weekly), by the time they arrived the food had already been eaten and some of the members (most likely the richer ones with more leisure time) were actually drunk (11:21). Paul is incensed at such behavior. That is not what the Lord's Supper entails (11:22). He reminds them of the reality of the sacred meal, which did not originate with him but with the Lord (v. 23a). The meal, he instructs them, is rooted in the salvific actuality of Christ's death. It was instituted on the night when he was handed over according to God's plan. Paul goes on to interpret the meal as an act that remembers the new eschatological covenant established through Jesus' death. The concept of remembrance is rooted in a Jewish understanding of the Passover meal. To remember is not a simple act of mental recall on the part of the participants. Rather remembrance means that the meal's participants are actually participating in the divine liberation highlighted in the meal. To eat the bread and to drink the cup entails a horizontal participation in the oneness of community fellowship and a vertical participation in the saving event of Jesus' death (vv. 24-25; also see 10:16-17). Paul also understands the meal to be an act of proclamation. In celebrating this meal the community proclaims Christ's death and its saving benefits in the period between the cross and the parousia. The meal, then, does not belong to the community but has been given to the community by its Lord so that the community can experience intimate fellowship with one another and participation in the reality of the cross.

> TO EAT THE BREAD AND TO DRINK THE CUP ENTAILS A HORIZONTAL PARTICIPATION IN THE ONENESS OF COMMUNITY FELLOWSHIP AND A VERTICAL PARTICIPATION IN THE SAVING EVENT OF JESUS' DEATH.

THE GOSPEL
LUKE 9:11b-17 (RC)

Interpreting the Text

The form of miracle stories in the ancient world consisted of three parts: problem, solution, proof of the solution. Generally the emphasis in the miracle story would be in the solution, and that is the case in this particular feeding miracle. The problem of the story is that an immense crowd is gathered in a wilderness location. The day is winding down, and the desolate location does not have the resources to provide room and board for so many. The disciples propose a very logical solution to Jesus. They command Jesus to dismiss the crowd so that people can procure their own provisions and lodging (v. 12). Their solution is practical and reflects the ways of the world. People need to take care of themselves. Ironically, it completely overlooks what 8:11b declares. Jesus welcomes people and brings them the saving reality of God's reign through word and deed. Note that Jesus proposes that the disciples provide the solution when he commands them to give the people something to eat (v. 13a). The disciples know they cannot provide help because they have inadequate resources at their disposal (five loaves and two fish, v. 13b). At this point, Jesus takes over as host. He creates an orderly banquet setting for the thousands of people in the wilderness (vv. 14-15). As banquet host, he offers the blessing, portions the food appropriately, and then continuously gives the food to the disciples to set before the banquet guests (v. 16). Therein is the solution to the problem: Jesus is the host who invites, oversees, and feeds the hungry guests. The disciples thought that a solution was to be found in the nor-

> JESUS IS THE HOST WHO INVITES, OVERSEES, AND FEEDS THE HUNGRY GUESTS.

mal ways of the world: let people go off and fend for themselves. Jesus thinks in terms of the in-breaking of God's kingdom. Jesus is the solution. People are not sent away to fend for themselves. God has sent Jesus into the world to bring God's extravagant reign of abundant life, and Jesus welcomes people into that heavenly reality now on earth. Indeed, the proof of the solution is not only that all ate and were satiated, but there were more resources at the end of the banquet than there had been at the beginning of the banquet (v. 17). This is what happens when Jesus is the solution to the problem of human need.

Responding to the Text

As the Gospel reading for the Solemnity of the Most Holy Body and Blood of Christ festival, it is natural and appropriate for this text to be given significant eucharistic overtones. Jesus is the host of the meal who welcomes us to come and feast on the divine reality of forgiveness, life, and salvation. Jesus is the literal host of the meal in that his body and blood are the substance of this feast of salvation. God does not think that the solution to our human dilemmas and hungers can be found in that which we provide for ourselves. God has provided the solution to the deep hungers of humanity. Jesus is the divine solution. In Christ's death, God has poured out salvation, life, and forgiveness. In the sacred meal, we are welcomed to the divine banquet and invited to feast on the salvific reality of Christ's death. Life is not a matter of fending for ourselves but finding lasting satisfaction in the true resources for living that Christ continuously gives to us, his own self.

The lections in the RCL and the BCP follow a different track.

First Reading
2 SAMUEL 11:26—12:10, 13-15 (RCL, BCP)

This lection opens with the perfect royal cover-up already in place. Hence unless congregants are familiar with the story, the reason for the divine disapproval announced in 11:27 will be surprising and perhaps confusing. The events depicted in 11:1-25 show David at his worst as he abuses both his royal power and God's gracious election of him as king. David had sexual intercourse with the wife of Uriah the Hittite. After she became pregnant, he went to great lengths to cover up the affair, ultimately arranging to have Uriah killed in battle. Interestingly enough, these details are reported rather neutrally without any moral judgments being made in 11:1-27a. Note too that there is no mention of David's love for Bathsheba. It was lust from the start. Initially he had no desire to marry her, just to have sex with her. Only when he had to eliminate Uriah did he take Bathsheba as his wife and so create the illusion of proper marital relations (11:26-27a).

The first notation of God's perspective does not come until 11:27b, and it too is tersely presented: the thing David had done displeased the LORD. Whereas David had been the sender throughout chapter 11 (11:3, 4, 14, 27), God now becomes the sender as Nathan is dispatched to David. Nathan reports of the abuse of power and exploiting actions of an unnamed rich man against a poor person. David falls into Nathan's rhetorical trap by pronouncing judgment against the merciless rich man (11:6). Nathan springs the trap by announcing, "You are the man!" He then goes on to speak the LORD's word in this matter. David's sin is primarily not against an abstract or impersonal law code but against God's graciousness and God's word (12:7-9). The irony of God's judgment is that as David utilized the sword of his external enemies to kill Uriah (12:9), the sword will never depart from David's own house. His enemies will not be external but internal, from his own family (12:10-11). What David sought to perpetrate as cover-up, God will execute as public event (12:12). After the divine pronouncement of guilt, judgment, and long-term consequences, David confesses his sin not in hopes of avoiding the consequences of his sin but simply because the reality of sin has been uncovered (12:13). On the one hand, God's graciousness is still at the forefront. God has put away David's sin so that he will not die (12:13b). On the other hand, consequences of sin do not always go away as God's forgiveness comes forth. Those consequences remain (12:14), and that which Nathan prophesied in 12:11-12 will be the tenor of David's life and story until his death. David's sin is no more from God's perspective, but the fallout of his sin does remain and will spread.

1 KINGS 21:1-10, (11-14), 15-21a (RCL, alt.)

This reading tells of the abuse of royal power, although the culprits (King Ahaz and Queen Jezebel) neither confess their sin nor receive God's forgiveness. The situation is this: Naboth has a vineyard in Jezreel that borders the king's palace (v. 1). The king thinks this would be a nifty place for a royal vegetable garden and so makes Naboth what he considers a rather generous offer (v. 2). To King Ahab, land is a self-serving commodity. Naboth, however, refuses to sell the land for theological reasons. The land is more than a piece of disposable property. It is a sacred legacy for his entire family (past, present, and future) that God has bequeathed (v. 3). He cannot sell what is a family heirloom from God, and thus land is to be stewarded wisely rather than cashed in for a quick buck. When Ahab hears Naboth's theological perspective, he goes into a blue funk (v. 4). Jezebel, his wife, cajoles her husband and plots against Naboth (vv. 7-8). She does not make

Naboth an offer he cannot refuse but arranges to have him whacked by manipu-
lating the elite of the city (vv. 9-13). Naboth is stoned to death, thus allowing the
king clear deed to the vineyard (vv. 14-16). Or so King Ahab thinks. When God
hears of this, Elijah the prophet is sent to confront Ahab regarding the nefarious
real estate scam. Secret business deals do not escape God's eye. God placed Ahab
in his position, and God will remove Ahab from his position because of the evil
way he has used it for personal gain. Not only does the land belong to God first,
last, and always, but God remains the measure of justice and the punisher of
exploitation in the land.

Responsive Reading
PSALM 32 (RCL, BCP); 32:1-8 (BCP, alt.)

The theological foundation of this psalm is built on two realities. First,
human beings are sinful. Second, God is a God of grace and forgiveness. Thus the
righteous one who shouts for joy and rejoices at the psalm's end (32:11) is not one
whose life is spotless or whose conduct is always and completely above reproach,
but one who has honestly and openly confessed their sinfulness to God (v. 5). The
forgiven psalmist is able to celebrate God's graciousness (vv. 6-7, 11) as well as to
instruct others to give up a stubborn, mule-headed attitude and to trust in the all-
encompassing love of God (vv. 8-10). The contrast between Simon the Pharisee
and the sexually suspect woman at the heart of the Gospel from Luke 7 for this
Sunday reflects the psalm's contrast between a closed-in life silently refusing to
acknowledge one's sin and the joy-filled life that openly celebrates the forgiveness
that God extravagantly showers on sinners.

PSALM 5:1-8 (RCL, alt.)

Teamed with the story of Naboth's vineyard (1 Kings 21), this psalm
presents an appropriate posture of prayer as righteous indignation. The psalmist
does not present an attitude of sinlessness to God but comes to God in unceasing
prayer, supplication, worship, and watchfulness (vv. 1-3) because of God's abundant steadfast love (v. 7). Vindication is not to be found in matching evil for evil,
slander for slander, but in prayer and trust that God hears our prayers and answers
out of righteousness and love.

GALATIANS 2:15-21 (RCL);
GALATIANS 2:11-21 (BCP)

In these verses, Paul recounts an incident in Antioch to his Galatian audience, not to set the historical record straight or to defend his apostolic ministry but to help them understand how the truth of the gospel is continuously at stake in the theology, life, and fellowship of the church. Very early on, a Christian community was formed in Antioch of Syria that included believers of both Jewish and Gentile backgrounds. Somewhere in 48-49 C.E., Paul and Barnabas went to Jerusalem for what might well be called the first ecumenical council of the church (see Acts 15; Gal. 2:1-10). The major decision of that council was that circumcision was not required of male Gentile Christians. From Paul's perspective, this meant that no requirements of law observance were to be placed on Gentile believers. For him, not only does a person come into a right covenant relationship with God via the gospel, one also remains in that right relationship via the gospel and not the law. Similarly, the ongoing fellowship that Christians share with each other is an enactment of the gospel and not the observation of the law. This radical theological perspective, however, was severely tested in events following the Jerusalem conference. Cephas (i.e., Peter) came to Antioch, and though he was Jewish in background he continually enjoyed table fellowship (which would have included celebration of the Lord's Supper) with both Jewish and Gentile Christians apart from observance of the law (e.g., dietary restrictions). Subsequently, when people under the influence of James (Jesus' younger brother, not the son of Zebedee) Cephas continually withdrew from such inclusive fellowship as did the other Jewish Christians (including even Barnabas). Evidently their perspective was that Gentile Christians must observe minimal dietary laws in order for Jewish and Gentile Christians to have table fellowship (cf. Acts 15:19-20, 28-29). For Paul this was anathema. To Paul, this violated the truth of the gospel (2:14) as well as the Jerusalem accords. Thus he recounts in 2:14ff. how he confronted Cephas, reminding him that a person (whether Jew or Gentile) is brought into a right relationship (i.e., justified) not by works of the law (vv. 15-16). Thus a Jewish Christian cannot insist on even minimal law observance by Gentile Christians, because that would mean rebuilding the wall of the law (v. 18), nullifying the grace-filled effects of the cross (vv. 19-21) and establishing something other than faith as the grounds of a right relationship with God and with other Christians (vv. 15-16). The gospel is not only how one comes into a right relationship (rather than the law) but also how one maintains/remains in a right relationship (rather than the law).

Justification by grace through faith is a radical notion whether it is the first century, the sixteenth century, or the twenty-first century. The law is not the means for entrance into a right relationship or the contours of maintaining that relationship. It is first, last, and always justification by grace through faith alone. No additions. No hidden codicils. Even faith is not a human initiative. Paul is not arguing we that substitute the human effort of believing for the human effort of doing works of the law. Rather, faith begins with the divine initiative of the proclamation of the cross through which God's Spirit works to create the response of faith. Another radical component of the vision of justification in this text is that it is not a private matter. For Paul, justification is communal. The issues of the text are communal (and Paul most certainly would have included the inclusive celebration of the Lord's Supper). Even Paul's use of himself as personal example in vv. 18-21 is meant to depict universal Christian experience and not his private experience. The gospel brings us into fellowship with other Christians—all other Christians, even if their background or piety or theology is not exactly the same as ours. To withdraw from fellowship and require other Christians to be/act like us before we acknowledge the validity of the cross in their lives is to threaten the unity God has wrought through the cross. Our fellowship and life together are established and maintained by the cross. That is the radical nature of justification.

> THE GOSPEL BRINGS US INTO FELLOWSHIP WITH OTHER CHRISTIANS—ALL OTHER CHRISTIANS, EVEN IF THEIR BACKGROUND OR PIETY OR THEOLOGY IS NOT EXACTLY THE SAME AS OURS.

THE GOSPEL

LUKE 7:36—8:3 (RCL);
LUKE 7:36-50 (BCP)

Interpreting the Text

The third Gospel often employs the literary method of comparison and contrast (called *synkrisis*). Sometimes the comparison and contrast is between characters of consecutive stories (e.g., Zechariah and Mary), sometimes it is between characters in a parable (e.g., the rich man and Lazarus), sometimes between parallel events (e.g., the birth of John the Baptist and of Jesus). Through this technique, differing perspectives, responses, theological responses, etc. are presented for the audience's evaluation and enlightenment. In this text, the comparison/contrast deals with two radically different characters who embody the contrasting theological stances presented in 7:29-30. One of the characters is depicted as having relatively high social and religious status. He is a male, a Pharisee named Simon, who invites Jesus to a dinner in his own home. The character held in contrast to him is depicted as having low social and religious status. She is an unnamed female, a sinner who barges into the scene completely uninvited and displaying scandalous behavior. Through the contrast of their status, attitudes, and actions the text is making a surprising theological claim regarding the relationship between forgiveness and love as it involves Jesus' person and activity.

After the brief introduction of v. 36, the story unfolds as a chiasm (antithetical parallelism) to highlight the *synkrisis*.

A		Woman's stance toward Jesus (vv. 37-38)
	B	Simon's stance toward Jesus (v. 39)
	B'	Jesus' response to Simon (vv. 40-47)
A'		Jesus' response to the woman (v. 48)

The woman's stance toward Jesus is socially scandalous. She is described as a woman in the city who was a sinner. Though her sin is not listed, her uninvited and unexpected actions have blatant sexual overtones as she goes to great lengths to bathe and anoint Jesus' feet using her tears, her hair, and perfume. The depiction of such extravagant touching of Jesus by a sinful woman would have made a first-century audience extremely uncomfortable. Simon the Pharisee does not respond to the woman's actions. Instead, he takes a theological stance toward Jesus. Though he had invited Jesus into his home as honored guest, he now concludes that Jesus cannot possibly be a prophet (i.e., God's authorized spokesperson), because a prophet would have known the theological reality of that woman. So the sinful woman's stance of elaborate devotion to Jesus is contrasted with the religious leader's dismissive stance toward Jesus.

Jesus responds first to Simon even though Simon had only expressed his theological conclusions to himself (thus indicating to the audience that Jesus indeed has prophetic powers of insight). He presents a situation to Simon regarding the correlation between forgiveness and love (vv. 41-42) in the form of a question that forces Simon to come up with the correct answer: the one who is forgiven more will, in turn, love more. Jesus then turns Simon's correct answer against him by pointing out that Simon did not perform any of the basic obligations of hospitality (e.g., water for feet, greeting kiss, anointing for the head) even though Simon is the one who had invited Jesus as guest. The theological point is that Simon saw neither his own need for forgiveness nor Jesus as one who bestows forgiveness. He even treated Jesus with a degree of theological disdain because of Jesus' apparent inability to make theological discernments regarding the character of the woman. Jesus then presents the woman as a model of how great forgiveness begets great devotion and love. Here there is an important point of Greek grammar in v. 48 that is not evident in our English translations. Jesus says to her, "Your sins have been forgiven." The verb here is in the perfect tense (mistranslated in the English as a present tense, "your sins are forgiven") indicating that forgiveness previously has been bestowed on her. Here she continues to live in the reality of divine forgiveness by recognizing from whom divine forgiveness comes and responding with extravagant devotion. This is what faith and salvation entail. The story tacks on a dénouement (8:1-3), noting that among those accompanying Jesus and continuously offering service to him from their own resources are a great number of women who had experienced healing and restoration from Jesus. Again divine benefaction begets devotion and service.

Responding to the Text

There is a degree of salvation calculus presented in this text, but it is important to see how the formula works. Forgiveness generates love (not vice versa). If one perceives little forgiveness, then little love is demonstrated. If one receives immense, unexpected, and totally unmerited forgiveness, then one is going to respond with immense devotion and gratitude. The in-breaking of divine love, acceptance, and forgiveness is a given in the person of Jesus. This is the stuff of his mission as he first announced in his inaugural sermon in Luke's story (4:16-30). What is not a given is how that impacts human lives. Those who see neither their need for such unmerited divine extravagance nor how Jesus uniquely and truly brings this reality of divine acceptance into human lives are not going to respond in overwhelming joy and thanksgiving. While some might not take seriously their sinfulness and others might so wallow in his or her sin that they do not take seriously God's forgiveness poured out in Jesus, the response is quite similar. Limited joy; limited devotion. When one rightly perceives their own sinful reality and that Jesus is the agent of divine forgiveness and grace, then a response of continual service and devotion that includes one's emotional and economic resources results.

God's forgiveness in Jesus Christ is a scandal. It goes out to sinners regardless of their religious or social standing. It breaks into human existence without prior invitation. It transforms who we are, whom we understand God to be, and how we are to live our lives and utilize our resources. It touches every aspect of our existence. It seeks to generate not just an intellectual acknowledgment or a polite thank you but blubbering, messy, wholehearted, continual, gushy devotion. It is not something that we control but something that slams into our lives and takes control. It is not given to us as a result of our love but generates love in us to God and to others. Too often in an effort to be morally upright, the church has forgotten that it is a community for sinners only; those who are not sinners need not apply for membership.

> GOD'S FORGIVENESS IN JESUS CHRIST IS A SCANDAL. IT GOES OUT TO SINNERS REGARDLESS OF THEIR RELIGIOUS OR SOCIAL STANDING.

THIRD SUNDAY AFTER PENTECOST

TWELFTH SUNDAY IN ORDINARY TIME / PROPER 7
JUNE 20, 2004

REVISED COMMON	EPISCOPAL (BCP)	ROMAN CATHOLIC

Isa. 65:1-9
  or 1 Kings 19:1-4,
  (5-7), 8-15a
	Zech. 12:8-10; 13:1	Zech. 12:10-11; 13:1

Ps. 22:19-28 or Psalms 42, 43	Ps. 63:1-8	Ps. 63:2-6, 8-9
Gal. 3:23-29	Gal. 3:23-29	Gal. 3:26-29
Luke 8:26-39	Luke 9:18-24	Luke 9:18-24

FIRST READING
ISAIAH 65:1-9 (RCL)

This passage most likely dates from the period when the nation is returning from exile to a land that is ruin and to a Jerusalem that has no temple (ca. 515 B.C.E.). Theologically, it follows the nation's lament of chapters 63–64 (especially 63:7—64:12), in which the people are asking God to be active and self-revealing as in the good old days (63:15-17; 64:1-2, 10-12). Isaiah 65:1-2 introduces the divine answer. It is not God who has been absent and indifferent. God has been there, ready to be found, calling, "Here I am! Here I am!" to the nation. No, the distance that now exists between God and the nation is not because of what God has done; it is due to the attitudes and actions of the nation. It is a rebellious nation that sets its own agendas for life (v. 2). In vv. 3-5 a laundry list of examples is presented by God detailing the ways the nation has continuously provoked God's indignation; so now the nation is going to get a divine communiqué—only the divine message does not contain hearts, smiling faces, and wishes of "have a nice day." It is a message of divine retribution in which the former and current sins of the nation land right back in their own laps as the divine punishment is in equal measure to their sinfulness (v. 7). Yet at the very moment when all might seem doom and gloom for the nation's future because of its sinful past, the tone of the prophetic utterance shifts to a radical pronouncement in v. 8, as the LORD announces that some bad grapes do not automatically spoil the wine that comes from the whole cluster. This time divine judgment will be more selective so that those who have sought God will inherit the land and all its blessings (vv. 9-10). Thus the postexilic period begins a new chapter in God's dealing with the people of God. Divine integrity is not being compromised. God is not suddenly becoming soft on sin. But God's execution of judgment within Israel is not a blanket judgment. Here begins the theological movement toward the reckoning of sin more to individuals than to a people as a whole so that not all will be destroyed (v. 8).

1 KINGS 19:1-4, (5-7), 8-15a (RCL, alt.)

For the presentation of this text see the first lesson for St. James Elder, Apostle (July 25, 2004), below.

ZECHARIAH 12:8-10; 13:1 (BCP);
ZECHARIAH 12:10-11; 13:1 (RC)

Zechariah 12–13 presents significant divine promises that stand in stark contrast to the preceding prophecy of devastation against the corrupt leadership of God's people (11:4-17). On the coming day of the LORD, just when things look hopeless because the nations have besieged Judah and Jerusalem (12:1-3), God will be the divine warrior bringing full victory against all the nations that have come against Jerusalem (12:4-9). Interestingly enough, the divine triumph will not result in great victory celebrations by the people but mourning as God will pour out a spirit of compassion and supplication (12:10a). This divine outpouring also indicates that the spirit of recognition and repentance will come over the people, leading to cleansing from idolatry and phony prophecy introduced in 13:1. Thus the movement of the pericope is from divine deliverance to divinely induced recognition of sin to divine cleansing from sin. When linked to the Gospel lesson from Luke 9:18-24, it is clear that Jesus is the royal figure whom God's people will pierce, but God's overarching plan for repentance and forgiveness will flow out of the death of the pierced one.

RESPONSIVE READING
PSALM 22:19-28 (RCL)

Christians are most familiar with the first half of this psalm from its quotation in the passion narratives in Matthew and Mark. That portion of the psalm is an intense lament in the midst of afflictions and the terror of abandonment by

God. The pericope boundaries for this psalm pick up the action at the point of transition from lament to praise (vv. 19-21). Words that had previously been used in a sarcastic or frantic way (i.e., help, deliver, save, rescue) now form the contents of petition and affirmation as the tormented psalmist declares the LORD's rescue (especially see v. 21b). Such transcendent sovereignty manifested in God's merciful deliverance is also at the heart of the presentation of Jesus as he rescues the foreign demonic from the imperial clutches of the power of evil.

PSALMS 42, 43 (RCL, alt.)

These two psalms actually form one unit that is riveted together through its note of isolated longing and its hopeful refrain repeated in 42:5, 11; 43:5, 11. Thus the themes of despair and hope are held together in deep, profound ways. Despondency does not squash or eliminate hope but makes it even more fervent as the refrain makes clear. Hope, then, is not wishful thinking or simply desiring that things will turn out differently. Hope is holding on in the midst of desolate feelings to God's future in which praise will be the final note of the living, ongoing relationship with our Savior, our help, our God.

PSALM 63:1-8 (BCP);
PSALM 63:2-6, 8-9 (RC)

Psalm 63 is an acclamation of God's complete, sovereign, and magnanimous reign. God cannot be manipulated or influenced to act for the people through the right form of worship. Rather, God's presence, majesty, and attentive care mean the people of God respond with resplendent exultation and unceasing praise.

SECOND READING
GALATIANS 3:23-29 (RCL, BCP);
GALATIANS 3:26-29 (RC)

Early in this chapter Paul had introduced Abraham into his argument that a right relationship with God is determined not by works of the law but stems from the gospel, which brings about faith (3:6-9). Beginning in v. 23 Paul describes the present, post-law reality to his Gentile audience, which is struggling with the place of the law in their own lives. His use of faith here refers not first to our human faith but to the revelation of Christ's faithfulness (i.e., Christ's death as the center of God's salvific plan; cf. 1:3-4; 2:19-21; 3:1, 13-14; 4:4-5; 5:11, 24; 6:12-15). The coming of faith means the coming of Christ as fulfillment of God's promises to Abraham and the opportunity for the Gentiles to enter into a right covenant relationship with God as heirs of Abraham via faith. Paul tells us that we are incorporated into this salvific reality and its relationships via baptism into Christ. Baptism is thus imaged here as an event of negation and inauguration. Former identity markers that classified, divided, and stratified humanity based on religious affiliation (Jew or Greek), economic status (slave or free), and gender (male and female) have been abrogated in baptism. It should be noted that his final paring of male and female negates any reliance on circumcision since with the coming of faith it does not even matter if one has a penis to be circumcised. In baptism, one puts on Christ (i.e., one is immersed into Christ and his saving death through which we are liberated from the law's curse; cf. 2:19-21; 3:14) so that the promises to Abraham are fulfilled in Christ (3:16) for those who now dwell in the oneness of the Christ-reality (3:29).

> THE COMING OF FAITH MEANS THE COMING OF CHRIST AS FULFILLMENT OF GOD'S PROMISES TO ABRAHAM AND THE OPPORTUNITY FOR THE GENTILES TO ENTER INTO A RIGHT COVENANT RELATIONSHIP WITH GOD AS HEIRS OF ABRAHAM VIA FAITH.

Paul would agree with the adage that "clothes make the person." For Paul, our clothing as Christians is none other than Christ (v. 27), in whom God's plan of salvation and radical inclusivity comes to full fruition. Whereas Paul holds up baptism as the event that eradicates that which had divided humanity, subsequent Christian practices and arguments have often made baptism a point of divisiveness. What is the proper form of baptism—sprinkling or immersion? Who is the one allowed to baptize? What is the proper age of baptism? While these are not inconsequential or irrelevant issues for theological discussion, the answers to those questions have often become determinative to the meaning, power, and place of baptism. Baptism is not about age or denominational affiliation. It is about God immersing us into the salvific reality of Jesus Christ that defines who we are and gives us our common identity. Thus all Christians wear the same baptismal garb, Jesus Christ.

THE GOSPEL

LUKE 8:26–39 (RCL)

Interpreting the Text

The story of Jesus' battle with the Gerasene demoniac is one of the most vivid miracle stories in the Gospels. Some previous texts in Luke's story serve as an interpretive backdrop for this particular story. In 4:16-30 Jesus announced that his Spirit-endowed mission of divine jubilee would include releasing those held in bondage (see especially 4:18-19). In 4:31-41 various exorcisms were narrated to demonstrate that the captives being released through Jesus' mission included those held in bondage by Satan. In the preceding text, Jesus' power over chaotic forces was displayed as he stilled the storm. Nonetheless, whereas demons had recognized him as Son of God (4:41), his own disciples are left pondering Jesus' identity in light of his power over wind and wave (8:25). Hence Jesus' identity and his power to free captives function prominently in this miracle story.

The setting for this story alerts the reader to the fact that in crossing the lake, he has also crossed a theological boundary. He is now in unclean territory where he will encounter demons, pigs, and tombs. Thus for the first time in Luke's story, Jesus is bringing the mission of divine liberation beyond the boundaries of Israel. The first person he encounters on this alien turf is a man of sorry plight (v. 27). He is naked (signifying shame) and cut off from community, living as a dead man and being in bondage for a long time. This man has lost all social and religious status. He is truly a nonentity. The reason for this is that thousands of demons hold him in captivity (a Roman legion contains 5,600 troops). They are so strong that mere chains and shackles cannot confine them (v. 29). The demons resist Jesus' initial command to come out of the man and then seek to fend off Jesus in two ways. First, they point out that there is a gap separating them and Jesus, which is tantamount to telling Jesus that he should leave them alone. Second, they launch a preemptive strike by naming Jesus in order to gain authority over him (v. 28). Ironically, the demons are the ones who answer the question previously put forth by the disciples, who had seen Jesus' power over the forces of chaos (v. 25). Jesus, however, turns the tables by forcing them to name themselves. Once they acknowledge Jesus' superior power, their only recourse is to throw themselves upon Jesus' mercy (v. 31) and seek to negotiate a deal. Instead of being sent into the abyss (i.e., a prison reserved for demonic spirits; see 1 Enoch 10:4-6; 18:11-16; Jubilees 5:6-10; Rev. 20:1-3), they implore Jesus to send them into a herd of pigs grazing on the hillside. On the one hand, Jesus grants their request. On the other hand, this does not guarantee their survival but seals their doom as the pigs run down a cliff and drown in the lake.

The rest of the story presents two distinct reactions to Jesus' triumph over the legion of demons. One reaction is that of fear. First the herders and then the local populace are overwhelmed with fear (note its repetition in vv. 35, 37), and so ask Jesus to depart. Evidently the Gentile world is not quite ready for the mission of divine liberation Jesus is unleashing. The other reaction is that of the healed man. His plight has been completely reversed by Jesus (cf. vv. 27-28, 35). He had been naked, now he is clothed; he had fallen down shouting at Jesus, now he sits at Jesus' feet; he had been seized by demons and out of control, now he is in his right mind. Whereas the local folk had begged Jesus to depart from their area, the former demoniac implores Jesus that he might be allowed to go with Jesus. While Jesus had granted the requests of the demons (to be sent into the pigs) and the local populace (that he depart their area), Jesus does not grant this man's request. Instead, he restores the man to community, the place where he belongs. Jesus also instructs him to declare how much God did for him, but the healed man returns to community preaching how much Jesus did for him. The man might not be allowed to accompany Jesus, but he is fulfilling the role of a disciple by preaching Jesus. Jesus might be leaving alien territory, but a Gentile is preaching about him in that territory.

Responding to the Text

Preaching on demon possession and exorcisms in a postmodern era is never an easy task. Yet powers of evil are still in existence (be they political, social, or economic in nature) that seek to dominate, isolate, and alienate their victims. At times such powers can even try to negotiate with the church, to strike a deal so that if the church does not name them and their tyranny of oppression, then the powers will leave the church alone. This story, however, announces anew that the mission of the gospel includes liberation, wholeness, and restoration. In naming the powers of evil that hold others in captivity, the gospel seeks to bestow status, peace, and belonging to community. Perhaps the greatest challenge in proclaiming this text is not in demythologizing its demonic elements but in having the courage to name the powers that seek to enslave people for their own ends and in announcing anew the liberation that Jesus' mission of wholeness and restoration brings to the captives of today's world.

> IN NAMING THE POWERS OF EVIL THAT HOLD OTHERS IN CAPTIVITY, THE GOSPEL SEEKS TO BESTOW STATUS, PEACE, AND BELONGING TO COMMUNITY.

LUKE 9:18-24 (BCP, RC)

Interpreting the Text

Jesus' identity and his mission have been inextricably connected from the beginning of Luke's story. He is the royal figure, the anointed Son of God whose reign will have no end (1:32-33). His anointed role (the title Messiah/Christ literally means "anointed one") involves the ministry of liberation as part of God's acceptable year (4:16-21). Up to this point in the story, the interrelationship between Jesus' identity and mission has manifested itself in his authoritative preaching, teaching, welcoming/forgiving sinners, healing, exorcising demons, and calling disciples to follow him. To properly understand his identity is to properly understand his mission. Of course, to miss one is to miss the other. This is exemplified by the perspective of Herod the tetrarch who, upon hearing all that Jesus did, wonders just who is Jesus (9:7-9).

Beginning in v. 18 this identity/mission connection takes a new turn for the reader. The scene opens with a familiar Lukan scene: Jesus is praying (cf. 3:21; 5:16; 6:12). In Luke, prayer involves opening oneself fully to the power and will of God. (Just what that entails will be revealed shortly.) Jesus then conducts a brief popular opinion poll, asking the disciples about his identity among the populace. The general opinion about Jesus' recalls what Herod had heard about him (vv. 7-8). Jesus then asks the disciples about their own opinion (note that in v. 20 the word "you" is emphatic). Peter responds by claiming that Jesus is God's Messiah. To the reader, this information is no surprise. An angel, Simeon, and demons had already said as much (2:11, 26; 4:41). It might be a bit surprising that for the first time one of the disciples understands his anointed, royal identity. What is much more surprising than Peter's confession of Jesus' identity, however, is Jesus' revelation of the mission that lies ahead for him. He who has bested demons, windstorms, a hometown lynch mob, and obdurate religious leaders is on a mission leading to suffering, rejection, and death. Such a mission is not happenstance or simply the outcome of evil human designs against Jesus. This mission is the stuff of divine necessity (the "must" of v. 22 is from the Greek word *dei,* referring to God's necessary plan; cf. 2:49; 4:43; 13:33; 17:25; 19:5; 22:7, 37; 24:7, 26, 44).

Then comes perhaps the biggest surprise of all for the reader. Not only is Jesus' identity and mission now linked to suffering and death but so too is dis-

> NOT ONLY IS JESUS' IDENTITY AND MISSION NOW LINKED TO SUFFERING AND DEATH BUT SO TOO IS DISCIPLESHIP.

cipleship. To follow Jesus entails denying self, picking up the cross on a daily basis, and following Jesus on his divinely decreed path unto death (v. 23). This path is not just for the Twelve or for other characters in the story; it is for anyone who is a disciple. Thus the reader of the text suddenly finds themselves to be a participant in the way of the cross for that is the way of discipleship day in and day out.

Responding to the Text

To recognize Jesus' messianic identity and mission is to recognize one's own path of discipleship as following Jesus. To confess that Jesus is the Christ entails embarking on the way of the cross. Denying oneself does not mean snuffing out any sense of self-esteem that we might have. Rather, it means that we stop living by our agendas and start living by God's agenda. It means acting out of selflessness rather than out of self-interest. Instead of daily life being a matter of my surviving or thriving, daily living means taking on God's agenda exemplified in, by, and through Jesus the crucified Messiah. Popular opinion does not determine

RICHARD P.
CARLSON

Jesus' identity or mission. Our identity and mission is not determined by what makes us popular, successful, or satisfied. The way of the Messiah is the way for the disciple, and here it is revealed that this is the way of the cross.

FOURTH SUNDAY AFTER PENTECOST

THIRTEENTH SUNDAY IN ORDINARY TIME / PROPER 8
JUNE 27, 2004

REVISED COMMON	EPISCOPAL (BCP)	ROMAN CATHOLIC
1 Kings 19:15-16, 19-21 or 2 Kings 2:1-2, 6-14	1 Kings 19:15-16, 19-21	1 Kings 19:16b, 19-21
Psalm 16 or 77:1-2, 11-20	Psalm 16 or 16:5-11	Ps. 16:1-2, 5, 7-11
Gal. 5:1, 13-25	Gal. 5:1, 13-25	Gal. 5:1, 13-18
Luke 9:51-62	Luke 9:51-62	Luke 9:51-62

FIRST READING

1 KINGS 19:15-16,19-21 (RCL, BCP);
1 KINGS 19:16b,19-21 (RC)

This lesson presents the call of Elisha through the prophet Elijah, to which oblique reference is made in the Gospel reading for the day (especially Luke 9:61-62). Elijah was instructed by God to commission Elisha to be a prophet in his place (v. 17). Elijah finds Elisha working as part of an immense farming crew. He thrusts his mantle onto Elisha as a mark of commissioning and then heads off without telling Elisha what he should do (v. 19). When Elisha catches up to Elijah, Elisha

> WHILE ELIJAH IS A VETERAN OF PROPHETIC BATTLES AND ELISHA IS JUST A ROOKIE IN THIS DANGEROUS VOCATION, BOTH GO DOWN THE ROAD OF MINISTRY TOGETHER.

requests that he be allowed to bid farewell to his parents, and Elijah grants his request with a tone perhaps bordering on sarcasm (v. 20). Then it is Elisha, not Elijah, who offers a community meal/sacrifice, after which he follows Elijah and becomes his servant without knowing exactly why or what God has in store (v. 21). While Elijah is a veteran of prophetic battles and Elisha is just a rookie in this dangerous vocation, both go down the road of ministry together, called by God with different roles to play in the impending divine drama.

2 KINGS 2:1-2, 6-14 (RCL, alt.)

This is a story in which the mantle of leadership is literally passed from one generation to another. Elijah had been God's major prophetic spokesperson in Israel. Now the time has come for Elijah's departure, and so he begins his final journey (v. 1). Three different times he tells Elisha to stay behind, and three times Elisha refuses to leave Elijah's side (vv. 2, 4, 6). It is not that Elisha is ignorant or in denial about Elijah's impending departure (vv. 3, 5). Rather, he is like a loyal son who is going to stick with his prophetic parent unto the end. When the two of them stand alone on the other side of the Jordan, Elijah inquires what he might do for his prophetic protégé. Elisha's request is tantamount to the inheritance the oldest son receives, and all that he wants from "father" Elijah is double his prophetic spirit (v. 9; cf. Deut. 21:15-17). Elijah cannot guarantee it but says that if Elisha sees him being taken up, the request for the prophetic inheritance will be granted (v. 10). Elijah is then taken up into heaven by a whirlwind (note that the chariot separates the two but the whirlwind provides the means by which Elijah is transported to heaven, v. 11. Elisha sees his master no more and mourns that loss (vv. 12-13). Yet the changing of the guard has been accomplished. Elisha has seen the departure. He now possesses double the prophetic spirit. He picks up Elijah's mantle (thus Elijah's prophetic vocation is now literally in Elisha's hands) and returns into the land the same way he had left it (v. 14). The next generation of prophets is now set to proclaim the word of God to the people because God has provided leaders for that mission (v. 15).

RESPONSIVE READING

PSALM 16 (RCL, BCP);
PSALM 16:5-11 (BCP, alt.);
PSALM 16:1-2, 5, 7-11 (RC)

As the so-called baby-boomer generation enters into their fifties, there are more and more commercials advertising retirement investments. The key to the good life in the future lies in choosing the right investments in the present. The author of Psalm 16 would not disagree with that broad principle but would have definite ideas regarding the right place to invest for the good life. To the psalmist, God is the place where one invests for the good that is life. At a time when there are such overwhelming concerns for security both for our nation and our personal finances and futures, Psalm 16 redirects our attention and grounds us anew in the ancient belief that true security and true goodness for life are not by-products of our achievements or might, but flow out of a living, ongoing, intimate relationship with God.

PSALM 77:1-2, 11-20 (RCL, alt.)

We live in a "But what have you done lately?" society. Artists and athletes are measured by their most recent accomplishments. Four straight quarters of bottom-line loss means that corporate heads will roll. Politicians make decisions based on current polls so as not to upset their constituencies. This is a time of instant results, analysis, and gratification. The author of Psalm 77 is in deep, distressful contemplation with somewhat the same attitude toward God. Times are difficult, and so the question is asked, "God, what have you done for me lately?" The second half of the psalm (vv. 11-20) does not really provide the answer to that question. Rather, it shifts the focus from the immediate to the extensive past of God's mighty and redemptive activity for the people of God. By focusing on where God has compassionately worked redemption, one dares to be led by God into an uncertain future. This psalm gives voice to the experience of praying the Lord's Prayer at a deathbed, of reciting the Apostles' Creed at a funeral, or of remembering one's baptism in the midst of depression and despair. God's unseen footprints in the past help us walk by faith in a troubled present.

SECOND READING

GALATIANS 5:1,13-25 (RCL, BCP); GALATIANS 5:1, 13-18 (RC)

Crucial for interpretation of this passage is a proper understanding of Paul's Spirit-flesh antithesis. Too often this has been understood anthropologically, so that "flesh" is connected to our lower nature as humans (e.g., our appetites, cravings, sexuality) while "spirit" is linked to our higher nature (e.g., intellect, spirituality). This is not the dualism Paul has in mind here. The Spirit-flesh antithesis, for Paul, is cosmic. It relates to forces far beyond the ability or power of any human to control. The Spirit (note the use of a capital "S" to communicate this) is God's presence and activity by which we are given the gift of faith, made children of God, and live in a right relationship with God. The flesh is the locale of sin's presence and activity in a person's life by which we are enslaved. It has the power to shape our relationships with others (and ourselves) so that we seek to satisfy our needs, wants, and desires to the detriment of others, ourselves, and God. To live by the flesh is to live under the power of sin. To live by the Spirit is to live in a faith-filled relationship with Jesus.

Paul is quite intentional in utilizing this Spirit-flesh antithesis at this juncture in his letter to the Galatians. All along he has been calling on the Galatians to remain in the gospel-based reality of freedom to which they were called based not on works of the law but the power of the Spirit to bring forth a right relationship with God via the faithfulness of Jesus Christ (1:3-9, 11-17; 2:1-5, 14-21; 3:1-14, 21-29; 4:1-11, 21-31; 5:1-6). Now as the letter's argument is climaxing, Paul is telling the Galatians about what Christian freedom does and does not entail in terms of conduct. Christian conduct is not a matter of intentionally living by the law since the law is a yoke of slavery from which we have been set free (v. 1). Our conduct, however, does not mean using one's gospel-based freedom as a license to do whatever one chooses. That would mean living not by the gospel's freedom but by the flesh's desires (vv. 13, 16-17) and carrying out works of the flesh (vv. 19-21). Paul's list of these works is reminiscent of the vice lists employed by moral philosophers of that age (including some Jewish Hellenistic philosophers such as Philo) and would have been regarded as representative not exhaustive. This fifteen-word list puts the works of the flesh into four broad categories: sexual immorality (three items), idolatry (two items), communal discord (eight items), and self-indulgence (two items). The distribution is significant and shows that Paul main concern is how the flesh seeks to rip apart the fabric of the community's life together (also note his warning in v. 15).

In counterdistinction to the works of the flesh is the fruit of the Spirit (vv. 22-23), which is divinely and holistically grown in the lives of each Christian. It is significant that the first (love) and final fruit (self-control) point to how we live in community with one another. This holistic, growing fruit is not under the law, the product of the law, or guided by the law. It is the growth, work, and product of the Spirit making our lives and conduct fruit-

> IT IS SIGNIFICANT THAT THE FIRST (LOVE) AND FINAL FRUIT (SELF-CONTROL) POINT TO HOW WE LIVE IN COMMUNITY WITH ONE ANOTHER.

ful and whole. It is part of our cruciform reality in Christ (cf. 5:24; 2:19-21). Thus Paul is very concerned about how Christians live, but he is just as concerned to show that this is not a matter of returning to the law. The Spirit sets the standards for Christian conduct and also empowers us to live out and by those standards as individuals and as community in Christ.

THE GOSPEL
LUKE 9:51-62 (RCL, BCP, RC)

Interpreting the Text

Luke 9:18-50 had foreshadowed an impending shift in the drama and direction of this story: Jesus announced that out of divine necessity he would suffer many things, be rejected by the temple leadership, be killed, and be raised on the third day (9:22; also see 9:44). He then discussed with Moses and Elijah his impending exodus that he would fulfill in Jerusalem (9:30-31). The shift itself is enacted in v. 51, a brief verse brimming with theological importance that is not always noticed. For example, the typical English translation "when the days drew near" (v. 51a) does not fully capture the thrust of the Greek. It would be better to render it as "when the days were made full," thus stressing that the timing of the move toward Jerusalem is in fulfillment of God's plan. Similarly the expression "to be received up" will be the same term used to describe Jesus' ascension in Acts 1:2, 11, 22 so that God's plan will include his death, resurrection, and ascension accomplished in Jerusalem. Finally, the expression "set his face" depicts an absolute vocational resolve or determination to follow God's mission (recalling its use in Isa. 50:7; Jer. 3:12; 21:10; Ezek. 21:1-2). Thus Jesus is not just starting a trip toward Jerusalem. Rather, he is on a mission journey in accordance with God's plan. For him there is no turning back, only the turning toward his destiny that awaits him as decreed by God.

Juxtaposed with Jesus' unflinching resolve to journey to his destiny are four vignettes on responses to Jesus and his journey. The first is a response of rejection (vv. 52-56). Messengers are sent head of Jesus into a Samaritan village to prepare his way (v. 52 recalling John's mission of preparation in 1:17, 76; 7:27). The Samaritans, who were perceived in that day and age as religious traitors and outcasts, are now graciously being invited to participate in the ministry of God's kingdom as it comes in the person of Jesus. Because they wrongly conclude what his journey to Jerusalem entails, they do not receive him into their midst. James and John (two of the three disciples who had recently participated in the events of the Transfiguration, 9:28-36) take a judgmental stance against the Samaritans, reminiscent of Elijah who twice called down fire from heaven against those opposing him in Samaria (2 Kings 1:9-12). Jesus issues a rebuke; surprisingly it is not directed at the obduracy of the Samaritans but at the judgmental zeal of the two disciples (v. 55). Evidently Jesus has greater insight into God's long-term plan and mission for the Samaritans than do James and John (cf. Acts 1:7-8; 8:4-25).

The next three vignettes all revolve around the theme of following Jesus (note its repetition in vv. 57, 59, 61). While this stress on the concept of following recalls how the first disciples called by Jesus left everything and followed him (5:11, 28), it especially echoes Jesus' recent instructions on following in 9:23. Hence these verses serve as snapshots of what it means to deny self, pick up one's cross on a daily basis, and follow Jesus on his journey to his God-given destiny. In vv. 57-58 we are told that following Jesus includes complete displacement so that even common animals have refuge and shelter that Jesus lacks (and so will be lacking for those who follow him). In vv. 59-60 we discover that following Jesus takes precedence over everything. A prime Jewish obligation was to bury one's own parents. Indeed, this was an ultimate act of obeying the commandment to honor one's father and mother (cf. Gen. 25:7-10; 50:5-6; Tobit 4:3). Even priests were allowed to bury their parents (Lev. 21:1-2). Yet now following Jesus supersedes even that fundamental obligation to family. Verses 61-62 recall but also reverses 1 Kings 19:19-20 wherein Elijah called Elisha but then permitted him to kiss his mother and father goodbye prior to following. Here following Jesus is so pressing that what Elijah permitted Elisha to do is not permitted to those following Jesus. Focus is the key. When one plows, one needs to look ahead and not behind. In this story looking ahead means watching/following Jesus as he journeys to Jerusalem and his destiny in fulfillment of God's plan.

Responding to the Text

Following Jesus is not a part-time job. It is not something we fit into our crammed schedules. It is not one obligation among several others in our hurried, multitasking lives. Following Jesus involves a radical reorientation and redirecting of ourselves, our obligations, and our loyalties. Following Jesus is not the key to having it all but involves leaving it all behind. Following Jesus is not even the top priority in our lives but is a way of living and relating to others that permeates every aspect of our lives including vocation, family, finances, and relaxation. Jesus'

> FOLLOWING JESUS IS NOT A PART-TIME JOB.

journey to Jerusalem in obedience to God's salvific goals patterns the way for those who follow him, those who remove themselves from the center of their existence and pick up their cross on a daily basis. Whether the analogy is plowing or perhaps driving a car on a busy interstate highway, the point is the same. One cannot move forward by setting one's focus backwards. Following Jesus means looking forward. And what do we see in such a forward-looking vision? We see Jesus who is leading the way to his own death; Jesus who is drawing us out of ourselves and even beyond ourselves to ventures we cannot fully plan or always anticipate. In this text James and John thought that loyal following meant destroying those who did not respond positively to Jesus and his mission. Jesus, however, operates with the big picture of God's salvific plan for all humanity so that raining fire on the Samaritans would only have burned up a future field for the mission of the gospel. Thus following Jesus does not mean that we can always calculate where we are going on the expedition of faith or even when we are going to get there. Rather, it entails trusting that Jesus is leading to places, people, and ways that God's grace, gifts, and salvation will blossom through our journey of discipleship.

FIFTH SUNDAY
AFTER PENTECOST

FOURTEENTH SUNDAY IN ORDINARY TIME / PROPER 9
JULY 4, 2004

REVISED COMMON	EPISCOPAL (BCP)	ROMAN CATHOLIC
Isa. 66:10-14	Isa. 66:10-16	Isa. 66:10-14c
or 2 Kings 5:1-14		
Ps. 66:1-9 or Psalm 30	Psalm 66 or 66:1-8	Ps. 66:1-7, 16, 20
Gal. 6:(1-6), 7-16	Gal. 6:(1-10), 14-18	Gal. 6:14-18
Luke 10:1-11, 16-20	Luke 10:1-12, 16-20	Luke 10:1-12, 17-20
		or Luke 10:1-9

FIRST READING
ISAIAH 66:10-14 (RCL);
ISAIAH 66:10-16 (BCP);
ISAIAH 66:10-14c (RC)

The final chapter of Isaiah contains prophecies related to Jerusalem and proper worship therein and uses maternal images to depict the impending divine activity of restoring Jerusalem. The purpose of such an incredible birth is that God's people could be delightfully breast-fed and nourished by the divine *shalom* (translated "prosperity" in v. 12) that will flow forth from the restored Jerusalem and its temple (vv. 12-14a). Such birthing and nourishing divine activity for God's people

> THROUGH THE MISSION OF THOSE SENT BY JESUS, THE REIGN OF GOD HAS COME UPON PEOPLE AND, DEPENDING ON THEIR RESPONSES, THAT ANNOUNCEMENT CAN BE GOOD NEWS OR BAD NEWS.

has a flip side according to the prophet. God's indignation is against those who stand opposed to Jerusalem. God shall come against them as a divine warrior, resulting in their utter decimation. Thus in the same passage two radically different sides of divine action are presented. Although the imagery of the day's Gospel is not nearly so stark, the two-sided result of the gospel's mission is also being presented in Luke 10:8-12. Through the mission of those sent by Jesus, the reign of God has come upon people and, depending on their responses, that announcement can be good news or bad news.

2 KINGS 5:1-14 (RCL, alt.)

In the ancient world, miracle stories generally had three parts: problem, solution, and proof that the solution worked. This healing story from the career of Elisha the prophet includes all three components, but the stress is on the problem (which compounds as the story unfolds), whereas the solution and its proof are reported together in the final verse of the pericope. The problem seems simple and straightforward: a guy named Naaman was a leper (v. 1b). In reality the problem is much more complicated. He is a Syrian general who worships foreign gods and leads attacks against Israel. This is not the typical candidate for God's healing touch. This is the type of arrogant and idolatrous person whom God would more typically strike down with leprosy than heal of the disease. Nevertheless, through a set of circumstances, Naaman heads out with a letter from his king for their king and with immense and elaborate gifts of favor (vv. 4-5). This, however, only complicates the problem in two new ways. The readers know that God's benefactions are not for sale to the highest foreign, royal bidder. Also, the Syrian king screws up the request so that it sounds as if he expects the king of Israel to heal Naaman (v. 6).

A potential solution seems to present itself when Elisha the prophet summons Naaman (v. 8). Naaman and his entourage go to Elisha's house but are not granted an audience (v. 9). Instead, the prophet sends a message that he bathe seven times in the Jordan and the solution will take hold (v. 10). Instead of being grateful and obedient, Naaman is indignant at being put off by the prophet with such a ridiculous suggestion (vv. 11-12). He is in the process of returning home and thus turning his back on the solution when his servant persuades him to give it a try (v. 13). Naaman does as the prophet commanded, and the solution occurs (v. 14). How often do we figure that God would not or cannot work outside the boundaries of faith and in the lives of nonbelievers or that God's benefactions are reserved for us insiders? How often does God present a simple solution for our wholeness and restoration, and we tend to make it so complicated that we almost prevent God's simple solution from occurring?

Responsive Reading
PSALM 66:1-9 (RCL);
PSALM 66 or 66:1-8 (BCP);
PSALM 66:1-7, 16, 20 (RC)

It is enlightening to have Psalm 66 as the responsive reading on the Fourth of July. On a day when Americans celebrate their independence and their national identity, this psalm invites us to recognize and celebrate God's sovereign

reign over all the earth and its nations. God's awesome deeds are not the privileged possession of any single nation or people, because God is the God of all peoples so that the entire earth worships God (vv. 1, 4, 5, 8). Any nation that exalts itself over all others or claims to have favored nation status before God or sees itself uniquely blessed by God to the exclusion of others is in danger of an arrogance and self-centeredness that violates God's creation-wide rule (v. 7). For each nation on earth is but one of the pantheon of nations past, present, and future over which God rules and holds accountable.

PSALM 30 (RCL, alt.)

If one is not careful, Psalm 30 can be shallowly interpreted as an act of praise when life is good. Instead, this psalm presents the profound realization that praise to God is central in all circumstances because life from and with God is good. The psalmist claims that one always praises God because God is present and at work in all circumstances (vv. 5, 12). Deliverance from adversity is not the cause for praise but a circumstance for praise. The cause for praise is God's character as Lord of all life whose goals are for life (vv. 1-3, 10-11). We do not praise God only when things go well in life. We praise God because God gives life, and life with God is good no matter what the circumstances may be.

SECOND READING
GALATIANS 6:(1-6),7-16 (RCL);
GALATIANS 6:(1-10),14-18 (BCP);
GALATIANS 6:14-18 (RC)

This text forms the epistolary climax to the letter's argument. It is akin to a lawyer's closing statement in that these words are meant to form the final (and lasting) impression of the communiqué in the minds of the audience. The culmination of Galatians entails the antithesis between what is outwardly popular and what is essential. Following some broad instructions on Christian conduct (vv. 1-10), Paul introduces his climax by writing it himself (most likely a scribe had been writing Paul's words up to this point). The stress on writing in large letters in v. 11 has nothing to do with faulty eyesight on Paul's part but is tantamount to saying, "Read my lips!" He recapitulates the castigation of his mission opponents by claiming that they are operating with a hidden agenda. What they really seek in compelling the Galatian Christians to receive circumcision (and other elements of the law) is their own glory as well as the avoidance of persecution that goes with life marked by the cross (vv. 12-13). In distinction Paul holds up the reality of the cross as God's (and his) open agenda. On the one hand, the cross means losing one's achievements as the standard for determining self-worth. On the other hand, the cross means removing oneself from the center of one's own existence (v. 14; also cf. 2:20-21). To be made a participant in the cross of Jesus Christ means that one now participates in a whole new creation. This bold claim in v. 15 summarizes everything Paul has said throughout the letter about whom we no longer are and who we are made to be in the cross of Christ. To walk in the new created reality of the cross means to experience divine peace and mercy as the people of God (v. 16). This new creation is the salvific reality into which we have been incorporated so that Christ and his cross mark our lives in their entirety. This is the truth of the gospel on which Paul's whole ministry and the argument of Galatians stands.

> TO BE MADE A PARTICIPANT IN THE CROSS OF JESUS CHRIST MEANS THAT ONE NOW PARTICIPATES IN A WHOLE NEW CREATION.

THE GOSPEL
LUKE 10:1-11, 16-20 (RCL, BCP);
LUKE 10:1-12, 17-20 or 10:1-9 (RC)

Interpreting the Text

The first verse in this Gospel lection raises some eyebrows, in that Jesus is now sending seventy-two others (the number seventy-two instead of seventy is attested in the earliest manuscript evidence as well as in some other strong manuscripts) for mission. How did Jesus go from twelve to at least eighty-four followers? In Luke's story Jesus has a large group of disciples accompanying him. The Twelve are a subset selected by Jesus to serve as apostles (6:12-16). This larger group includes men and women (8:1-3; 23:49, 55). By the time of Jesus' ascension the group will number about 120 (Acts 1:12-15). The number twelve, of course, signifies the number of tribes in Israel, and the twelve apostles will be the eschatological judges over the twelve tribes of Israel (23:29-30; thus also the need for the twelfth apostle in Acts 1:15-26). The number seventy-two recalls the number of nations in the world in the list of the descendants of Noah in Genesis 10 (Septuagint). Nevertheless, the real focus of the text is not on the exact number of disciples Jesus now sends out but how this sending involves an extension of Jesus' mission. Jesus had initially announced his messianic mission of jubilee restoration and liberation in line with Isaiah 61 and 58 in his so-called hometown sermon in Nazareth (4:16-30). In 9:1-6 Jesus empowered and sent out the Twelve as participants in his mission. Now Jesus is extending his mission even

> THE REAL FOCUS OF THE TEXT IS NOT ON THE EXACT NUMBER OF DISCIPLES THAT JESUS NOW SENDS OUT BUT HOW THIS SENDING INVOLVES AN EXTENSION OF JESUS' MISSION.

more as he sends out seventy-two others who are also to announce and enact God's reign (vv. 9, 17-19). Hence this new wave of mission workers is an answer to the prayer Jesus mentions in v. 2. They are the Lord's workers sent by the Lord of the harvest to extend the Lord's mission movement.

The welcome they will meet cannot be assured. As Jesus is heading to Jerusalem to face his own rejection and death (9:22, 44, 51), he is sending out followers into potentially ravenous settings (v. 3). Theirs is a mission of urgency and dependency so that they travel light without worrying about provisions (v. 4). While they deserve whatever hospitality they receive on their mission endeavors, they are not to jockey for the best lodging or provisions (vv. 7-8). They bring God's peace to those who receive them and announce the advent of God's reign in their coming (vv. 5-6a, 9). Yet they will not always be received positively. Sometimes they will encounter rejection, in which case they are to shake off the town's dust because it is an unclean place and are to announce impending judgment against that locale (vv. 10-12). On the one hand, Jesus' prediction of positive and negative receptions recalls Simeon's prophecy in 2:34 and foreshadows the contrasting receptions apostles and witnesses will encounter throughout the book of Acts. On the other hand, negative receptions do not retard the spread of God's kingdom. The reign of God goes out regardless of the reception (vv. 9, 11), because its spread is not dependent on how it is received but on the faithfulness of those whom Jesus empowers to extend his mission. Likewise, even when Jesus' disciples carry out their mission in a right and faithful manner, not everyone will rightly receive it. Finally, vv. 17-20 bring an additional reminder that joy comes not from our power, success, or status in doing mission work but flows out of our participation in God's heavenly victory of life over Satan. This is the true reason for this mission and why Jesus is continually commissioning his followers to participate in such a heavenly mission on earth.

Responding to the Text

The precise style of the mission of the seventy-two is probably not the same as mission in most of our twenty-first-century congregations. Generally most congregations do not send out itinerant preachers/healers in pairs who go from town to town, staying in one particular house for a short period of time before moving to another town. Nevertheless, this text does provide some important mission insights for us today. First, this text reminds us that it is the Lord's mission first, last, and always. Because we are called by the Lord to participate in his mission, a key question we should be asking is not really, "What is our mission?" but, "What is the Lord's mission, and how is the Lord empowering and sending us to participate in that larger mission?" Second, this is a mission call for faithfulness that does not necessarily guarantee success. What we see here and throughout Luke-Acts is that God's mission in Jesus Christ brings forth both positive and negative responses. We should not judge the importance and value of our mission endeavors on quantifiable rates of success/failure but on faithfulness to Jesus and his saving mission. Third, this is a mission of dependence not of independence. It is the Lord's mission, and he (not we) remains in charge. We do not always know where that will take us. We go not by ourselves but in community (here exemplified in the two by two of v. 2). We do not always provide for ourselves but are somewhat dependent on the kindness of strangers who turn out to be children of peace (vv. 5-6). The goal of mission is not the elevation of power or status of those sent by Jesus but the joy that comes in participating in Jesus' mission of life now and life eternal both for us and for those who receive the fruits of our mission labors.

SIXTH SUNDAY
AFTER PENTECOST

Fifteenth Sunday in Ordinary Time / Proper 10
July 11, 2004

Revised Common	Episcopal (BCP)	Roman Catholic
Deut. 30:9-14	Deut. 30:9-14	Deut. 30:10-14
or Amos 7:7-17		
Ps. 25:1-10	Psalm 25 or 25:3-9	Ps. 69:14, 17, 30-31, 33-34,
or Psalm 82		36-37 or 19:8-11
Col. 1:1-14	Col. 1:1-14	Col. 1:15-20
Luke 10:25-37	Luke 10:25-37	Luke 10:25-37

First Reading
DEUTERONOMY 30:9-14 (rcl, bcp);
DEUTERONOMY 30:10-14 (rc)

At first glance, this might seem like a strange first lesson to pair with the parable of the Good Samaritan (Luke 10:25-37). Two Old Testament passages that seem to be a better fit are Lev. 19:18-19 and Deut. 6:4-6, since those passages are given direct reference in Luke 10:27. Nevertheless, this lesson does provide a significant hermeneutical complement to the Gospel for this Sunday through its stress on "doing" the commandment (for the importance of this in Luke 10:25-37 see the discussion below). The Hebrew word "do" is the final word in vv. 12, 13, 14. The whole focus of the text is on the importance and very real possibility of "doing" the commandment God has given.

In Deuteronomy 29–30 Moses places two alternatives before Israel, blessing/life and curse/death (cf. 30:1, 15-20). The thrust, however, is a bit more complex than simply asserting, "If you do the commandment, then it will mean blessing and life; and if you do not do the commandment, then it will mean curse and death." This text was composed and addressed to a people in exile, reminding them of how they ended up in their dire predicament and holding up the promise that God will return them to the land. Our text, then, is not a "do the law, or else" type threat but encouragement for the fundamental praxis of the commandment, a praxis the text assumes God's people have previously ignored with disastrous consequences. That which God desires for the praxis (i.e., the "doing") of every member of the community is not rocket science. It is not a matter of hidden, esoteric knowledge. It is accessible to all and close at hand. It means doing the commandments and statutes written in the book of Deuteronomy (v. 10). Thus the text is not saying, "If you do the commandments, then God will return you to the land and you will enjoy blessings." It is saying that when God returns you to the land, when God reverses the devastation of the exile, you know the praxis for which God is calling. You know how to live in a way that reflects the divine blessings God has graciously bestowed. It is a matter of doing that which is commanded because that word is placed in your mouths and hearts (v. 14). Doing the commandment is not a hidden trick geared to get something from God. In essence, then, Moses is saying that our praxis in life embodies the Nike slogan, that is, because God has placed this in our hearts and minds, we just do it.

DOING THE COMMANDMENT IS NOT A HIDDEN TRICK GEARED TO GET SOMETHING FROM GOD.

AMOS 7:7-17 (RCL, alt.)

This powerful prophetic text entails the vision of a plumb line, its meaning, the reaction to Amos's prophetic mission by the royal chaplain, and Amos's pronouncement against Israel and its royal chaplain. It begins in v. 7 when Amos sees the Lord standing by a wall holding a plumb line, a common builder's tool to assure that a wall is built at a proper ninety degrees. God's plumb line of judgment reveals that Israel is no longer living at the proper angle, and so its two fundamental structures, its religion and its monarchy, are going to be destroyed. In vv. 10-13 we hear the reaction to Amos's prophecies by Amaziah, the royal chaplain at the cultic site of Bethel. He informs King Jeroboam II that Amos is causing social and political unrest. Amaziah tells him to go back to Judah whence he came and make his prophetic living there (v. 12). To him Amos is an outsider who has no business saying such things to Israel. In addition, Amaziah forbids him from prophesying in the cultic center of Bethel, because that is a royal place of worship (v. 13). Amos responds to Amaziah with an explanation and another prophecy. Amos's vocational background was as a herdsman and husbandman, not a prophet (v. 14). It was God who took him from that background and gave him this prophetic vocation (v. 15), which Amos continues to carry out by announcing personal doom on Amaziah (vv. 16-17a). When God is finished, this priest, whose job is to mediate purity in the land, will end up in an unclean land along with all of Israel (v. 17b). Thus we hear in this text that the political and religious elite do not determine what word of the LORD they want given to meet their needs or to serve their own interests. The LORD 's word will go out even if it is one of judgment and impending doom, even if it takes someone from the outside without the proper credentials to deliver this divine word.

PSALM 25:1-10 (RCL, BCP); PSALM 25:3-9 (BCP, alt.)

This is an acrostic psalm; the opening word of each verse follows the sequence of the Hebrew alphabet. Using the parlance of our alphabet, this psalm presents the A to Z of God's character and what that means for us. Its very nature as an acrostic seems to give the psalm a "catch-all" tone, but at its very heart is the realization that our identity and actions in life are not determined by whom we are or what we achieve but by whom God is and what God achieves.

PSALM 82 (RCL, alt.)

The theological vision of this psalm gives cosmic significance to the claims of the Good Samaritan parable. The setting for Psalm 82 is the divine council in which God now acts as presiding judge, prosecuting lawyer, and jury over all other gods (v. 1). God brings the charges against the gods in vv. 2-4 because of their unjust impartiality. In ancient Near Eastern thinking, the gods of a given nation were the gods of the privileged elite. The upper class of those societies had the gods in their back pockets and justified their exploitative social structures as divinely sanctioned ways of life. God, however, sees through the sham and now holds those gods accountable (v. 5). The sentence is handed down in vv. 6-7. The divine status of the gods does not exempt them from the fundamental principles of justice and the divine predisposition for the poor. The gods will fall and die as if they were mortal monarchs. Yet their removal could mean a juridical vacuum in the cosmos that would be chaos, and so the psalm closes with a call by the psalmist for God to step forward and forever more be the judge of the earth since all nations (and their gods) belong to God. Love of neighbor, particularly of the neighbor in need, is thus a reflection of cosmic justice.

PSALM 69:14, 17, 30-31, 33-34, 36-37 (RC)

This psalm is a prayer for deliverance. In vv. 1-29 petition and lament are woven together. Beginning in v. 30 there is a stark turn in the psalm as pervasive praise becomes the tone. Interestingly enough this praise, which is more significant than sacrifice (v. 31) and which covers the heights and depths of the cosmos (v. 34), comes about not because God has rescued the psalmist but because the psalmist trusts that God will rescue the psalmist (vv. 33, 35-36). Thus in the midst of distressful circumstances, prayers imploring God's help and praises trusting in that divine help are equally important.

PSALM 19:8-11 (RC, alt.)

Psalm 19 spotlights the central significance of God's word and ways for all life and daily living. Verses 1-6 center on God's creative and sustaining work with regard to celestial space. In particular, the sun is a consistent witness to God's power and purposes. In vv. 7-11 God's law is the consistent witness to God's intentions for life. While the heavens endure as God's eternal handiwork, so too do God's instructions endure as God's intention for our daily conduct (vv. 9, 11).

SECOND READING

COLOSSIANS 1:1-14 (RCL, BCP);
COLOSSIANS 1:15-20 (RC)

The opening section of New Testament letters is generally not the most scintillating component of scripture. Openings tend to lack the drama of a Gospel narrative or the theological punch often found in the body of a letter. The opening of Colossians might seem even more mundane when we consider the fact that a majority of scholars do not think Paul wrote the letter (but we do not know who the author really is), that the letter might not have been written to Christians in Colossae in present-day Turkey (which had been destroyed by an earthquake in the year 61 C.E.), and that vv. 3-17 are actually just two long sentences overflowing with subordinate clauses. Nevertheless, the theological foundation of the entire letter is being laid here for the audience to understand their identity in connection with what God has accomplished in Jesus Christ.

Verses 1-2 tersely identify the sender and addressee and provide the salutation. The letter's thanksgiving begins in v. 3 and extends through v. 23. The central focus of the thanksgiving involves what God has done through Jesus Christ and what that means for the audience as they participate fully in the cosmic, salvific reality of the gospel. Through God's activity in Jesus Christ, Christians were rescued from the dominion of darkness and transferred to the kingdom of God's beloved Son as an act of divine redemption and forgiveness (vv. 13-14). Thus Christians are saintly

GROWTH INVOLVES FRUITFULLY LIVING OUT OUR GOD-GIVEN REALITY IN ALL ASPECTS OF OUR LIVES, AND KNOWLEDGE MEANS RECOGNIZING ANEW HOW CHRIST'S DEATH AND RESURRECTION DETERMINE WHO WE ARE AND HOW WE LIVE AS A COMMUNITY AND AS INDIVIDUALS.

heirs of a future already awaiting them in heaven (vv. 5, 12). Christian knowledge and insight (stressed in vv. 6, 9, 10) are not mere intellectual qualities possessed only by the wise but flow out of the gospel's declaration of God's activity in Jesus Christ, which Christians manifest in faith, love, patience, and joy on a daily basis.

Christian growth does not mean becoming something we have not yet attained. Rather, growth involves fruitfully living out our God-given reality in all aspects of our lives, and knowledge means recognizing anew how Christ's death and resurrection determine who we are and how we live as a community and as individuals.

THE GOSPEL
LUKE 10:25-37 (RCL, BCP, RC)

Interpreting the Text

Most people know this story as the parable of the Good Samaritan, which, in Jesus' day, would have been an oxymoron. A better title for the whole text, however, might well be "A Lesson on Compassionate Praxis." The Greek word meaning "do" (*poieo,* whose cognate noun forms our word *praxis*) stands at the text's beginning (v. 25), middle (v. 28), and end (v. 37). The parable becomes a hermeneutical lens through which Jesus gives us a vision for compassionate praxis. The two parts of the text (vv. 25-28, 29-37) are carefully and intentionally constructed to flow in a parallel format:

Flow	Part One, vv. 25-28	Part Two, vv. 29-37
Lawyer's motive	v. 25a	v. 29a
Lawyer's question	v. 25b	v. 29b
Jesus' response		
and counter-question	v. 26	vv. 30-36
Lawyer's answer	v. 27	v. 37a
Jesus' conclusion		
on praxis	v. 28	v. 37b

Note also the context of this pericope. Jesus had been speaking privately to his disciples (10:23-24) when this lawyer seems have intruded with his own questions and motives. Jesus had told his disciples to rejoice because their names had been written in heaven (10:20) while the lawyer asked how he could inherit eternal life (v. 25). Jesus thanked God for hiding these things from the wise and intelligent (10:21) while the lawyer seems to have represented such supposedly learned people who were actually clueless as to that which God was doing in and through Jesus. Note too that he did not come to Jesus in sincerity but in order to test *(ekpeirazon)* Jesus (v. 25a). His actions duplicated those of the devil (4:2) and recall Jesus' final instructions to Satan that one is not to test *(ekpeiraseis)* the Lord (4:12). Thus the lawyer is presented as interrupting Jesus and having his own hidden agenda. The question he first asks Jesus, "What must I do to inherit eternal life?"

(v. 25b) is not a negative question in itself. Note that it will be asked again with sincerity by the rich ruler in 18:18. For heirs of the sixteenth-century hermeneutical traditions, an immediate response might be, "Nothing!" In its first-century context, however, the question could be very appropriate (even though it is here asked by a negative character). The question is focusing on covenantal praxis appropriate for resurrection reality. Jesus responds with a counterquestion regarding the interpretation of the law ("reading" in 10:26 includes interpretation as is also the case in 6:3; Acts 13:27; 15:21). Hence Jesus is asking the lawyer to do exactly what lawyers are trained to do, i.e., interpret the law.

The lawyer immediately displays his professional acumen by answering Jesus' question (v. 27) with a combination of the *Shema* (Deut. 6:5) and Lev. 19:18. The appropriate covenantal praxis emblematic of divine life is comprehensive love— that is, loving God with the whole self and loving the neighbor as one's self. Jesus does not congratulate the lawyer for his answer but declares his answer to be the right one (literally the "orthodox" one) in v. 28. While the lawyer came to render judgment on Jesus, Jesus turns the tables and renders judgment on the lawyer. This could be the end of the story if not for the fact that the lawyer will not let the matter go, and so the text moves into its second (and parallel) part, which again opens with the lawyer's motive. In saying that the lawyer was "wanting to justify himself" (v. 29a), the writer is telling us that the lawyer is seeking to assert his status over Jesus as the one who rightly knows/interprets the implications of the law. He is now playing a game of one-upsmanship against Jesus as he asks (v. 29b), "And who is my neighbor?" He has attempted to shift the main focus of discussion away from appropriate covenantal praxis to covenantal boundaries. Who is the one inside the boundaries of God's covenantal people (i.e., the neighbor) whom we are to love as ourselves? If one takes clues from Lev. 19:18, the answer is quite clear. One's neighbor would be other members of God's holy covenant people, Israel. Jesus' response and counterquestion, however, take the lawyer's question in a very different direction.

The parable (though it is not explicitly identified as a parable in the text itself) that Jesus now tells is the longest part of this pericope and carefully forms the hermeneutical lens not simply for understanding the category of neighbor but for understanding the dynamics of compassionate praxis. Jesus' mini-story begins with a common situation. A certain person was going down from Jerusalem to Jericho. Nothing is said about the person's status, but trouble befalls him when he falls among thieves who leave him beaten, naked, and half-dead (v. 30). Thus he had literally been stripped of all status and could potentially be a threat to the cleanliness of others if he becomes completely dead. Hence it should not be surprising that when two religious figures (first a priest, then a Levite) whose vocation involves mediating purity in Israel come down the road (evidently returning from worship or service in the Temple in Jerusalem), they each see him and pass by on the other side (vv. 31-32). In this way their praxis indicates that their primary covenantal loyalty is to purity, and so they do not risk contamination from the naked (and potentially dead) person they encounter. Next comes a Samaritan who has no religious status within Israel. Samaritans were regarded as religious traitors and outcasts. In fact, the last time Samaritans were mentioned in Luke's story, they were portrayed as rejecting Jesus on his journey to Jerusalem (see 9:51-55). The Samaritan's first two actions of coming and seeing replicate those of the priest and Levite (cf. vv. 31, 32, 33), but his next action breaks the pattern and becomes the key to the whole text. He has compassion (the NRSV translation "moved with pity" does not fully capture the crucial dynamics of the word *esplagchnisthe* in v. 33). The reference to his compassion recalls prior references to God's compassionate mercy (1:78) and Jesus compassion (7:13) and foreshadows the compassion of the father in another parable (15:20). This word is literally in the middle of the parable (sixty-eight words had proceeded it and sixty-seven words will follow) and presents the stuff of covenantal praxis. It is having compassion for others in the manner of God and Jesus. As presented in the story, this compassion includes risk to one's own self (recall that this spot is portrayed as a high crime area) and religious status (contamination if he is dead) and the extravagant use of one's resources for the well-being of another with no thought of being repaid (vv. 34-35). Through this hermeneutical lens Jesus has shifted the focus from who is worthy of one's love to what it means for one to act lovingly for another. This is brought home when he asks the lawyer not about the object of one's love but about the doer of love (v. 36). The lawyer is forced to conclude that the neighbor is the one who *did (poiesas)* mercy (often mistranslated as "show" in v. 37a), to which Jesus responds, "Go and *do (poiei)* likewise." This, the text claims, is the praxis of love to be emulated by all. It is the boundaryless praxis based on compassion for others. It is the praxis of compassion which is extravagant and selfless. It is a compassion first enacted by God and modeled by Jesus.

Responding to the Text

Sometimes the most challenging texts for preaching are those that are most familiar. The text of the Good Samaritan is a prime example of that. To us, the term "Good Samaritan" is neither an oxymoron nor an insult but a high compliment. We even have civil laws bearing this title. Thus one challenge for the preacher is to discover ways to let the shock of such an unsavory character be a paradigm for compassionate praxis. Even more of a challenge is to keep the focus on compassionate praxis as does the text (especially in the lawyer's forced conclusion on doing and Jesus' final instruction on doing in v. 37). When we let the text's stress on compassionate praxis become our hermeneutical lens, we suddenly discover that the true, lasting motivation for our praxis (either individually or corporately) is not need. Too often we let need motivate us as Christians. We see people in need (be it physical, social, or spiritual), and so we respond. The problem with need as the motivation for our Christian praxis is that the world will always produce more need than we can satisfy. When need becomes our fundamental motivation for praxis, ultimately we will end up feeling guilt-ridden, hopeless, bitter, or burned out because we as individuals and as the church can never meet nor solve all the needs of this world. Likewise, when need motivates us, we are treating others as objects rather than neighbors. Note well how the text shifts the focus away from need and away from neighbor as an object. Instead, the text holds up compassion as that which motivates praxis so that neighbor is defined as the one who enacts compassionate praxis instead of the one who is in need. Thus the motivation for our praxis is grounded in the divine compassion poured out to us in Jesus. This is an unending storehouse of compassion that allows guilt-free, extravagant, selfless action for others. Neighbor is no longer that person out there who is in need; now neighbor is I who have received God's compassion in Jesus Christ and who enacts compassionate praxis for others.

SOMETIMES THE MOST CHALLENGING TEXTS FOR PREACHING ARE THOSE THAT ARE MOST FAMILIAR. THE TEXT OF THE GOOD SAMARITAN IS A PRIME EXAMPLE OF THAT.

SEVENTH SUNDAY AFTER PENTECOST

SIXTEENTH SUNDAY IN ORDINARY TIME / PROPER 11
JULY 18, 2004

REVISED COMMON	EPISCOPAL (BCP)	ROMAN CATHOLIC
Gen. 18:1-10a	Gen. 18:1-10a, (10b-14)	Gen. 18:1-10a
or Amos 8:1-12		
Psalm 15 or 52	Psalm 15	Ps. 15:1-5
Col. 1:15-28	Col. 1:21-29	Col. 1:24-28
Luke 10:38-42	Luke 10:38-42	Luke 10:38-42

FIRST READING

GENESIS 18:1-10a (RCL, RC);
GENESIS 18:1-10a, (10b-14) (BCP, alt.)

A dynamic that runs throughout scripture is the tensive relationship between God's promises and outward circumstances. God had promised to make a great nation of Abraham (12:2), but Abraham is getting old as is Sarah, his wife, who also happens to be barren. In the prior chapter, Abraham was told that God would provide a son through Sarah (17:15-16). Abraham takes this as a divine joke (even falling on his face in laughter) because he can only see outward circumstances: he is one hundred, and Sarah is ninety (17:17); they are the least likely candidates to be new parents. Chapter 18 opens with another appearance of the LORD to Abraham in the form of three men (vv. 1-2). It is not clear at this point in the text if Abraham perceives that this is a divine visit, but he does regard the visitors as men of significant stature. He bows to

"IS ANYTHING TOO WONDERFUL FOR THE LORD?"

the ground before them and goes to great lengths to provide not just a morsel of bread but a banquet for them (vv. 2-8). During the meal, the LORD announces anew that in the spring Sarah will have a son (v. 10). Sarah, who was eavesdropping from the tent door, reacts just as Abraham had reacted. She takes this announcement as a joke and laughs to herself because she knows that the outward circumstances of their advanced age mean that this cannot possibly happen (vv. 10-12). Nevertheless, God persists in operating from the perspective of promise, not outward circumstances, and so asks the theological $64,000 question in v. 14a:

140

THE SEASON
OF PENTECOST
─────────
RICHARD P.
CARLSON

"Is anything too wonderful for the LORD?" God fulfills divine promises in ways that seem improbable, if not impossible, from our human point of view. God does not operate according to outward circumstances but according to divine faithfulness. While Abraham and Sarah are laughing at a birth announcement that is folly to them, God plans to come again in the spring, at which time Sarah will be holding her laughter in the person of a son named Isaac, which means "he laughs." Who says God does not have a sense of humor?

AMOS 8:1-12 (RCL, alt.)

Although we live in an era of refrigeration, we can imagine a basket of fruit at the end of the season as it is puckering, getting squishy and growing brownish. It is not quite rotten, but before too long it will no longer be edible and so will be tossed in the trash. This is the image God shows to the prophet Amos at the beginning of the lesson (v. 1). It indicates that the end has come upon Israel (in Hebrew there is a play on the words "summer fruit" and "end"). On the impending day, celebratory songs in the temple will be replaced with mourning wails; corpses will strew the landscape to be discarded in utter silence (v. 3). In the midst of this prophecy regarding the day of doom, the cause for such dire judgment against Israel is interjected. Whereas the target of previous prophetic indictments had been the religious and royal elite (e.g., 7:8-17), here those who control the market economy are condemned for exploiting the underclass of Israel (v. 4). They cannot wait for the holy occasions to finish so they can resume their profitable but fraudulent practices (v. 5a). They openly acknowledge how they manipulate the tools of the marketplace (here weights and scales); how the poor are commodities to be cashed in for personal gain; and how food is distorted to an unnatural state to make a profit (v. 5b-6). God, however, is not deceived by such clever economic manipulations and so swears a divine oath that the land will quake and shake at the divine retribution that is coming (vv. 7-8). Day will become night; festive occasions shall become mournful occasions; famine and thirst will come upon the land. Yet it will not be a famine and thirst for physical food but for the very food by which people are to live, that is, a thirst for the words of the LORD that will no longer be found because the LORD's presence has been removed from the land (vv. 11-12).

One's piety and one's ethics in business are not separate entities. Both are to be guided by the word of the LORD; both involve acknowledging God's sovereignty; both include concrete expressions of concern for the underclass. One's business practices involve vocational service of love toward God and love toward neighbor.

PSALM 15 (RCL, BCP);
PSALM 15:1–5 (RC)

The opening of Psalm 15 poses a question (v. 1), which the subsequent verses answer (vv. 2–5b), and concludes with an affirmation (v. 5c). The question focuses on who may live in God's presence (tent and Mount Zion) as a resident alien. Similarly, the answers that make up the body of the psalm are not requirements for sojourning (i.e., they are not a theological "green card") but depict the moral integrity of those who do dwell in God's presence. Indeed, the moral integrity of such people is a reflection of God's moral integrity. The theology at work here recalls how Moses reflected God's glorious presence after spending time in that presence (Exod. 34:29–35). Here, however, the reflection involves the actions, attitudes, and character by which a person lives and conducts his or her life. If one is graciously allowed to sojourn in the moral integrity of God, one will reflect the moral integrity of God.

PSALM 52 (RCL, alt.)

Psalm 52 is socially and politically subversive as it indicts the so-called mighty. Purportedly, David sings this psalm against a servant of Saul named Doeg, who notified the king about David's whereabouts and then launched a deadly retaliatory raid that killed priests, men, women, children, infants, oxen, asses, and sheep (1 Sam. 21:7; 22:9–23). Nevertheless, it applies to situations throughout history in which those in power seek protection in wealth and exercise their might at the expense of others. Such people operate with an "the end justifies the means" mind-set so that violence, treachery, and duplicity are acceptable ways to safeguard their own position, home, land, and security (vv. 1–5, 7). The alternative way to security is to be rooted in God; to trust and reflect God's steadfast love; to give thanks for God's ways and means; and to participate in a faithful community that bears the goodness of God's identity (vv. 8–9). The psalmist knows that in the end God's love and justice will triumph, and so these are the means by which one experiences and lives life.

SECOND READING

COLOSSIANS 1:15-28 (RCL);
COLOSSIANS 1:21-29 (BCP);
COLOSSIANS 1:24-28 (RC)

Colossians 1:15-20 is one of the most profound christological statements in all of scripture. It utilizes an early Christian hymn that itself had drawn upon Jewish Hellenistic understandings of Wisdom as the preexistent, divine agent of creation (Prov. 8:27-31; Sir. 24:5-6) that holds all things together (Wis. of Sol. 1:6-7; Sir. 43:26). This hymn can be broken into two interrelated parts. Part one, vv. 15-17, focuses our attention on the preeminent place of Jesus Christ before and in creation. It declares that Christ is before all things (v. 17a); is the visible manifestation of the invisible God (v. 15a); is the firstborn of all creation (v. 15b); is not only the agent of creation so that all things were created through Christ (v. 16a), but is also the goal of creation, i.e., all things were created for him (v. 16b). Thus Jesus Christ, not Wisdom, is God's agent of creation and the divine principle that holds creation together. Jesus Christ, not Adam or Eve, bears the indelible image of the invisible God. Jesus Christ, not the law, is the goal for which everything has been created. Christ is the glue holding everything in heaven and earth together (note the emphatic, fivefold use of all/every in vv. 15-17).

The second part of the hymn, vv. 18-20, shifts the focus from Christ and creation to Christ and God's ultimate salvific activity. It begins by claiming that Christ is the head of the body, which is the church (v. 18a). The hymn moves on to extol Christ's role and position in God's salvific activity. Not only is he the firstborn of all creation (v. 15b), he is also the firstborn from the dead (v. 18b). That is, in his resurrection Christ is the beginning of God's new creation. Verses 19-20 expand on this by explaining that the fullness of God's own being dwells in Christ (v. 19) and that as everything was created through Christ (v. 16), so too through him is everything reconciled to God (v. 20a). Hence God has resolved cosmic enmity through Christ. In the cross the peace treaty between God and everything (both on earth and in heaven) is signed by means of Christ's blood (v. 20). The cross of Christ, then, is the divine act that puts the expanse of all reality back into the equilibrium it had when it was created through Christ.

CHRISTIANS ARE CALLED TO LIVE STEADFASTLY AND DILIGENTLY IN THE HOPE OF THE GOSPEL AS MATURE AND INSIGHTFUL MEMBERS OF CHRIST'S BODY, THE CHURCH.

The rest of this lection goes on to present the impact this cosmic christological activity has for the lives of the audience and the ministry of the author. Whereas before the audience had been hostile in attitude and action toward God

(v. 21), they now enjoy the status of moral purity and innocence (v. 22b) as a result of the reconciling activity of the cross. In vv. 24-29, the author focuses on the role he has been called to play in God's cosmic saving activity. His appointed ministry is to make the Christ hymn known throughout the world even though that means suffering and affliction due to the nature of their ministry. Christians are called to live steadfastly and diligently in the hope of the gospel as mature and insightful members of Christ's body, the church. In this way, the reality of the Christ hymn forms the foundation and the guidepost for Christian life and ministry, which the rest of the letter will explicate.

THE GOSPEL
LUKE 10:38-42 (RCL, BCP, RC)

Interpreting the Text

The depiction of Martha "welcoming" Jesus into her house (v. 38) presents her as a patron of some independent means who extends hospitality to Jesus. This recalls the story of Simon the Pharisee (7:36-52) who had invited Jesus to his house as a guest but failed to extend proper hospitality to him, whereas an unnamed sinful woman modeled extravagant hospitality and devotion as a response of love for divine forgiveness (see the discussion of this for the Second Sunday after Pentecost). It also recalls the varied expressions of hospitality and welcome presented in 9:51—10:37 (9:52-53, a negative picture of hospitality; 10:8-11, both positive and negative pictures of hospitality; 10:31-35, both negative and positive pictures of hospitality). Thus the scene at hand is fraught with narrative possibilities on how one will welcome Jesus. The initial picture of Martha is positive in that she has welcomed Jesus and seeks to carry out the services of a host to an important guest (also recalling the many women who followed Jesus and served him out of their means, 8:1-3). Martha is fulfilling cultural expectations. Her sister, Mary, however, is not acting in terms of cultural norms and expectations. She is not involved in either the domestic chores of a woman or the hospitality roles of a host. Instead, she sits at the Lord's feet and listens to his word (v. 39). She has assumed the position of disciple (reinforced by describing Jesus as "Lord" in v. 39) that normally would be reserved for men, especially in light of the domestic and hospitality chores at hand. Thus one sister is acting according to social norms and one sister's actions violate such expected social norms. This contrast between the actions of Martha and Mary is portrayed more vividly in the Greek through the use of imperfect verbs to present repeated/continual action. Mary keeps listening to Jesus' word (*ekouen*, v. 39) while Martha keeps being distracted (*periespato*, v. 40) over her serving.

The crux of the problem is presented in Martha's words to Jesus in v. 40. First, she asks Jesus if he does not care that Mary has abandoned her to do all the serving. The way she phrases her question shows that she expects a positive answer from Jesus (through the use of *ou* in a question). She thinks that Jesus does care that Mary has abandoned her to perform the proper hospitality. Second, she commands Jesus (*eipe*, "tell," is a second person singular imperative) to tell her sister, Jesus' supposed disciple (note her use of "lord"), to be of assistance to her and thus fulfill the cultural norm and her social obligation. So whereas Mary's focus is on Jesus and his teaching, Martha's focus is on her obligations in doing so much serving (note too that in v. 41 Martha says "me"/"my" three times). It is very important to pay close attention to what Jesus does and does not say in his response to Martha in vv. 41-42. He does not assess her serving activity as negative. Rather, he assesses her anxiety as negative (cf. 8:14; 12:22-31; 21:34-36). Her anxiety over her social obligations is causing her to have a dissipated, agitated perspective. Mary's focus, however, is on hearing the Lord's word. She is doing exactly what God commanded in the transfiguration scene ("listen to him," 9:35). This recalls how Jesus told the devil that a person does not live by bread alone (Luke 4:4, referencing Deut. 8:3). This is the one thing that is needed. This is the good portion that Mary has chosen. Inactivity is not being commended (recall the stress on praxis in the previous story, 10:25-37). Serving is not being condemned (note that at the Last Supper Jesus will present himself as one who serves, 22:27). Rather, it is the frenzied and frazzled anxiety that comes with seeking to fulfill cultural expectations and social norms at the expense of focused discipleship that is being critiqued. Martha thinks that relief for her anxiety will come when Mary leaves her position at Jesus' feet and joins her in carrying out what is expected of hosts and women. Jesus tells her that relief from her anxiety comes in choosing the position of focused discipleship that Mary has assumed. This text, then, is indeed trying to put women in their place, but that is the place of focused discipleship that begins for both women and men in hearing the Lord's word.

> IT IS THE FRENZIED AND FRAZZLED ANXIETY THAT COMES WITH SEEKING TO FULFILL CULTURAL EXPECTATIONS AND SOCIAL NORMS AT THE EXPENSE OF FOCUSED DISCIPLESHIP THAT IS BEING CRITIQUED.

Responding to the Text

Welcoming Jesus means welcoming him as the bringer of God's reign whose word is the focus of life. In this story, the guest and his word are the true and needed portion of food for life. Discipleship includes doing, but it is the doing of Jesus' word and not the frenzied activity of doing what others expect of us. In Luke 6:46-49, the order of activity for disciples is quite clear: hearing Jesus' words and doing them. The doing is grounded in and guided by the hearing of

Jesus' word. This text seeks to free us from anxiously struggling to fulfill the cultural norms that dictate how we act and how we do not act. It seeks to free us for authentic servanthood in which Jesus' word takes priority as it defines us and our praxis. Martha's anxiety over seeking to be the proper host becomes a trap for her in which she focuses in on herself, on all that she is expected to do to succeed, and on how another (in this case her sister) is not aiding her in that which is causing so much anxiety. As Jesus revealed in the parable of the four soils (8:14-15), relief from such anxiety does not come in getting more help to get the job done (or, perhaps, in being rich enough to afford hiring others to do the work) but in being fully and continually rooted in the word. This is the portion Mary has chosen and the food Jesus offers to Martha since he is the host who feeds anxious lives with his word of life.

EIGHTH SUNDAY AFTER PENTECOST

Seventeenth Sunday in Ordinary Time / Proper 12
July 25, 2004

Revised Common	Episcopal (BCP)	Roman Catholic
Gen. 18:20-32	Gen. 18:20-33	Gen. 18:20-32
or Hos. 1:2-10		
Psalm 138 or 85	Psalm 138	Ps. 138:1-3, 6-8
Col. 2:6-15, (16-19)	Col. 2:6-15	Col. 2:12-14
Luke 11:1-13	Luke 11:1-13	Luke 11:1-13

First Reading
GENESIS 18:20-32 (RCL, RC); GENESIS 18:20-33 (BCP)

God has given Abraham promises of blessings and a vocation of blessing (Gen. 12:1-3). In this text Abraham models what it means to have a vocation of blessing. Unfortunately, the lectionaries obscure some of this by beginning the text at 18:20 instead of 18:16. In 18:17-19 we are privy to a divine inner dialogue as God contemplates whether or not to disclose to Abraham the impending judgment of Sodom and Gomorrah. God's decision to reveal the divine intent to Abraham rests on the vocation that God has given to Abraham. In the ensuing conversation between God and Abraham in vv. 20-32, we learn much about both God and Abraham as well as what a vocation of blessing might include for us today. God is a God of justice toward all humanity and not just toward a chosen few. Likewise, God's judgments are not arbitrary but are based on the very righteousness and justice God charges Abraham and his posterity to model. Consequently, God is not at all displeased with Abraham when Abraham begins to dicker with God over how divine judgment shall be executed. Abraham holds up God's character and intentions back to God, reminding God that the divine will to save the righteous far exceeds the divine will to destroy the unrighteous. The narrative drives this point home again and again as Abraham slowly negotiates the number of needed righteous persons from fifty (v. 26) to forty-five (v. 28) to forty (v. 29) to thirty (v. 30) to twenty (v. 31) to ten (v. 32). God is indeed moved by

GOD IS A GOD OF JUSTICE TOWARD ALL HUMANITY AND NOT JUST TOWARD A CHOSEN FEW.

the intercession and advocacy of God's chosen even when it is on behalf of those outside the chosen family.

To have a vocation of blessing means that one does not seek God's favor in a self-serving way but that one advocates and intercedes for others. It means taking seriously both God's stature as executor of divine judgment and God's will to save, which exceeds the divine will to destroy. It includes modeling God's justice and righteousness as well as holding up God's justice and righteousness even to God. It means that one does not celebrate the destruction of the unrighteous (even if it be deserved), but one has compassion and care for the innocent who also would suffer in the process. It is a vocation in which one does not smugly judge others in light of one's own character but in which one looks to the character of God as the paradigm for justice, righteousness, and blessing. This paradigm will take on new dynamics in Jesus' teaching about prayer in the Gospel lesson for the day.

HOSEA 1:2-10 (RCL, alt.)

God is doing a strange job of matchmaking for the prophet Hosea. Hosea is instructed to marry a woman of known sexual promiscuity (not necessarily a prostitute but certainly a shameful woman) and to have children with her. This unusual family planning serves as a divine message that God is speaking through Hosea to Israel (Hos. 8:2a). The sexual promiscuity exemplified by Gomer is a theological symbol for the religious promiscuity exemplified by Israel, i.e., idolatry (8:2b). Hosea does not ask about details and discuss God's matchmaking (in fact, in chapter 1 Hosea does not say a single word that is unusual for a prophet) but instead does as he is instructed. The result of their unusual marriage is the birth of a son. Once again God instructs Hosea that he is to carry out an act of prophetic symbolism by naming his son Jezreel. On the one hand, this name could be a sign of prophetic reassurance because it means "God sows" and is the name of the fertile valley that is the breadbasket of Israel. On the other hand, it is actually a portent of defeat, because God will put asunder Israel's military might in the valley of Jezreel and so end its dynasty (vv. 4-5). Hosea and Gomer have two more children whose names (which mean "not pitied" and "not my people") continue to stand as prophetic symbols of destruction (vv. 7-9). Yet in the midst of this fourfold act of prophetic doom a distant note of hope is raised. At some future point in time the very ones now classified as "not my people" will be called "children of the living God." Those who are not pitied by God will one day be pitied beyond measure (v. 10) so that Israel's impending defeat in Jezreel (vv. 4-5) will one day be reversed on the great day of Jezreel (v. 11). The details of God's coming activity are not spelled out in the first chapter of Hosea, but the dialectic of divine judgment followed by divine restoration is introduced here and will be the ongoing theme in the rest of this prophetic work.

RESPONSIVE READING

PSALM 138 (RCL, BCP);
PSALM 138:1-3, 6-8 (RC)

Verse 8 not only provides the climax of the psalm but also its theological foundation. In the end, God will fulfill God's purposes. In the end, God's steadfast love carries the day. God's ultimate will and character do not guarantee a safe, smooth life but stand as the bedrock for our thanksgiving, our worship, and our hope (vv. 1-2, 5, 7-8). For the psalmist this is not the stuff of private piety but of public witness (even before other gods, v. 1) and policy (kings are to reflect this, vv. 4-6). Out of steadfast love and faithfulness God is intimately involved in human lives (more for the downtrodden than for the elite, v. 6) so that in the end God's purposes will be accomplished.

PSALM 85 (RCL, alt.)

This psalm is a wonderful paradigm of what a prayer for deliverance should entail. The prayer is not mired down with how bad things are, nor does it present a grocery list of things God should be providing but has not. The prayer's opening focus is on God's past graciousness (vv. 1-3), because what God has done engenders trust in what God will do. The prayer acknowledges how God takes sin seriously, not casually (vv. 4-6), but also celebrates a vision of the future brought into existence by God's promissory word (vv. 7-9). Thus the paradigm of prayer is not a "me, me, me" shout for attention but a presentation of our present in light of God's past and in anticipation of God's graciousness in the future.

> THE PARADIGM OF PRAYER IS NOT A "ME, ME, ME" SHOUT FOR ATTENTION BUT A PRESENTATION OF OUR PRESENT IN LIGHT OF GOD'S PAST AND IN ANTICIPATION OF GOD'S GRACIOUSNESS IN THE FUTURE.

SECOND READING

COLOSSIANS 2:6-15, (16-19) (RCL);
COLOSSIANS 2:6-15 (BCP);
COLOSSIANS 2:12-14 (RC)

Colossians 2:6-15 is a tightly packed argument (only five sentences make up these ten verses). The author holds up the fullness of salvific reality in which the audience already exists so that they will not be suckered into seeking salvation through other philosophical systems and ascetic practices. The theological backdrop of the text is the profound claims of the Christ hymn in Col. 1:15-20, to which this text makes connections again and again (see the discussion of this hymn for the Seventh Sunday after Pentecost). The opening exhortation to live in Christ (v. 6b; though literally it is a call to walk in him) means that they are to continue being rooted in the reality of reconciliation and salvation that God has accomplished in Christ (1:18-23), as they were first taught (v. 7). Verse 8 opens with a warning that such continuation involves diligence since others seek to take the audience captive through deceitful, philosophical systems. Here the author refers to unnamed opponents who have been promoting a theology that says that the way to find protection from hostile spirits and to obtain true understanding and salvation is through the particular philosophy, worship practices, and ascetic piety they propagate (vv. 8, 16-18). In opposition to what he considers humanly designed philosophies, traditions, and practices, the author puts forth the cosmic reality that is Jesus Christ, in whom all the fullness of God's being dwells bodily (v. 9, recalling 1:19). Christians do not need to chase after close encounters with the divine through other philosophical systems or ascetic practices. They already experience the fullness of divine reality as a result of being in the church, the body of Christ (v. 10). In vv. 11-15, the theme of continuation draws on the common, crucial experience of Christian baptism. As circumcision was the rite marking covenantal inclusion in Judaism, so baptism (imaged as the circumcision of Christ done without hands, v. 11) marks covenantal inclusion into the Christ-reality. In baptism, our former standing in the flesh was negated as we were buried and raised with Christ (vv. 12-13). Thus the theme of continuation includes understanding how baptism has fully included us in God's complete victory over all principalities and powers achieved in Christ's death and resurrection (vv. 14-15, recalling 1:18-20).

The theme of the religious quest or the quest for the ultimate meaning of life is common in the ancient and contemporary worlds. It is not unusual to hear that by diligently following this theological system or those ascetic practices one can advance into the higher plans of reality and so discover true peace, harmony, and meaning in life. This text claims something quite

> ULTIMATE MEANING IS FOUND IN JESUS CHRIST. THIS IS A REALITY NOT FOR WHICH WE STRIVE BUT WHICH IS FREELY AND GRACIOUSLY GIFTED IN BAPTISM.

different. Ultimate meaning is found in Jesus Christ. This is a reality not for which we strive but which is freely and graciously gifted in baptism. We already dwell in the ultimate and eternal meaning of life because we are participants in the body of Christ in whom the fullness of God's being dwells. Hence we are not called to be anything other than who God has already made us in Christ.

THE GOSPEL

LUKE 11:1-13 (RCL, BCP, RC

Interpreting the Text

In Luke (as well as in Acts) prayer is the act of fully opening oneself to the power and will of God. Jesus has continually modeled this prayer posture in Luke's story. He was praying when the Spirit descended onto him (3:21-22) following his baptism. Just prior to naming the twelve apostles, Jesus spent the night in prayer (6:12-13). Peter confesses Jesus to be the Messiah in a prayer setting (9:18-20). The transfiguration occurs while Jesus is praying (9:28-29). Prayer will precede Jesus' passion (22:39-46). Thus the text presents not only instructions on prayer but also a vision of prayer as a crucial dynamic in one's relationship with God. Indeed, note that the disciples ask Jesus to teach them to pray just after he himself has been praying (11:1).

The Lukan version of the Lord's Prayer in vv. 2b-4 is not to be regarded as the be-all and end-all of prayer; it is the paradigm for prayer. It is grounded in the reality of the God-Jesus-disciple relationship. Jesus, God's Son, has modeled prayer and now teaches a prayer pattern for his followers. Prayer opens by acknowledging this relationship as disciples address God as "Father." From Luke's perspective, one does this not because God's name is Father but because one lives in a relationship with God that is modeled on right/ideal parent-child relations. That also means that the title "Father" is culturally conditioned. In that social world a father had virtual control over the household as long as the father lived (not as long as his children were minors). He was the one responsible for providing the household with sustenance, security, a legacy, status, and honor. This first-century text draws on that social reality and its relationships to image something far greater, that is, the ongoing and eternal relationship between God and the disciples of Jesus. God relates to us and we relate to God in a parent-child relationship of sustenance, nurture, guidance, and love. Given the social norms of first-century reality, it is understandable that this text uses the image of father to communicate that reality and how prayer is a vital component of the relationship.

The passive imperatives of v. 2b call on God to make God's own name holy (i.e., to be set apart by God for God's own special purposes) and to let God continue to bring forth God's kingdom, which has dawned in the royal advent of Jesus (1:32-33; 2:10-11; 4:43; 8:1). The request of bread (v. 3) could possibly be understood in terms of the food of the eschatological banquet (cf. Luke 14:15-24) but most likely is a petition for daily provision so that one relies on God for basic sustenance in daily life (cf. Exod. 16:9-21). Forgiveness has been a fundamental mark of divine activity in the coming of God's kingdom (1:77; 5:20-24;

7:47-49), and so a proper posture of prayer is to request divine forgiveness for our own lives and to make forgiveness a hallmark of our relationship with others (v. 4a). Finally, the request that God not bring us into temptation (or testing) recalls the lawyer in 10:25 who sought to establish his own honor and status by testing Jesus. This petition means that we live in reliance on God not in reliance on self. Likewise it is an admission that in the battle with Satan we cannot stand on our own but live only by divine intervention, protection, and care (cf. 4:1-11; 10:17-20; 11:18-26; 22:31-32).

Verses 5-13 offer parallel reflections (vv. 5-10, 11-13) on the prayer paradigm of vv. 2b-4 in the form of illustrations followed by ramifications. The key to understanding the first illustration in vv. 5-8 is to realize that this is a no-brainer drawn from the daily life in the narrow confines of a first-century village wherein hospitality is a prime matter of honor and to refuse hospitality brings shame within village society. A request of a friend (note "friend" is used four times in these few verses) for bread so that one can provide hospitality to a visitor will be granted even if it is in the middle of night, not necessarily out of friendship but because refusal would bring shame since everyone else in the village would know of the request and the response (be it positive or negative). The point of the illustration is not that prayer is a matter of persistently haranguing God to give us what we want. The illustration focuses not on the one who does the asking but on the one who responds to the request. Hence it is meant to show us that God

> GOD'S HONORABLE CHARACTER HELPS US UNDERSTAND WHY WE CAN PRAY AS JESUS TEACHES AND MODELS.

will most definitely act honorably in our relationship so that we can confidently ask, seek, knock in full trust that God will give, provide, and open (vv. 9-10). Thus God's honorable character helps us understand why we can pray as Jesus teaches and models. The second illustration (vv. 11-13) utilizes a "lesser to greater" argument. The lesser is human (sinful) fathers; the greater is our divine Father. Human fathers do not act malevolently to the requests for sustenance from their children. Since that is true of sinful human fathers, how much more is that true in regard to God who will answer the requests for sustenance from God's own children. The ultimate gift for sustenance in our lives as the children of God is the Holy Spirit (so that this is an anticipation of Pentecost; cf. 24:49; Acts 1:5, 8; 2:1-39).

Responding to the Text

From this text we discover that prayer is much more than a particular formula or talking to God or bringing a laundry list of concerns, needs, or wants to God's attention. First and foremost, it shows us that prayer lives from the relationship we share with God in Christ Jesus. The paradigmatic prayer that Jesus teaches his disciples looks to God to vindicate God's own self, to bring forth

God's own reign, to provide for the needed stuff of daily life, to forgive us as we seek to embody forgiveness to others, and to protect us from being led away by Satan's allures. Hence in prayer we participate in God's own character. That is, we trust God to be a loving God who mercifully cares for us and provides not only for our physical sustenance in this age but the ultimate sustenance of the eschatological age, the Holy Spirit. While this text images our relationship with God via father-child realities, God transcends all our images and cannot be limited by or to a particular gender. The image of this text does not seek to limit God to "Father" but to use parent-child language of its day to help our feeble minds comprehend the dynamics of the relationship we have with the almighty, transcendent divine being we call God; and prayer is an intimate, vital, daily aspect of this relationship.

ST. JAMES THE ELDER, APOSTLE

JULY 25, 2004

REVISED COMMON
1 Kings 19:9-18
Ps. 7:1-10
Acts 11:27—12:3a
Mark 10:35-45

FIRST READING
1 KINGS 19:9-18

This story from the life of Elijah does not tell how we can find God in the quiet moments of life but of how God relentlessly finds us and calls us to tasks neither of our own choosing nor which always appeal to us. One would have thought that Elijah had just reached the pinnacle of his prophetic career. Previously, God had miraculously sustained him during an extensive drought (1 Kings 17:1-16). Elijah had interceded for a dead widow's son so that God revived him (17:17-24). Elijah was victorious in a head to head contest on Mount Carmel against the combined forces of 850 priests of Baal and Asherah to demonstrate whose God is true God (18:17-40). After all of these monumental occurrences, it comes as quite a surprise that Elijah goes into an immediate tailspin when Queen Jezebel vows to have Elijah killed within twenty-four hours (19:1-2). Suddenly the boldness and trust that had marked Elijah's ministry vanishes as he fearfully flees into the wilderness (19:3-4a). Feeling forlorn he considers himself as good as dead (19:4b). Ultimately, he flees even further from his prophetic vocation by traveling forty days and forty nights to Horeb, God's mountain (19:8). Note well that he does not do this because of God's command. Instead, he goes there to hide out because he considers himself to be the last loyal worshiper of God and a hunted man to boot (19:9-10). According to Elijah's perspective, when the going gets tough the tough get going to safety, isolation, and privacy where one's devotion to God and fidelity to God's covenant will not attract the attention (or potential animosity) of others.

It is important to pay attention to how the text presents the next scene and not simply rely on past pious interpretations of the text. In v. 11, God commands Elijah to stand upon the mountain before the LORD, but note that Elijah does not do that. Elijah remains hiding in his cave. Nevertheless, God passes by with trappings typical of a theophany (cf. 19:11-12; Exod. 19:16-19; 20:18; Deut. 4:11; 5:23; Judg. 5:5; Pss. 18:12-14; 29:7-9; 68:8). God is never in such striking theophanic signs. They mark God's passing by but never contain God's presence. Thus to preach a sermon whose point is to declare that we should look for God in our inner voices or in quiet solitude rather than in dramatic outward signs misses the thrust of the text. Elijah does come out of his hiding place when he hears what the NRSV translates as "a sound of sheer silence" (vv. 12-13), but that phenomenon no more contains God's presence than the wind, earthquake, or fire. It is merely the vehicle that lured Elijah out of his hideout. A voice then comes to Elijah asking him exactly the same thing the Lord had asked him while he was still in the cave: "What are you doing here, Elijah?" (cf. vv. 9, 13). Elijah, in turn, gives the exact same excuse of being the last loyal worshiper of God and a hunted man to boot (cf. vv. 10, 14). God, however, does not buy Elijah's self-pitying attitude, his excuses, or his assessment of the situation. Instead, he recommissions Elijah for a new stage in his prophetic ministry while also letting Elijah know that he is not God's last great hope. Whereas Elijah went into hiding because he was threatened by the enemy, God is now calling him to be the vanguard of a movement by which God will decimate those enemies (vv. 15-17). Whereas Elijah saw his leadership in isolation, God is now calling him to anoint new political and religious leaders. Whereas Elijah considered himself to be the last loyal worshiper, God informs him that God has seven thousand loyal worshipers (v. 18). Whereas

THIS IS NOT THE STUFF OF QUIET, HUMAN, INNER VOICES BUT THE BRASH, INTRUSIVE, BOLD INITIATIVES FOR MINISTRY BY A GOD WHO DOES NOT QUIT ON US EVEN WHEN WE THINK OUR CALL TO MINISTRY IS OVER.

Elijah was bringing his ministry to an abrupt end through his self-absorbed outlook and attitude, God is calling Elijah out of himself and into a whole new direction for ministry through which God's goals and purposes will be accomplished not in isolation by a solitary figure but in public by a whole cadre of folk empowered by God. This is not the stuff of quiet, human, inner voices but the brash, intrusive, bold initiatives for ministry by a God who does not quit on us even when we think our call to ministry is over.

RESPONSIVE READING
PSALM 7:1-10

In Psalm 7 we hear the psalmist standing at the bar of divine justice pleading for God's vindication from unspecified but clearly unjust, carnivorous enemies (vv. 1-2, 7-8). Divine justice is celebrated as being both transcendent and intimate so that what is a basic governing principle of the cosmos is also something for which the psalmist personally seeks in very real ways and in very dire circumstances. Seeking to stand in truth, justice, and the divine way, however, does not make one a superman or superwoman. It makes one utterly trusting in God's vindicating activity especially when injustice seems to be the order of the day. It is this theological reality that makes this psalm so appropriate on a day honoring the memory of James the Elder, Apostle.

SECOND READING
ACTS 11:27—12:3a

This text tells of two crises the early Jerusalem church faced. The first crisis involved a worldwide famine. When the church in Antioch is foretold of this impending event, they do not stockpile supplies for their own survival or well-being. Rather, they respond with generous open hearts on behalf of the Christians in Judea who were evidently in more dire economic straits (vv. 27-29). This is also an act of reciprocity in that the church in Jerusalem first sent Barnabas to Antioch to help in their mission endevours (vv. 19-26). Thus Christian bonds of fellowship address the first crisis. The second crisis is political in nature. In the early forties, Herod Agrippa I (grandson of Herod the great and nephew of Herod Antipas, who beheaded John) assumed the position of king in Judea and perpetrated violence against some in the Jerusalem church including James, the brother of John and the son of Zebedee (Acts 12:1-2). While this was not the first time church leaders suffered violence and death (see 5:40-41; 7:54—8:3), it is the first time that one of the twelve apostles is killed. When this brought a popular reaction from the populace, Herod proceeded to arrest Peter, the head apostle, with the same ends in mind (vv. 3-4a). This crisis is also addressed by Christian bonds of fellowship as the church earnestly and continuously offers prayers to God on his behalf (v. 4b). Christians are not immune from natural or political crises but are fully susceptible to the hardships of life and persecutions from political powers. It is the bonds of Christian faith and fellowship that allow the church to stand together and address such difficulties.

THE GOSPEL

MARK 10:35-45

Interpreting the Text

There are five people in the New Testament who bear the name James (which is actually the name Jacob in the Greek): James, the son of Zebedee and brother of John; James, the son of Alphaeus (Matt. 10:3; Mark 3:18; Luke 6:15; Acts 1:13); James, the brother of Jesus (Mark 6:3; Acts 15; Galatians 2); James, the father of Judas (not Judas Iscariot, Luke 6:16); and James, the author of one of the catholic epistles. July 25 in the church calendar honors the first of these five people.

In Mark's Gospel, James along with his brother, John, are the third and fourth disciples called by Jesus (Mark 1:16-20). He has been following Jesus from the very beginning and along with John and Peter is a member of the inner circle of disciples. They are the three who accompany Jesus when he raises Jairus's daughter from the dead (5:35-43) and are the ones at the scene of Jesus' transfiguration (9:2-13). So if any of the disciples is expected to have additional insights to Jesus, his power, and his destiny, it would be one of these three. Thus in some ways it should not be too surprising that James and his brother perceive that Jesus will one day be in glory. Guided by that perception they try to get in on the ground floor by demanding that Jesus give them positions of honor in his glorious state (v. 37). Their demand is very problematic in light of who Jesus is, what Jesus is about, and what it means to be a disciple of Jesus. That is why Jesus tells them that they do not know what they are asking (v. 38). They can only see Jesus in terms of power, glory, and honor and thus want to claim these things for themselves. Jesus, however, understands himself in terms of the cross and the attendant humiliation, rejection, and lowliness accompanying it. Three times he has spoken of this to his disciples (8:31; 9:31; 10:32-34). He also told this to Peter, James, and John an additional time as they were descending from the transfiguration experience (9:9-13). Yet James and John continue to see things from a human perspective rather than from God's perspective (cf. 8:33; 9:32). Their ultimate concern is how they can get the highest status possible through their association with Jesus. They even go so far as to seek to impose their will on Jesus (v. 35). Their affirmative answer to Jesus' question about being baptized with his baptism and drinking the cup he will drink belies both arrogance and ignorance as to just what these actually entail (v. 39). Yet the Zebedee brothers are no worse than the other disciples. The indignation of the ten toward the two (v. 41) is not because of what James and John asked but because the brothers dared ask before any of them, as if whoever popped the question first got dibs on the best seats in glory. None of the disciples perceive Jesus' destiny as his passion. Indeed, none of them will be capable of true insight prior to that event because it is such a radical, unworldly perspective.

In the divine perspective of the cross with which Jesus operates and is at the center of this particular Gospel text, everything is literally tipped upside down. Honor is in shame. Glory is in suffering. Power is in servanthood. Being first means being enslaved. This is definitely not the way the world operates. The great supposedly are the rulers who exercise power and authority over underlings (v. 42). In God's system, however, things are radically different. That is what Jesus had taught again and again (cf. 8:34-38; 9:33-50; 10:23-31, 42-44) and what Jesus embodies in his own mission unto the cross. In many ways, v. 45 is perhaps the most profound statement of this in all of Mark. On the one hand, Jesus is the one whom the angels served in the wilderness (Mark 1:13). Jesus is the son of humanity who has God's authority to forgive sins upon earth (2:10), who is lord even of the Sabbath (2:28), and who will come in God's glory with the holy angels (8:38). On the other hand, the mission for which Jesus has come and to which he is going is one of absolute servanthood to the point that he gives his life as an act of liberation for so many others. Thus his baptism is his death. The cup is that of suffering and death (14:23-24, 36). The positions on Jesus' right and left will be occupied by those crucified with him (15:27). The paradox that is true for Jesus remains true for those who follow Jesus. To be a leader in God's mission to liberate the world from its bondage to sin and Satan is to be a servant whose actions, attitudes, and values are defined by the cross rather than the ways of the world. At this point in the story, though he remains a member of the inner circle (cf. 14:32-33), James just does not get it. He understands discipleship in terms of personal privilege and what is in it for him rather than how he is to serve others for the sake of God's agenda in the cross.

Responding to the Text

It is somewhat ironical that on a day that honors the memory of James the Elder and Apostle, the Gospel pericope does anything but honor him. It presents a picture of an aggressive, somewhat overbearing disciple, who is using insider information about Jesus for the enhancement of his own status, a status that would put him in a position of authority even over his fellow disciples. Clearly he is not a paradigm for true discipleship. In fact, he is a paradigm of how power and leadership operate in the world. He is replicating within the circle of faith the style of leadership they always see in the world in which leadership means exercising authority and lordship over underlings. This Gospel text recognizes the tension in models of leadership that existed in the church in the first century and has continued to confront and confound the church into the twenty-first century. Time and again, the church has sought its

> SERVANT LEADERSHIP IS TO MAKE THE AGENDA OF THE CROSS THE VISION BY WHICH ONE LEADS AND THE GOAL FOR WHICH ONE LEADS.

models for leadership in what works in the world and has only paid lip service to a cruciform model of leadership exemplified by and in Jesus. This is not a call to approach leadership in terms of a "What would Jesus do?" style but a call to take seriously what Jesus has done as the son of humanity who came not to be served but to serve by giving his life for our liberation. Servant leadership is to make the agenda of the cross the vision by which one leads and the goal for which one leads. It does not mean being a doormat or an ecclesiological Jeeves in which others tell us what to do and how to do it. To be a servant leader is to be unconcerned with one's personal authority or status and to take one's place at Jesus' right or left at the foot of the cross. In this text James shows us how not to lead while Jesus' vision of the cross shows us what leadership truly entails.

THE SEASON OF PENTECOST

NINTH THROUGH SEVENTEENTH
SUNDAYS AFTER PENTECOST/
PROPERS 13–21

JEANNE STEVENSON-MOESSNER

Advent has come and gone. Christmas and Epiphany have been celebrated. Lent has been endured. Christ's resurrection has been proclaimed. The coming of the Holy Spirit has been commemorated with Pentecost. Now the church year is in the post-Pentecost period, a part of the religious calendar that could be seen as lacking in liturgical significance and excitement.

In some ways, these lectionary texts are the most vital to our everyday lives as Christians because they answer the query: How then shall we live? This question is posed after the birth of Christ, after his death, resurrection, and ascension, and following the coming of the Holy Spirit to believers. How then shall we, as Christians, live?

> HOW THEN SHALL WE, AS CHRISTIANS, LIVE?

These texts will carry us from the psalmist's "Pit of Sheol" to the preacher's portrayal of a heavenly "cloud of witnesses" (Heb. 12:1). We are shown a range of emotions, from David's remorse over his adultery and participation in murder to Paul's exuberance over his conversion experience. There is talk of conversion (Paul) in these selections but even more comment on how to live a life with Christ. In some ways, the ninth through seventeenth Sundays after Pentecost coach us in how to walk through the "wilderness experience" and then on through "Canaan" with its many gods and temptations. There is reference to the giving of commandments and injunctions; there is frequent mention of the breaking of these. How we receive God's forgiveness and how we offer God praise are recurrent motifs as well.

Many in your congregation will be interested in the "journey to maturity" as Christians. In some circles, this will be described as Christian spiritual formation. These lectionary texts offer much for those who are growing in the Holy Spirit following their Pentecost experience. The lectionary readings have wandered between God's *hesed* (compassion, mercy) and life's *hebel* (vanity). Always, God's mercy and compassion have offered a way for the weary pilgrim who was claimed in baptism.

I have followed this format for all Sundays: First Reading, Responsive Reading, Second Reading, and The Gospel. Interwoven in my textual and exegetical work, you will find reflections on the readings with possibilities for your sermon preparation and sermon topics. The Holy Spirit has come, and we are growing in maturity with the help of that intervention. These texts were selected to overcome the pretenses of all who read, to loosen the "stiff-necked," and to warm all our stubborn hearts.

NINTH SUNDAY AFTER PENTECOST

EIGHTEENTH SUNDAY IN ORDINARY TIME / PROPER 13
AUGUST 1, 2004

REVISED COMMON	EPISCOPAL (BCP)	ROMAN CATHOLIC
Eccl. 1:2, 12-14; 2:18-23 or Hos. 11:1-11	Eccl. 1:12-14; 2:(1-7, 11), 18-23	Eccl. 1:2; 2:21-23
Ps. 49:1-12 or 107:1-9, 43	Psalm 49 or 49:1-11	Ps. 90:3-4, 5-6, 12-13, 14, 17
Col. 3:1-11	Col. 3:(5-11), 12-17	Col. 3:1-5, 9-11
Luke 12:13-21	Luke 12:13-21	Luke 12:13-21

FIRST READING

ECCLESIASTES 1:2, 12-14; 2:18-23 (RCL); ECCLESIASTES 1:12-14; 2:(1-7, 11), 18-23 (BCP); ECCLESIASTES 1:2; 2:21-23 (RC)

The first reading offers the startling and despairing reflections of the Teacher (*Qoheleth*), sometimes called the Preacher, who is a son of David. These reflections are a depressing assessment of all the deeds done under the sun, that is, the work of humankind. The Teacher gives the verdict: All is vanity.

It is not that the ensuing text gets more difficult; rather, the assessment gets worse. Not only is daily toil and effort meaningless and futile. The results of such toil and labor will eventually be turned over to others, perhaps undeserving and foolish! They inherit easily what others have toiled for laboriously. The undeserving may inherit what I have worked for so diligently. This is not only foolishness or vanity, it is a great evil. What, then, is the point of all the strain of the everyday work world? For what does my labor—and my life—count?

Those who have stood on the brink of disillusionment with their purpose in life have asked this same question. Interestingly, scholars place Ecclesiastes, a piece of wisdom literature, between 250 and 167 B.C.E., and yet the pervasive question as to the meaning of life's toil is as contemporary as the congregation gathered to hear a sermon on the Ninth Sunday after Pentecost. "Ecclesiastes" derives from

162

THE SEASON
OF PENTECOST

JEANNE
STEVENSON-
MOESSNER

the Greek *ekklesia*, a public gathering. The Teacher or Preacher offers a debilitating conclusion: Life is a striving after wind, a futile chasing after air. All is vanity *(hebel)*, breathlike, vaporous.

A modern reader and a contemporary preacher cannot help but compare this futile feeding on wind with the intensity of the Day of Pentecost as described in Acts 2:2 with its in-breaking of the sound of a violent rush of wind and an infusion of the Holy Spirit. Yet, in the liturgical year, we are nine weeks past Pentecost, when the absurdity of our best efforts, the despair of our best-formulated plans, and the uncertainty of our world have engulfed us. All does appear to be in vain.

The Teacher in vv. 1-7, 11 (BCP) makes a test of pleasure and becomes in the telling the wise fool. His account of his search for self-fulfillment in these opening verses of Ecclesiastes 2 utilizes language that is reminiscent of ancient Near Eastern despots who accumulated land, gardens, pools, vineyards, slaves, and herds. A ruler in the ancient Orient took pride not only in physical conquest on the battlefield, but of horticultural expertise in growing lavish gardens. Thus, a ruler could master nature and often experience sexual pleasure when the gardens were used as settings for lovemaking.

Yet, as the Teacher considers all that he has done and created, he as a Wise One knows the opposite of wisdom, and that is folly. In Eccl. 2:11, a verse of pivotal insight, the Teacher confesses: "All was vanity and a chasing after the wind, and there was nothing to be gained under the sun." This lament that seeking after pleasure is vanity will be echoed in the Lukan parable of the rich fool who seeks an abundance of possessions.

HOSEA 11:1-11 (RCL, alt.)

The LORD God agonizes over the punishment of God's wayward and wandering children. Hosea offers a picture of a loving God, an image of a nurturing parent, a parent who suffers even as a child is disciplined. Hosea had two sons and a daughter and could have functioned for a time as a single parent. Thus, the depiction of a parent helping a toddler walk, picking a child up in an embrace, lifting an infant to the cheek, could have been drawn from Hosea's familial circle. "I led them with cords of human kindness, with bands of love"

> HOSEA OFFERS A PICTURE OF A LOVING GOD, AN IMAGE OF A NURTURING PARENT, A PARENT WHO SUFFERS EVEN AS A CHILD IS DISCIPLINED.

(Hos. 11:4). Hosea describes raising children with its risks, for example, the possibility of rebellion. Even as God's children turn away, God does not react in fierce anger, but with tender compassion. The closing verses in the Hosea passage depict a homecoming, when God's trembling children return to their homes.

It is almost as if there has been a progression from the narcissism of spiritual infancy (in Ecclesiastes) with its focus on "me" and "mine," to toddlerhood with its proclivity to individuate from the parent, to adolescent arrogance with its open rebellion (in Hosea). Through all these stages of Christian formation, God as parent has remained steady in *hesed*, loyal compassion. When the rebel children grow weary, when their souls faint within them, when their thirsty lips and their hungry mouths cry out, "All is vanity," the Lord who is good satisfies this thirst and hunger with good things. All is not vanity.

RESPONSIVE READING

PSALM 49:1-11 (RCL);
PSALM 107:1-9, 43 (RCL, alt.);
PSALM 49 (BCP)

The psalmist reiterates the folly of trusting in riches. Those who trust in their wealth and boast of the abundance of their riches will not avoid the grave. Mortals will perish just as animals do. There is no price that can be paid to God that will preserve one's life. There is no ransom that can be found to prevent one's banishment to the grave.

PSALM 90:3-4, 5-6, 12-13, 14, 17 (RC)

Psalm 90 elaborates on that which is not vanity: God's steadfast love and favor. It is God's love each morning that produces pleasure and joy. It is God's favor that brings meaning to the work of our hands. Human frailty is contrasted with God's permanence. We are like dust, like grass that withers. Psalm 90 is often used at funerals, over the gravesite, when those gathered are vulnerably aware of their own mortality.

Psalm 90 affirms the fact that we will die. It is not a psalm of denial. It acknowledges that shattering moment in our journey of faith when we truly must accept the fact that our days are not endless, as youth mythologize, but our days are numbered. The psalm contains a prayer for help and a request in vv. 13 and 14 that God turn from anger to compassion, or *hesed*. This request and the confidence of God's loyalty in this psalm go beyond the refrain "All is vanity" found also in Ecclesiastes. All is not vanity when one's days are meted out and favored by God.

164

THE SEASON
OF PENTECOST
—————
JEANNE
STEVENSON-
MOESSNER

SECOND READING

COLOSSIANS 3:1-11 (RCL);
COLOSSIANS 3:(5-11), 12-17 (BCP);
COLOSSIANS 3:1-5, 9-11 (RC)

This lection prompts us to invoke the significance of our baptism in three ways. First, we are to remember that we have died to a life that worships earthly creations and revels in vices. Second, we have been raised with Christ, hidden with Christ in God, and given a new life that centers in the person of Christ and ensues in virtues that are Christlike. Third, this new self of ours is being renewed in knowledge according to the image of the creator God, and in that renewing of the mind and soul we participate in a spiritual family, which overcomes racial, cultural, ritualistic, and social divisions.

In many ways I am reminded through this passage in Colossians of injunctions and exhortations, of a young adult's passage away from the family of origin, perhaps to college or a new geographical location or to marriage or employment away from the birthplace. I can imagine the loving warnings of those who have raised this child, this adolescent, this young adult: Remember who you are, be careful, take care of yourself. In comparable fashion, the author of Colossians is firm with his readers: Remember your new life in Christ, put to death whatever in you is earthly and a vice, clothe yourself with your life in Christ and all its virtues. This advice is given to Christians who will be navigating passages on this earth with all its snares and temptations. These words of godly wisdom are offered to all those Christians who are serious about their Christian spiritual formation.

WE ARE OFFERED IN THE READING OF THIS TEXT A REFRESHING RESTATEMENT OF WHO WE ARE AND WHOSE WE ARE.

These are words of exhortation any Christian might need to hear. A dramatic and definitive conversion may be long in the past. A reminder of the working of the Holy Spirit could seem distant. Yet we are offered in the reading of this text a refreshing restatement of who we are and whose we are: "For you have died, and your life is hidden with Christ in God."

Colossians 3:1-11 is analogous to the baptismal font that is often placed near the altar in a worship service. Whether or not a formal baptism occurs as a sacrament in a service, the placement of the font serves as a visual aid, a prompt, of the essential demarcation of who Christians are: We are alive in Christ. This reminder is particularly needed when the vices of this earth and the memory of the "old self" start to exert a power over the believer.

Vices are listed in Col. 3:5-9, and vv. 12-17 (BCP) contain the desired virtues. Although earlier verses had used rather uncomfortable language of "stripping off the old self," these exhortations gracefully offer covering and clothing that is gentle, compassionate, and loving.

THE GOSPEL
LUKE 12:13-21 (RCL, BCP, RC)

Laws of inheritance were found in the Torah. It would have been natural for one heir to ask a religious teacher like Jesus to settle a disagreement among heirs. A family dispute does occur, and one member of the family asks Jesus to intervene. Jewish custom allowed one heir the opportunity to demand that an inheritance be divided among all heirs. Jesus, however, resists the triangulation or the attempt to pull him into the divided situation. Jesus was witnessing a predicament that so many of us as pastors have seen divide a family: an argument over inheritance.

As in the admonitions of Colossians, Jesus warns: "Take care! Be on your guard against all kinds of greed." Jesus develops the understanding of the "new self" when he adds that one's life does not consist in the abundance of possessions. The vice of greed is singled out here in this family controversy. Then Jesus tells the story, the parable, of the greedy rich man whose land produced abundantly.

Are we to assume this rich fool in the parable is a man who never found the new life in Christ? Or, and this is a more distressing interpretation, is this rich landowner perhaps a Christian who neglected the care of his or her soul and instead put all energy into material acquisitions? Perhaps the landowner remained in an infantile spiritual posture of "Give me, give me, gimmeee!" He is described as in poverty toward God. He is a poor and wayward pilgrim in the journey of faith.

> IS THIS RICH LANDOWNER PERHAPS A CHRISTIAN WHO NEGLECTED THE CARE OF HIS OR HER SOUL AND INSTEAD PUT ALL ENERGY INTO MATERIAL ACQUISITIONS?

Coming full circle now to the cry of Ecclesiastes, we find that all is vanity. For in the moment of earthly abundance, the rich fool could not enjoy his bounty, because his life was demanded. He died. We are left with the haunting question: Who will inherit what he worked for so diligently? Is all vanity?

Even we as pastors and religious leaders have at times questioned the meaning of our life and ministry. We have wondered, "Does my life really count?" This is a search for meaning that even mature Christians articulate. There will be parishioners listening for a message of hope in the spectrum that has despair at one pole and meaning at the opposite. Your audience, your congregation, will be at different places on that spectrum and in various positions in faith stages of development.

THE SEASON
OF PENTECOST
─────────
JEANNE
STEVENSON-
MOESSNER

These texts are rich in developmental imagery: the baby and toddler (Hosea), the rebellious adolescent (Hosea), the midlife queries (Ecclesiastes, Psalms). Your sermon can be a vehicle of hope, that even with the pulls of pleasure and greed, with the inevitability of the grave, God as loving parent is with us in the temptations and in the transitions. There is no greater antidote to the hopeless cry, "All is vanity," than the prayerful petition, "Satisfy us in the morning with your steadfast love, so that we may rejoice and be glad all our days" (Ps. 90:14).

TENTH SUNDAY AFTER PENTECOST

NINETEENTH SUNDAY IN ORDINARY TIME / PROPER 14
AUGUST 8, 2004

REVISED COMMON	EPISCOPAL (BCP)	ROMAN CATHOLIC
Gen. 15:1-6 or Isa. 1:1, 10-20	Gen. 15:1-6	Wisd. of Sol. 18:6-9
Ps. 33:12-22 or Ps. 50:1-8, 22-23	Psalm 33 or 33:12-15, 18-22	Ps. 33:1, 12, 18-19, 20-22
Heb. 11:1-3, 8-16	Heb. 11:1-3, (4-7), 8-16	Heb. 11:1-2, 8-19 or 11:1-2, 8-12
Luke 12:32-40	Luke 12:32-40	Luke 12:32-48 or 12:35-40

FIRST READING
GENESIS 15:1-6 (RCL, BCP)

In a seminary class in preaching, a middler, a second-year student, took his turn and rambled and ambled through a maze of words that was meant to be a sermon. The text was the narrative of Jesus in the boat with the disciples during a terrible storm. Slowly, the sermon sunk in the fierceness of the storm. Afterwards, fellow students offered "room for improvement" as gently and as forcibly as they could. Yet one student remained silent throughout the critique. Because it was not normally the student's nature to be so quiet, the professor asked her "Mary, would you like to offer a comment?" Slowly, Mary turned to face the novice preacher and said: "I just wanted you to throw me the life preserver."

Abraham was also in a life-threatening situation. He was facing the equivalent of death in this passage, Genesis 15. He had no heir. He had been obedient in leaving his home in Haran, but he was given no son. The lack of descendants in the Hebrew lineage was the equivalent of death. One's life really did not go on. In this battle against death, the cessation of one's lineage without biological heirs, God offered Abraham a shield. "Do not be afraid, Abram, I am your shield." This shield is not so far removed from a life preserver.

Your congregation will be facing death, loss, and fear in its many guises. They will surely relate to Abram in his inability to make things come out right.

168

THE SEASON
OF PENTECOST
_____

JEANNE
STEVENSON-
MOESSNER

Granted, Abram had Eliezer of Damascus, a slave born in his house. Granted Eliezer could function as a son, inherit property, and beget children himself. However, the blood lineage would cease. Abraham's plans would come to an end. The members of your congregation will identify with plans gone awry.

Sarai, not mentioned in these verses, was also suffering. She would be stigmatized as a barren matriarch. This barrenness would be seen as a curse upon her. Bearing offspring, especially a male child, was interpreted as God's blessing and approval. It is very possible that Sarai felt she had failed her purpose in life. She, too, was floundering and ashamed.

In the night vision described in Gen. 15:1-6, Abraham was told to count the stars in heaven. The stars were as plentiful as the number of his future descendants. With the help of this visual aid, Abraham moved from his protest in vv. 2-3 to trust in v. 6. Abraham believed God, and this belief was counted as righteousness.

The development of trust, according to developmental psychologist Erik Erikson, is the core task in the first stage of spiritual formation, as well as the rudimentary stage of psychosocial development. Abraham, like any spiritual pilgrim, met additional challenges. Yet his initial positive response to God's challenge,

IN THE POLARITY OF TRUST VERSUS MISTRUST, ABRAHAM HAD FOUND A POSITIVE RESOLUTION, A RIGHT RELATION.

"Do not be afraid, Abram," gave him a foundation upon which to develop and redevelop a profoundly decisive trust. In the polarity of trust versus mistrust, Abraham had found a positive resolution, a right relation. This right relation God reckoned as righteousness.

WISDOM OF SOLOMON 18:6-9 (RC)

The sage describes the night when the angel of death passed over the land of Egypt, sparing the firstborn of families whose doorposts and lintels were marked with the blood of a male lamb. After this Passover, Moses, who himself as an infant had been abandoned and rescued, led the Israelites out of Egypt. Many Egyptian children died during the final plague, firstborn children from the house of Pharaoh to the hovels of slaves. Egyptian families who did not have faith in the God of the Hebrew people were destroyed by various earlier plagues. Egyptian livestock and crops were devastated as well.

People of faith have shared in both blessings and dangers. Shortly after Jesus was born, many innocent children in Bethlehem under the age of two were massacred by Herod. Thirty-three years later, on the night of the Passover, Jesus was abandoned, killed, and later resurrected. Many holy people, from biblical times to the present, have known blessings and dangers as they followed their ancestors. Christians hearing your sermon are called into this tradition.

ISAIAH 1:1, 10-20 (RCL, alt.)

God is great. God is good. But as Jeffrey Zurheide points out in *When Faith Is Tested,* evil is real. The first chapter of Isaiah elaborates on this last reality. The rulers and population of Jerusalem are addressed as "Sodom and Gomorrah" in these verses. The Holy City had been renamed a despicable name. There is an element of horror and a note of judgment in this chapter. Evil is real.

The eighth-century prophet Isaiah, son of Amoz, wrote of his vision of the wickedness of Judah. Isaiah 1:1 cites four kings, a list that includes the weak ruler Ahaz and the reliable king Hezekiah. Isaiah's mention of a vision reminds us of Abraham's vision earlier. A vision is not only a dreamlike condition but also a new way of seeing. Whereas Abraham was told not to be afraid, Isaiah's contrasting vision of a recalcitrant and rebellious Judah might have resulted in a startling realization: Be afraid—for Judah and Jerusalem.

As crime and corruption are recounted in Isa. 1:10-20, various attempts to placate God are recited: sacrifices, burnt and blood offerings, incense, assemblies and festivals, prayers. God does not see them; God does not hear them.

God asks for cleansing, for cessation of evil. When a bad habit is taken away, a new habit must be learned. In similar fashion, God asks for reorientation toward good, for a beginning of acts of justice. These gestures of mercy are toward those marginalized in Israel's history: the widows, the orphans, and the oppressed.

God asks to be in relationship, in dialogical relationship with the former offenders. These are the words your congregation wants to hear:

Come now, let us argue it out, says the LORD:
Though your sins are like scarlet, they shall be like snow;
though they are red like crimson, they shall become like wool. (v. 18)

RESPONSIVE READING
PSALM 33:12-22 (RCL);
PSALM 33 or 33:12-15, 18-22 (BCP);
PSALM 33:1, 12, 18-19, 20-22 (RC)

God is great. God is good. Psalm 33 elaborates these two foundational truths. The greatness was manifested when God gathered the waters of the sea as in a bottle, as the heavens were made by God's word and the host of heaven was created by God's breath. These expansive images are used by the psalmist to encourage the earth to stand in awe of this God.

170

THE SEASON
OF PENTECOST

JEANNE
STEVENSON-
MOESSNER

God is good. The "eye of God" is on those who stand in awe, on those who hope in God's love, to deliver their bodies from famine and their souls from death. God is described as a help and a shield. Again, the theme of *hesed*, God's steadfast love, runs through this hymn of praise. This psalm has the same number of lines as there are letters in the Hebrew alphabet, which is a signal that this psalm is to be as comprehensive as an alphabet, according to James Luther Mays in his *Interpretation* commentary on the Psalms.[1]

As the psalmist describes God's greatness, the images could be frightening; in the first half of the psalm, God brings the counsel of the nations to nothing. God frustrates the plans of peoples. However, due to *hesed,* God establishes hope: God's counsel endures. God has a plan for people.

In vv. 12-22 God is described as "looking down from heaven" and watching humankind. Military might is depicted as ineffectual when compared in vv. 16 and 17 with what God has to offer. God is both help and shield. As shield, God is great. As help, God is good. The psalmist uses anthropomorphic language to describe this heavenly potentate who sits enthroned above the earth. Yet this same Lord fashions the hearts of earth's inhabitants and is worthy of our trust.

PSALM 50:1-8, 22-23 (RCL, alt.)

God does not need the flesh of bulls, the blood of goats, the charred remains of burnt offerings. God abhors religious pretense and feigned spirituality. What God does desire is a sacrifice of thanksgiving, an offering of righteous living, and the incense of loyal obedience. Taken together, these constitute an acceptable sacrifice.

There is so much that demands our attention to keep a local church going. May this psalm serve as a reminder of what it is that God desires from us at the heart of our covenantal relationship. In the flurry of church business and in the fervor of church maintenance, this psalm beckons us to pause and remember the acceptable sacrifice.

SECOND READING

HEBREWS 11:1-3, 8-16 (RCL);
HEBREWS 11:1-3, (4-7), 8-16 (BCP);
HEBREWS 11:1-2, 8-19 or 11:1-2, 8-12 (RC)

Abraham was as good as dead. He had no son. "But by faith he received the power of procreation . . ." (v. 11). Many in the congregation will find it difficult to muster up the faith they perceive Abraham must have had. They will be waiting for a word, your word, God's word, to help them engender this sort of faith. After all, Abraham left all that was familiar, without a road map or final destination, to enter a land that was unfamiliar to him and to Sarah. Sarah was a barren woman, and she was expected to have faith, too. From these two unlikely people, one as good as dead and the other a complete failure by virtue of her barrenness, came a line of descendants so numerous that they are compared to the stars of heaven. We recall Abraham's night vision in Gen. 15:1-6.

"Now faith is the assurance of things hoped for, the conviction of things not seen" (v. 1). How can the average Christian hope for such faith as that portrayed in this passage in Hebrews? Verse 11b offers the only way such faith was attainable for Abraham and Sarah. Abraham considered the one faithful who had promised. Faith hangs on the faithfulness of God. As we learn to trust this faithfulness, we gain the assurance of things hoped for, and this is faith. The burden of faith is thus transferred to God, the author of our faith.

FAITH HANGS ON THE FAITHFULNESS OF GOD.

Those who trust in God's faithfulness are described as sojourners or pilgrims on this earth. We seek a homeland, a resting place. We are never quite content to settle fully anywhere on this earth, because we desire a better country, a heavenly one. This passage in Hebrews, with its list of the faithful, ends with the stark statement: All of these strong people of faith died without receiving the promises but saw at a distance the city God had prepared for them. Jesus was born to bring them home.

How do we know all of this to be true? Several times recently someone has said to me, "My word is bond." That means I can count on his or her word as if it were a bond in a courtroom proceeding. What you have to offer your congregation is this: God's faithfulness is bond. To understand this concept and to rely upon it is to have the faith of Abraham.

In the chapel at Samford University in Birmingham, there is a dome encircled by the "cloud of witnesses" painted on the ceiling and looking down at worshipers. In some ways, other verses in Hebrews 11 paint this picture. In vv. 4-7 (BCP), the examples of Abel, Enoch, and Noah are given to motivate us and to encourage us to have faith. When we have faith in God's faithfulness, we are seen by God as righteous.

In the Roman Catholic lection, vv. 17-18 are extremely difficult for some because there appears to be an instance of child sacrifice. What kind of a God would ask Abraham to offer up his long-awaited son? It appears to be a macabre manipulation of the circumstances to squeeze out a test of faith. It has been suggested that Abraham had faith in God's faithfulness to raise Isaac from the dead, a possible prefiguration of God's only son, Jesus.

172

THE SEASON
OF PENTECOST

JEANNE
STEVENSON-
MOESSNER

THE GOSPEL

LUKE 12:32-40 (RCL, BCP);
LUKE 12:32-48 (RC)

God is great. God is good. Evil is real. For example, a thief can rob you of your earthly possessions, but no thief can come near your treasure in heaven. These verses in Luke remind us that our heart should be attached to our treasure in heaven. We should not be afraid, even as the economy around us fluctuates. In fact, Jesus asks us to be proactive with our material resources and give some away!

Evil is real. Be watchful! Be ready! The images for this readiness center on being dressed for action and keeping lamps lit. In this Lukan parable, the images are suited for watchful slaves who do not know when the master will return from the wedding banquet. If they are alert to his coming and ready to open the door to him, they will not only receive his approval but a blessing. The slaves will become guests at a meal, which the master serves them.

> THESE VERSES IN LUKE REMIND US THAT OUR HEART SHOULD BE ATTACHED TO OUR TREASURE IN HEAVEN.

This Lukan parable bears similarities to the parable in Matthew 25 of the ten bridesmaids. They were waiting for the bridegroom also with lamps. However, five of the ten were not ready, for they had no oil for their lamps. They were not allowed into the wedding banquet to eat in festivity. The common themes are to be watchful, to be ready, for the master like the bridegroom may knock on the door at any hour.

Luke tries one more approach to illustrate this point of readiness. A thief can be successful in accomplishing evil by appearing unexpectedly and breaking into a home. The owner of this home had not prepared for such an event. Yet the reality of the in-breaking of evil is always present.

Are we Christians being watchful? Are we guarding our hearts as well as our homes of being robbed? Are we putting our treasures and valuables in a place where no thief comes near, no moth destroys? In a time of anxiety, it is a natural move to rely on the familiar. Will the familiar be our material securities? This Lukan text is a timely way to take interior inventory. This you can adapt in your sermon and offer to your congregation.

The Roman Catholic lection includes vv. 41-48, which make clear our responsibility as leaders of the church. Places of spiritual leadership are not immune from temptations to misuse power and abuse privileges. There are some harsh implications and consequences for imprudence, mismanagement, improper conduct, and abuse. These consequences differ in accord with the degree of awareness that the spiritual leader possesses, awareness of what was required of him or her by the master. Some leaders will even be cut off and relegated to the unfaithful. Evil is real, and a God who is both good and great will act accordingly.

MARY, MOTHER OF OUR LORD

AUGUST 15, 2004

REVISED COMMON	EPISCOPAL (BCP)	ROMAN CATHOLIC
Isa. 61:7-11	Isa. 61:10-11	Rev. 11:19a; 12:1-6a, 10ab
Ps. 45:10-15	Psalm 34 or 34:1-9	Ps. 45:10, 11, 12, 16
Gal. 4:4-7	Gal. 4:4-7	1 Cor. 15:20-27a
Luke 1:46-55	Luke 1:46-55	Luke 1:39-56

The celebration of Mary, mother of Jesus, is particularly important for Protestants, because the Protestant tradition has generally downplayed the ministry of Mary. Following Jesus' ascension and the Holy Spirit's descent, the only physical link with Jesus was Mary, his mother. All Christian traditions have this

> THE PROTESTANT TRADITION HAS GENERALLY DOWN-PLAYED THE MINISTRY OF MARY.

understanding in common: God's incarnation in Jesus occurred in the body of a woman named Mary. The maternity of Jesus has not been questioned even when the virgin birth has been disputed. Thus Jesus' paternity has been argued but not his maternity.

Incarnation theology asserts that God became flesh. God became incarnate in the body of a woman from Nazareth. This assertion underscores the inseparable unity of spirit and body and negates a possible dualism. Incarnational theology values woman's experience and her body. It affirms the importance of Mary as

> JESUS' PATERNITY HAS BEEN ARGUED BUT NOT HIS MATERNITY.

Theotokos (God-bearer) as affirmed by the Council of Ephesus in 431 C.E.. Protestants recite the Apostles' Creed, "I believe . . . in Jesus Christ, God's only Son, . . . born of the virgin Mary," and often fail to incorporate this creedal statement about Mary into their daily spirituality and worship. This brief section on Mary is my own attempt as a Protestant to offer a Marian middle ground.[2]

FIRST READING

ISAIAH 61:7-11 (RCL);
ISAIAH 61:10-11 (BCP)

God promises restoration. In Isa. 61:1-11three speakers address the issues of repair, recompense, and blessing. The first is a preacher (vv. 1-3), the second an administrator (vv. 4-7), and the third is Yahweh (v. 8a). Each speaks of dedication to the rebirth and invigoration of Jerusalem. Yahweh establishes an everlasting covenant with the people of God and their descendants. Whereas Luke 4:14-21 contains Jesus' reading of the first portion of Isaiah 61, Luke 1:46-55 is Mary's song of praise or *Magnificat,* which is similar in tone to the song of praise found in Isa. 61:10-11. Just as the portion of Isaiah 61 chosen for this Sunday testifies to God's great reversals for those who are shamed and dishonored, so does the life of Mary offer a lasting example of how God can lift the lowly. Thus the theme of Isaiah 61 will be illustrated later by Mary who acclaimed: "for the Mighty One has done great things for me" (Luke 1:49).

RESPONSIVE READING

PSALM 45:10-15 (RCL);
PSALM 45:10, 11, 12, 16 (RC);
PSALM 34 or 34:1-9 (BCP)

On one level, Psalm 45 is a wedding song. The lectionary verses chosen for this Sunday center more on the bride of the king, this daughter soon to be a celebrated princess. From this union will come royal ancestors. On a second level, this psalm may be the basis of the allegory of Christ, the king, and the church, the bride. Thus, the themes become love, loyalty, and progeny. This last theme becomes prominent in the Second Reading.

SECOND READING

GALATIANS 4:4-7 (RCL, BCP)

"But when the fullness of time had come, God sent [God's] Son, born of a woman, born under the law" (Gal. 4:4). The woman is Mary, God-bearer. She bore the one who was the fulfillment of the law yet chose to be born under the law. Through this one's life, death, and redeeming work, "we"—Jew or Greek, slave or free, male or female—may receive adoption as sons and daughters of God, as royalty, as children of promise. Christ has created a multiracial, diverse-strata, and across-gender family of promise and progeny. The mechanism for this royal lineage is that of adoption.

An adopted family is aware that it is not constructed by biological ties. An adopted family cannot expect physical similarity or genetic sameness. In fact, for an adoptive family to be healthy and functional, there will be a shift into an acceptance of differences of all family members. The church will want to model its life after healthy adoptive families. Instead of divisiveness and rejection of differences, the church is encouraged to grow into a stance of acceptance of differences of its "heirs of God."[3]

THE GOSPEL
LUKE 1:46-55 (RCL, BCP);
LUKE 1:39-56 (RC)

The Holy Spirit filled Elizabeth's soul and she cried, "Blessed are you (Mary) among women, and blessed is the fruit of your womb" (Luke 1:42). Elizabeth was six months pregnant with John the Baptist, who leaped within the womb at the sound of Mary's voice. It is this same voice of Mary that burst forth in a song of praise called The Magnificat. This Psalter of an unwed mother,

> CHRIST HAS CREATED A MULTIRACIAL, DIVERSE-STRATA, AND ACROSS-GENDER FAMILY OF PROMISE AND PROGENY.

Mary, has been echoed by those in "lowly" positions and has been the theme song for many working for justice and liberation of the downtrodden and mistreated.

It has taken me many years to realize that Mary was not a passive, helpless woman who crumpled at the foot of the cross out of weakness. I have found in recent years, perhaps through my own motherhood, a fierce and strong Mary. Dorothee Soelle, in *The Strength of the Weak: Toward a Christian Feminist Identity*, described Mary as one who stood against the forces of a violent society, earning her—in Polish legends—the title "Madonna of the rogues."[4] Rosemary Radford Ruether wrote on Mary's receptivity, true receptivity being only possible for a person with self-esteem and independence.[5] Even Mary Daly and Sojourner Truth thought the Marian symbolism

> THE GOD-WHO-BECAME-FLESH WAS CARRIED IN THE WOMB OF A WOMAN. WE WOULD BE BLESSED TO HONOR THE WOMAN WHOM GOD SO HONORED.

might be a prophetic sign of a new, strong woman. The virgin birth suggested to them that women need not be identified with men.

Women are appreciative of the strength of Mary. Mary is among the cloud of witnesses mentioned in Heb. 12:1, praying for us, urging us on. Mary embodied the unity of body and soul. She remains a model of a wounded, pierced heart and of the courage to endure with such pain. With Mary, the physical is inseparable from the spiritual. She would understand that hysterectomy, mastectomy, child loss, and childbirth are spiritual matters. She would also understand that rape, battering, incest, and child abuse are theological and religious issues that should be seen as such by the church.

The God-who-became-flesh was carried in the womb of a woman. We would be blessed to honor the woman whom God so honored.

ELEVENTH SUNDAY AFTER PENTECOST

TWENTIETH SUNDAY IN ORDINARY TIME / PROPER 15
AUGUST 15, 2004

REVISED COMMON	EPISCOPAL (BCP)	ROMAN CATHOLIC
Jer. 23:23-29 or Isa. 5:1-7	Jer. 23:23-29	Jer. 38:4-6, 8-10
Psalm 82 or 80:1-2, 8-19	Psalm 82	Ps. 40:2-4, 18
Heb. 11:29—12:2	Heb. 12:1-7, (8-10), 11-14	Heb. 12:1-4
Luke 12:49-56	Luke 12:49-56	Luke 12:49-53

FIRST READING
JEREMIAH 23:23-29 (RCL, BCP)

God's character, as Walter Brueggemann notes in *To Pluck Up, to Tear Down*, a commentary on Jeremiah 1–25, is at the heart of this passage.[6] God is a great God whose word is like a scrutinizing fire that blazes and a judicious hammer that breaks a rock in pieces. The fire is a discerning fire that burns ineffectual straw, not useful wheat. The hammer smashes graven

> GOD'S CHARACTER IS AT THE HEART OF THIS PASSAGE.

images and idols. This great God whom Jeremiah serves is not a local figure or cultural idol. This God is far away from the temple cult. This God is sovereign, filling heaven and earth, unbounded by temple walls. This God is transcendent and aware of what occurs even in the secret places. This God is observant of what Judah and Judah's prophets are doing.

Jeremiah portrays God in such a way, hovering over the true and false prophets, seeing into the recesses of their hearts and their dreams. The artist Salvador Dali created a cosmic Christ in 1978 in his painting titled "The Christ of Gala." Christ is made to appear floating over the earth through the creation of two slightly varying picture panels that give a three-dimensional effect. This stereoscopic work, when viewed with special mirrors or glasses, presents Christ as hovering over the world, floating in space, filling heaven and earth. Using words instead of

178

THE SEASON
OF PENTECOST

JEANNE
STEVENSON-
MOESSNER

brush strokes, Jeremiah attempts in similar fashion to describe God as omniscient, omnipotent, and benevolent. God is great. God is good.

Yet, unlike the prophet Jeremiah, false prophets appear in many charming ways. Your sermon might elaborate on some of the more seductive lies that would align us with the character of the culture rather than the character of God. False prophets would have us forget God's name, and in doing so, forget whose we are. Then our allegiance is somewhere else, and our lives are lived with reckless abandon.

It is the character of God that determines the true from the false prophets. God sends and appoints the true prophets. As Charles Gerkin relates in his book, *An Introduction to Pastoral Care,* a pastor's role is to be a priest, prophet/ess, and a wise man/woman.[7] God calls a pastor to speak God's word faithfully, to live righteously. In so doing, a true prophet/ess is formed and reformed. This passage may be offered to the congregation as a gauge for discernment. In addition, it is a reminder and a self-check to us who pastor that in this vocation we are called to be, like Jeremiah, true prophets.

ISAIAH 5:1-7 (RCL, alt.)

This passage is much like a sermon with a surprise ending. There is a question left dangling, a piece of the puzzle missing, until the last words are spoken.

This passage has also been likened to a poem or love song that contains a plea for justice and righteousness. We do not know at the beginning of this love song who the parties are. We know that the narrator speaks on behalf of a friend, the owner of a vineyard, who is loving and careful in character. The imagery of caring is connected to the planting, maintenance, and protection of some choice property on a fertile hill. This friend of the narrator was so confident that the vines would yield choice grapes that a wine vat was installed in anticipation. Yet the shocking development came when the vines bore wild grapes!

In v. 3 the narrator recedes, and the friend speaks instead. This friend, as owner of the vineyard, appeals to the inhabitants of Jerusalem and the people of Judah. What more could have been done to yield good fruit? Now the owner gets angry and decides to allow the vineyard to be overrun with briers and thorns. It will not be pruned or hoed. And furthermore, this owner will not let the clouds give rain. Then comes the surprise ending: The owner is God, the Rainmaker, the Lord of hosts!

The people of Judah and the house of Israel are God's pleasant planting. Yet the wildness, the variance from what was expected, is sown by the injustice and bloodshed of this chosen people. God expected a refrain of righteousness from them but heard instead the cry of social injustice.

PSALM 82 (RCL, BCP)

We move now from false prophets to false gods. Psalm 82 utilizes the language of court proceedings and is written in the style of liturgical drama. The setting is a divine assembly with a deity presiding. This staging would have been understandable to an ancient culture that believed in a pantheon of gods. In Psalm 82, the Lord is presiding over the assembly; the other "gods" are subordinate and held accountable. As Psalm 82 unfolds, as the liturgist or psalmist narrates, God metes out judgment. The "lesser gods" have failed to perpetuate the divine dance that always circumambulates outward—toward those not in the inner circle of power, toward those not in the pantheon of privilege. These would be the weak, the orphans, the lowly, the destitute. Those in the divine council are told to rescue these needy ones. For although those in the divine council are privileged, some day they will die like mortals and fall like any ruler.

This psalm can be used first to help us refocus our ministry, then to reenvision the audience for our sermon. Have we positioned ourselves to show partiality to the strong, the affluent, the powerful in our congregation? Are we willing to preach and to reach the marginal ones in our congregation, marginal by whatever description? Only by answering these questions ourselves in the affirmative can we then preach with passion and conviction on this text as it seeks to motivate our congregation with a plea for justice toward the destitute and needy.

PSALM 80:1-2, 8-19 (RCL, alt.)

God is great. This psalm of Asaph describes God as enthroned upon the cherubim. God is good. Psalm 80 likens God to the shepherd of Israel who led Joseph out of Egypt like a compassionate shepherd leading a flock of sheep. Then the psalmist mixes metaphors. Once again, the vine and vineyard imagery is evoked as the psalmist depicts God tenderly planting a vine brought out of Egypt. God clears the ground as the vine takes deep root. The vine grows, and its branches and shoots reach to the sea and river.

However, it appears from the corporate lament within this psalm that this good and great God has allowed the cherished vineyard to go to waste. Not only do wayfarers pluck fruit from the vine, but the wild boar from the forest ravages the vineyard while other animals also dine on the fruit. Furthermore, it is mentioned that the vine stock has been burned down and cut! The appeal to God in the psalm is to restore favor once again to Israel, the stock of Joseph.

180

THE SEASON
OF PENTECOST
—————
JEANNE
STEVENSON-
MOESSNER

The members of your congregation will identify with these feelings of being overwhelmed, overcome, forgotten, useless. These are the feelings expressed in Psalm 80.

Verses 14-17 contain a series of petitions with a promise of renewed faithfulness (v. 18). What is noticeably lacking is a statement of repentance or confession. In a time of great loss and stress, a common response is: Why is this happening to me (us)? Rarely, in a time of pain, is there a careful analysis of the causes of calamity. We seek relief from pain, not a discourse on causality. Israel is in great distress in this psalm. Israel wants relief or restoration quickly! Israel appeals to God's doting love. Israel promises never to be unfaithful again.

The spiritual posture of the members of this psalmic chorus reminds me of an adolescent who disobeys parental rules, drives too fast or too far, wrecks the family car, then calls home: "Dad, Mom, I'm okay, but I totaled the car." In the trauma of this initial exchange and in the relief that ensues, causality, confession, remorse, and forgiveness may be absent in the discourse. Psalm 80 is an exchange much like the one described. Those suffering are relying on the love of the parent (the shepherd of Israel) to come "pick them up at the police station."

In this corporate prayer, Psalm 80, the psalmist and people appeal to God to repent or change from wrath to grace. In this way I agree with James Luther Mays in his *Interpretation* commentary on the Psalms. This hope is not based in the lives of the flawed and prodigal people. The trust is in a God who will hopefully not abandon what God planted. Thus, hope is placed in the character of God, the shepherd of Israel.

SECOND READING
HEBREWS 11:29—12:2 (RCL)

Each year in our "Foundations of Christian Education" class, my seminary students make a fabric or felt tapestry of their role models in the faith. Many of the role models were (are) grandparents, coaches, Sunday school teachers, relatives, or pastors who took an interest in the person's spiritual formation and encouraged growth in faith. Such a tapestry is verbally presented in the opening verses of Hebrews 12. The tapestry is comprised of role models in the faith who cheer us on in the race that is set before us by Jesus.

MANY MOVING STORIES CAN BE FOUND IN THE BIBLE AND IN CHURCH HISTORY TO INSPIRE YOUR CONGREGATION, TO GIVE THEM EXAMPLES OF SPIRITUAL STAMINA.

The roster of faithful Israelite heroes and heroines is a needed balance to Psalm 80 with its theme of unfaithfulness. Hebrews 11:29-39 is replete with sermon examples, including less well-known biblical figures like Rahab the prostitute.

This text in Hebrews gives you the occasion to tell stories of faith: for example, women like Martha and Mary, who received their dead relative back again through a miracle of resurrection. Others like Perpetua and Felicitas in Carthage who were mocked and massacred in the arena because of their stance for Christ. Many moving stories can be found in the Bible and in church history to inspire your congregation, to give them examples of spiritual stamina. However, it is also important to honor the everyday, personal heroes and heroines of your parishioners. For all who point us to Jesus as the pioneer and perfecter of our faith will be honored by the one who now sits "at the right hand of the throne of God" (12:2).

HEBREWS 12:1-7, (8-10), 11-14 (BCP);
HEBREWS 12:1-4 (RC)

"Lift your drooping hands and strengthen your weak knees." Remember you are running a race with perseverance. Make straight paths for your feet!

In this race, there will be trials, discipline, correction, and chastisement. The author of Hebrews, the Preacher, now affects a connectional move in order to involve his listeners. The Preacher recalls their childhood. Parents discipline those they love. So does God chastise every spiritual child. If we respected our human parents' discipline, why not that of God? God's goal is our maturation into the joy of winning the race of life with holiness, righteousness, and peace.

There are many forms of discipline. It is important that members of your congregation recall positive discipline and in no way confuse discipline with abuse or neglect. There will be some in the congregation who did not receive healthy parenting. The bounty of this segment of Heb. 12:1-14 is the double imagery: running the race and disciplining the child. Taken together, there is a fuller picture of what it means to grow in Christian spiritual formation.

THE GOSPEL
LUKE 12:49-56 (RCL, BCP);
LUKE 12:49-53 (RC)

The fire imagery employed in Luke is a symbol for the divisiveness Jesus' incarnate presence on earth will bring. There is reference to a future baptism that Jesus is anxious to effect. The coming of the Holy Spirit at Pentecost was a type of baptism with divided tongues "as of fire" (Acts 2:3) appearing among the believers. As a "tongue" rested on each, a different language ensued as the Spirit gave ability. Those assembled were divided linguistically.

182

THE SEASON
OF PENTECOST
———
JEANNE
STEVENSON-
MOESSNER

In Luke 12:49-53, Jesus speaks of a division based on his person. Those who believe in him will form a new spiritual family, causing alienation from some members in their adoptive, foster, step, or biological families. Those in your congregation who are serious about Christian growth or sanctification will find a realistic assessment in these verses of the cost of primary allegiance to Christ. For those serious in their Christian faith, this passage prepares them for future demands in their spiritual development. Jesus will be the cause of division.

FOR THOSE SERIOUS IN THEIR CHRISTIAN FAITH, THIS PASSAGE PREPARES THEM FOR FUTURE DEMANDS IN THEIR SPIRITUAL DEVELOPMENT.

Allusions in Luke to water and fire, baptism and subsequent divisions among people remind us of similar references in the description of Pentecost in Acts. The presence of Christ and the coming of the Holy Spirit are the decisive events in the life of your congregation.

TWELFTH SUNDAY AFTER PENTECOST

TWENTY-FIRST SUNDAY IN ORDINARY TIME / PROPER 16

AUGUST 22, 2004

REVISED COMMON	EPISCOPAL (BCP)	ROMAN CATHOLIC
Isa. 58:9b-14	Isa. 28:14-22	Isa. 66:18-21
or Jer. 1:4-10		
Ps. 103:1-8	Psalm 46	Ps. 117:1-2
or 71:1-6		
Heb. 12:18-29	Heb. 12:18-19, 22-29	Heb. 12:5-7, 11-13
Luke 13:10-17	Luke 13:22-30	Luke 13:22-30

FIRST READING

ISAIAH 58:9b-14 (RCL)

Pastors often preach on God's unconditional love. This passage from Isaiah, however, presents God's conditions for authentic worship. This pericope is constructed with a series of "ifs" and "thens." For example, "If you refrain from trampling the Sabbath . . . then you shall take delight in the LORD." Thus conditions are set for true spirituality in worship. There is conditional assurance of blessing "if" certain moral acts, social practices, and public signs are in evidence.

This prophetic passage, written in the sixth century B.C.E., targeted religionists and religious professionals who sought to impress others with their meticulous observances and strict adherence to privatized piety. This message critiques our contemporary worship services today as accurately as it did in the Third Isaiah circle where Amos, Hosea, Isaiah, and Jeremiah all addressed proper worship and justice issues.

> PROPER WORSHIP OCCURS AT THE INTERFACE OF THE INDIVIDUAL'S SPIRITUALITY AND THE COMMUNITY'S NEEDS.

Proper worship occurs at the interface of the individual's spirituality and the community's needs. When hunger is satisfied and when the needs of the afflicted are met, then the ancient ruins of God's *basileia,* or intended kingdom, are rebuilt and foundations of *koinonia* are re-laid. In this way, those whose spirituality is tied to justice will be called "repairers of the breach" and "restorers of streets" in the cities of God.

184

THE SEASON
OF PENTECOST
─────────
JEANNE
STEVENSON-
MOESSNER

As we work for this repair and restoration, we as co-laborers with God are asked not to trample the Sabbath. We are asked not to pursue our own interests or affairs on this holy day, but to take delight in God alone on this day and be rejuvenated. "I will make you ride upon the heights of the earth," says Yahweh. This imagery is reminiscent of some of the ecstasy language of the mystics. It evokes a sense of transcendence in our spirituality. It comes, however, not from privatized devotion, but from honoring God's Sabbath and from pursuing the needs of the community.

ISAIAH 28:14-22 (BCP)

Scoffers are ones who resist this invitation. Using graphic images, vv. 14 through 22 present not only the scoffers' "state of denial" but the terror and devastation as a result of this refusal and mockery of the LORD's invitation. The corrupt rulers, priests, and prophets of Israel have made a "covenant with death" instead of one with the Lord; they have accepted an invitation to Sheol instead of the offer of Yahweh. Walter Brueggemann, in his commentary on Isaiah 1–39, writes: "Jerusalem has exhausted all of the kind inclination of Yahweh, and there is now only devastation." In contrast to God's grace, this passage presents "alien work" (v. 21).[8] Perhaps this is another way of explaining both the door that is too narrow or the door that has closed to late guests (see The Gospel, Luke 13:22–30, below).

JEREMIAH 1:4-10 (RCL, alt.)

Jeremiah was only a youth when God called him and appointed him a prophet to the nations. The pastoral and prophetic initiative was God's. The call of God originated before Jeremiah's conception, before his birth. Jeremiah did not seek this status of prophet. In fact, like Moses' response to God's call, Jeremiah feared it. He was afraid. He had cause to be terrified. During the forty years that Jeremiah warned the people of Judah of the dangers facing them, he lived these forty years, R. E. Clements observes in his commentary on Jeremiah, "as an isolated and derided prophet."[9]

God asked him not to underrate himself. God asked him to be bold. God "touched his mouth" and promised the words would come—from God.

We learn a "ministry of presence" in pastoral care. We are trained to expect this in our classes at seminary. A ministry of presence, we learn, is being with the person who needs our care; it is also expecting God to be with us as we minister. It is oftentimes when we feel most inadequate, when we are at a loss for words, that

God allows us to hear the words beneath the silences, the words of those suffering and the words of God: "For I am with you to deliver you, says the Lord" (v. 8).

According to John M. Bracke, in his commentary on Jeremiah 1–29, Jer. 1:1-10 "expresses a central theme of the book, that God is sovereign over the nations and directs history."[10] The action verbs in v. 10—plucking up, pulling down, destroying, overthrowing, building, planting—reveal God's activity to judge and restore nations. God is portrayed as directing history. Although not all will agree with this view of history, it is a dominant and recurrent view in the Bible. This perspective can be used to affirm God's initiative in our lives and that of the people we serve, to confirm our appointment by God, and to be firm in the conviction, "I am with you, says the Lord" (v. 8).

ISAIAH 66:18-21

God is the object of worship. This is what we as pastors proclaim each Sunday. The vision of the reign of God presented in Isaiah 66 portrays all nations and tongues gathered around God's glory. Just as prophets urged Israel to return to a worship of the one true God, so does the prophetic nature of our pastoral vocation commission us to forthtell God's glory to all nations. This foretelling is of a time when all socioeconomic groupings—depicted in Isaiah as the wealthy in chariots, the sick or pregnant on litters, the oppressed on mules, and the tradespeople on dromedaries—will rally around the fame and holiness of God. This image or vision impels our preaching toward the promise and the coming of a new heaven and a renovated earth.

RESPONSIVE READING
PSALM 103:1-8 (RCL)

God is good, and this goodness is praised in Psalm 103. There is a very uplifting tone to this psalm, an upbeat mood, a positive outlook. It is, to quote James Luther Mays, the "favored praise of sinners."[11]

A reader could make the assumption that this psalm was written in a period of triumph, personal victory, or communal accomplishment. As I read this psalm lauding God's *hesed* or steadfast love, I am reminded of a meditation that was given to me during a period of discouragement.

GOD'S BLESSING IS TRULY REMARKABLE. OUR SINS ARE FORGIVEN, OUR DISEASES HEALED, AND OUR YOUTH RENEWED LIKE THE EAGLE'S.

The message of the meditation was this: Praise God in the most difficult times

186

THE SEASON
OF PENTECOST

JEANNE
STEVENSON-
MOESSNER

because it is the only hope for survival. It is probable that the psalmist knows of the "Pit" as mentioned in v. 4. It could even be the case that the psalmist praises God from the "Pit," the mire of desolation.

God's blessing is truly remarkable. Our sins are forgiven, our diseases healed, and our youth renewed like the eagle's. God vindicates the oppressed as God did for the people of Israel in the time of Moses. When Israel sinned by worshiping the golden calf in the wilderness experience, God related to them with anger but continued the relationship because of steadfast love. It is in such a time of shame, in our own rendition of idolizing "the golden calf," in our guilt over a broken commandment, that we ask for God's forgiveness and recognize God's mercy, and we truly sing with the psalmist, "Bless the Lord, O my soul." Such praise, especially from the Sheol-like Pit of torment, is our only hope for survival.

PSALM 71:1-6 (RCL, alt.)

In almost any Christian bookstore, one of the most popular images of God as protector and comforter is depicted by a small child nestled safely in the open oversized hand of a parent. In some ways, the opening verses of Psalm 71 expound upon this image.

The psalmist takes refuge in God, who is asked to be a rescuer from the hand of the wicked and the grasp of the unjust and cruel (v. 4). Similar to the small child in the palm of God's hand, the psalmist declares: "Upon you (Yahweh) I have leaned from my birth."

There are other images of God's protection and help in the opening of this psalm: God as listener (v. 2), God as rock and fortress (v. 3), God as midwife (v. 6b). This last depiction of God is least used in our hymns and sermon materials: "It was you (Yahweh) who took me from my mother's womb." The congregation will be blessed to learn of the many metaphors used in praise of God.

PSALM 117:1-2 (RC)

This shortest of all the psalms is perhaps the most comprehensive in its appeal to all the nations to praise the Lord. It is evangelism in world context. It is the invitation that we as pastors offer to all people: "Extol the LORD, all you peoples!" (v. 1). The reason for this praise is God's steadfast love for us and God's faithfulness. This is God's timely and universal invitation.

HEBREWS 12:18-29 (RCL);
HEBREWS 12:18-19, 22-29 (BCP);
HEBREWS 12:5-7, 11-13 (RC)

Lest we think that our many metaphors for God are illuminative of and adequate for God, the preacher of Hebrews reminds us that God is like a con-

suming fire, like a force that cannot be fully grasped or contained, like an energy that cannot be suppressed. God cannot be encompassed any more than darkness, a tempest, or gloom can be confined. God cannot be restrained any more than the

> THE PREACHER OF HEBREWS REMINDS US THAT GOD IS LIKE A CONSUMING FIRE, LIKE A FORCE THAT CANNOT BE FULLY GRASPED OR CONTAINED, LIKE AN ENERGY THAT CANNOT BE SUPPRESSED.

sound of a trumpet piercing the silence. On Mount Sinai, the voice of God made even Moses tremble with fear. This God cannot be cloistered.

This passage in Hebrews introduces Jesus as the mediator of a new covenant, which is symbolized by Mount Zion, the heavenly Jerusalem. In contrast to the somber atmosphere surrounding the portrayal of Mount Sinai, the depiction of Mount Zion is of a festive gathering, with innumerable angels and the assembly of Jesus as firstborn of a royal family. Although Sinai and Zion are contrasted with each other, there is actually only one mountain. As Thomas G. Long points out in *Hebrews,* there are two ways to travel, two paths on the same mountain.[12]

The contrast of Sinai and Zion provided in Hebrews 12 offers comforting insight for those on the pilgrimage of faith with Christ as guide. In our Christian formation, we often try to take "stones from Sinai" with us. These stones can be broken commandments, fallen idols, faithless formations with jagged edges. Our backpacks are heavy-laden.

I have seen this heaviness on several occasions in the foundational course in pastoral care at seminary. In this course we learn the importance of truly listening to others, of "attending" to them, of respecting silence, of avoiding "bromides" (i.e., a truth presented in an unhelpful manner and at the wrong time), of being at a loss for words. I have had well-meaning students come to me in deep remorse over something that might have been done or something that could have been said better. At times this retrospection turns up in their case studies. Their backward look has at times bordered on spiritual self-flagellation. This is when I am compelled to comment: "God would not have you carry that burden." This is to carry a "Sinai stone," and there comes a time on the journey of faith when Christ asks us to hand that over to him. Our load is lighter, and we not only climb more easily with Christ, but we begin to run the race that is set before us toward the heavenly Jerusalem.

188

THE SEASON
OF PENTECOST

JEANNE
STEVENSON-
MOESSNER

The Gospel

LUKE 13:10-17 (RCL)

She comes to worship, crippled with cares, bent with burdens that only her Maker could carry. It may look like she is weighted down with "Sinai stones." Her body is weary from a restless sleep, but still she comes to worship in your congregation. Her face, which is angled to the ground, shows signs of her aging. Is she perhaps suffering from a disease? She comes to you on the Sabbath, to worship. There are many others like her, you notice, men and women of all ages in your congregation, crippled with care.

You have worked diligently on your sermon. You have coordinated the hymn selections to match the mood of the sermon and the lectionary texts. The altar flowers are especially appealing; they were used in a tasteful wedding ceremony on Saturday. The hand-bell choir has selected some favorites. You and your associate have carefully reviewed all the cares and concerns, making certain no items were overlooked. You have attended to every pastoral detail to ensure that these moments in worship will be welcoming, life-sustaining, and life-changing. Slowly she comes, crippled with care and bent with burdens. All that you have prepared, all that you have prayed for is realized in the moment she is aware of Jesus' presence with her. All of the liturgical resources, all of the homiletical skills, have leaned into this encounter of the "daughter of Abraham" with Jesus. This is your pastoral task, to create the Sabbath space where Jesus can be met, time and again.

In Luke 13:10-17, a stooped woman entered the synagogue. She had been doubled over for eighteen years, half of her adult life, as the result of a "spirit of weakness," notes Sharon H. Ringe, in her commentary on this passage.[13] The stooped woman demanded nothing from Jesus; he took the initiative and came to her, laying hands on her and healing her. She immediately stood up straight and praised God. The leader of the synagogue was furious and accused Jesus of breaking the Sabbath with his act of cure. In the debate which ensued, Jesus taught an object lesson, using an analogical method. If an ox or donkey is worthy of being untied to receive water on the Sabbath, how much more appropriate to untie this woman from her bondage and revive her! Jesus calls her a "daughter of Abraham," a term found only here in all of the Gospels. In contrast, Ringe points out, the masculine parallel "sons of Abraham" is used frequently to identify God's people. The woman released from the bondage of weakness and Satan and newly named "daughter of Abraham" had reason to stand tall.

JESUS CALLS HER A "DAUGHTER OF ABRAHAM," A TERM FOUND ONLY HERE IN ALL OF THE GOSPELS.

LUKE 13:22-30 (BCP, RC)

As is common in the Gospel of Luke, someone asks Jesus a question: "Lord, will only a few be saved?" Whereas in the preceding verses of this chapter the issue centered on the understanding of Sabbath, the concern in this passage hovers around those included in the heavenly banquet. Thus we move in Luke 13 from a volatile debate over Sabbath etiquette to concerns over the guest list at the Lord's eschatological banquet. Who exactly will be included?

Jesus tells a story involving a door. The door to the banquet hall appears to be quite narrow. Many will try to enter and will not be able to squeeze through the aperture, even with great personal effort. Others will postpone their RSVP to attend this great feast, open to all people, from whatever geographical or genealogical location. There will be a moment when the reservations are closed. Our task as pastors is to make certain the invitation of Christ is heard clearly; our prayer is that the invitation will be received and responded to before the narrow door is shut.

THIRTEENTH SUNDAY AFTER PENTECOST

TWENTY-SECOND SUNDAY IN ORDINARY TIME / PROPER 17

AUGUST 29, 2004

REVISED COMMON	EPISCOPAL (BCP)	ROMAN CATHOLIC
Prov. 25:6-7	Sir. 10:(7-11), 12-18	Sir. 3:17-18, 20, 28-29
or Sir. 10:12-18		
or Jer. 2:4-13		
Psalm 112	Psalm 112	Ps. 68:4-7, 10-11
or 81:1, 10-16		
Heb. 13:1-8, 15-16	Heb. 13:1-8	Heb. 12:18-19, 22-24a
Luke 14:1, 7-14	Luke 14:1, 7-14	Luke 14:1, 7-14

FIRST READING
PROVERBS 25:6-7 (RCL)

This chapter of Proverbs opens with the superscription: "These are other proverbs of Solomon that the officials of King Hezekiah of Judah copied" (v. 1). Some of the concerns for proper protocol could have been directed to young courtiers of the king or to youth in a royal school. Verses 6 and 7 advocate humility and deference in the presence of the king. Admonitions include the following: Do not go forward into the king's presence without being summoned, and do not stand in the place of the great. It is better to be summoned by the king than to overstep one's position and be demoted in rank. Leo G. Perdue, in his commentary on Proverbs, surmises that these helpful hints are meant for "aspiring young scribes" in the court of an ancient Israelite king.[14]

This protocol of humility could be adapted not only to sermon preparation, but entrance into sacred space or daily devotional time. After a period of self-emptying, we allow ourselves to be summoned by the message of the biblical text and by the Holy Spirit as messengers of God. As we enter the antechamber of illumination, we are immersed in the glory of God. Then we reenter the world of the sermon, the congregation, or parish rejuvenated as "aspiring young scribes."

SIRACH 10:(7-11, 12-18 (BCP);
SIRACH 10:12-18 (RCL, alt.)

Readings from Sirach (or the Wisdom of Jesus ben Sirach, also referred to as Ecclesiasticus) appear infrequently in the lectionary. Jesus ben Sirach was a second-century B.C.E. Jewish scribe and teacher in Jerusalem. Verses 6 to 18 of Sirach 10 focus on human pride as sinful and explicitly relate pride to those who exercise political power (the Egyptian and Syrian kings of Sirach's time). Earlier in this chapter (v. 4), Sirach makes it clear that "the government of the earth is in the hand of the Lord"—not in the hands of political operatives. The Lord overthrows the "rulers" and "enthrones the lowly in their place" (v. 14). Human pride in any form is not the divine intention for humanity. "Arrogance is hateful to the Lord and to mortals, and injustice is outrageous to both."

This reading provides the basis for preaching about human pride and its inevitable, disastrous consequences. It also opens the door for commenting on contemporary political decisions that are based on arrogance rather than justice. Recall the psalmist's words: "Do not put your trust in princes" (Ps. 146:3).

SIRACH 3:17-18, 20, 28-29 (RC)

As in the reading from Proverbs 25 (RCL first reading), the emphasis here is also on humility. All of our affairs in life should be conducted with humility (v. 17), and in so doing, we "will find favor with God" (v. 18). We are also summoned to intellectual modesty since some matters are "too sublime" for us and "beyond our strength" to understand (v. 20). Moreover, God's glory is made manifest in humility that recognizes our mortal limitations. The reading from Sirach concludes (vv. 28-29, NAB) by extolling the value of almsgiving, that is, showing mercy and kindness toward the poor by relieving their burdens. God will respond favorably to such kindness. Here, then, is an opportunity for the preacher to tell stories of genuine humility (Mother Teresa, for example) and to make the connection between humility and acts of kindness toward the poor.

JEREMIAH 2:4-13 (RCL, alt.)

"Cracked cisterns" or faulty pumps have been chosen by Israel instead of the fountain of living water that is their Lord. In this shocking choice, there has been an abandonment of God and a faulty alliance with evil.

Jeremiah's account of this reckless negligence starts with a history lesson, recalling the choices of the ancestors who first entered the land of Canaan. They forsook the Lord and wed themselves to the gods of Baal, fertility gods. As in

192

THE SEASON
OF PENTECOST

JEANNE
STEVENSON-
MOESSNER

modern-day genograms or family histories, we see repetitive patterns within families. The Lord also accuses the grandchildren of the first generation to enter Canaan; they, too, have found other gods. Jer. 2:4-13 reads like a legal indictment against Israel. In his commentary on Jeremiah, John Bracke observes, "In this lawsuit, God is the prosecutor and, finally, the judge; God's people are the accused. God brings charges against the people (vv. 4-9), conducts an interrogation (vv. 10-11), appeals to witnesses (v. 12), and finally renders a verdict (v. 13)."[15] Bracke views this passage as an occasion to consider our own unfaithfulness. Have we abandoned the Lord for lesser gods? Have we aligned ourselves with someone or something else that requires our primary allegiance? Are we truly living as if Christ was a living, gurgling fountain of life to us? Or are we operating out of cracked cisterns? There are many contemporary applications of this appalling text.

RESPONSIVE READING
PSALM 112 (RCL, BCP)

The same psalmist wrote Psalms 111 and 112, intending them to be a pair. Psalm 111 is a series of praises *by* those who delight in the Lord. Psalm 112 is a series of praises *for* those who delight in the Lord. In his commentary on the Psalms, James Luther Mays has noted that the external forms are similar: both are acrostic poems with twenty-two measures, each measure starting with the next letter of the alphabet (Hebrew).[16] Psalm 112 opens with a beatitude, "Happy are those who fear the Lord." This happiness is tied to keeping the commandments. Blessings such as wealth, riches, descendants, admirable qualities, righteousness, strength, and victory are enumerated. As pastors, we can surely preach on the truth of the text, but how can we utilize the particulars? We will see many from the pulpit who do fear the Lord and are bereft of many of the "blessings."

> BY FEARING THE LORD ONE ENTERS INTO THE WORKS THAT THE LORD BOTH MODELS AND EXTOLS.

I am reminded of an interview I observed at a private boys' school that utilizes military regimen and protocol for the life and discipline of its cadets. Happy are those who keep the rules of the school. I sat in on one interview and heard about the daily schedule starting with 6:00 A.M. reveille and shoe shining and ending with compulsory study hall and taps. I heard a lot of rules and an equal number of rewards. As I looked out of the commandant's window during this parallel presentation of both codes and kudos, I noticed five cadets in their athletic attire picking dandelions from the campus lawn. These boys were picking bags of dandelions! Unhappy are those who break the rules! When the interviewee asked what would happen when there was snow on the ground, the commandant replied: "I provide a shovel."

In Psalm 112, the psalmist is trying to say that by fearing the Lord one enters into the works that the Lord both models and extols. The hinge verse between the two psalms is Ps. 111:10. "The fear of the LORD is the beginning of wisdom; all those who practice it have good understanding." Mays makes this connection: "By their fear of the Lord, they (the upright) enter into the works of the Lord, who works on and on and through their lives. Their goodness is godliness."[17] Those picking dandelions or shoveling snow see this goodness, are angry, and gnash their teeth (v. 10).

PSALM 81:1, 10-16 (RCL, alt.)

This psalm is an elaboration of the first commandment: "I am the LORD your God, who brought you out of the land of Egypt . . . you shall have no other gods before me" (Exod. 20:2-3). This first commandment is quoted in Ps. 81:10. The narrator speaks in first person; thus the psalmist addresses the reader not only as an oracle of Yahweh, but as Yahweh, the LORD.

Yahweh delivers a narrative sermon. The narrative sets the historical background by reminding the listeners of their deliverance from the bondage of Egypt. Yahweh feeds stubborn Israel with the oral tradition. Yahweh wanted to feed them with the finest of wheat and with honey from the rocky crags (see Deuteronomy 32). "Open your mouth wide, and I will fill it," says Yahweh. Israel did not listen.

In locating prime real estate, the three criteria are "location, location, location." In pastoral care and in pastoral ministry, the emphasis is on listen, listen, listen. This listening is modeled by the request of God in Psalm 81 to listen to God's voice. This is the most important step in sermon preparation, for an inspirational sermon cannot proceed from a stubborn heart. A sermon proceeds from listening to God. In this way, a preacher and a congregation can be moved to open their mouths and echo the psalmist: "Sing aloud to God our strength; shout for joy to the God of Jacob" (v. 1).

PSALM 68:4-7, 10-11 (RC)

Psalm 68 is a very difficult and obscure psalm. In some ways, it appears to be a catalog of lyric poems consisting of the first lines of a series of ancient hymns. In general, the psalm is a communal song of thanksgiving -- an Israelite processional celebration of God's reign in the Temple. "Sing to God, chant praise to his name (v.5, NAB). God is generous to his people – a "defender of widows" (v.6, NAB); giver of "a house to the forsaken" (v. 7, NAB); one who restores "the land when it languished," providing it "for the needy" (vv. 10-11). God is generous and good – sing praises to his name!

SECOND READING

HEBREWS 13:1-8, 15-16 (RCL);
HEBREWS 13:1-8 (BCP);
HEBREWS 12:18-19, 22-24a (RC)

There are various types of learners: auditory, visual, kinesthetic, tactile, etc. In some ways, Hebrews 13 helps us "visualize" what it means to listen to God's voice. In other words, if the stubbornness of heart (as mentioned in Psalm 81) was replaced with a willing heart, if the deaf ears were replaced with receptive ones, what might one expect?

Hebrews 13 gives corporeality to the willingness and humility that God requests (Psalm 81). If a congregation were to "listen to God's voice," there would be hospitality to strangers, remembrance of those imprisoned and tortured, faithfulness in marriage, lack of greed, the dethronement of the idol mammon or money, and an appreciation for spiritual leaders and mentors. A spirit of contentment would settle upon parishioners as well as a sense of safety. "The LORD is my helper; I will not be afraid" (v. 6). There would be a sharing of wealth and a proliferation of good works. This abundance of Christian actions and this adherence to a Christian lifestyle would be "through him (Jesus)" (v. 15), and it would be deemed both a sacrifice within this relationship with Christ and the fruit of this union. Thus we are encouraged by the text to offer not only praise, but a sacrifice of praise. This, in turn, becomes the fruit of lips that confess the name of Jesus.

> THIS PASSAGE OF HEBREWS HELPS US "VISUALIZE" WHAT IT MEANS TO LISTEN TO GOD'S VOICE.

There will be some in your congregation who want to know how to have this relationship with Christ. Many others are really seeking to develop that relation. They seek spiritual and personal maturity. They hope to grow healthily in spiritual formation. They desire to live out in authentic ways their faith and commitment. This passage in Hebrews gives many specifics for the process of sanctification, a worthy topic for numerous sermons.

THE GOSPEL

LUKE 14:1, 7-14 (RCL, BCP, RC)

This Lukan text is of revolutionary caliber. If preached with passion and precise application, it could cause quite a stir in an established, staid, or traditional congregation. It is designed for those serious about spiritual formation and Christian maturity. It heralds a reversal of positions of power.

Jesus was being watched closely as he went to eat at the home of a Pharisee, a religious leader in a position of power. Jesus noticed how guests chose the places of honor, on the right and left hand of the host. He taught by a parable involving a wedding banquet. This parable is familiar, but the movement within the parable always goes against the mainstream movement of our culture. Christians are to seek the lowest places in the "seating order"; they are to move to the margins of privilege. It is not enough to stand patiently in a queue; we are told to go to the end of the queue or line. Furthermore, we are to associate through table fellowship with those who could never repay our invitation or initiative. The jockeying for power that we observe all around us—in seminaries, churches, judicatory bodies, theological circles, and academic guilds—is in contradistinction to what Jesus is teaching. Fyodor Dostoyevsky illustrates the origin of this countercultural movement in a parable of his own, spoken through Marmeladov in *Crime and Punishment:*

THIS LUKAN TEXT IS OF REVOLUTIONARY CALIBER. IF PREACHED WITH PASSION AND PRECISE APPLICATION, IT COULD CAUSE QUITE A STIR IN AN ESTABLISHED, STAID, OR TRADITIONAL CONGREGATION.

And when He (Christ) has finished judging all, He will summon us, too: "You, too, come forth," He will say, "Come forth, you drunkards; come forth, you weaklings; come forth, you shameless ones!" And we will all come forth unashamed. And we will stand before Him, and He will say: "You are swine, made in the image of the Beast, with his seal upon you: but you, too, come unto me!" And the wise and the clever will cry out: "Lord! why dost thou receive these people (men)?" And He will say: "I receive them, O wise and clever ones, because not one among them considered himself worthy of this. . . ." And He will stretch out His hands unto us, and we will fall down before Him and weep . . . and we will understand everything.

FOURTEENTH SUNDAY AFTER PENTECOST

TWENTY-THIRD SUNDAY IN ORDINARY TIME /
PROPER 18
SEPTEMBER 5, 2004

REVISED COMMON	EPISCOPAL (BCP)	ROMAN CATHOLIC
Deut. 30:15-20	Deut 30:15-20	Wisd. of Sol. 9:13-18b
or Jer. 18:1-11		
Psalm 1	Psalm 1	Ps. 90:3-6, 12-17
or 139:1-6, 13-18		
Philem. 1-21	Philem. 1-20	Philem. 9-10, 12-17
Luke 14:25-33	Luke 14:25-33	Luke 14:25-33

FIRST READING

DEUTERONOMY 30:15-20 (RCL, BCP)

Several lections in the Pentecost season have been constructed around the First Commandment: "I (Yahweh) am the LORD your God. . . .You shall have no other gods before me." Deuteronomy 30 calls for a decisive commitment to uphold this commandment. A preference will not do. A choice must be made.

In hortatory style, Moses closes this section of his address with an impassioned appeal. He equates loving God and following God's commandments as choosing life. Life is not only a quantity of days on this earth, but a qualitative relationship with Yahweh, the giver of life. Thus the spiritual meaning of this exhortation interlaces with the physical reality. The same is true of the term "death"; not only is material death meant, but a life that refuses to enter into a covenant with Yahweh is another and more potent form of demise.

IN MOSES' MESSAGE TO ISRAEL AND IN ITS APPLICATION TODAY, THERE IS NO WAVERING. ONE EITHER CHOOSES TO SERVE GOD OR DIE.

This section of Deuteronomy, Ian Cairns observes in *Word and Presence,* a commentary on the book of Deuteronomy, is like a "transcript of a covenant renewal ceremony in the plains of Moab."[18] The covenant ceremony contains a climactic moment: a choice of "grounding" the self and the nation is presented. There is life and prosperity on one side, death and adversity on the other. There is no middle ground. If the Promised Land or Canaan can be used to illustrate the side of blessings, then Egypt represents curse. It is either/or. One either leaves Egypt or remains in it. The demarcation line is the Red Sea, which represents no neutral zone or middle option.

It is quite common today to attempt to avoid either/or thinking by finding alternatives or options to problems and choices. Pastoral counselors and ministers often seek a middle way or third alternative in a situation that appears "stuck." In Moses' message to Israel and in its application today, there is no wavering. One either chooses to serve God or die.

WISDOM OF SOLOMON 9:13-18b (RC)

How can mere mortals discover and discern God's will? In this pericope from the Wisdom of Solomon, the sage asserts that the reasoning of mortals is worthless. It is Lady Wisdom who can teach what is right and set the paths of righteousness. As commentator James Reese states, Lady Wisdom communicates God's grace.[19] Wisdom's holy spirit is contrasted with the perishable designs of humankind. This passage attempts to address the question: How do we live out the godly life? (v. 13).

JEREMIAH 18:1-11 (RCL, alt.)

How does God shape the human soul? Jeremiah is given the image or prophetic parable of "the potter and the clay." Jeremiah visits a potter's house. The potter is working clay on a wheel, trying to shape something beautiful by design. However, the potter notices the vessel is misshapen. The potter, who is God, has the ability and power to rework and reshape the vessel on the wheel. This characteristic of the potter points to God's sovereignty. The potter can smash the vessel or pot that is malformed on the wheel.

A second theme of choice, however, is introduced by the "but if" construction in v. 8: "But if that nation (i.e., the vessel or Judah), concerning which I have spoken, turns from its evil, I will change my mind about the disaster that I intended to bring on it." Thus, while retaining and claiming the same sovereignty over outcome, God indicates that a nation has a role to play in the way that sovereign power is exerted over that nation. God is potter. God is also the wheel on which all clay is formed and all souls are shaped. Some clay may be too hardened to be fashioned in the way God had desired.

RESPONSIVE READING
PSALM 1 (RCL, BCP)

The either/or language continues in Psalm 1. Either you are with the wicked or with the righteous. Only two ways are presented: follow the advice of the wicked, take the path of the sinners, and sit in the seat of the scoffers, or delight in and meditate upon the Lord's law. The wicked will perish like chaff blown away by the wind; the righteous will prosper and be protected. Whereas the sinners are likened to dry chaff, which is subject to the vagrancy and capriciousness of the wind, the righteous are compared to a well-grounded tree that drinks deeply of water and bears luscious fruit and vibrant leaves in rhythm with the seasons.

Psalm 1 is a beatitude, a literary form popular in the postexilic period. The "law of the LORD" or Torah is being praised. Torah is instruction, given through commandments and proclamations, laid out in written form in various canonical texts, including this psalm. The Torah was given as a means of following the way of the Lord, a prosperous way into a safe place in this journey of life. The Torah of the Lord, James Luther Mays notes in his commentary on Psalms, is a body of tradition in which God "reaches, touches, and shapes the human soul . . . torah is a means of grace."[20]

PSALM 139:1-6, 13-18 (RCL, alt.)

Psalm 139 has two parts. The first part, vv. 1-18, is a groundswell of praise to God, the one who knows each person intimately. This knowledge is more intimate than found in any other relationship, whether marriage or partnership or friendship or parent-child relation. This God provides the context of who we are.

Psalm 139 gives a basis for an understanding of the self, a theological anthropology. The self is a wonderful work of God (v. 14), a design and not an accident of creation. The psalmist speaks in terms of I-Thou, me-you, addressing the creator God with both awe and familiarity. After all, this God both formed the inward parts of the psalmist and knit them together in the womb (v. 13). This, of course, is true for each person created by this inescapable God.

Psalm 139 is a favorite among women. It offers images of safety (v. 5a), loving caresses (v. 5b), and a doting gaze (vv. 3, 16). We all need to be the object of the gleam in someone's eye. Our earliest recollection of this ideally would be from a devoted parent. We all desire to be known, fully known and accepted. This is a universal desire, most eloquently expressed by certain mystics. God is offering such a comprehensive embrace, such a beaming look, such a vast sum of weighty thoughts (v. 17). This is the God whose way we follow, whose commandments we keep. This is the God who wins over our stubborn hearts and inspires us to praise.

SECOND READING

PHILEMON 1-21 (RCL);
PHILEMON 1-20 (BCP);
PHILEMON 9b-10, 12-17 (RC)

In many ways, this short letter illustrates or witnesses to life in Christ. The attitude of Paul toward the slave Onesimus is more than a matter of following a law or commandment. It is a movement of the heart, resulting in a controversial yet incontrovertible act: a petition to exonerate a runaway slave, to right his wrong or pay his debt, and to accept him in Christian fellowship as an equal. Paul offers to "stand in for him" as regards consequences for his misdeed. Furthermore, Paul asks Philemon, a Christian living in Colossae, to welcome the runaway slave "as you would welcome me." This bold petition is followed with no embarrassment or strain in the relationship. Rather, Paul advises Philemon to prepare the guest room for him (Paul).

> THE ATTITUDE OF PAUL TOWARD THE SLAVE ONESIMUS IS MORE THAN A MATTER OF FOLLOWING A LAW OR COMMANDMENT. IT IS A MOVEMENT OF THE HEART, RESULTING IN A CONTROVERSIAL YET INCONTROVERTIBLE ACT.

This is the shortest letter in the Pauline corpus but one of the most compactly passionate. The sequence of actions referred to in the letter is as follows: Philemon incurs a debt to Paul, who was the instrument of his conversion; Paul is in prison, and during his imprisonment, he meets the runaway slave Onesimus, whom he converts; Paul sends Onesimus back to Philemon as well as the letter which is carried by Tychicus. Two debts are referenced: Philemon's debt to Paul and Onesimus's debt to Philemon. Paul is inferring that both be canceled and any residue of debt be covered by himself (Paul).

During this period of time, household codes stipulated relationships between masters and servants. Under the rubric of these stylized codes of conduct, a master could arrest and brutally beat a runaway slave like Onesimus. Yet Paul is subverting these household codes by introducing "the family of faith" in which the slave will be treated as if he were the esteemed apostle and evangelist! Paul is so fervent in this hope and plea that he implores Philemon: "Refresh my heart in Christ." If Philemon acts as a brother in Christ to Onesimus, his actions will refresh the imprisoned Paul.

This is a post-Pentecost occurrence. It can happen again, this movement of the Spirit, this vision of forgiveness and equanimity, this refreshment of the heart.

THE GOSPEL
LUKE 14:25-33 (RCL, BCP, RC)

This Lukan passage centers on what it costs to enter a life with Christ. It reminds me of an incident when I was in my twenties and part of a singles group in a Protestant church. Several of us were given the assignment to pick up a well-known speaker at the airport and drive him to our church, which was a well-endowed congregation in a thriving urban setting. This speaker had his ministry on the streets of Newark, New Jersey. He ministered out of a plain coffee shop that would have been accessible to those of low income, or less. My friends and I prattled on and on about the blessings we enjoyed as Christians, the benefits we received, and the bounty of lively fellowship and activities in our singles group. About halfway home from the airport, our guest speaker swiveled around in the passenger's seat, turned to the three of us seated behind him, and quietly said: "And what has it cost you?"

> THIS LUKAN PASSAGE OFFERS YOU AS PASTOR THE OPPORTUNITY TO EXTOL THE BENEFITS OF FOLLOWING CHRIST AND TO EXTEND THE CHALLENGE: WHAT WILL IT COST YOU?

Jesus was traveling with large crowds, and he swiveled and told them: "It will cost you." Jesus spoke about the ostracism and misunderstanding and emotional cut-off that occurs when families of origin do not understand why their offspring are following Christ. Hating family would be committing an act of disgrace that would injure the honor of the nuclear family. Jesus talked about "hating life itself"; his cross would have to be carried through places where the refrain would be "crucify." Jesus asked his followers to count the cost ahead of time, like a builder estimating his expenses on a tower, or like a king tabulating the numerical strength of his military might. Then, as if an afterthought, Jesus drew one more boundary: possessions must be left behind. In the early church, the traveling missionaries were asked to shoulder these costs. This Lukan passage offers you as pastor the opportunity to extol the benefits of following Christ and to extend the challenge: What will it cost you?

FIFTEENTH SUNDAY AFTER PENTECOST

TWENTY-FOURTH SUNDAY IN ORDINARY TIME / PROPER 19
SEPTEMBER 12, 2004

REVISED COMMON	EPISCOPAL (BCP)	ROMAN CATHOLIC
Exod. 32:7-14 or Jer. 4:11-12, 22-28	Exod. 32:1, 7-14	Exod. 32:7-11, 13-14
Ps. 51:1-10 or Psalm 14	Ps. 51:1-8 or 51:1-11	Ps. 51:3-4, 12, 13, 17-19
1 Tim. 1:12-17	1 Tim. 1:12-17	1 Tim. 1:12-17
Luke 15:1-10	Luke 15:1-10	Luke 15:1-32 or 15:1-10

FIRST READING

EXODUS 32:7-14 (RCL); EXODUS 32:1, 7-14 (BCP); EXODUS 32:7-11, 13-14 (RC)

While Moses was on Mount Sinai, the Israelites waiting on him to return grew anxious. They did not know what had happened to him. Moses had brought them up out of the land of Egypt and now, for all they knew, he was gone. Perhaps he was the victim of a wild beast or of lightning and smoke. Perhaps he gazed on the LORD and perished. The Israelites were fearful and alone. They approached Aaron and requested that he build something they could count on to last, to go before them in procession, to stay with them. Aaron was to fashion gods for them, gods they could control.

The LORD God was very angry with the image of the golden calf that Aaron formed, with the altar that was built for it, and with the festival to celebrate this "dependable, predictable god," this golden calf. As stiff-necked people, the Israelites could walk proudly behind the calf on their wilderness journey.

The LORD God was so angry that God's wrath was hot and ready to consume the Israelite people. Moses, however, would be saved and would be the progenitor of a nation. Yet Moses pleaded with God to avert the disaster. First, he pleaded the case of continuity: Why would God bring them this far to destroy them? Second, Moses argued the point of perception: The Egyptians would falsely perceive

202

THE SEASON
OF PENTECOST

JEANNE
STEVENSON-
MOESSNER

that the Israelites' God had evil intent in luring the Israelites out of Egypt. Third, Moses advocated from ancestry: Remember the oath of longevity sworn to Abraham, Isaac, and Israel. Then follows one of the most debated and enigmatic statements in the Hebrew Bible: Yahweh's mind was changed (v. 14). Here is a God whose laws are immutable, whose commandments are not to be broken, yet a God whose mind can be swayed. Is Moses standing before an unpredictable God?

The Second Reading for this Fifteenth Sunday after Pentecost, 1 Tim. 1:12-17, and the Gospel in Luke 15 offer insights into this puzzlement. God's "unpredictability" is evidenced by overflowing grace, mercy, and utmost patience in light of our own sinfulness and that of the Israelites. The golden calf was predictable with its immovable response to the folly of its worshipers. In fact, one could say that God's "unpredictable response" to the breaking of the first commandment was the heart of God's dependability. As Paul confessed: "But I received mercy because I had acted ignorantly in unbelief" (1 Tim. 1:13b).

Is Moses standing before an unpredictable God?

There are many places in this Exodus text for your sermon to center: our tendency to fashion substitutions for God in our anxiety and fear; God's wrath; the efficacy of prayer; God's mercy. We cannot overlook the pastoral anguish expressed by Moses for his people, a passion felt so deeply that Moses boldly implored God. This passion is a profoundly spiritual place, a space from which a sermon originates.

JEREMIAH 4:11-12, 22-28 (RCL, alt.)

Jeremiah begins with a reference to the invasion of the land of Judah. He employs both militaristic and meteorological images to describe God's wrath toward Jerusalem: a hot wind, clouds, chariots like the whirlwind, horses swifter than eagles (vv. 11-13). God, through the spokesperson Jeremiah, is proclaiming judgment on the wickedness in Judah.

Jeremiah feels such sorrow for the foolish people of Judah, his people, God's people. Jeremiah himself is a citizen of Judah. Now he speaks from the heart of a prophet who is filled with grief, anguish, and anger. He calls his people foolish, stupid children. Verse 23 introduces a vision of chaos Jeremiah imagines: a void, a waste, absence of light, quaking mountains, no inhabitants, no birds, a desert of desolation. It is an Armageddon, a catastrophic conflict. There are many levels on which to read this doom for the nation. The LORD implies, however, that it is not the final denouement, the grand finale. The hint of hope is given in v. 27: "For thus says the LORD: The whole land shall be a desolation; yet I will not make a full end."

Pastors fulfill the role of priest, wise person, and prophet/ess. There are times when we do feel the sorrow of Jeremiah. We anguish and "writhe in pain" (v. 19). That is perhaps why John Bracke, in his commentary on Jeremiah 1-19, writes, "Prophets are those among us who give expression to the anguish we all should feel."[21] This text gives you as pastoral prophet the occasion to express for society and for your congregation the pain that God must feel when foolishness, stupidity, and evil are practiced on this earth.

203

FIFTEENTH
SUNDAY
AFTER PENTECOST
─────────
SEPTEMBER 12

RESPONSIVE READING

PSALM 51:1-10 (RCL);
PSALM 51:1-11 (BCP, alt.);
PSALM 51:3-4, 12, 13, 17-19 (RC)

The responsive reading is a psalm of deep remorse. David broke two commandments by committing adultery with Bathsheba and by arranging for Uriah the Hittite, Bathsheba's husband, to be slaughtered. David begs for mercy on the basis of God' steadfast love and abundant mercy toward him, the sinner.

Imagery of cleansing and washing flow through and through this psalm. David asks to be washed thoroughly, cleansed, purged with hyssop, scrubbed whiter than snow. David had the sweat and scent of an adulterous relationship on his skin and the blood of an innocent soldier/husband on his conscience and heart. It is with heavy remorse that David cries: "Wash me thoroughly from my iniquity, and cleanse me from my sins" (v. 1).

Although the superscription identifies this psalm as one of David's, its usage has been varied. It has been sung or spoken as a general penitential prayer, not only during and after the exile of Israel but in contemporary worship as a standard prayer of confession for the community. John Calvin, Martin Luther, and Karl Barth saw Psalm 51 "as a text for reflection on Christian doctrine," notes Psalms commentator James Luther Mays. Mays has aptly underscored the fact that, in the Old Testament, it is inconceivable that a person could sin without injuring others.[22] Thus Psalm 51 is an individual lament but one that affects the well-being of the sinner's community.

In pastoral ministry, we are trained to help people express their feelings by speaking in the first person. For example, "I feel sad," "I feel hurt," "I am responsible," "I am an alcoholic." These statements show ownership. In this psalm of confession and petition, David proclaims: "I am guilty," "I am the problem." In the imperative, David or the psalmist speaking for David rightly addresses the source of the solution: "(You, O God) Create in me a clean heart." (v. 10). With one moment of panic, he also exclaims: "Do not cast me away from your presence, and do not take your holy spirit from me."

This is a psalm with a range of emotion, disarming honesty, and serious sins. Your congregation will connect readily with all of these aspects.

PSALM 14 (RCL, alt.)

We have all sinned and gone astray; we have all fallen short of what God intended for us. The psalmist targets a particular group: fools or people who deny the existence of God. The Hebrew for fool, *nabal,* is illustrated by the story of a man named Nabal in 1 Samuel 25. It is not that he was the dunce or class clown; it is not that he was incompetent, silly, or dumb. In fact, Nabal was successful and very rich in sheep and goats. However, Nabal made a very great miscalculation, and he died for it. This is the way of a "nabal" or fool: to live life in a miscalculation of reality. To say there is no God, and to act accordingly, is to play the fool.

THIS IS A PSALM WITH A RANGE OF EMOTION, DISARMING HONESTY, AND SERIOUS SINS.

SECOND READING
1 TIMOTHY 1:12-17 (RCL, BCP, RC)

Is there hope for the sinner? For the fool? Paul uses himself as a personal example of the foremost or grandest of sinners. Before Paul's conversion to the Christian faith, he had persecuted Christians; he had been a blasphemer and a perpetrator of violence. He had played the fool. According to Acts 8:3, "Saul (Paul) was ravaging the church by entering house after house; dragging off both men and women, he committed them to prison." He created an Armageddon.

PAUL OFFERS HIS LIFE AS A "HYPOTYPOSIS" OR PARADIGM OR PROTOTYPE FOR ALL WHO DESIRE TO RECEIVE CHRIST'S MERCY.

Paul describes a drastic behavioral conversion as the result of God's intervention: "Christ Jesus came into the world to save sinners" (v. 15). This theological truth is at the core of what we preach and believe. If we do not believe it, we really should not preach at all.

For all of the post-Pentecost lections we have read that describe the breaking of commandments and the ungodliness of God's people, here is a vivid description of the hope on which our faith rests: Christ Jesus came into the world to save sinners. Paul offers his life as a "hypotyposis" or paradigm or prototype for all who desire to receive Christ's mercy. Paul was converted. The grace of the Lord overflowed for him with the faith and love that are in Christ Jesus (v. 14).

LUKE 15:1-10 (RCL, BCP, RC)

When I was a child, I was taught that if I were the only person on earth, Christ would have died for me. The reaction I had to this statement was awareness that I must be very special to God. These two parables in Luke, one lost sheep out of one hundred and one lost coin out of ten coins, impress me in the same way.

The setting of these parables in Luke holds significance for its interpretation and application. The swirls of people around Jesus now include "all the tax collectors and sinners," the undesirables, the unclean, and the unpopular. The Pharisees and scribes, who were desirable, clean, and popular were very upset. Recalling Luke 14, we remember that Jesus had earlier eaten in the home of a prominent Pharisee.

> JESUS AFFECTS A REVERSAL; HE IS NOW THE HOST OF A BASILEIA BANQUET THAT WELCOMES THE LONE SHEEP AND MISSING COIN (I.E., THE SINNERS), TO TABLE IN GOD'S PRESENCE.

He had told parables in this setting, parables that attempted to illustrate humility and inclusiveness at God's table of fellowship. The religious dignitaries around him in this setting of Luke 15 obviously had not heard or accepted the message and meaning of these parables. Instead, the ecclesiastical authorities murmured: "This fellow welcomes sinners and eats with them" (v. 2).

Jesus uses three parables of "lost and found," two of which are in the lectionary for this Sunday. In the first parable, the worried shepherd leaves ninety-nine sheep in the wilderness to hunt for the lost one of the flock. In the second parable, a woman loses one of ten silver coins, possibly her dowry; then in darkness, she lights a lamp, sweeps the house, and searches meticulously until she finds it (v. 8). Like the shepherd, she is so relieved and joyful that she calls in friends and neighbors to celebrate. What was lost has been found.

The Pharisees probably liked these parables or stories with a hidden meaning. When the meaning, however, became evident, they surely were defiant and resistant. "In both instances," David P. Moessner writes in his treatment of this passage in *Lord of the Banquet*, "Jesus does not allow the point to escape his Pharisees-scribes audience: He is like the shepherd and the woman by seeking out the lost and separated folk from society and bringing them to the table fellowship of repentant sinners (15:7, 10)."[23] Thus Jesus affects a reversal; he is now the host of a *basileia* banquet that welcomes the lone sheep and missing coin (i.e., the sinners), to table in God's presence. The question to your congregation through the sermon can be: Who is missing from our table?

SIXTEENTH SUNDAY AFTER PENTECOST

TWENTY-FIFTH SUNDAY IN ORDINARY TIME /
PROPER 20
SEPTEMBER 19, 2004

REVISED COMMON	EPISCOPAL (BCP)	ROMAN CATHOLIC
Amos 8:4-7	Amos 8:4-7, (8-12)	Amos 8:4-7
or Jer. 8:18—9:1		
Psalm 113	Psalm 138	Ps. 113:1-2, 4-6, 7-8
or 79:1-9		
1 Tim. 2:1-7	1 Tim. 2:1-8	1 Tim. 2:1-8
Luke 16:1-13	Luke 16:1-13	Luke 16:1-13 or 16:10-13

FIRST READING
AMOS 8:4-7 (RCL, RC);
AMOS 8:4-7, (8-12) (BCP)

This passage from Amos addresses a particular group of people, the prosperous and immoral businesspeople of the city, probably Samaria or Bethel. "Hear this" cries the indignant prophet, "the LORD God will not forget your misdeeds." These misdeeds include "trampling the needy" and ruining the poor by false business practices: the ephahs or baskets were undersized, thus the indignant customer did not receive the full amount of purchase; the shekels or weights placed in the scales were too heavy for the true quantity being purchased; and the scales or balances were false and rigged (v. 5). The prophets Hosea and Micah, too, speak of such dishonesty in the business community of the eighth century. And Amos points out the travesty of the slave trade where slaves were sold for the equivalent of a pair of sandals. And Amos exposes the practice of impure merchandise when sweepings or trash is mixed in with the good wheat to add bulk (v. 6).

> AMOS IS MAKING THE POINT THAT ONE'S FAITH IN GOD CANNOT BE SEPARATED FROM ONE'S DAILY LIFE AND PRACTICE.

Amos is making the point that one's faith in God cannot be separated from one's daily life and practice. These businesspeople actually "keep the Sabbath" by worshiping in the synagogue and observing a holy day of rest. Their minds are not at rest, however, because they are focused on getting the Sabbath over with so they can make more money (v. 5a). Amos concludes that these "devout" people are really worshiping the god of money and the goddess of greed.

The consequence is deadly. Verses 8-12 follow as the aftermath of Armageddon. The sun disappears, as will the word of the LORD. The land will be in upheaval, reminiscent of the tossing and sinking of the Nile River waters in Egypt. The people will run from north to east, from sea to sea, but they will not find the word of the LORD for which they thirst and hunger. It will be so great a loss that it will be as losing an only son. The people will remain desolate, with shorn hair, draped in sackcloth, despairing and alone.

This lectionary text points to the connection between our Sunday worship and our weekday practices. Faith and daily living cannot be disassociated. Rather, our worship on Sunday and other practices of Sabbath-keeping should give us not only Christian insight into our professional practices, but the principles to undergird our workplace. Furthermore, Sabbath-keeping empowers us through the indwelling of the Holy Spirit to put this insight and these principles into effect. The coming of the Holy Spirit at Pentecost enables us to do so.

JEREMIAH 8:18—9:1 (RCL, alt.)

Gilead, meaning "strong" and "rocky," was a mountainous region east of the Jordan River. It was the home of Elijah; it was the last meeting place between Jacob and Laban, and was the scene of the battle between Gideon and the Midianites. Gilead was known for its balm, an odiferous resin of the styrax tree; the balm was used as a famous medicinal ointment.

In the biblical text, Jeremiah cries out with great agony and pathos: "Is there no balm in Gilead? Is there no physician here?" His grief is pervasive, his heart is sick within. Jeremiah calls the inhabitants of Judah "my poor people" and shows the brokenheartedness that a parent can feel over a child, in this case, an oppositional defiant child. Jeremiah loves Judah as one would love a child. Frederick Buechner in *Now and Then,* calls this vulnerable loving. "To love another, as you love a child, is to become vulnerable in a whole new way . . . when it comes to the hurt of a child you love, you are all but helpless. The child makes terrible mistakes, and there is very little you can do to ease (the) pain."[24] Jeremiah calls out in suffering for these people who are like children to him: "Is there no balm in Gilead?" And the answer is no. There is no balm for Judah, for their wound is infected with pride, gangrenous with idolatry, and terminal with unrepentance. In short, Judah will not give up her idols, repent, and turn to God. Jeremiah is sick at heart, for he knows of the unrepentance. Without repentance, there is no balm in Gilead to heal a nation of sin-sick souls.

We gather together in worship for this very purpose: to repent, to give up idols, to confess, to prepare our hearts for healing, to turn to God. We cry out: "Is there

208

THE SEASON
OF PENTECOST

JEANNE
STEVENSON-
MOESSNER

a balm in Gilead?" We cry out in need of renewal: "Is there no physician here?" It is easy to feel trapped and overcome by adversity, imprisoned with self-doubt and recriminations.

Yet the good news we preach is that there is a balm in Gilead. We receive the poultice of prayer, the elixir of fellowship as we break bread together and drink of Christ's cup. Confessing our unworthiness to approach Christ's table, we are anointed as with balm from Gilead. The open sores of doubt and guilt, the lacerations of fear and lostness, the bruises of competition and power, the blisters of vain quests are all tended—one by one—by the Great Physician. There is a balm in Gilead.

RESPONSIVE READING

PSALM 113 (RCL);
PSALM 113:1-2, 4-6, 7-8 (RC)

God sets the example of acting to correct injustices and inequities. God shows us how to live out our faith as discussed above in Amos 8:4-7. The sovereign of the universe tries to give us object lessons by raising the poor from the dust and by lifting the needy from the ash heap and placing them with the princes. How is this done today without our assistance? The coming of the Holy Spirit at Pentecost has enabled us to see this vision. It is a vision from God's perspective, described by the psalmist as a perspective from one "who is seated on high," looking down on the heavens and the earth (vv. 5, 6). The psalmist praises the name of this God who is incomparable.

GOD REVERSES THE FORTUNE OF THE MARGINALIZED AND HELPS THE NEEDY.

The psalm is a movement in three parts. The first movement is a praise hymn to God who is high above the heavens (vv. 1-3). The second movement describes the exalted position of this sovereign (vv. 4-6). The third movement, James Luther Mays notes in his commentary on Psalms, describes the "condescension" of God to help the lowly and needy (vv. 7-9).[25] The barren women of scripture, the matriarchs like Sarah, Rebekah, Rachel, Samson's mother, and Hannah, after years of infertility and embarrassment, were all blessed by God with fertility and sons. Thus God reverses the fortune of the marginalized and helps the needy.

One approach to this text through the sermon is to contrast the movement within this psalm to the reality all around us. The needy remain in their need and the poor in their poverty. The contrast will underscore the responsibility of Christians to help God close the gap between the intended basileia and the uneven world in which we live. The Holy Spirit given at Pentecost empowers us to close the gap.

PSALM 79:1-9 (RCL, alt.)

The fall of Jerusalem in 587 B.C.E. to the Babylonians is the situation out of which this psalm arose. The holy Temple in Jerusalem was defiled; Israelites were slaughtered and left as vittles for the birds and wild animals. Their blood was poured out like water all around Jerusalem. The land was devastated. The people of Israel were shamed and mocked. They cry out: "How long, O Lord?" "Will you be angry forever?" "Will your jealous wrath burn like fire?" (v. 5). There is true repentance in this psalm as the Israelites appeal to God's glory. The honor of God's name is at stake. They ask to be pardoned for the sins of their ancestors, and they appeal to God's compassion.

Second Reading
1 TIMOTHY 2:1-7 (RCL);
1 TIMOTHY 2:1-8 (BCP, RC)

First Timothy is known as one of "The Pastorals," because it was written to give pastoral advice to church leaders. There is a direct link between doctrine and behavior; for example, Christ gave himself as a ransom for all, therefore we should pray for everyone. Hoping that Christians could lead a quiet and peaceable life in all godliness and dignity (v. 2), the writer of 1 Timothy advocates for prayers for those in high government positions.

The Christology is central in this passage. Just as there is one God, there is one mediator between God and humankind, Christ Jesus (v. 5). This does not lead to a universalist view, but to an outreach to all people, that they might know the One who was a ransom for all. Instead of lifting up hands to hurt or hit, the writer desires that men lift up their hands without anger or argument, thus, as "holy hands" (v. 8).

The Gospel
LUKE 16:1-13 (RCL, BCP, RC)

In this complex and often confusing parable, it is important to remember the message: You cannot serve or be devoted to both God and wealth (v. 13). Jesus gives a parable to his disciples, while the Pharisees are listening. Jesus is trying to prepare his followers to be responsible and shrewd managers of their communal resources. To quote Sharon Ringe in her Luke commentary, "For the disciples, this parable provides a 'management model' for their own role as leaders . . . ; it challenges them to manage wealth in the role of justice."[26]

210

THE SEASON
OF PENTECOST
_____

JEANNE
STEVENSON-
MOESSNER

The parable opens with the firing of a manager by the manager's employer, a rich man with a lot of property. The owner was something of an absentee landlord; in other words, the tenants did not see him or deal with him directly. Before word got out that the manager was to be dismissed, the manager acted quickly and shrewdly. Since he was facing unemployment, he wanted to leave on a popular note with the tenants in the hopes they would welcome him with hospitality into their homes. So he summoned his master's debtors one by one and reduced all their debts. He had them rewrite the bill of debt in their own hand.

WE AS MANAGERS OF GOD'S WEALTH ARE ALSO CALLED TO REDUCE THE DISPARITY BETWEEN THE POOR AND WEALTHY.

Commentators have suggested that the owner was perpetuating an unjust system, perhaps by charging usurious interest in violation of Torah. We are really not clear on the internal accounting system of the owner. What is clear by the end of the parable is that the manager has righted an injustice. As Ringe concludes: "By reducing the amount owed by the (obviously poorer) debtors to the rich man, the manager is doing justice—a way of doing his job as a 'manager of injustice' that no longer aims at perpetuating and even adding to old inequities, but instead reflects the new 'economy' of which Jesus is the herald."[27]

In the season of Pentecost, we as managers of God's wealth are also called to reduce the disparity between the poor and wealthy. We are expected to act quickly and shrewdly in such a way that we, like the manager, will be welcomed by those who have less. This parable is a teaching about God's desired economy.

SEVENTEENTH SUNDAY AFTER PENTECOST

TWENTY-SIXTH SUNDAY IN ORDINARY TIME /
PROPER 21
SEPTEMBER 26, 2004

REVISED COMMON	EPISCOPAL (BCP)	ROMAN CATHOLIC
Amos 6:1a, 4-7	Amos 6:1-7	Amos 6:1a, 4-7
or Jer. 32:1-3a, 6-15		
Psalm 146	Psalm 146	Ps. 146:7, 8-9, 9-10
or 91:1-6, 14-16	or 146:4-9	
1 Tim. 6:6-19	1 Tim. 6:11-19	1 Tim. 6:11-16
Luke 16:19-31	Luke 16:19-31	Luke 16:19-31

FIRST READING
AMOS 6:1a, 4-7 (RCL, RC);
AMOS 6:1-7 (BCP)

As I write these comments on Amos 6, the seminary carillon is playing "God Bless America." How ironic that Amos is announcing that God will not bless the "ruin of Joseph" because the ruling classes of Israel (at ease in Zion) and the privileged of Judah (secure on the hill of Samaria) are self-indulgent, proud, ensconced in their material superiority, and indifferent to social realities around them. As commentator Bruce C. Birch notes, "Elsewhere Amos has described social conditions in which the poor and weak are exploited, the law courts are corrupted, illegal business practices abound, worship has grown hypocritical, and justice is not honored."[28] However, the "notables" of Israel and Judah have a nationalistic arrogance (v. 2b) that Amos feels is unfounded and dangerous. This false assessment of superiority and might could result in "a reign of violence."

> WILL GOD BLESS AMERICA? THIS TEXT FROM AMOS OFFERS US WARNINGS AND CONDITIONS FOR THIS BLESSING.

Granted, Israel and Judah were experiencing a period of political peace and material prosperity; the powers of Egypt and Assyria were not being invasive and trade was going well for the upper classes of Israel and Judah. However, a sense of security based on material advantage had set in for those rich enough to eat meat, amuse themselves with music, drink wine from bowls instead of more modest

212

THE SEASON
OF PENTECOST
———
JEANNE
STEVENSON-
MOESSNER

cups, bathe and anoint themselves with oil, and be at leisure and lounge on their fine couches. Their minds were preoccupied with their well-being and sense of national invulnerability. Amos prophesies that they will be the first to go into exile. He predicts the end of "the revelry of the loungers."

Will God bless America? This text from Amos offers us warnings and conditions for this blessing. Although Amos was targeting the indifferent privileged of Israel and Judah, Birch observes, "God's wrath will be directed equally at churches who sought only the comfort of their own sanctuaries and the resourcing of their own programs without regard to the brokenness of the world to which they were sent."[29]

JEREMIAH 32:1-3a, 6-15 (RCL, alt.)

Our ultimate trust in God is based upon God's character. God is good; God is great; God is just; God is faithful. It is this last characteristic that is best illustrated by Jeremiah in an object lesson—the purchase of a family field. This field was located in his hometown of Anathoth. Jeremiah's cousin Hanamel must have lost possession of this field due to personal financial difficulties. In ancient Israel, family land was considered a gift from God, a sacred trust, and a holy inheritance. To lose family land was to lose part of the family's "inheritance." One's relationship to the land was not the sum total of one's relationship to God, of course, but it was a part of that relationship. When a family member lost land, therefore, the relatives had an obligation to "redeem" it. God told Jeremiah that Hanamel would say, "Buy my field, . . . for the right of possession and redemption is yours; buy it for yourself" (v. 8). Verses 9-14 contain details of the transaction of purchase and redemption.

The timing of this purchase is important because it was not the time to buy land! The opening verse gives us the historical setting: the last year of King Zedekiah of Judah's reign—587 B.C.E.—just before Judah fell to Babylon. Jeremiah had been predicting this fall to Babylon and had consequently come into disfavor with the leadership of Judah. In fact, he had been rejected as a prophet of God and was imprisoned. Thus this public act of "redeeming land" was the illustration of Jeremiah's sermon: God would allow Babylon to overtake Jerusalem. God would pluck up and pull down Judah (Jer. 1:10), but the import of Jeremiah's real estate transaction was that God would someday "redeem" Judah. This is the message of hope that constitutes the ending of this "sermon." It is where sermons should end. There will be times when we are overthrown by evil and the consequences of our actions; but God promises to rebuild and restore us, to redeem us, because God holds the "deed of purchase" in Christ.

PSALM 146 (RCL, BCP);
PSALM 146:7, 8-9, 9-10 (RC)

Psalm 146 is the first of the five "Hallelujah psalms" that conclude the Psalter. Its central message is a reminder to put our ultimate trust in the God of Jacob and not in princes, rulers, presidents, congressmen and women, governors, and other mortals. Only God keeps faith and lives forever. Earthly leaders can only carry out short-term plans and reforms. It is God alone who executes justice for the oppressed, gives food to the hungry, sets prisoners free, restores sight to the blind, lifts the lowly, watches over strangers, orphans, and widows, loves the righteous, and ruins

> THE PSALMIST SUMMONS US TO PRAISE THIS GOD AND GROUND OUR TRUST IN THIS GOD'S CHARACTER, RATHER THAN MISPLACING OUR PRAISE AND TRUST IN GOVERNMENT OFFICIALS.

the wicked. The psalmist summons us to praise this God and ground our trust in this God's character, rather than misplacing our praise and trust in government officials. This God of Jacob has long-term plans for reform. Our allegiance belongs to this God who will "stand beside us and guide us" in this re-formation.

PSALM 91:1-6, 14-16 (RCL, alt.)

Many dangers surround our lives. As Christians, we do not resort to charms, magic, superstition, amulets, formulas, and psychics to deal with anxieties. We look to God as our ultimate refuge and protection. There are many and mixed images of God's protection in Psalm 91: the shelter of the Most High, the shadow of the Almighty, refuge, fortress, God's wings and pinions (the end joints of a bird's wings), shield, and buckler (a small ground shield). Danger stalks both day and night, yet God promises, "Those who love me, I will deliver" (v. 14). God promises to answer those who call, to rescue and to protect. This is a place of trust that is often difficult to reach. As pastors, we are asked not only to state this place of trust, but to stand in it.

I am reminded of a visit I made to Wittenberg Lutherstadt in 1979. Wittenberg was in East Germany at that time. I wanted to see the university where Martin Luther and Melanchthon had taught. The church door on which Luther had nailed his theses was also in Wittenberg. Across from these doors were military canons aimed in the direction of the church. In some ways, Psalm 91 is like this setup. We and the members of our congregations are surrounded by many terrors. We cannot preach on how God will rescue us from all our individualized trou-

JEANNE
STEVENSON-
MOESSNER

bles. But we can preach that no matter what is aimed against us, the church of Jesus Christ will stand and be delivered.

SECOND READING

1 TIMOTHY 6:6–19 (RCL);
1 TIMOTHY 6:11–19 (BCP);
1 TIMOTHY 6:11–16 (RC)

The advice to Timothy is the advice to all Christians: There is "great gain in godliness combined with contentment" (v. 6). There will not be one person in your congregation who does not desire contentment. What counsel will your sermon provide for them to live the contented life?

This passage of 1 Timothy offers wisdom and cautions for the Christian journey. We were all born as naked, vulnerable infants. We entered this world from the uterine fluids with no possessions, no land, no jewels, no money markets, no investments, no homes, no clothing. That is exactly the way we shall exit. If we have food and clothing while on this earth, we should be content with these. Contentment is being satisfied to travel this Christian path with the necessities and be at peace. We travel light and lighthearted. When the love of money and possessions roots in our hearts, it encumbers our journey, it endangers our sense of direction, and we can wander away from the faith (v. 10). If a Christian happens to be rich, she is not to set her hopes on the uncertainty of riches, but to share and be generous with that wealth (v. 18).

> CONTENTMENT IS BEING SATISFIED TO TRAVEL THIS CHRISTIAN PATH WITH THE NECESSITIES AND BE AT PEACE.

Timothy is asked to recall his "ordination" as a follower of God, as a pastor to his people (v. 12). Timothy made a "good confession" of faith before many witnesses. Timothy is reminded of Jesus' "good confession" before Pilate (see John 18:36–37). Jesus tells Pilate that his kingdom or *basileia* is not of this world. Otherwise Jesus' followers would be fighting on his behalf. By inference, Jesus claims to be king. This reference in 1 Tim. 6:13 to the "good fight of faith" makes sense in light of Jesus' words to Pilate. Timothy is to "fight" or struggle on Christ's behalf by pursuing godliness, righteousness, faith, love, endurance, and gentleness. Timothy's allegiance is to the king of kings, to Christ as the only sovereign. The military imagery of fighting and the language of "kingship" will not work well in all homiletical settings. The question of this passage is to whom do we give our heart: to the god of riches or to the God who richly provides us with everything for our enjoyment (v. 17)?

LUKE 16:19-31 (RCL, BCP, RC)

This passage relates to the previous concern in Luke 16, the responsibility of the wealthy for the poor. The Pharisees who were lovers of money (16:14) heard Jesus tell a story about a rich man and a beggar named Lazarus. It is noteworthy that the beggar has a specific name in this text; we are already alerted to the bias of the story. The beggar, Lazarus, will be favored.

The story begins with a tantalizing description of the rich man who is dressed in sumptuous apparel and who dines lavishly. In contrast, at his gate lies a poor, ulcerated beggar named Lazarus. The dogs dine on Lazarus as they lick the pus oozing from his sores. Possibly the rich man had stepped over the languishing corpus of Lazarus. We do know, from later in the parable, that the rich man had noticed him at his gates. Then, both men receive equal treatment: They die. Lazarus is carried away by angels to be with Abraham. The rich man is transported to Hades where he is tormented and dehydrated. With calculated manipulation in his voice, he calls out "Father Abraham." The rich man would like to acquire Lazarus as his servant to run to and from and fetch him some drops of water for his parched tongue. Abraham announces the great reversal that has occurred and addresses him as "child" in response to his plea to "Father Abraham": "Child, remember that during your lifetime you received your good things, and Lazarus in the like manner evil things; but now he is comforted here, and you are in agony" (v. 25). To make matters worse, for the rich man in Hades there was a great inseparable chasm between them.

It was even too late for the rich man's five brothers, who had not heeded Moses and the prophets. The rich man had hoped to command Lazarus as servant to run back to his mansion and warn his five brothers. Alas, the wealth that had afforded him such power to command people on earth survived neither death nor the flames of hell. Sharon Ringe, in her *Luke* commentary, elucidates this concern for the rich man's five brothers: "The biological family, and not a wider or more inclusive community, continues to function

> LUKE 16 REMINDS US THAT OUR TENACITY IS NOT TO GREED, AND OUR WAY IS NOT EMPOWERED BY PERSONAL MIGHT TOWARD ECONOMIC INJUSTICE.

as his principal, (even his only) point of reference, security, and concern."[30] Used as a post-Pentecost sermon text, Luke 16 reminds us that our tenacity is not to greed, and our way is not empowered by personal might toward economic injustice; rather, our tenacity is to the risen Christ and our way is empowered by the Holy Spirit toward economic and social justice.

216

THE SEASON
OF PENTECOST

JEANNE
STEVENSON-
MOESSNER

Notes

1. James Luther Mays, *Psalms,* Interpretation (Louisville: John Knox, 1994).

2. Jeanne Stevenson-Moessner, "Incarnational Theology: Restructuring Developmental Theory," in *In Her Own Time: Women and Developmental Issues in Pastoral Care,* edited by Jeanne Stevenson-Moessner (Minneapolis: Fortress Press, 2000).

3. Jeanne Stevenson-Moessner, *The Spirit of Adoption: At Home in God's Family* (Louisville: Westminster John Knox, 2003).

4. Dorothee Soelle, *The Strength of the Weak: Toward a Christian Feminist Identity,* trans. Robert and Rita Kimber (Philadelphia: Westminster Press, 1984).

5. Rosemary Radford Ruether, *Mary, the Feminine Face of God* (Philadelphia: Westminster John Knox, 1977).

6. Walter Brueggemann, *To Pluck Up, to Tear Down: A Commentary on the Book of Jeremiah 1–25* (Grand Rapids: Eerdmans, 1988), 206.

7. Charles V. Gerkin, *An Introduction to Pastoral Care* (Nashville: Abingdon, 1997).

8. Walter Brueggemann, *Isaiah 1–39* (Louisville: Westminster John Knox, 1998), 228.

9. R. E. Clements, *Jeremiah,* Interpretation (Atlanta: John Knox, 1988), 15.

10. John M. Bracke, *Jeremiah 1–29* (Louisville: Westminster John Knox, 2000), 18.

11. Mays, *Psalms,* 326.

12. Thomas G. Long, *Hebrews,* Interpretation (Louisville: John Knox, 1997).

13. Sharon H. Ringe, *Luke* (Louisville: Westminster John Knox, 1995), 187.

14. Leo G. Perdue, *Proverbs,* Interpretation (Louisville: John Knox, 2000), 224.

15. Bracke, *Jeremiah 1–29,* 25–26.

16. Mays, *Psalms.*

17. Ibid, 360.

18. Ian Cairns, *Word and Presence: A Commentary on the Book of Deuteronomy* (Grand Rapids: Eerdmans, 1992), 263.

19. James M. Reese, *The Book of Wisdom, Song of Songs* (Wilmington, Del.: Glazier, 1983).

20. Mays, *Psalms,* 42.

21. Bracke, *Jeremiah 1–29,* 49.

22. Mays, *Psalms,* 198.

23. David P. Moessner, *Lord of the Banquet: The Literary and Theological Significance of the Lukan Travel Narrative* (Harrisburg, Pa.: Trinity Press International, 1998), 159.

24. Frederick Buechner, *Now and Then* (San Francisco: Harper and Row, 1983), 54–55.

25. Mays, *Psalms,* 361.

26. Ringe, *Luke,* 214.

27. Ibid.

28. Bruce C. Birch, *Hosea, Joel, and Amos* (Louisville: Westminster John Knox, 1997), 228.

29. Ibid, 229.

30. Ringe, *Luke,* 217.

EIGHTEENTH SUNDAY
AFTER PENTECOST

TWENTY-SEVENTH SUNDAY IN ORDINARY TIME /
PROPER 22
OCTOBER 3, 2004

REVISED COMMON	EPISCOPAL (BCP)	ROMAN CATHOLIC
Hab. 1:1-4, 2:1-4	Hab. 1:1-6, (7-11),	Hab. 1:2-3; 2:2-4
or Lam. 1:1-6;	12-13; 2:1-4	
3:19-26		
Ps. 37:1-9	Ps. 37:1-18 or 37:3-10	Ps. 95:1-2, 6-9
or Psalm 137		
2 Tim. 1:1-14	2 Tim. 1:(1-5), 6-14	2 Tim. 1:6-8, 13-14
Luke 17:5-10	Luke 17:5-10	Luke 17:5-10

God expects great things of us. God calls us to live faithful, compassionate lives that demonstrate and proclaim the love and justice of the one who created us. We also expect great things from God, that same compassion, love, and justice. Yet we live in a world that frequently shows forth more pain and suffering than justice or love. Living in the intersection of expectations and reality frequently proves challenging for the people of faith. What does God see us doing? What do we see God doing? What keeps us from doing what God wants us to do? What keeps us from seeing God's justice and mercy in a world filled with pain and sorrow?

FIRST READING
HABAKKUK 1:1-4; 2:1-4 (RCL);
HABAKKUK 1:1-6, (7-11),12-13; 2:1-14 (BCP);
HABAKKUK 1:2-3; 2:2-4 (RC)

Unlike many of the other prophetic writings, the date of this book is difficult to pin down. While it clearly alludes to historical events and situations, scholars have been unable to identify a specific time or place. Some suggest that it was written in the waning years of the Assyrian domination and that empire was the wicked one. Although quite brief, the book employs three genres. The first section (1:1—2:5), from which this reading is taken, is a conversation between the prophet and God. The second section (2:6-20) consists of five woes directed at the wicked one. And the final section (3:1-19) is a prayer or hymn that reminds those listening to the words of the prophet of the greatness of God and God's powerful deeds. While the final section is not heard in today's reading, it is important to remember that the book concludes with this strong reminder of the great things God has done and continues to do.

Those reading the text will want to find ways to differentiate between the complaints of the prophet and God's responses. This is a time when reading aloud makes it much easier to appreciate the movement of the text. It is important that the listener understands this is a dialogue.

Our lives are a dialogue with God. Like the prophet, we see pain and suffering and wonder why these things are happening. The book opens not with the words of God but with the prophet's complaint against God. Looking at the world about him, the prophet sees only destruction and violence. It is no wonder that many preachers and liturgists immediately turned to these words on September 11 to voice their despair and agony in those dark days. The prophet's cry is all too often our cry.

Where is God and what is God doing? Why are we suffering?

Where is God and what is God doing? Why are we suffering? And like the prophet, we often wonder if God is deaf to our cries for help. But God quickly answers the prophet with the assurance that the wicked will not triumph. If the prophet will only be patient and look about, he will see God's gracious deeds.

It is not enough for the prophet to see and recognize what God is doing. God, according to Habakkuk, understands that we all need to hear words of comfort and reassurance. The final section of today's reading is the call to spread abroad this good news, that God has not forgotten us. The prophet gives us the image of a messenger running from place to place. We are to record—and this is not metaphorical—the vision in such a way that the messenger will be able to read the message while on the run. Think of Paul Revere riding through every "Middlesex village and farm" spreading his important message. Like the prophet, we too must be prepared to spread this crucial message—that no matter what tragedies and disasters befall us—we must hold before us the good news that the day of God's triumph "will surely come."

LAMENTATIONS 1:1-6; 3:19-26 (RCL, alt.)

We grieve at how often these words of lament over Jerusalem have been able to describe the destruction experienced by others who experience similar tragedy. The author has anthropomorphized Jerusalem, comparing the ruined city to a woman whose husband has died and left her with nothing. Many will be able to relate to the sense of desolation and despair, some on a communal level, others on a personal level. Whether the former or the latter, these are powerful words of sorrow that relate to the theme of desperation about our world that runs through this set of lections.

The theme of patience and endurance in the face of suffering is not easy for a contemporary congregation to hear. When we find ourselves in painful situations, our desire is to get out or get it "fixed" as soon as possible. Notice that the writer does not call for vengeance or retribution. Instead, the writer's gaze is fixed firmly on God, the only one in whom we can place our trust. Is this our response when we experience overwhelming destruction and devastation at the hands of others?

RESPONSIVE READING
PSALM 37:1-9 (RCL);
PSALM 37:1-18 or 37:3-10 (BCP)

This wisdom psalm mirrors the book of Proverbs. The psalmist presents the listener with advice or directions for living a faithful, well-ordered life. Do good, do not be angry, be patient writes the psalmist. The psalmist knows that we are tempted to anger when we see that it is the evildoers, not the good, who flourish. Like Habakkuk, the psalmist does not deny the presence of evil in the world but rather offers the assurance that the success of the wicked will be short-lived. Ultimately it will be the people of God who will flourish and live forever.

PSALM 95:1-2, 6-9 (RC)

The psalmist sings of God's faithfulness and care, using the image of God as the constant and trusted shepherd of his sheep. While our response to this love should be one of joy and trust, all too often we test God. The preacher may want to expand on the link between the image of "rock of salvation" with the water that came from the rock (Exod. 17:1-7). How do we test God today?

PSALM 137 (RCL, alt.)

Two events in the lives of the Jewish people shaped them most profoundly: the escape from Egypt and wandering in the wilderness, and their exile into Babylon. In each of these experiences of dislocation they saw the hand of God at work. But, as this psalmist observes, it was not without pain. How, the writer asks, can we sing the songs of faith when our faith is being tested to its limit? How can we, as Psalm 95 declares, "make a joyful noise to the rock of our salvation," when the rocks of our very walls have been broken? Like those in exile, we often wonder how we are to live faithful lives in an age that ignores religious faith.

The preacher and worship leaders will need to wrestle with the decision about including v. 9. Violence and retaliation are human responses, but do we voice them within our worship? Clearly the psalmist thought it was appropriate. Do we?

SECOND READING
2 TIMOTHY 1:1–14 (RCL);
2 TIMOTHY 1:(1–5), 6–14 (BCP);
2 TIMOTHY 1:6–8, 13–14 (RC)

Timothy was a colleague and companion of Paul's (Rom. 16:21; 1 Cor. 4:17; 16:10), but we are not sure whether this is in fact a letter of Paul to Timothy or a letter from a senior pastor to a junior worker in the vineyard who cast it as a letter from Paul. What is important is the advice of one further in his journey, one who has endured much for the sake of the gospel, to one who is facing the possibility of suffering for his faith.

LIKE HABAKKUK AND THE PSALMISTS BEFORE HIM, TIMOTHY IS CONFRONTED WITH THE REALITY THAT LIFE DEALS HARSHLY WITH US AND WE MUST DECIDE WHAT OUR RESPONSE WILL BE TO THIS VIOLENCE.

While we might never face imprisonment or death for our faith, we can relate to Timothy's plight. Because we are hearing only one side of the conversation, we do not know exactly what was happening to Timothy, but we can read between the lines. Timothy was raised in a family of faith and experienced the laying-on of hands. It may have been an early form of confirmation or it may have been ordination. It was the writer of the letter who laid his hands on Timothy. In spite of this strong foundation, however, Timothy seems to be suffering a crisis of faith.

Like Habakkuk and the psalmists before him, Timothy is confronted with the reality that life deals harshly with us and we must decide what our response will be to this violence. The writer reminds this young one in the faith that we are all heirs of a strong tradition. Those who have gone before us have testified to God's faithfulness, and we are to add our strong, not timid, voices to that chorus of the faithful.

The preacher may wish to focus on the importance of the witness of family members. Timothy is a preacher in part because of the teaching of his mother and grandmother. Recent studies have begun to explore the importance of grandmothers. One study pointed out that a child's survival is closely linked to the presence in his or her life of a maternal grandmother. We do make a difference in the lives of others, and this writer calls us to accountability.

The Gospel
LUKE 17:5-10 (RCL, BCP, RC)

The Gospel readings of the previous weeks have introduced us to a number of interesting characters—the rich man and his shrewd if somewhat unscrupulous steward, and another rich man who ignored the poor man Lazarus who sat by his gate. These parables explore themes of faithfulness and forgiveness in rather unsettling ways. But they serve as the backdrop for Jesus' examination of faithfulness. After employing parables to teach by indirection, Jesus turned to direct commands.

When we begin to study a portion of the lectionary, it is important not only to remind oneself about the passages read in the previous weeks but also to read what has been ignored. In this case, following the parable of the rich man and Lazarus come some rather harsh words of Jesus concerning our relationship with others. There is no parable to soften the words of judgment. Jesus instead directs his followers to care for others and not to lead people into

> IT IS IMPORTANT NOT ONLY TO REMIND ONESELF ABOUT THE PASSAGES READ IN THE PREVIOUS WEEKS BUT ALSO TO READ WHAT HAS BEEN IGNORED.

sin. Death by drowning would be preferable to that. He also charges them to forgive their brother every time he repents and asks for forgiveness—every time. The unspoken message is that failure to forgive will also call for the millstone around the neck and being tossed into the sea. While our listeners will not have heard these commands, we must keep them in mind, for it is because of them that the apostles cried out, "Increase our faith!"

How often do we—like Habakkuk, Timothy, and the disciples—feel uncertain of the journey and inadequate for the task that has been set before us? Which of the injunctions created such feelings of inadequacy in the followers of Jesus? Was it being admonished not to lead others to sin, or was it the charge to forgive others over and over and over again?

The disciples who followed Jesus along the way as he taught and lived the ethic of God's reign must have continually faced the reality that they fell far short of their master. He may have spoken with Samaritans, eaten with tax collectors, and healed the outcasts, but they were the ones who tried to keep the public away from their beloved teacher. They wanted the women to be quiet, the children to leave Jesus alone, and for them to avoid lepers. How could they watch out for these "little ones" and forgive everyone who insulted and offended them? And so they ask or beg Jesus to increase their faith, the faith that will allow them to measure up to the task.

We expect great things from God, and God expects great things from us. Jesus tells us that God expects us to have the faith and the confidence that we can keep from causing our brothers and sisters to fall into sin. God expects us to forgive our neighbors over and over again. And God expects us to have the faith that would enable us to order trees to throw themselves into the sea. But if you are like me, while you can imagine the first two, you have great difficulty when it comes to the third. I have enough trouble pulling out dead shrubbery, and I don't "speak" "Sycamineze."

Could it be that Jesus is reminding them—and us—that the ability to do the great things that God expects from us does not depend upon us but upon God? Is Jesus telling us that we already have the power to do what God wants us to do? While this sounds like an impossible command, it is because of the ridiculous impossibility of the task that we are supposed to hear this as good news.

There is a wonderful scene at the end of *The Wizard of Oz*. Dorothy has gone through many trials in her effort to please the wizard with the hope that he will send her back to her beloved Kansas. She has battled the Wicked Witch of the West and triumphed with the help of her friends. But when she returns with the witch's broomstick, she discovers that the wizard is nothing more than a man, a carnival huckster who has no more power than she. Yet her disappointment is short-lived; Glinda arrives, the good witch who tells her that the power to return home already lies within Dorothy herself. Naturally, Dorothy is upset: "Why didn't you tell me that at the beginning? Why did you make me go through all of this?" "Why?" the witch replies. "Because you would not have believed me."

Do we believe Jesus when he tells us that we have the power to care for our brothers and sisters? Do we believe Jesus when he tells us that we can forgive our neighbor over and over again? Or do we see only our weakness and failures? Do we focus on the possibilities or the impossibilities? What would you do if you knew that you would succeed?

To reinforce his message, Jesus offers us a very quotidian image of discipleship—working in the field, taking care of the flock, and serving at table. There is nothing unreasonable or extraordinary about that. And, in fact, these are the very images we use to describe the ministry.

We expect great things from God and receive no less. Likewise, God demands great things from us and should receive no less than our very best. "I can do all things in him who strengthens me" (Phil. 4:13).

NINETEENTH SUNDAY AFTER PENTECOST

TWENTY-EIGHTH SUNDAY IN ORDINARY TIME / PROPER 23

OCTOBER 10, 2004

REVISED COMMON	EPISCOPAL (BCP)	ROMAN CATHOLIC
2 Kings 5:1-3, 7-15 or Jer. 29:1, 4-7	Ruth 1:(1-7), 8-19a	2 Kings 5:14-17
Psalm 111 or 66:1-12	Psalm 113	Ps. 98:1, 2-3, 3-4
2 Tim. 2:8-15	2 Tim. 2:(3-7), 8-15	2 Tim. 2:8-13
Luke 17:11-19	Luke 17:11-19	Luke 17:11-19

Perhaps one of the most difficult challenges to people of faith is saying thank you to God. We seemingly have no difficulty expressing our anger or our fears. Our prayers are filled with our concerns about what is happening to us or to those whom we love. But how many times do we, like the Samaritan who is healed, return to God to give thanks for the blessings that have been poured into our lives? I have long remembered a story told to us in Sunday school. Two angels went to earth to collect all of the prayers. One was sent to retrieve petitions, the other, thanksgivings. Each was given a basket, and the one picking up thanksgivings chose a much larger basket, thinking that was what would be needed. The one who was collecting petitions and appeals had to return over and over to get another basket. But the angel picking up thanksgivings, in the end, returned with the same basket not even half full. How grateful are we?

FIRST READING

2 KINGS 5:1-3, 7-15 (RCL); 2 KINGS 5:14-17 (RC)

There are some stories in the scriptures that make the preacher's job easy. The meeting of Naaman and Elisha is one such story. The only difficulty is choosing among the many sermon possibilities.

One possible thread is the miracle of healing. Elisha had important messages for the people of Israel. But why should people listen to him? How were the people to know that this was, in fact, a man of God? Chapters 4 through 8 represent

224

THE SEASON
OF PENTECOST
‾‾‾‾‾‾‾‾
LUCY
LIND HOGAN

a wonderful collection of miracle stories that serve to validate Elisha's credentials. Whether it is an ever-flowing supply of oil or the resuscitation from the dead, these stories point to the holiness of Elisha.

In this story the prophet seeks to rescue two people. First, there is Naaman, the famous warrior who suffers from leprosy. Curing the leprosy is so easy for Elisha that he doesn't even have to come out of his house. He only has to give the directions to his servant who can pass them on to Naaman, and it will be done. But we should also note how Elisha saves the unnamed king of Israel.

When Naaman is sent to the king by the equally unnamed king of Syria for healing, the king of Israel panics. Knowing that healing is not within his power, the Israelite king thinks that this is really a plot by the king of Syria to provoke armed conflict. Fortunately, Elisha comes to the king's aid and sends word that the king should send the general to him.

Another theme on which preachers might focus is the interfaith dimension. Naaman was not a Jew, and yet the healing mercies of God were extended to him through God's prophet Elisha. We also note that it was a young Jewish slave, the maid of Naaman's wife, who served as an "evangelist," pointing her master toward the true source of life and healing. Naaman's healing precedes his conversion and confession. It is only when he sees that he has been cured that he returns to the prophet to declare in the presence of the holy man that he now knows who is the true God: "I know that there is no God in all the earth but in Israel."

NAAMAN'S HEALING PRECEDES HIS CONVERSION AND CONFESSION. IT IS ONLY WHEN HE SEES THAT HE HAS BEEN CURED THAT HE RETURNS TO THE PROPHET TO DECLARE . . . THAT HE NOW KNOWS WHO IS THE TRUE GOD.

The story also presents us with an almost humorous example of human arrogance meeting divine power. We think that we know better than God and we are not willing to accept the profoundly simple ways that God seeks to give us life. When given the charge to "wash in the Jordan seven times," Naaman is furious and is ready to storm off to Syria. First, the prophet wouldn't do him the honor of coming out to meet him. Now he is given a task unworthy of a great general. He is like the people who prefer to pay more for a car or house, thinking that the higher price makes it better and them more important. God comes to us and gives us new life in simple, everyday ways—the plain water of baptism, the bread and wine of communion, the healing touch of someone who cares for us. Those are the humble ways that the great God of all the universe chooses to act upon our lives. Only when Naaman was willing to humble himself did he finally meet the living God.

Finally there is the theme of gratitude. Naaman returned to Elisha. While Naaman wanted to offer his thanks and gifts to Elisha, the prophet knew to whom thanks belong and would not accept them. It was God, not Elisha who had cured the general. And it was God who deserved the thanks. This theme of gratitude will be picked up in our Gospel text—and we will note the difference between Elisha's and Jesus' reactions to the grateful man.

RUTH 1:(1-7), 8-19a (BCP)

There are only two books in the Hebrew scriptures (Ruth and Esther) and two in the Apocrypha (Judith and Susanna) that bear the names of women. For Christians, Ruth, who is the great-grandmother of David and named in Matthew's genealogy, provides Jesus with a Gentile grandmother. While Ruth's pledge, "Where you go I will go," is a popular wedding text and therefore familiar to many, it is important to place her pledge in the proper context (exile and death) and remember to whom she is speaking—not her husband but rather her mother-in-law.

The story is one of hardship and tragedy. Elimelech, Naomi, and their sons must become refugees in Moab because famine has gripped their land. While there seems to be a period of relative calm and hospitality during which they prosper and their sons marry local women, tragedy soon strikes again with the death of Elimelech and both of Naomi's sons.

After the death of her sons, leaving Naomi with no male heir or relative to support her and save her from ruin and death, she has no choice but to return to her homeland. Not wanting to see the same fate befall her daughters-in-law, Naomi, who now calls herself Mara ("bitter") begs them to return to their families. One follows her wishes, but Ruth refuses and dedicates herself not only to her mother-in-law, but to the God of Naomi as well. This is conversion born out of love and an abiding relationship and commitment.

JEREMIAH 29:1, 4-7 (RCL, alt.)

While the beginning of Jeremiah's prophecy is certainly one of "fire and brimstone," once the people had been sent into exile (another seminal experience), the prophet's message changes to that of comfort and encouragement. However, it is important to note the irony in the message.

We could find Jeremiah's reporting of God's directions to be comforting—build houses, plant gardens, eat produce, have sons and daughters. But would we find this very comforting if what we really wanted to do was go home? God is telling those in exile to settle in. They will be there for a long time, long enough to do all of those things. Is that what they wanted to hear? Didn't they want to hear that they would be going home shortly? God continually reminds us that

God's ways are not our ways, and what we want may not be what God has in store for us.

RESPONSIVE READING
PSALM 111 (RCL)

The psalmist may declare that "fear of the LORD is the beginning of wisdom," but this psalm and today's lessons would help us to understand that the end lies in love and gratitude. We do not have a vicious, vindictive God who demands our cowering obedience but a God who lavishes great gifts upon us and asks only that we revel in their glory returning thanks and praise.

Psalms like this were written to thank God for a particular favor or release from an illness or grief. One may have had an opportunity to visit churches that have a tradition of memorial plaques. The walls of the church will be covered with such messages—"Thanks be to God for Healing, Maria, 1859." The visitor is intrigued but frustrated.

GOD HAS "CAUSED HIS WONDERFUL WORKS TO BE REMEMBERED."

We will never know what happened to the person. We will not know her story. All we know is that God has "caused his wonderful works to be remembered."

PSALM 113 (BCP)

Psalms 113-118 are used during the Passover meal. Psalms 113–114 are sung before the start of the meal.

The psalm of praise is filled with opposites. God is to be blessed "from this time . . . for evermore." There is the opposite of sunrise and sunset, heavens and earth, the poor who become princes, and the barren woman the mother of many children. For our God, nothing is impossible.

PSALM 98:1, 2-3, 3-4 (RC)

Those for whom God has done great things need a song to sing. Psalm 98 provides a chorus for all with overflowing hearts. God's arm is strong and has done great things, and our response should be one of thankfulness and praise.

PSALM 66:1-12 (RCL, alt.)

The people of God had seminal moments to which they return over and over again. Those moments remind us not only of who God is but also of who we are. The exodus is one such moment in the life of God's people, and the psalmists frequently lift up the image of the children of Israel marching through the sea with dry feet. In this moment of terror and fear, God saved the people, and the psalmist testifies that what God has done, God is ready to do again.

The preacher may be able to connect the image of the Israelites passing through the waters with Elisha's command for Naaman to "pass through" the waters of the Jordan River.

227

NINETEENTH
SUNDAY
AFTER PENTECOST
───────
OCTOBER 10

Second Reading
2 TIMOTHY 2:8-15 (RCL);
2 TIMOTHY 2:(3-7), 8-15 (BCP);
2 TIMOTHY 2:8-13 (RC)

In the introductory preaching course that I teach, I encourage students to enter into a conversation with the preachers who have preceded them, reflecting on the preachers they know, thinking about their denominational and cultural understandings of preaching and developing their theology of preaching—all of this in order to answer an important question: Who are they as preachers? Timothy and the community to whom he was preaching seem to have had a disagreement about who was to preach and what should have been preached.

Timothy's mentor, a senior preacher, understands the importance of preaching the word, the gospel, and also understands what happens when congregations "dispute about words." It "ruins those who are listening," and the "profane chatter" will lead people to "impiety." In the end, this senior pastor charges his young colleague to be a "workman" (RSV) who handles the "word of truth." Earlier in the letter he had raised up images of soldiers, athletes, and farmers. A preacher, he argues, must be the same kind of person—not be distracted by worldly fame and adulation, breaking the rules, or avoiding hard work.

I must confess that I do not usually think of being a preacher in terms of being a "workman." That, for me, conjures up images of overalls with tools hanging off of the loops on the pant leg and grease from the chores attacked. But in the end, preaching is messy and down to

IN THE END, PREACHING IS MESSY AND DOWN TO EARTH.

earth. We are dealing with the everyday, troublesome parts of life, and a preacher who doesn't want to get her or his hands dirty is going to have a hard time "handling the word of truth" (RSV).

All of us have a duty to preach the gospel, as in vv. 11-13. This was probably a well-known hymn. This message of life in Christ and the faithfulness of God makes an excellent connection for the preacher who wishes to pursue the baptismal thread that appears in the story of Naaman. Through our baptism we are all sent out to proclaim this good news.

THE GOSPEL
LUKE 17:11-19 (RCL, BCP, RC)

Place is an important aspect of any writing. Where did you grow up? Was it in the hot, humid regions of the South or the arid regions of the Southwest? I grew up in frozen Minnesota. It was not until my family traveled to Florida during the Christmas holiday in the mid-1950s that I realized not everyone had snow from November to April. It was a wonderful revelation. Places shape who we are, what we think is important or not important, and stand as synecdoche—a particular for the whole.

At the opening of this Gospel pericope, we must not gloss over Luke's observation that Jesus was "on the way to Jerusalem." This serves more than just a way of introducing a new story or advancing the plot. Luke wants to remind us that, while Jesus might be preaching, teaching, and healing people, he is always focused on the end, the goal. Jerusalem is more than just a city. It presents us with a reminder of the entire life, ministry, and death of Jesus. Jesus, Luke is telling us, is on his way to the cross, and we must never forget that.

Along the way, however, Jesus encounters a group of leper, which includes both Jews as well as a Samaritan. Again Luke employs the rhetorical device of the synecdoche. The Samaritan serves to represent the outsider, the outcast, the enemy of the Jews. When Luke wants to preach the good news that God's love and healing through Christ extend beyond the boundaries of God's chosen people, he introduces the Samaritans here in this story and earlier in the story of the man beaten by robbers (Luke 10:29-37).

This is a somewhat confusing story that seems to pull together two stories and make two different points. The first scene (vv. 11-14) presents us with the healing of ten lepers. As Jesus was entering an unnamed village, he encountered ten lepers. At this point we are not told any more about them other than the fact that they are standing at a distance, which is in accord with the Jewish law regarding lepers, "He shall live alone; his dwelling shall be outside the camp" (Lev. 13:46b). But, disregarding the injunction that the leper cry, "Unclean, unclean," when encountering others, these lepers proclaim Jesus to be their master: "Master, have mercy on us." Luke is the only one who uses the term *epistates,* which means

> WHEN LUKE WANTS TO PREACH THE GOOD NEWS THAT GOD'S LOVE AND HEALING THROUGH CHRIST EXTENDS BEYOND THE BOUNDARIES OF GOD'S CHOSEN PEOPLE, HE INTRODUCES THE SAMARITANS.

"commander" or "overseer." The disciples also call Jesus master, the one who has authority over them.

The lepers ask for mercy, and mercy is shown to them. Jesus does not touch them. There is no spit and mud, no washing in pools. They are told to show themselves to the priest, which would indicate that they have already been healed. Do we believe that God can heal us without a theatrical display? Jesus' simple command to go is quite different from the dramatic flair of a healing evangelist like Benny Hinn or like Oral Roberts in his younger days. If someone whispered to us that we were healed, would we be disappointed like Naaman and want more of a show?

The first story ends as the lepers follow Jesus' command and head off to see the priests. Yet in the second half of the story they are seemingly scolded for doing just that. One of the lepers, a Samaritan we are told, realizes that he has been healed and returns to Jesus before he even reaches the priests. (Since he is not a Jew and in fact an enemy, wouldn't it make more sense for him to return to Jesus than to go to hostile Jewish officials?)

Presumably the others were also already healed. Jesus never retracted their healing. But in this moment Luke wants us to recall the story of another outsider who found healing from the God of the Jews, Naaman. As in 2 Kings, the message is preached that our God is the God of all people, healing Jews and Samaritans alike. But there is a significant difference. If we put these two stories together as Luke intends, we must compare the reactions of Elisha and Jesus. Elisha, you will recall, refused Naaman's thanks and gifts, demanding that the Syrian give thanks to God, not him. Jesus accepts the thanksgivings of the Samaritan and makes a startling admission: "Was no one found to return and give praise to God?" In returning to give thanks to the man Jesus, the Samaritan has met and given praise to the living God.

Every day we encounter the living God who gives us life anew each day, yet do we return and give thanks? Or do we continue to fill only the baskets of the angel who is collecting our petitions and requests?

TWENTIETH SUNDAY AFTER PENTECOST

TWENTY-NINTH SUNDAY IN ORDINARY TIME / PROPER 24
OCTOBER 17, 2004

REVISED COMMON	EPISCOPAL (BCP)	ROMAN CATHOLIC
Gen. 32:22-31	Gen. 32:3-8, 22-30	Exod. 17:8-13
or Jer. 31:27-34		
Psalm 121	Psalm 121	Ps. 121:1-8
or 119:97-104		
2 Tim. 3:14—4:5	2 Tim. 3:14—4:5	2 Tim. 3:14—4:2
Luke 18:1-8	Luke 18:1-8a	Luke 18:1-8

The story is told of a rabbi who once counseled a woman who came to him grieving over and complaining about all of the pain and sorrow in her life. He listened sympathetically but told her that, before he could help her, she would first have to go and find a person whose life involved no troubles or hardship. As you can imagine, the story ends with the woman returning to tell him that in all of her travels, she never found such a person. And, in fact, she discovered that her problems and burdens were much lighter than many of the people she encountered in her journey. Like that woman, our journey through life is often marked by struggles and conflict. Like Jacob and the widow, we find that we are wrestling with the powers that would overwhelm us. But the good news of today's lessons is that God hears our cries, and is present in our struggles, and that the people of God can live in hope knowing that with God we will triumph.

FIRST READING
GENESIS 32:22-31 (RCL);
GENESIS 32:3-8, 22-30 (BCP)

Wrestling has a rather notorious reputation these days. Ask people to picture a wrestling match and most will conjure up images of Hulk Hogan (no relation) and wildly costumed muscle men. Nothing could be further from this intense, pivotal moment in the life of Jacob. Throughout his life, Jacob's actions frequently placed him in dangerous situations. This night was no different. He is getting ready to do the right thing—reconcile with Esau. He had decided to return to confront and at the same time appease the brother whom he had cheated out of his inheritance. It would seem that sibling rivalry is built into our very bones, and many people seated in the congregation will be able to commiserate with either Jacob or Esau. Why at this time would God choose to challenge and confront him? Why is life difficult and challenging when we seek to do good?

The central moment of this story is the wrestling match between Jacob and an unnamed "man." Who or what this being is, we are never told. The confused arrangement of the story seems to indicate that this may be constructed from multiple ancient stories. For example, this would seem to be an etiological tale for two different things: (1) a dietary restriction that does not appear anywhere else and (2) a place name. While in the original story the "man" may have been a demon, hence the vampire-like need to flee before sunrise, in this version it would seem that Jacob is wrestling with none other than God.

In the dark of night, after placing his family in safety, Jacob suddenly finds that he is engaged in a wrestling match. Most of us find it difficult to image that an opponent could sneak up on him unawares. Couldn't he see him, even in the dark? Today we have grown accustomed to electric lights and rarely experience true darkness. My husband was a navy doctor and tells of his nights on a supply ship. Navy ships run completely dark; otherwise they would be sitting targets. He would go out on the deck at night but would stay only a little while because it was so dark he could not see his hand in front of his face. That kind of darkness, he said, was palpable and oppressive.

Jacob could not identify his antagonist; he only knew that he had to fight for his life. How often do many of us find ourselves in a similar situation? All he could do was fight. And in the end he prevailed, but not without suffering—a dislocated hip. When his opponent perceived that he would not win and demanded to be released, Jacob exacted a payment. Jacob

> THIS RICH STORY INVITES US TO THINK ABOUT OUR RELATIONSHIP WITH GOD IN A NEW WAY. IT IS AN INVITATION TO STRIVE OR WRESTLE WITH GOD.

would stop the fight if the "man" would bless him. This is the first inkling we have that this being is anything but a "man." In the end not only does Jacob receive a blessing, but also a new name and new identity. He is now "Israel," a man who has "striven with God."

This rich story invites us to think about our relationship with God in a new way. It is an invitation to strive or wrestle with God. In the moments of darkness, when we are afraid for our life, God comes. So it is God, not Jacob, who initiates the wrestling match. God can take it, and, in fact, God encourages us to engage in the confrontation.

EXODUS 17:8-13 (RC)

An important theme of this week's lections is fortitude—keep going beyond the limits of our physical, emotional, or spiritual strength. This passage from the life of Moses and the people of Israel presents us with an amazing story of human possibility and the importance of community.

Israel, the people of the covenant, must do battle with Amalek and his tribe who controlled an area in the Kadesh. While Moses sent Joshua and his men into the battle, Moses took his place at the top of the hill to raise his hands in supplication to God, calling down divine assistance. And, as the story tells us, with Moses' aid, the Israelites were successful, but only with Moses' aid. For the battle was long, and whenever Moses lowered his arms his fighters began to lose.

Have you ever worked on a project for which you had to keep your arms raised above your head? You know that you can't do it for long before you have to lower your arms and give them a rest. How could Moses rest if that meant losing the battle? This is a story of Moses' fortitude and perseverance—he kept his arms raised. But it is also a story of community. Moses couldn't do what he needed to do without the help of others. Only when Aaron and Hur held up Moses' arms were the Israelites successful.

I think that I had a Moses moment when I was in labor. Both of my labors were quite long and arduous. As you get to the end of your labor, there is no let-up, no break from the intense contractions—you can't "lower your arms." While they couldn't hold up my arms, my husband and the nurses could encourage me by holding my hands and shouting at me to keep going. They called forth from me more strength and more energy than I thought I had. How often do others help us to keep on going long after we think we can go no further?

JEREMIAH 31:27-34 (RCL, alt.)

In Jeremiah 29, the prophet's letter to the exiles that is filled with hope and comfort, God reminds the people: "I know the plans I have for you, says the LORD, plans for welfare and not for evil, to give you a future and a hope" (Jer. 29:11). No matter what the people of God had done, even if they had turned away and rejected God, God would not reject them. There is always a new covenant to be made. There is always the possibility of a new start, a new beginning. When we grow weary and our arms fail, God is there to pick us up and carry us along.

Jeremiah gives us the image that we become the very witnesses to the covenant. We do not need to depend upon tablets of stone or a temple in Jerusalem to know that our God is with us always: "I will put my law within them, and I will write it upon their hearts; and I will be their God and they shall be my people" (v. 33). This was wonderful news to a people who felt rejected and cut off from all that they knew.

Yet this is still a call for accountability and faithfulness. People will "die for their own sin," not the sin of their fathers and mothers. God's message pulls us into the present, our present, and asks us to be responsible for our actions. Can we do this? While we don't want to be responsible for what our parents and grandparents did, we have long memories and we continue to want to punish people for the sins of their ancestors. Think of conflicts around the world that point to centuries-old atrocities as their justification. That is "sour grapes."

RESPONSIVE READING
PSALM 121 (RCL, BCP, RC)

"Next year in Jerusalem." At the end of the Passover Haggadah, those participating in the Seder meal express the longing, the hope of all Jews, that they will be able to observe one of the holiest festivals within the walls of the hallowed city Jerusalem. The Temple at Jerusalem was the center of all feasts and festivals, and for millennia pilgrims have been streaming through its gates. Psalm 121 was a song that the pilgrims sang as they were getting ready to leave their home and make the pilgrimage.

This psalm is not a prayer, for it is not addressed to God. Rather, it serves to encourage the pilgrims as they set off on a long, difficult, and dangerous journey, reminding them that God is with them every step of the way.

When we lift our eyes to the distant hills, knowing that we will have to walk that long way, we know that our help comes from God. And this is not just any god—who would be responsible for only one thing, i.e., the god of the woods, the god of the waters, or the god of the weather. Our God is the God of heaven, earth, day, night, light, dark, life, and death. And our God will not fall asleep. Our God's arms will not grow weary and fail. Our God's outstretched arms will keep us in safety every step of the way.

> THIS PSALM REMINDS US THAT GOD IS WITH US FROM BIRTH TO DEATH AND TO ETERNAL LIFE.

The journey to Jerusalem was difficult and demanded the divine assistance. So, too, are our lives. This psalm reminds us that God is with us from birth to death and to eternal life.

PSALM 119:97-104 (RCL, alt.)

This is a psalm that teachers would rather their students didn't read. I am not sure that I want my students thinking they are wiser than I because they read and follow God's ordinances. But it just might be true.

This psalm presents us with a wonderful image for studying scriptures—dessert. Plunging into the story of God's law and love is, for us, sweeter than honey in our mouths. The psalm also reminds us that God's commandments supersede or trump anything that the world has to offer—academic achievement, physical strength, and age all pale when compared with the greatness of our creator.

SECOND READING
2 TIMOTHY 3:14—4:5 (RCL, BCP); 2 TIMOTHY 3:14—4:2 (RC)

Do we look only backwards to the past or only ahead to the future? We, like Timothy, live in challenging times. Pick up any book about the future of the church and you will read the admonition that the old ways are dead and will not work with those raised with the computer and the internet. Everything has to be new, new, new. With those challenges ringing in our ears, we hear the call to Timothy: "Continue in what you have learned . . . the sacred writings."

The way to the future is only through the lessons of the past. This letter gives the impression that Timothy or his congregation was being lured by those who were preaching a different lesson and demanding a break with the past. Could it be that they were preaching "cheap grace" and an easy road ahead? This passage includes two similar lists. The first list lays out what scripture can do for us. It will teach, reprove, correct, and train. And we hear a similar refrain when we are told the task of the preacher: "Convince, rebuke, and exhort, be unfailing in patience and in teaching."

The message of the church, Paul tells Timothy, must build up and strengthen, and it must do so with the lessons of the past. We cannot tell people only what they want to hear. Nor can we look only ahead while ignoring our past. There was a Roman god, Janus, that was the god of doorways and gates—entrances into something new. Janus was always depicted as a two-faced god. One face was looking to the past and one to the future. Perhaps this is a good image for preachers. We look to the past and the future at the same time, knowing that ours is the God who is the God of the past and the future, our alpha and omega, our beginning and our end.

THE WAY TO THE FUTURE IS ONLY THROUGH THE LESSONS OF THE PAST.

THE GOSPEL
LUKE 18:1-8 (RCL, BCP, RC)

Luke is the only Gospel writer who presents us with the wonderful characters of the pestering widow and the detestable judge. Luke also tells us how we are to hear and interpret this parable. It is, he tells us, about the need "to pray and not lose heart." But is that what this parable is, in fact, all about? Verse 1 may tell us that this is a parable about our persistent need for prayer, even when we feel that we cannot go on. But this does not seem to be a parable about faith or prayer. What happens if we pull the parable (vv. 2–5) out of its frame? It then becomes a parable about justice and human persistence and triumph over injustice and oppression. How do we connect this with prayer and hope in the face of hopelessness?

There is a significant portion of Luke's Gospel that is not heard in this cycle of the lectionary. Luke 17:20 introduces an important theme with a question that is asked by the Pharisees: When will we see the kingdom of God? Jesus then explores this important question by assuring them that the kingdom will indeed come, but not according to any human timetable, or with any signs that they will recognize. The kingdom will come suddenly and unexpectedly, like Lot's wife being turned into a pillar of salt. Jesus concludes his teaching with images of the rapture. People will be going about their daily affairs, and astonishingly, one will be gone and one will remain.

These images are quite popular today with Jerry Jenkins and Tim LeHaye's "Left Behind" series. But do those books accurately portray Jesus' and Luke's teaching? The question about the return of the kingdom and the uncertainty surrounding that time is the setup for the parable, and these teachings challenge us to live into the uncertainty. But they also present us with an image of our discipleship in this in-between time.

Like the Christian community to whom Luke was writing, we wait and pray for the return of the Son of Man. But that community may have waited with even more fervor and more distress. Today, after two thousand years, we have come to terms with the delay of the parousia. But remember, the early church expected Christ to return at any moment and agonized when, each moment, his return did not occur. We may say and sing, "Come, Lord Jesus," but for them it was a heartfelt plea. And so they felt like the widow who was waiting for vindication. How were they to live when they expected any moment to be their last? How were they to continue wrestling with a world of sin and evil when their strength was failing? How were they to continue to hold up their arms to welcome the returning Christ when their arms were growing weak and weary? With this important question echoing in our ears, "When will the kingdom of God come?" we can hear this story in a very different way.

THE EARLY CHURCH EXPECTED CHRIST TO RETURN AT ANY MOMENT AND AGONIZED WHEN, EACH MOMENT, HIS RETURN DID NOT OCCUR.

We must also be careful that we do not read it analogously, i.e., we are the widow, God is the dreadful judge. Unfortunately, when the passage from Genesis is read—Jacob wrestling with God—it is difficult not to hear it that way. But the parable wants us instead to focus on the persistence of the widow in spite of her frustration. There is no way that she can appeal to the judge's humanity or good sense; he has none. That is why the parable tells us twice that this judge "neither feared God nor had respect for people." He was beyond her control.

The coming of God's reign is also beyond our control. We may pray, "Thy kingdom come," every day, but Jesus reminds us that only God, not we, will make that happen. He also tells us that we must continue to make that our prayer. We must pray and pray and pray, seventy times seven. We must be like the widow who never gives up. We have a God who does listen, who "will neither slumber nor sleep" (Ps. 121:4b).

In her culture, the widow was one of the most vulnerable of creatures. She did not have a man to support her and depended upon others for her sustenance. She is an image of pain and suffering. She reminds us of the agony of losing someone we love and all of the distress that goes with it. She is wrestling with the judge, with life, with that which would deprive her of true justice.

Throughout our history we have known many "widows." One such persistent voice against injustice was Edith Stein. She was born an Orthodox Jew in Germany in 1891. A brilliant philosopher, Edith came upon the biography of St. Teresa of Avila, and on New Year's Day, 1922, she was baptized a Christian, much to her family's pain. The Vatican has recently released papers and letters revealing the Vatican's involvement with the German atrocities against the Jews. Among the released letters are ones that Dr. Stein wrote to the pope in the early 1930s describing the barbarism and calling for his intervention lest even worse events occur: "Vindicate me against my adversary." In 1934 Edith entered a Carmelite convent in Holland, and it was there that the Germans arrested her. She died in the gas chambers of Auschwitz in 1942. Edith Stein stands for us as a reminder that we must always raise our voice to cry out for justice and peace.

The widow is humanity wrestling with the "slings and arrows of outrageous fortune" (Shakespeare, *Hamlet*). The widow is us. We are called to wrestle with life. But the good news is that through our wrestling we will eventually prevail. We will be vindicated. We will be blessed, and we will be given a new name—the one who has striven with God.

> Those who wait for the Lord
>   shall mount up with wings like eagles,
> they shall run and not be weary,
>   They shall walk and not faint. (Isa. 40:31)

TWENTY-FIRST SUNDAY AFTER PENTECOST

THIRTIETH SUNDAY IN ORDINARY TIME / PROPER 25
OCTOBER 24, 2004

REVISED COMMON	EPISCOPAL (BCP)	ROMAN CATHOLIC
Jer. 14:7-10, 19-22 or Sir. 35:12-17 or Joel 2:23-32	Jer. 14:(1-6), 7-10, 19-22	Sir. 35:12-14, 16-18
Ps. 84:1-7 or Psalm 65	Psalm 84 or 84:1-6	Ps. 34:2-3, 17-18, 19, 23
2 Tim. 4:6-8, 16-18	2 Tim. 4:6-8, 16-18	2 Tim. 4:6-8, 16-18
Luke 18:9-14	Luke 18:9-14	Luke 18:9-14

When beholding the glorious splendor of a crisp autumn day, it is not difficult to shout God's praises: "How lovely is your dwelling place, O LORD of hosts!" (Ps. 84:1). In those moments our hearts do, indeed, "sing for joy to the living God" (Ps. 84:2). And on those days, we can more easily see that everything in our world is infused with the mark of the maker, affirming that, like the sparrows and swallows, we are nestled

> PRAYER COMES EASILY WHEN WE ARE COMFORTABLE WITH OUR RELATIONSHIP TO THAT LOVING GOD. BUT WHAT ABOUT THOSE MOMENTS OF DESPAIR AND DESPERATION?

in the hands of a loving God whose bounty overflows. Prayer comes easily when we are comfortable with our relationship to that loving God. But what about those moments of despair and desperation? Is God there? Does God care for us and listen? And what of those moments when we are overwhelmed by our failures and faults? Who are we, sinful creatures that we are, to come before almighty God? Are we able to face our true nature? Perhaps God has every right to "turn aside like a wayfarer" (Jer. 14:8).

FIRST READING
JEREMIAH 14:7-10, 19-22 (RCL);
JEREMIAH 14:(1-6), 7-10, 19-22 (BCP)

One of the most difficult problems encountered by those who would read scripture before a congregation is what is known as "first-timeness." That is, as a passage is read, the end of the story is implied or betrayed. This happens frequently when reading the passion accounts. One may be reading the description of the crucifixion, but the tone of voice is calm and assuring: "I know this sounds bad, but don't worry, there is a happy ending." It is difficult not to do this because we do know the end of the story. The same is frequently the case when we read passages such as this lament from Jeremiah.

Drought, famine, starvation, death—these were the crises facing the people of God. Things were desperate, and they did not know when or if things would get better. Some of you will be preaching in congregations filled with those who work the soil. They have a firsthand knowledge of the ravages of drought. For them this is not a symbolic or metaphorical concept; it is all together too real. And what else is real is the uncertainty about how long this will last. Oh, they know that eventually the rains will return, but will it be a month, a year, several years? So we don't want our reading of the passage to ignore the seriousness of the situation or their uncertainty.

While we may be able to empathize with Judah's plight, a challenge for us comes when assigning blame. Weather patterns have recently been affected by an El Niño off the west coast of North America. For some that has meant more rain and more snow, for others a drought. That weather phenomena affects precipitation and temperatures. Meteorologists also tell us that this pattern comes and goes in cycles. If we just wait, things will change. But, unlike insurance companies, we don't claim the drought is "an act of God." Nor do we locate the blame on ourselves, on our backslidings and sins. But Jeremiah did. The rains had dried up and the crops withered because the people of God had turned away from God. In return, God had turned away from them and become "like a stranger in the land."

Jeremiah is seeking to make sense of a "natural" disaster that has befallen his people. (Would he call it a "natural" or a "divine" disaster? The way we describe it locates blame—and today we no longer attribute these crises to God.) Jeremiah also knows that an even bigger disaster is looming, and he is there to proclaim that the people deserve everything that is coming to them. They have, he declares, brought this on themselves and they have no one to blame but themselves.

The people of Judah did not want to hear Jeremiah's laments and prophecies. Because of his message, or rather God's message, he was beaten and imprisoned. We likewise are very uncomfortable with attributing causality for disasters, either

THE GOOD NEWS FOR JEREMIAH WAS THAT THE GOD WHO PUNISHED WAS ALSO A GOD WHO FORGAVE.

natural or personal, to God. Think of the reaction when Pat Robertson and Jerry Falwell suggested that the disaster of 9/11 was God's way of punishing homosexuals, feminists, abortionists, and all sorts of liberals. Likewise, most of us would protest if a pastor preached that a town's destruction by a tornado, flood, or hurricane was God's way of chastising a wayward community.

The good news for Jeremiah was that the God who punished was also a God who forgave. While "the anger of the LORD will not turn back until he has executed and accomplished the intents of his mind" (Jer. 23:20), that same God would eventually welcome them back: "I will turn their mourning into joy, I will comfort them and give them gladness for sorrow" (Jer. 31:13).

This presents us with a problem. Can we celebrate the loving God who lavishes us with grace and mercy without also accepting God's punishments? Are we able to confront and confess our sinfulness and wickedness? This is not an easy message to preach in today's intellectual and theological climate. Also, because we do not locate the cause of disasters, hurricanes, droughts, and tornadoes in God's wrath, we are left passive and defenseless, at the mercy of the weather.

SIRACH 35:12-17 (RCL, alt.); SIRACH 35:12-14, 16-18 (RC)

An exemplar of wisdom literature, the writings of Jesus ben Sira appear infrequently in the RCL but are more common in the Roman Catholic lectionary. Sirach (ben Sira) wrote about 180 B.C.E., and the book is a compilation of his thoughts and lectures on ethics and various religious matters. The book is also known by its Latin name, Ecclesiasticus ("the church book").

Sirach 35:12-18 expounds on God's response to our prayers. But within this teaching is an unexpected revelation. All sorts and conditions of men and women may come before God with their requests and petitions, and God will listen to them all, rich and poor alike. God will listen to the greatest and the least. God hears the cries of those who have been wronged, and God will vindicate them.

This is good news and bad news. The good news is that God will hear the prayers of all. The bad news is that God will punish us if we are not kind to our neighbor. Indirectly, Sirach is passing judgment and issuing a warning to those who would crush the least among them, widows, and orphans. God will do "justice for the righteous, and execute judgment."

It is important for us to remember the connection between prayer and justice. A faithful and devoted prayer life does not excuse us from taking care of our neediest sisters and brothers.

JOEL 2:23-32 (RCL, alt.)

We may long for and pray that we see the "day of the Lord" (Joel 2:1), but do we really know what will happen on that day? There is much speculation and interest in the popular press about this. A number of authors are getting rich providing their readers with blow-by-blow descriptions of what they might expect. Whether or not Joel was a rich man, we cannot know. What we do know is that he reminds us that on that day everything will experience a dramatic change.

Joel paints an amazing picture. First, the earth will be completely restored and renewed. What had been desolate and devastated will be lush and productive. We will have wine, oil, and grain, and have them abundantly. Vats will overflow. We will be able to feed everyone. Our God does everything on a grand scale. Think of the feeding of the five thousand at Matthew 14. When all had been fed, twelve full baskets were left over. (I have a similar experience when I cook for guests; I always make enough food to feed an army. I don't want to run out, so I run over.)

Not only will the material world overflow with God's grace, so too will God's people. They will be so filled with God's Spirit that even those not usually allowed will be able to speak. Not only sons, but daughters as well will prophesy.

Peter incorporated this passage into the sermon he preached when he experienced the outpouring of God's Spirit on the day of Pentecost (Acts 2:14-24). Joel may have been speaking of a future event, but Peter declared that the day had finally come. Through the death and resurrection of Jesus, we are able to experience the "day of the Lord" and live into its possibilities. How do you experience that overflowing?

RESPONSIVE READING

PSALM 84:1-7 (RCL);
PSALM 84:1-6 (BCP)

If you have access to it, you might listen to the fourth movement of Brahms's *Requiem*. Following a movement that confronts us with our mortality and the brief span of our life, Brahms uses the opening of this psalm to express the good news that even though we die, in God our souls have a home and will find rest.

This psalm may have been another in the series of psalms sung while people journeyed to Jerusalem. When they sang about the loveliness of God's dwelling place and the longing to be in God's court, they were speaking of the Temple in Jerusalem. They were not speaking metaphorically when referring to the highways to Zion. But we are.

THIS PSALM GIVES US WONDERFUL, COMFORTING IMAGES OF A TENDER GOD WHO CARES FOR EVEN THE SMALLEST OF CREATURES.

This psalm can be a wonderful opportunity to reflect on our cosmology. Sirach made the point that the "prayer of the humble pierces the clouds [and will] reach the Lord" (Sir. 35:17a). Where does God live? How many people, when speaking about or thanking God, look up? Yet none of our space exploration has bumped into the gates of heaven. Like the children of Israel, we long to dwell in God's presence. But how do we go about doing that—where should we, must we go? The preacher might turn to Jesus' discussion with the woman at the well that explored these questions (John 4:20-24).

However we answer these questions, this psalm gives us wonderful, comforting images of a tender God who cares for even the smallest of creatures. Sparrows and swallows can safely rest in God's presence. Desolate places, the Valley of Baca, become lush waterholes through God's mercies. We all have moments of desolation in our lives when we feel as fragile as a sparrow. In those moments we need to hear the good news that this psalm provides. God loves us and cares for us, no matter in what desolate or dry place of life we find ourselves.

PSALM 34:2-3, 17-18, 19, 23 (RC)

A thread running through today's lessons is the good news that no matter who we are, God encourages and listens to our prayers. God saves the righteous, those who are right with God, but God also rescues the brokenhearted. We cannot hear this news too often. Altogether too many people do not go to church because they do not think they are good enough. Rather than understanding the church as the refuge of those whose spirits have been crushed, they mistakenly see it as the club of the perfect who don't need any help.

But we have a God who lifts us up no matter how far we have fallen or how much weight has fallen upon us. The most interesting part of all of this, however, is that very often we do not realize that God has been with us until it is all over. I know that there have been difficult times in my life, serious illnesses or painful conflicts, when I felt that God had abandoned me. Only when the crisis had passed was I able to understand that I could never have made it through without God.

The good news is that God's ways are not our ways. Human beings may condemn and abandon one another, but "none of those who take refuge in God will be condemned."

PSALM 65 (RCL, alt.)

Some have suggested that this communal psalm of thanksgiving is actually three psalms, vv. 1-4, vv. 5-8, and vv. 9-13. What is clear is that this psalm is directed entirely to God and uses expansive language and images to praise God's mighty powers. We worship the God who not only created the very mountains but who also can still the sea. The Gospel writers hoped that we would hear echoes of this psalm when they told us the stories of Jesus stilling storms.

In the midst of these larger-than-life images comes the recurring theme that the same God who can do this can also hear the prayers of sinners. When we come to God on our knees asking forgiveness, our prayers will be answered; and look what we will be given—deliverance, salvation, joy, water, grain, more than we could ever hope or pray for.

SECOND READING
2 TIMOTHY 4:6-8, 16-18 (RCL, BCP, RC)

What does one say to those who follow in one's footsteps? How does one build them up, encourage them, and pass on the important information that they will need after you are gone? This friend, colleague, teacher, and pastor to the young Timothy knows that he will not be there much longer, so he has been imparting those final bits of wisdom. At the end of the letter, however, he speaks about himself, both his pride in what he has done, his faithfulness in the face of torment and travail, and his testimony that God has remained faithful through all of this.

The writer is honest about his situation. He recognizes that death is near. Then, mixing metaphors, he compares his life to that of a soldier who has "fought the good fight" and an athlete who has "finished the race"—images that Paul uses throughout all his letters. We are soldiers in the army of Christ, sent out with our swords and shields. And we are athletes who must train and practice in order to do the work that God has called us to do. Christians do this not for an earthly crown of laurels, not for human fame or fortune, but for the crown that we know will be ours "on that day" (4:8), the day of final judgment when we will enter into heavenly glory. This is a message of joy and confidence in God's gift of eternal life. The knowledge of that allows Timothy's mentor to live and proclaim this good news—right up to the end!

As I am writing this, a very dear friend of mine is coming to the end of her "good fight." She has lived, and I mean lived, with cancer for two years. She has been valiant through surgery, rounds and rounds of chemotherapy, and through it all remains cheerful and hopeful, even when the news is not good. She was a colleague of mine at the seminary, and we were recently speaking of the importance of theological reflection, a process our students learn. She stopped, almost mid-sentence, and exclaimed, "You know, one thing I have come to realize is that all of this *really matters!*" She told me that she could not have done any of this without God and God's strength. My friend has expressed, both in word and deed like Paul that "the Lord stood by me and gave me strength to proclaim the message fully." Thank God for giving us such wonderful messengers.

LUKE 18:9–14 (RCL, BCP, RC)

It would be so easy to read this parable and understand it simply as instructions for prayer. That is, we are to be like the tax collector who sits at the back of the church (which many people do already) and pray the magic words: "God, be merciful to me a sinner!" (18:13). We would also like to think that we are off the hook because we are not Pharisees.

The parable of the Pharisee and the tax collector follows immediately after the parable of the widow and the unjust judge, and they both follow the introduction of a recurring question: When will we see the advent of the reign of God? Jesus tells the Pharisees who have asked the question that there will be no signs or portents as they assume. Rather, he announces to them: "In fact, the kingdom of God is among you" (Luke 17:21).

What does it mean if the kingdom of God is already here? How are we to live if we are living in the reign of God? Both the parable of the widow and the judge, and the Pharisee and the tax collector give us pictures of what that reign looks like, and how we are to live in that reign. It is a

> WHAT DOES IT MEAN IF THE KINGDOM OF GOD IS ALREADY HERE? HOW ARE WE TO LIVE IF WE ARE LIVING IN THE REIGN OF GOD?

reign of justice and mercy. It is a reign in which the ways of the world are turned upside down.

We know how *we* look at people—heroes and villains, sinner and saved, blessed and cursed. But how does *God* look at people? When Samuel went to the home of Jesse the Bethlehemite to anoint the new king who would rule over Israel, he was assured that God would show him who was to be anointed. As Samuel saw all of Jesse's sons, each more handsome and worthy than the next, Samuel was sure that he had found the one. But he was warned, "Do not look on his appearance . . . for the LORD does not see as mortals see; they look on the outward appearance, but the LORD looks on the heart" (1 Sam. 16:7).

If we were to look at the Pharisee and the tax collector with human eyes, we would be sure that we knew who was favored by God and who was scorned. The Pharisee was the man who kept the law, gave alms, said his prayers, and had found both worldly and (he hoped) divine success. The tax collector, on the other hand, was certainly scorned by women and men and was probably scorned by God. He made his money by cooperating with the Roman oppressors and stealing from his fellow citizens. Jesus' listeners would have been shocked to hear Jesus report that it was the tax collector and not the Pharisee whose prayers were heard and who "went down to his house justified" (v. 14). God's ways are not our ways.

All throughout his Gospel, Luke is trying to proclaim an important message about the reign of God. Those who have found favor in the sight of the world, who have power and riches in human kingdoms, are not automatically or necessarily privileged in the kingdom of God. Mary introduces this theme in the song that she sings after answering her call. Mary also announces to us that we are to rejoice because God has found favor with her, and with us. The mercy of this God is "on those who fear him . . . exalted those of low degree; he has filled the hungry with good things" (Luke 1:50, 52-53). Likewise, this same God "has scattered the proud . . . put down the mighty from their thrones . . . the rich he has sent empty away" (Luke 1:51-53). It was the tax collector, not the Pharisee, who found favor that day. This is a parable about God's abundant grace and mercy as much as it is about the proper attitude of prayer. It is a parable that shows us that God's justice looks nothing like human justice, but central to God's justice is our willingness to admit and confess who we truly are.

We may not be cheating our fellow citizens out of their hard-earned cash, but Jesus is reminding us that we must all recognize that, like the tax collector, we should come before God recognizing our sinfulness and our failure to live up to God's expectations. The good news is that our God is merciful and not only listens to our cries, but is willing to wipe the slate clean, welcoming home repentant children and sending us away justified.

REFORMATION DAY

OCTOBER 31, 2004 (OR TRANSFERRED TO THE
TWENTY-SECOND SUNDAY AFTER PENTECOST)

Jer. 31:31-34
Psalm 46
Rom. 3:19-28
John 8:31-36

A note of full disclosure is in order. Although a daughter of the broader Reformation (the Anglican branch), I am not a Lutheran. Take that into account as you prepare to preach on this pivotal day in Luther's ministry. If Americans speak of the "shot heard 'round the world," can Christians speak of the "nail pound heard 'round the church?" If so, we read these lessons with trifocal vision. First, we reflect on the context of the writer. Second, we think of our current context. And finally, on Reformation Day, we place these writings in the context of the events that happened almost five hundred years ago.

FIRST READING
JEREMIAH 31:31-34

For a fuller discussion of this passage from Jeremiah, see the comments for Proper 24.

This beautiful message is at once a message of judgment, of our disobedience and unfaithfulness, and of hope and new possibility. In spite of the fact that we break God's covenant with us, God remains faithful and continually seeks new ways to strengthen that relationship. If tablets of stone could be broken, then perhaps God had to write the law on our hearts so that those laws of love would become a very part of our being.

> IN SPITE OF THE FACT THAT WE BREAK GOD'S COVENANT WITH US, GOD REMAINS FAITHFUL AND CONTINUALLY SEEKS NEW WAYS TO STRENGTHEN THAT RELATIONSHIP.

On this day the preacher may want to focus on the understanding that God is always doing new things, looking for news ways to be our God and new ways for us to be God's people. God's dealings with us are never static. And, in return, we should always be thinking about and seeking new ways to be faithful children of the Creator. Whenever the church ceases to grow, change, reform, then it will die.

While this is surely good news, it carries within it a potential for arrogance and separation. If we reform, if we set off on a new path, we are tempted to believe that those who do not travel with us are on the wrong path. We may believe that God is ours and ours alone, and that the new covenant is better than the old covenant. That may become our attitude toward other brothers and sisters in the Christian faith. But it may also color our attitude toward our Jewish or Muslim brothers and sisters.

We live in a challenging world. God has written a law within our hearts—that we love our neighbor as ourselves. And who is our neighbor? Our neighbor is all of God's children. As we ponder God's desire to be our God and a part of our lives, we are called to recognize God's presence in all of the world and all of God's people.

RESPONSIVE READING

PSALM 46

This psalm was appointed because it provided Luther with the text for his famous hymn "A Mighty Fortress." Although the hymn will be sung on this day, what message does this psalm have for us today?

Apparently this psalm was sung at the autumnal Feast of the Tabernacles, celebration of a new year, a new beginning. In spite of the chaos that surrounds us on every side—earthquakes, floods, etc. (you will have no difficulty finding additional contemporary catastrophes)—we as the children of God dwell secure in the city of God.

The psalm opens with two descriptions. First, it describes the world we inhabit. Terrible things have happened, do happen, and will happen. When we experience natural disasters and political turmoil, in our fear and uncertainty we turn to God. As the psalmist describes our world, we are given a glimpse of another world, the city of God. With God at the center, this is a world of stability and plenty. It is a city in which a river, the symbol for the source of life, runs directly through it. It was only the advent of trains, and then airplanes, that made it possible for people to live easily without access to a river. Not only did people need a river for drinking water, but more importantly they needed it for transportation and transporting goods to others. What are our lives like if the river of God's love does not flow through us? We wither and die. We lose our connection with others.

FOR THOSE STRUGGLING WITH THE DESTRUCTION OF THEIR LIVES AND THE CRUMBLING OF THEIR FOUNDATIONS, CAN THERE BE ANY BETTER OR STRONGER PROCLAMATION THAN THAT GOD IS OUR GOD?

Into this description of God's presence among us comes God's voice, saying, "Be still and know that I am God" (v. 10; cf. 1 Kings 19:12). For those struggling with the destruction of their lives and the crumbling of their foundations, can there be any better or stronger proclamation than that God is our God? We cannot be reminded too often that God is with us and will overcome the chaos and disorder of our lives.

Second Reading
ROMANS 3:19-28

Is it possible to return to Paul's letter to the Romans without taking a detour through Luther's writings? We hear his admonition in the preface to his commentary on Romans that "this epistle is in truth the most important document in the New Testament, the gospel in its purest expression." In Romans 3 we hear Paul's and Luther's gospel within the gospel, that it is only through faith in Christ that we are justified and have new life. We cannot work out this righteousness. We cannot justify ourselves by works of the law.

> IN ROMANS 3 WE HEAR PAUL'S AND LUTHER'S GOSPEL WITHIN THE GOSPEL, THAT IT IS ONLY THROUGH FAITH IN CHRIST THAT WE ARE JUSTIFIED AND HAVE NEW LIFE.

Yet, even today, when we shout affirmations of Amen and Alleluia to this declaration, we go out into the world and continue lives that seek to work out our own salvation, our own justification. It may not be the way that Paul or Luther envisioned, but it is through works nonetheless. We believe that we hold our lives in our hands—our success, our health, our security. Our bookshelves are filled with books that tell us how to be more efficient, how to make our bodies lean and trim, how to make investments that will allow us to retire to a life of leisure. We are the captains of our own ships. We want to be better, stronger, richer, and more famous than others. And we are uncomfortable thinking that being right with God is a gift.

We are uncomfortable with gifts. They are unpredictable. What happens when someone gives you a gift at Christmas (if you have not gotten them a gift)? I know that my first response is, "Oh, you shouldn't have." My second response is to quickly go out and buy a gift for that person. I don't want to be indebted—for them to have the upper hand. And yet God's grace comes to us as a gift. We cannot earn it, we do not deserve it, we cannot repay God. This is a difficult message for us to hear.

THE GOSPEL
JOHN 8:31–36

John records a tense exchange between Jesus and his followers, those "Jews who had believed in him" (v. 31). Jesus is not speaking with his adversaries, the "scribes and Pharisees." No, John is very clear that this is a conversation, if not among friends, at least among supporters. Yet we can hear the indignant tone in their voices when they respond, or challenge Jesus' assertion that, as Jews, they have not known the truth and consequently have been slaves. While they have been willing to follow this new rabbi who preaches as one with authority, that does not necessarily mean that they are willing to abandon the life they have been following. They still understand themselves to be "descendants of Abraham," accepting all that that may entail. In fact, they say, we "have never been in bondage to anyone. How is it you say, 'You will be made free'?" (v. 33). And what is this truth that they have not already known or been privileged to? What does it mean to put aside or reject that which you have known, the way you have lived, your very identity, and follow something or someone new?

"You will know the truth, and the truth will make you free" (v. 32). We long to know, to hear, to discover the truth. We demand that witnesses tell "the truth, the whole truth, and nothing but the truth." The television program *X-Files,* however, enacts our postmodern dilemma. While Agent Mulder proclaims that "the truth is out there," what that truth is and where "out there" is located we could never be sure. Each week viewers see that truth is relative, slippery, and idiosyncratic. The truth can be manipulated, distorted, and certainly concealed. How can we know the "whole truth"? Will we even know the truth if we see it?

Law schools have a favorite exercise. When the students are learning about the reliability of witnesses, someone enters the hall while the professor is lecturing. The person runs over, steals someone's purse or brief case, then runs out. The professor plays along, running after the person and acting as though it is truly an incident of brazen theft. The professor returns to the classroom with the news that the person got away, but campus security has been called, thereby allowing some time to pass. When "security" arrives, the students are asked to describe the person— and the fun begins. Inevitably they discover that each person is "certain" about what he or she saw, and that none of their descriptions match. How short is short? How tall is tall? What was the person wearing? No one can agree, and yet they all saw the same person and are certain about what they saw. Eventually the "thief" returns and they are allowed to check their memories. The goal of the exercise is the realization that the "whole truth and nothing but the truth" is not as reliable or attainable as one might think.

Truth is an important issue in the Gospel according to John. While the word truth, *aletheia,* appears only six times in all three of the Synoptic Gospels and three times in Acts, John uses it twenty-two times. In fact, the Gospel is essentially a circular answer to a question that is posed by Pilate during the passion. As Jesus appeared in the praetorium, Pilate asked him if he was a king. Jesus responded: "You say that I am a king. For this I was born, and for this I am come into the world, to bear witness to the truth. Every one who is of the truth hears my voice" (18:37). This prompts Pilate to ask, "What is truth?" But of course we, the readers of the Gospel, already know the answer. We were told it at the beginning, for the Gospel opened with the declaration that, "the Word became flesh and dwelt among us, full of grace and truth . . . [and while] the law was given through Moses;

> TRUTH IS AN IMPORTANT ISSUE IN THE GOSPEL ACCORDING TO JOHN.

grace and truth came through Jesus Christ" (1:14a, 17). Jesus, the incarnate one, is the truth of God. If we know the truth, that is, if we know Jesus, that knowledge and that knowledge alone will set us free. Doing and living the law will not.

We may live in a time that hungers for the truth that is "out there," but the Christian proclamation is that we already know the truth. Following the way of Jesus, living in the faith of the Risen One is to live in the truth. "I am the way, and the truth, and the life," Jesus says (14:6). It is not out there, it is right here in the worship, the community, the fellowship of those who have died with Christ in their baptism and have risen to new life in the body of Christ. We find our freedom in living as a member, a part of that body.

Reformation Day is an opportunity to reflect upon the joys and challenges of being the body of Christ. How do we grow? How do we reflect the truth of the Risen One? How are we able to embody the amazing variety of those whom "the Son [has] made free"?

TWENTY-SECOND SUNDAY AFTER PENTECOST

THIRTY-FIRST SUNDAY IN ORDINARY TIME / PROPER 26
OCTOBER 31, 2004

REVISED COMMON	EPISCOPAL (BCP)	ROMAN CATHOLIC
Isa. 1:10-18 or Hab. 1:1-4; 2:1-4	Isa. 1:10-20	Wisd. of Sol. 11:22—12:2
Ps. 32:1-7 or 119:137-144	Psalm 32 or 32:1-8	Ps. 145:1-2, 8-11, 13-14
2 Thess. 1:1-4, 11-12	2 Thess. 1:1-5, (6-10), 11-12	2 Thess. 1:11—2:2
Luke 19:1-10	Luke 19:1-10	Luke 19:1-10

What does it mean to follow Christ? What does it mean to accept Christ into one's life? What does it mean to realize that Christ already loves us and accepts us? This All Hallows' Eve (Halloween), as we prepare to celebrate the saints of the church, those whose lives shone with the glory of God, we are right to reflect upon the challenge of responding to and living into Christ's call—as Zacchaeus does in today's Gospel.

FIRST READING
ISAIAH 1:10-18 (RCL);
ISAIAH 1:10-20 (BCP)

While today's Gospel presents us with a loving moment of acceptance, tenderness, and joy, this reading from the opening chapter of First Isaiah is a message of judgment. The voice of God that is heard through the writing of this prophet is a voice demanding the people to either "shape up or they will be shipped out."

Isaiah of Jerusalem was writing in the later half of the sixth century B.C.E., roughly between 740 and 700. The political situation was tense. The northern kingdom had been annexed by the Assyrian Empire. While Judah (southern kingdom) remained free, albeit a tributary of the large empire, nonetheless, those in Jerusalem lived under the constant threat of a similar fate. To a people who often seemed unaware of the possible danger, Isaiah exhorted them to repent of their evil ways and return to God's path. But it sounded as though they were doing the right things and following the law. What were they to do?

Today's passage opens with an unambiguous accusation. Isaiah announces that they are to "hear the word" and "give ear to the teaching of our God." The prophet is therefore speaking both a prophetic and priestly word. And who should listen? It is addressed to the "rulers of Sodom" and the "people of Gomorrah." This message, in other words, is being addressed to wicked sinners. Sodom and Gomorrah had long before been destroyed by God's hands. If the people of Jerusalem did not repent, they would suffer a similar fate. What contemporary places would evoke a similar response? What are today's Sodom and Gomorrah?

This challenging opening is further eclipsed by God's harsh rejection of the people's religious practices. I frequently caution student preachers against chastising the people in the pew about not coming to church. After all, they are there. But this is exactly what the prophet is doing. God rejects all of their religious offerings and rituals.

First, God tells them what is wrong. What they have been doing, the prayers and rituals, have been for themselves, not for God. They may have been making offerings, but they did it for show. (Refer to Jesus' similar charges in Matt. 6:5—"You must not be like the hypocrites; for they love to stand and pray . . . that they might be seen by others." Or in Mark 12:44, where Jesus chastises the rich who contribute out of their abundance, in contrast to the widow who gives out of her poverty. We will return to the rich in the Gospel.) God, who can see into the hearts of those "trampling the courts," sees that they are not hearts turned toward the God who created them and loves them.

Isaiah also presents us with a troubling image. God sees that the hands that are upraised in prayer are hands that are covered with the blood of the innocent. God, not bearing to see that, turns away. Can we look honestly at our hands? Are they, too, covered with the blood of the innocent? Do we ignore those who are in pain and

> GOD MAY DECRY OUR UNFAITHFULNESS, BUT GOD REMAINS EVER FAITHFUL AND OFFERS US A WAY BACK.

are oppressed? Do we turn our faces away from those who cry out for help? Are we like the people of Jerusalem who concealed the injustices committed in their name or by their hands?

While this is unambiguously a word of judgment and condemnation, it is also a word of forgiveness and hope. God may decry our unfaithfulness, but God remains ever faithful and offers us a way back.

The second half of the reading instructs us about those things that God desires. It is not empty prayers, feasts, or incense. Rather, God commands us to wash ourselves and "learn to do good." Notice that nothing is mentioned about ritual practices. All that God demands is directed, not toward God, but toward the neighbor.

We are to "seek justice, correct oppression; defend the fatherless, plead for the widow" (v. 17). Clearly we are hearing a message similar to that in Amos 5:21-24, Mic. 6:6-8, and Matt. 25:31-46: "As you did it to one of the least of these my brethren, you did it to me" (Matt. 25:40, RSV).

The message of good news is that, when we do this, we are washed clean— "though your sins are like scarlet, they shall be like snow" (v. 18). Although one may be reluctant to use it in the pulpit, we have an amazing biological analogy. When smokers quit smoking, their lungs very quickly wash themselves clean. They can become like the lungs of one who never smoked. What a message of hope.

WISDOM OF SOLOMON 11:22—12:2 (RC)

Sin and repentance are threads that run through all of today's lections, culminating with Zacchaeus's turn to Jesus and a new life. This passage from the Wisdom of Solomon reflects upon God's tender love. As great as God is, high above all that lives, God still sees all and loves all. It is a message that most of us need to hear yet a tension that is difficult to comprehend. How is it that we can believe in a God who knows all, sees all, for whom the "whole world . . . is like a speck that tips the scales" (11:22), yet cares about our individual lives?

The author declares the message we want to and need to hear, that this great and all powerful God is as close to us as our heart and mind—"thy immortal spirit is in all things" (12:1). God is in us, correcting and guiding us. If we travel the wrong path, doing what is wrong in God's sight, still God does not abandon us. Rather, "You spare all things, for they are yours, O Lord, you who love the living" (11:26). Again, this is a message of hope and comfort.

HABAKKUK 1:1-4; 2:1-4 (RCL, alt.)

See the discussion of this lection for October 22, Proper 22.

RESPONSIVE READING

PSALM 32:1-7 (RCL);
PSALM 32 (BCP);
PSALM 32:1-8 (BCP, alt.)

Sin is not a very popular topic in churches these days. "Experts" who offer help to those seeking to find ways to bring the unchurched into the pew counsel against mentioning sin or guilt. References to sin and guilt are, according to these experts, a major "turn off" and keep people from returning to the church if "preached" too often. Yet these same churches willingly welcome twelve-step programs into their buildings, where a first step is to acknowledge their addiction. Are these churches not struck by the irony that people are able to confess their weakness and failure during the week but not on Sunday? Why can we acknowledge our helplessness in a support group but not in worship service?

Psalm 32 is one of the seven penitential psalms. The author gives thanks for recovery from an illness, which, for the author, would have been God's punishment for sinful actions. Healing, the author understood, was a sign from God that those sins had been forgiven. As long as the author refused to confront and acknowledge that sin, "my strength was dried up" (v. 4).

But, when he finally did stand up before God to confess his transgressions, he was met with love and forgiveness. While we may no longer equate illness with sin (although many, for example, would "blame" those with lung cancer for their history of smoking), we cannot help but relate to the psalmist's lament. We do know what it means to live with unacknowledged sins.

In the opening of the psalm, the author uses three different words for sins. First, he declares that his transgression, his *pesa'*, has been forgiven. *Pesa'* is used to describe willful, open rebellion against God's ways. Next, he acknowledges that his sin *(hatta't)* is covered. *Hatta't* means that one is missing the mark or deviating from the path that God has set. And finally, he observes that he is now free from iniquity *('awon)*. *'Awon* is perversion or twisting of life and truth. When the psalmist was willing to confess his transgressions, his sins and iniquities, God was willing to take him back and forgive him. Are we willing to make the same stand? Are we willing, as a church, to even talk about the ways that we rebel against God and set off on our own path rather than walking the path that God has invited us to follow?

PSALM 119:137–144 (RCL, alt.)

We are tempted to blame God or turn away from God when we are faced with difficulties and trials. The psalmist declares that although "trouble and anguish and have come upon me" (v. 143), he has not turned away. He is still able to declare that God is just and faithful, and that God's way is the path to follow.

PSALM 145:1-2, 8-11, 13-14 (RC)

As we prepare for All Saint's Day, the psalmist reminds us that God's "compassion is over all that he has made" and that, as God's saints, we are to give thanks and bless God's holy name. God has done great things for us and we, in turn, cannot remain silent. We are to tell all the world that God is faithful, now and forever.

LUCY
LIND HOGAN

SECOND READING

2 THESSALONIANS 1:1-4, 11-12 (RCL);
2 THESSALONIANS 1:1-5,(6-10),11-12 (BCP);
2 THESSALONIANS 1:11—2:2 (RC)

How gratifying it must have been for the Christians struggling in Thessalonica to hear that their friend and pastor was bragging about them—"we ourselves boast of you in the churches" (v. 4). Why? Because in spite of all that they were going through, much like the psalmist in Psalm 119, they were able to remain steadfast and faithful. However, that does not mean that the Thessalonian congregation was not faced with its own internal problems.

As she was reflecting on her impending death, my very dear friend said, "You know, theology matters!" What we think about God, who God is, who Christ is, all makes a difference in the way we live every day. Paul knew this, and he also knew that mistaken beliefs about God would cause problems. So he wrote to help the Thessalonians get back on the right track.

The shorter reading of this letter focuses on the faithfulness of the Thessalonians and Paul's prayer that they continue to remain faithful. In all that they were going through, their lives were able to preach God's love and God's faithfulness.

Those who read all of 2 Thessalonians will confront the difficulty facing those who belonged to the community. They were going through difficult times, and Paul wanted to remind them that there would come a time when "God deems it just to repay with affliction those who afflict you" (v. 6), and in that same time, those who were suffering would find rest. Paul presents a terrifying and powerful image of Jesus coming "from heaven with his mighty angels in flaming fire, inflicting vengeance upon those who do not know God . . . and do not obey the gospel" (vv. 7-8).

The north apse of the Shrine of the Immaculate Conception in Washington, D.C., is covered with one of the largest mosaics in the world—"Christ in Majesty"

WHILE PAUL WANTED TO ASSURE THEM THAT THE DAY WOULD COME, HE ALSO WANTED TO REMIND THEM THAT IT WAS NOT YET.

by John de Rosen. His portrait is modeled after the Eastern tradition of *Pantokrator,* Christ as ruler of all. The face of Christ is fierce and he is, indeed, ready to inflict vengeance, recalling the words of Rev. 4:5, "From the throne issue flashes of lightning, and voices and peals of thunder." Christ's halo is made up of tongues of fire, and his outstretched arms fill the space. It is an overwhelming but not necessarily comforting portrait. To those who are suffering at the hands of others, however, the message that Christ will rescue them and punish their oppressors is certainly good news.

The problem confronting the church in Thessalonica was the preaching of some that the day of the Lord had already come. While Paul wanted to assure them that the day would come, he also wanted to remind them that it was not yet.

How often do we long for that day ourselves! When we look at the suffering of our world, when we see the pain and oppression, the wars and conflict that continue to rage, we cry out for God to come in glory and grant rest to us all. But until that day comes, Paul reminds us that we must live lives that glorify God and "fulfill . . . every good resolve and work of faith" (v. 11).

And what does that life look like? What are those good resolves, and what are the works of faith? Those are the questions that are explored and answered by our Gospel lesson.

THE GOSPEL
LUKE 19:1–10 (RCL, BCP, RC)

On All Saint's Day the church will remember those whose lives reflected the light of Christ. It will recall those who, as the old children's hymn said, were "patient and brave and true" and who "toiled and fought and lived and died for the Lord they loved and knew" ("I Sing a Song of the Saints of God," by Lesbia Scott). While the hymn may go on to say that doctors and soldiers, shepherds and queens were all saints of God, it does not say anything about tax collectors. How can, and should, one of the lowest of the low find forgiveness and acceptance in the kingdom of God?

The meeting of Jesus and Zacchaeus is paired with an incident that occurs just before it—Jesus meeting the blind man. The latter occurred on the road to Jericho; the former occurred after Jesus had arrived in the city itself, and all took place in the broader event of Jesus and the Twelve "going up to Jerusalem, and everything that is written of the Son of Man by the prophets will be accomplished" (Luke 18:31).

Can we not place ourselves in that same journey? Our lives are a journey toward the end that God has in mind for us, toward the kingdom of God. But unlike Jesus, we cannot always be sure that we will gain admittance.

In a conversation just before his decision to go to Jerusalem, Jesus told a rich young ruler that in order to inherit eternal life he must sell all that he had. Unwilling to do that, the young man "became sad" (18:23). It is not difficult to see Jesus shaking his head as he declares, "How hard it is for those who have riches to enter the kingdom of God!" (18:24). Jesus then goes on to present us with a troubling image: "It is easier for a camel to pass through the eye of a needle than for someone who is rich to enter the kingdom of God" (18:25). This is a ridiculous image that many have tried to explain away. Some suggest, for instance, that the eye of a needle was really a very small gate. But we should give ourselves over to the ridiculous impossibility of the challenge. Of course it is impossible, and that is Jesus' point! He wants us to admit that it is impossible for us to enter eternal life by our own efforts and our own merits. If we try to do that, we will never make it. Naturally, the disciples despair at this realization and cry out, "Then who can be saved?" The good news is that, "What is impossible for mortals is possible for God" (18:27). Luke proceeds to give us two instances of camels passing through that needle's eye, a blind man who receives his sight and a rich man who receives salvation.

The people despised tax collectors. Not only were they employees and collaborators with the Roman oppressors, they made their money from essentially legalized stealing. They had a certain amount that they were directed to collect from the people; if they were able to collect more, they were able to keep that and enrich their own coffers.

"Then who can be saved?" Luke presents us with the stories of two unlikely people to answer that question. The first is a blind man, the second, Zacchaeus. While we read only one story, it is important to compare and contrast these two. Both the blind man and Zacchaeus are outsiders. The blind man is literally "near" Jericho, not in the town, sitting on the roadside. Religious people would have considered him to be a sinner, his blindness being punishment for a sin that he or perhaps his parents had committed.

"THEN WHO CAN BE SAVED?" LUKE PRESENTS US WITH THE STORIES OF TWO UNLIKELY PEOPLE TO ANSWER THAT QUESTION.

Zacchaeus is also on the outside, but he is up in the air, in the branches of a tree, so he is not a part of the crowd. We are told that he climbed the tree because he was a small man and, although he wanted to see Jesus, would not have been able to do so if he stayed in the crowd. As the chief tax collector, it would seem unlikely that the crowd would welcome him in their midst. And they certainly wouldn't have let him go to the front of the crowd so that he could see.

Both men want "to see." The blind man cries out to Jesus, trying to get his attention and begging for mercy. When asked by Jesus what he wants, he implores Jesus to give him his sight. But Zacchaeus merely wants a chance to see this prophet. There is no indication that he wants anything more. Both of these men attract the attention of Jesus, and their lives are changed. The blind man does see, and because of him, others also see, "all the people, when the saw it, gave praise to God" (18:43).

Imagine how surprised Zacchaeus was when Jesus told him that he was coming to his home for dinner. (You notice that Luke doesn't say anything about Zacchaeus's wife and what she thought about this—but that is another sermon.)

Zacchaeus did not ask for anything, and Jesus did not do anything other than go to his home. Yet merely allowing Jesus in was enough to call forth a radical change in his life. This rich man, while not giving up *everything* he had, was going to give half of what he had to the poor and make restitution to any he had defrauded. So salvation came to this rich man. He had entered the kingdom of God. A camel had passed through the eye of a needle.

What does it mean to follow Christ? What does it mean to accept Christ into one's life, to allow him in? What does it mean to realize that Christ already loves us and accepts us? It means that impossibly wonderful things can happen in our lives. It means that we who are sinful, weak people who rebel against God and refuse to follow in God's way can find forgiveness and love. It means that new life is always possible because God is not only waiting for us, God is actively seeking us out to bring us home. "For the Son of Man came to seek and to save the lost" (v. 10), so that they will be lost no more.

ALL SAINTS DAY

NOVEMBER 1, 2004
(OR TRANSFERRED TO NOVEMBER 7, 2004)

REVISED COMMON	EPISCOPAL (BCP)	ROMAN CATHOLIC
Dan. 7:1-3, 15-18	Sir. 44:1-10, 13-14 or 2:(1-6), 7-11	Rev. 7:2-4, 9-14
Psalm 149	Psalm 149	Ps. 24:1-6
Eph. 1:11-23	Rev. 7:2-4, 9-17 or Eph. 1:(11-14), 15-23	1 John 3:1-3
Luke 6:20-31	Matt. 5:1-12 or Luke 6:20-26, (27-36)	Matt. 5:1-12a

Early twenty-first-century Americans live in an age that worships celebrities. There are many paths to celebrity status. One might get there through sports, television and movies (and that says nothing about the quality of one's work), or even by questionable activities. Monica Lewinsky was elevated from White House intern to international celebrity by dubious behavior. What seems to be important for celebrities, and those who follow them, is that they are news makers of some sort whose pictures are in magazines, newspapers, and on the screen, film or television.

> WE REMEMBER THEM NOT JUST TO CELEBRATE WHAT THEY DID IN THE PAST, BUT TO RECOGNIZE IN THEIR EXAMPLES CHALLENGES TO LIVE LIVES THAT SHOW FORTH THE GLORY OF GOD.

Celebrity status is also fleeting and fickle. As Andy Warhol noted, we will all have our fifteen minutes of fame, but for most of us it will be only that fifteen minutes. On All Saints Day the church lifts up those who are not celebrities. Rather, we remember people for the quality of their lives and works, people who were not seeking to be famous but to be followers of Christ. And we remember them not just to celebrate what they did in the past, but to recognize in their examples challenges to live lives that show forth the glory of God. What does it mean to be a saint of God? Are they special, unusual people, or are they ordinary people who are able to do special, unusual things through the grace of God?

DANIEL 7:1-3, 15-18 (RCL)

How does one encourage people who are experiencing a difficult period of terror and testing? Many preachers asked that and similar questions in the days after September 11, 2001. How could you preach hope and endurance in the midst of pain and suffering? The author of the book of Daniel wrestled with similar questions. How could he offer words of encouragement to those suffering under the persecution of Antiochus Epiphanes that occurred between 167 and 164 B.C.E.?

He did so by employing the apocalyptic literary form. He told the stories and visions of a faithful follower of God, Daniel (or Dan'el) during the Babylonian captivity. Those visions were of "future" events that were, in reality, the current events of the readers. The visions foretold of their eventual victory over their oppressors. With God's help they, the saints, would, "receive the kingdom and possess the kingdom forever—forever and ever" (v. 18).

Apocalyptic literature employs complicated symbolism and fantastic images to talk about common, everyday fears. Like the anxious Daniel, we too see terrifying things all around us. The seas do boil and beasts arise that seek to do us harm. But the message of his vision is that God will prevail and in the end triumph. This message is sent to the saints, *qaddish*, those set apart by God, the separate ones.

> THE AUTHOR WANTED TO ASSURE THESE TORMENTED SAINTS THAT THEIR VICTORY WAS CERTAIN. THIS IS CLEARLY A MESSAGE WE STILL NEED TO HEAR.

Isn't it easier to endure, to keep going, if you know that ultimately you are going to win, to succeed, to be vindicated? The author wanted to assure these tormented saints that their victory was certain. This is clearly a message we still need to hear.

SIRACH/ECCLESIASTICUS 44:1-10, 13-14 (BCP)

Joshua (Jesus) the son of Sira offers us words of comfort. If we are decent people who live merciful lives, we will not be forgotten. This passage begins with the wonderful, well-known phrase, "Let us now sing the praises of famous men" (v. 1, RSV). Then, after noting all of the ways that these famous men—kings, musicians, poets, men of wealth and power—could be remembered, the author goes on to note that, in spite of their fame, even these men may be forgotten.

How many things do we do to make certain we will be remembered? We even carve our tombstones out of granite to ensure that our name is there long after we have turned to dust. But this reading reminds us that neither wealth nor power nor talent are enough to guarantee that we will not be forgotten. Instead, it is because we are merciful and perform righteous deeds that our "posterity will continue for ever, and our glory will not be blotted out" (v. 13). So on All Saints Day, we do praise famous women and men, remembering them not for their wealth or even for their creativity, but for the lives of mercy and righteousness that they lived.

SIRACH (ECCLESIASTICUS) 2:(1-6), 7-11 (BCP, alt.)

Joshua son of Sira is a wise teacher who counsels us to prepare for our future by looking to our past. In the first six verses of the second chapter, he reminds those who would "serve the Lord" (v. 1) that they must prepare themselves to face temptations and trials, "for gold is tested in the fire, and those found acceptable, in the furnace of humiliation" (v. 5). When we find ourselves in the intense moments that test us, we should remember those who have gone before, those who have faced their tests and prevailed. But it is most important that we remember why they prevailed. It was not that they felt themselves to be superior, but because they put their trust in the Lord. And it was the Lord who was faithful and allowed them to triumph. So Joshua challenges us to do as they did, to wait for God's mercy, to trust in the Lord, and to "hope for good things, for everlasting joy and mercy" (v. 9).

REVELATION 7:2-4, 9-14 (RC)

My mother enjoyed speaking with Jehovah's Witnesses who would come to the door seeking to convince her that she had not been saved. (Since she had been confirmed both in the Lutheran church and the Episcopal church, she felt otherwise.) She particularly enjoyed the moment when they confronted her with the central question. Quoting from the book of the Revelation, they would remind her that only 144,000 people were going to get into heaven—was she one of them? She would observe that they had stopped reading too early. If they would only read a little further they would discover that John saw "a great multitude that no one could count, from every nation, from all tribes and peoples and languages" (v. 9). She thought that this offered great hope, and that she just might make it!

As did the author of the book of Daniel before him, John employed the fantastic, visionary forms of apocalyptic literature to offer hope and encouragement to a people suffering persecution and enslavement. Using the image of baptism, he declared that they, who had been sealed as the servants of God, would be set aside and kept from harm in the mighty wind that was to blow. And, he reminded them, they will be delivered, called out, to join the chorus singing around the heavenly throne.

This passage offers hope not only for our own future, but offers comfort to those who wonder what has happened to those who have proceeded them in death. I am frequently asked what heaven is like and, while we can't give an absolute answer, Revelation gives us a hint in this glorious picture.

RESPONSIVE READING
PSALM 149 (RCL, BCP)

An important image for All Saint's Day is that of the heavenly, unending chorus of those praising God. As the final verse of "Amazing Grace" observes, "When we've been there ten thousand years, bright shining as the sun, we've no less days to sing God's praise than when we'd first begun" (John Newton, 1779). This psalm draws us into the chorus.

As the people of God, we are invited to "Sing to the Lord a new song" (v. 1). We are to sing because God has given us something to sing about. Those who are suffering at the hands of nations and kings will find that God will "execute on them the judgment written" (v. 9).

PSALM 24:1-6 (RC)

What does it mean to be a saint of God? Who are the holy ones, set aside ones? Who will be able to climb the holy hill and stand before the throne of God? The psalmist declares that they are those with clean hands and pure hearts.

SECOND READING
EPHESIANS 1:11-23 (RCL);
EPHESIANS 1:(11-14), 15-23 (BCP, alt.)

What a joy it must have been for Paul to hear that communities of new Christians were growing and flourishing even after he left them. His peripatetic ministry demonstrated an intense faith and trust in the Holy Spirit. He knew that they were Christ's churches, not his. And their future was "sealed with the promised Holy Spirit"(v. 13), not Paul's administrative and preaching ability.

In the opening of his letter to them, Paul reminds the community at Ephesus that both their present as well as their future is "destined and appointed" by God in Christ. It is Paul's prayer that they will continue to grow in "a spirit of wisdom and of revelation in the knowledge of him [Christ]" (v. 17).

This Jesus, who "humbled himself and became obedient unto death, even death on a cross" (Phil. 2:8), has been raised "far above all rule and authority and power and dominion" (v. 21). God has made Christ "head over all things" (v. 22), now and forever, and has also called them, the saints, to share in his inheritance.

> PAUL REMINDS THE COMMUNITY AT EPHESUS THAT BOTH THEIR PRESENT AS WELL AS THEIR FUTURE IS "DESTINED AND APPOINTED" BY GOD IN CHRIST.

Paul continues the image of the church, the saints, as the body of Christ which he empowers. They are doing great things now, "your love toward all the saints" (v. 15), and will go on to great things, "the riches of his glorious inheritance in the saints" (v. 18). To be a saint of God is to know that we have a present and a future life together.

REVELATION 7:2-4, 9-17 (BCP)

See the First Reading for today, above.

1 JOHN 3:1-3 (RC)

This brief reading introduces an important idea that brings with it a troubling concern. The writer offers us a word of comfort. God loves us so much that we can be called the children of God. But a question remains: Why do we often not feel like God's children? How can we tell that we are the children of God? Why do bad things continue to happen to us? John invites us to live into the hope with the assurance that when Christ returns, we will see that we are like Christ.

THE GOSPEL
LUKE 6:20-31 (RCL);
LUKE 6:20-26, (27-36) (BCP, alt.)

"Blessed are. . . ." Both Luke's and Matthew's Gospels include a sermon delivered by Jesus—Luke's Jesus seated on a plain, Matthew's on a mountain. They are sermons that explore what it means to be a "blessed one," a holy one that is set apart and sanctified, a saint of God.

Each morning my husband and I rise early to say prayers together. We read scripture, but we also read the stories of God's holy ones who went before us. We listen to stories of the works and trials of those who make up the great cloud of witnesses. There are inspiring stories. There are humbling stories. And a few are unusual stories. Not infrequently, when we finish some stories, we both say with one voice, "He or she was certainly an odd duck."

The cloud of witnesses that stands before the throne of God singing God's praises and cheering us on in our journey is filled with every sort imaginable. We must remember that, as Samuel found out, "the LORD sees not as mortals see; they look on the outward appearance, but the LORD looks on the heart" (1 Sam. 16:7). We often have preconceived ideas of what a holy or godly person is like. Samuel was looking for someone who was handsome and king-like. It was through that lens that he looked at all of the sons of Jesse. Reminiscent of the Cinderella story, as the sons passed before him, while they were good looking and strong, none was just right. Samuel waited until he got the word from God, "Arise, anoint him; for this is he" (1 Sam. 16:12). David was the chosen one of God—the youngest son who was spending his time with the sheep. Samuel was seeing as mortals see; God was looking at the heart, and David had God's heart.

> THE CLOUD OF WITNESSES THAT STANDS BEFORE THE THRONE OF GOD SINGING GOD'S PRAISES AND CHEERING US ON IN OUR JOURNEY IS FILLED WITH EVERY SORT IMAGINABLE.

What does it mean to be a person whose life is pleasing in God's sight? How does one live a godly life? In both the Sermon on the Plain and the Sermon on the Mount, Jesus explores what it means to have a "God heart." The two sermons, while clearly working from a common tradition, are different in a number of ways. Therefore, it is important for preachers to make sure that they keep them separate and honor those differences.

The sermons of Matthew and Luke appear to be compilations of the sayings of Jesus that were given at different times and in different places. Luke's presentation of the sermon is shorter. It is divided into three sections. It begins with four "blesseds," then moves to four "woes." Luke's sermon takes place on a plain in order to identify with the downtrodden and dispossessed, which is further seen in his construction of the blessings.

> THE BEATITUDES ARE BLESSINGS RATHER THAN EXHORTATIONS.

The Beatitudes are blessings rather than exhortations. Jesus pronounces blessings upon those hearing his words rather than telling them that this is what they must do. He is saying, "Blessed are you who are poor," not, "You must be poor." He is assuring those who are hungry, mourning, and experiencing persecution that they will be vindicated by God. Nevertheless, these sayings of Jesus give us a picture of what it means to live in the kingdom of God. Jesus is inviting us to a life that looks very different from worldly success.

When my oldest son was little, he had only one answer when he was asked what he wanted to be—a movie star. He was, and still is, a "Star Wars" fanatic. (Little did

I realize that he would be true to his passion. He may not be a film star, but today he lives in Hollywood and works in television production.) But when he was young, he wanted to be in the movies because he wanted to be rich and famous.

I see that in many young people today. They want to do something that is going to make them a star, a celebrity. Look at the programs that are now on television—*American Idol, Survivor,* and countless programs about men and women seeking to date or marry various people. Why would someone participate in these programs? Because they want to see themselves on television, and in doing so become famous. They want to be set apart from the crowd. They want to be singled out, to be special. This is in part, I think, because they don't understand themselves to be valuable in and of themselves as children of God.

Jesus came to tell us that we are beloved children of God and to invite us to live in that knowledge. We don't need to become rich and famous according to the world's standards in order to be valuable in God's sight or in the sight of our brothers and sisters in faith. In fact, the "woes" reported by Luke tell us that those who find success in this world, those who are rich and famous already "have received your consolation."

On All Saint's Day we are invited to reflect upon the saintly virtues of love for God and for our neighbor. We are to remember those who have lived that life and, in turn, remind ourselves that God is asking us to follow their examples. We are surrounded by a great cloud of witnesses—people who put the lives of others above their own. We have the "official" saints of the church. We are able to lift up those who, in our own day, have lost their lives following the gospel imperatives— Martin Luther King Jr., Oscar Romero, and those who live lives of untiring devotion like Mother Teresa. But we can also point to the example of the countless people in the World Trade Center who lost their lives when they went up the stairs to help rather than down to escape.

MATTHEW 5:1-12 (BCP); MATTHEW 5:1-12a (RC)

Like Luke, Matthew has also drawn together a number of the sayings of Jesus and placed them in a "sermon." In addition to the setting, on a mountain rather than a plain, there are a number of differences, and it is interesting to compare and contrast the two sermons.

The Sermon on the Mount is considerably longer, 5:1 to 7:28. By setting it on a mountain, Matthew is hoping to remind his readers/listeners of Moses and Sinai. There are nine blessings and no woes. Furthermore, Matthew has spiritualized the conditions. Luke's Jesus speaks of the poor, but Matthew's Jesus speaks of the "poor in spirit."

While there are differences, Matthew, like Luke, is seeking to provide the followers of Jesus with the good news of the kingdom. God cares for and lifts up those who have been oppressed and rejected, and in that we find comfort and assurance.

As the church remembers the "official" saints who have gone before us, we are also invited to remember the people in our own lives whose examples are known only to us and their friends and families, but who are surely among the blessed. For example, we remember our own parents and grandparents who showed us the way of faith. Then there is the grandmother who took in her grandchildren after her son or daughter was killed. Or the teacher who spent many extra hours after school, making sure that the little boy would know how to read. Or the man who delivered meals and a joyful smile to shut-ins even in the midst of a snow storm. Blessed are they, for theirs is the kingdom of God. Their lives show forth their God hearts.

TWENTY-THIRD SUNDAY AFTER PENTECOST

THIRTY-SECOND SUNDAY IN ORDINARY TIME /
PROPER 27
NOVEMBER 7, 2004

REVISED COMMON	EPISCOPAL (BCP)	ROMAN CATHOLIC
Job 19:23-27a	Job 19:23-27a	2 Macc. 7:1-2, 9-14
or Hag. 1:15b—2:9		
Ps. 17:1-9 or Psalm 98	Psalm 17 or 17:1-8	Ps. 17:1, 5-6, 8, 15
2 Thess. 2:1-5, 13-17	2 Thess. 2:13—3:5	2 Thess. 2:16—3:5
Luke 20:27-38	Luke 20:27, (28-33),	Luke 20:27-38
	34-38	or 20:27, 34-38

When is the end truly the end? When is the end not the end? We are reminded in 1 Samuel that God sees not as human beings see. Likewise, God's understanding of endings is not the same as our limited human perception. Christian faith is centered in the belief of the resurrection, that death was not the end for Jesus and it is not the end of our lives, yet we have difficulty understanding what that means, what it looks like, and how we are to live into that reality. We have no difficulty picturing the incarnation—museums are filled with images of the Word made flesh, the infant Jesus. But depicting resurrection is more difficult. There are glowing pictures of the resurrected Christ standing in a beautiful garden outside a dark tomb. Yet somehow we know resurrection is much more than that. The lessons this week focus our attention on this central tenet of our faith, not just the resurrection of Jesus, but our own resurrection.

FIRST READING

JOB 19:23-27A (RCL, BCP)

The book of Job pushes our faith to the limit. It is one thing to look around the world, seeing the pain, suffering, and injustice, and ask, "Where is God in all of this?" It takes us to another level, however, when that God is the one who indirectly causes an apparently innocent man to lose all of his children and his property, and to suffer an excruciating illness. What kind of God is that?

The book of Job is a poem set within a narrative frame. It is crucial that listeners understand this is a work of fiction. Few portions of this book are included within the lectionary—perhaps with good reason.

In the opening of the book, God and Satan are engaged in a debate. Satan claims that Job loves and praises God only because God has blessed him. So, with God's permission, Satan wreaks havoc on the life of Job to test and see if he will still love and praise God. As each terrible thing happens, Satan observes that Job still "did not sin or charge God with wrong" (1:22). So he continues to inflict pain and suffering. Finally, Job is reduced to sitting on an ash heap, surrounded by his wife and three friends. "Curse God and die" (2:9), his wife implores. But he will not. So for seven days he and his friends sit in silence.

Finally, Job speaks to bemoan what has befallen him, to declare his innocence but not to curse God. Then, in turn, the friends speak. They seek to convince Job that surely he must have done something wrong; all persons are guilty, "human beings are born to trouble/as the sparks fly upward" (5:7). If only Job would confess and repent, surely his suffering would cease. (With friends like this, who needs enemies?)

> IT TAKES US TO ANOTHER LEVEL WHEN GOD IS THE ONE WHO INDIRECTLY CAUSES AN APPARENTLY INNOCENT MAN TO LOSE ALL OF HIS CHILDREN AND HIS PROPERTY, AND TO SUFFER AN EXCRUCIATING ILLNESS.

After each friend speaks, Job responds. The passage read today is the response to the second friend, Bildad the Shuhite, who reminds him, "the light of the wicked is put out. . . . For they are thrust into a net by their own feet" (18:5, 8). What is happening to Job is surely the result of his own actions. Bildad then rehearses the horrible things that happen to the wicked, such as disease and death: "Their memory perishes from the earth, and they have no name in the street" (18:17). All of these things are happening to Job, so he must be guilty.

"How long will you torment me, and break me in pieces with words?" (19:2), Job cries out to his friends. He has been brought low, but he begs them, "Have pity on me, O you my friends, for the hand of God has touched me!" (v. 21). No matter what his friends say, he maintains his innocence, and he also declares that he will write that in a book that can never be destroyed, or "graven in the rock for ever!" (v. 24).

Job then declares that there will come a time when he will be vindicated. Job casts life beyond the grave, "after my skin has been thus destroyed" (v. 26), as a final courtroom. And he knows that when he goes before the divine judge, he will have a *Goel,* an advocate and vindicator. "I know that my *Goel* (Redeemer) lives, and at the last he will stand upon the earth" (v. 25). At the end God will be on his side, not against him, and he finally will be exonerated. For Job, this apparent end in suffering and pain is not nor will be his true and final end.

For another fictional approach to life after death, you might watch Albert Brook's movie *Defending Your Life.* Brooks plays a man who finds himself in "Judgment City" after crashing his new BMW. There, as the name implies, one must defend one's life to judges who will decide where you go next.

After a startling conversation with God in which he is reminded that he, Job, was not the one who created the world, so how was he to say what would or would not happen in it, Job confesses that God is correct and that he is humbled. Then, in the concluding narrative, Job is vindicated. God restores his fortunes, he has seven sons and three daughters, and "dies, an old man, and full of days" (42:17). Job was correct: suffering and pain were not his true end. His end was in God who gives him new life.

2 MACCABEES 7:1-2, 9-14 (RC)

The sufferings of Job seem to pale in comparison to the torture and violence inflicted upon the woman and her seven sons in this lection (echoing the number in our Gospel reading). The only way we can get away with reading this in church is by ignoring vv. 3-8, which describe what the vicious king had done to the first son after he questioned what the king intended to learn from them.

Like those in the story of Daniel, the woman and her sons were arrested and tortured for preferring the heavenly king to the earthly one. They protested their innocence and stood firm in the face of the torment knowing that, like Job, in the end they would be vindicated.

Those who live with the knowledge of resurrection are able to "regard sufferings as nothing," for they know that they have "the hope that God gives of being raised again by him" (v. 14).

This is certainly good news. However, preachers must make sure that they do not use these images to encourage people to passively remain in or accept oppressive and unjust situations. For example, how one behaves when under arrest by a tyrannical ruler should not be applied to an abusive marriage. Unfortunately, too many wives have been told to remain with abusive husbands because they will be raised up at the last day.

HAGGAI 1:15b-2:9 (RCL, alt.)

After the children of Israel returned from their exile in Babylon, they were instructed to rebuild the Temple in Jerusalem. However, as anyone who has ever been involved in the building or restoring of a building knows, that can take forever. And so it did for the Israelites. Haggai was the prophet assigned the task of overseeing the reconstruction.

HUMANS MAY SEE AN END, BUT GOD DOES NOT. NEW LIFE IN GOD IS ALWAYS POSSIBLE.

In this passage, Haggai gives the people a pep talk. He reminds them of God's power and glory. If they complete the task, God will come and not only fill the temple, but will also fill their lives with prosperity. They are not to be defeated by what seems to be ruin and devastation. Humans may see an end, but God does not. New life in God is always possible.

RESPONSIVE READING

PSALM 17:1-9 (RCL);
PSALM 17 (BCP);
PSALM 17:1-8 (BCP, alt.);
PSALM 17:1, 5-6, 8, 15 (RC)

Job was certain that he was innocent and knew that eventually God would prove it. This psalm has an interesting history. What was a person to do when one felt wrongly accused and could not find justice? One was able to appeal the case directly to God. So this psalm was spoken at the beginning of a temple hearing,

> THIS PSALM WAS SPOKEN AT THE BEGINNING OF A TEMPLE HEARING, REMINDING GOD OF ONE'S INNOCENCE AND PLACING ONE'S LIFE AND ONE'S FATE DIRECTLY IN GOD'S HANDS.

reminding God of one's innocence and placing one's life and one's fate directly in God's hands.

The psalm picks up the judicial image of resurrection. God is our advocate, the only one who will hear our plea and judge our fidelity. But God is not an overpowering, distant jurist, as indicated in the intimate plea, "Guard me as the apple of the eye, hide me in the shadow of your wings" (v. 8). In the end, resurrection is about trusting in God's love and faithfulness.

PSALM 145:1-5, 17-21 (RCL, alt.)

How are we able to praise God's holy name? By continuously recalling and retelling all the great things God has done. We are assured about what writer Madeleine L'Engle calls "resurrection then" by witnessing "resurrection now." But she reminds us, "Resurrection now means little if after death there is nothing but ashes to ashes and dust to dust . . . the joyful God of love who shouted the galaxies into existence is not going to abandon any iota of his creation."[1]

PSALM 98 (RCL, alt.)

There is no way that one can whisper this psalm. It demands to be shouted with loud voices. What is important to note is that in the midst of declaring all of the wonderful things that God has done, is doing, and will always do, this is a message for the whole earth. God will "judge the world with righteousness," not just certain people in certain places in certain times. God will judge "the peoples," all peoples, with equity.

In her discussion of heaven, author Kathleen Norris recalls a story told by a friend. As the woman sought to comfort her dying mother, she reminded her that "in heaven, everyone we love is there." But her mother quickly corrected her, "No, in heaven I will love everyone who's there."[2] We will love as God loves—everyone!

Second Reading

2 THESSALONIANS 2:1-5, 13-17 (RCL);
2 THESSALONIANS 2:13—3:5 (BCP);
2 THESSALONIANS 2:16—3:5 (RC)

Paul is coming to the end of his letter. At the start of the second chapter, he cautions those who have begun to believe others who are teaching that the second coming has already arrived. Clearly and emphatically Paul declares, "Let no one deceive you." That day has not yet come. He also reminds them that they won't have to wonder when it does, for it will be unmistakable.

Paul then reminds them what a wonderful job that they are doing and why they are able to do that. It is because they have been chosen by God and filled with the Spirit. It is not their doing, but God's. If they remember what Paul has taught them and continue to trust in God, they will be able to do what they have been called to do.

The Gospel

LUKE 20:27-38 (RCL, RC);
LUKE 20:27, (28-33), 34-38 (BCP);
LUKE 20:27, 34-38 (RC, alt.)

The time delay between the writer (me) and the reader (you) always makes this type of writing interesting and challenging, since the act of preaching is so grounded in the "here and now." Because I am writing for a future time, I am constantly wondering what issues will confront the preacher. What will the world be like? Will the world still be in the grip of warfare and terrorism, or will there have been a resolution to these difficult challenges? I have also found it ironic that I am writing on this set of lessons dealing with resurrection as I, myself, am beginning Holy Week. This fortuitous timing has forced me to ask important questions. How do we understand the relationship between the events of that Thursday, Friday, and Saturday night/Sunday morning and our own lives? What is the connection between Easter morn and our own death and resurrection? After all, today's readings focus not on Christ's resurrection but on our own. They challenge us to think about and reflect on our understanding of eternal life.

We are uncomfortable contemplating death—any death, but particularly our own. Death has become invisible. Most people today are rarely, if ever, involved in the death of another. Deaths that are not accidental usually occur in a hospital or hospice, not at home. We no longer wash and prepare for burial the bodies of those we love. We leave that to the professionals. And the bodies they prepare look more like they are sleeping. In fact, we even avoid saying the word death, often preferring to observe that they have "fallen asleep."

> TODAY'S READINGS FOCUS NOT ON CHRIST'S RESURRECTION BUT OUR OWN.

Death is seen not only as an end, but as a failure. We try to do so much to keep death from happening. We watch our weight, exercise, eat healthy food, get the proper medical tests, all with the goal of postponing the inevitable as long as possible. We seem to live as though death is actually under our control, taking a "works righteousness" approach to our finitude. But of course, we know that we are not in control, and that is why it becomes a forbidden topic. So, I wonder, if by extension, the same is true of resurrection.

In preparing to write upon this week's lections, I looked through Kathleen Norris's book, *Amazing Grace: A Vocabulary of Faith*. As her adult faith began to grow and deepen, she realized that "in order to inhabit it, to claim it as mine, I had to rebuild my religious vocabulary" (p. 3). She needed to revisit words that were too abstract, too remote, and make them come alive again. I wondered what she wrote about "resurrection." She revisits salvation, incarnation, and prayer. She explores Christ, creeds, and the Trinity. She discusses both heaven and hell but, in nearly four hundred pages, she *never* mentions resurrection.

In the midst of her grief over the death of her brother, Lazarus, Martha was asked an important question by Jesus. I believe it is an important question for all of us. After declaring, "I am the resurrection and the life; he who believes in me, though he die, yet shall he live, and whoever lives and believes in me shall never die" (John 11:25-26), Jesus then asked Martha, "Do you believe this?" (John 11:26). Do we believe this?

In his foreword to Rowan Williams's book, *Resurrection: Interpreting the Easter Gospel,* Paul Minear recalls a meeting with students and faculty at a theological school. When he spoke about "the presence of the risen Jesus," one of the theological professors stopped him. That phrase, he noted, was "either meaningless or misleading. Either it has no intelligible referent or it expresses an illusion that encourages self-deception on the part of pious Christians who rely on it."[3] Do you believe this?

Resurrection and the understandings of life beyond the grave are the focus of today's reading. It is the issue or question with which the Sadducees attempted to trap Jesus. A number of things have occurred since Jesus' meal at the home of Zacchaeus. He entered Jerusalem on the back of a colt to the shouts and cries of the crowd. In Luke's Gospel, Jesus then enters the temple, ejecting those who were making it "a den of robbers."

Having cleansed the temple, Jesus then sat down, teaching the people and preaching the gospel. The portion read today is the third of four debates that Jesus had with the religious leaders. The first concerned questions about his authority, the second about whether they should pay taxes to Caesar. Most of the time Luke tells us that Jesus was being questioned by chief priests, scribes, and elders. But in this, the third exchange, it is a group of Sadducees who try to entrap Jesus. This is unusual because this is the only time they appear in Luke's Gospel.

The Sadducees were an elite, aristocratic, and conservative priestly group. They would accept only the Pentateuch, the five books of Moses. They did not believe in angels, and they did not believe in the resurrection of the body. (As a colleague loves to remind us, that is why they were "sad, you see").

In order to ask their question, they must first tell a ridiculous story of a woman who marries seven brothers as each, in turn, dies. "In the resurrection, therefore, whose wife will the woman be? For the seven had her as a wife" (v. 33). They are not really interested in what Jesus has to say. They are not seeking to engage in true conversation. They merely want to demonstrate that he is wrong in proclaiming that there is a resurrection. But Jesus turns around the encounter and uses their question as an opportunity to teach about resurrection.

He makes two points. First, he tells them that this is an inappropriate question because it misunderstands the character of life after death. They seem to think that things will continue in the next life just as they are in this one. But, Jesus reminds them, that is not the case. We will be equal to the angels (they don't believe in angels) because we are sons and daughters of God. We will not need to be concerned about marriage anymore.

Second, Jesus reminds them that Moses tells us that God is the God of the living and not the dead. Drawing on scripture acceptable to the Sadducees, Jesus reminds them that, from the burning bush, the voice announced: "I am the God of your father, the God of Abraham, the God of Isaac, and the God of Jacob" (Exod. 3:6). Notice, Jesus observes, God speaks of the fathers in the present tense, "He is not God of the dead, but of the living, for to him all are alive" (v. 38). There is a resurrection of the dead, Jesus declares. Our end is not the end. Our vision and understanding are too limited, and we refuse to see the gift God has given us.

Do we believe that we will experience a resurrection? Do we believe that death will not be the end? Do we accept that, if we believe in Jesus, we will have eternal life? Or are our modern sensibilities offended by this physical impossibility, so that it becomes the topic we would just as soon avoid? Nevertheless, resurrection, the resurrection of Jesus, and our resurrection are at the center of our Christian faith, and we must answer Jesus' question.

TWENTY-FOURTH SUNDAY AFTER PENTECOST

THIRTY-THIRD SUNDAY IN ORDINARY TIME / PROPER 28
NOVEMBER 14, 2004

REVISED COMMON	EPISCOPAL (BCP)	ROMAN CATHOLIC
Mal. 4:1-2a	Mal. 3:13—4:2a, 5-6	Mal. 3:19-20a
or Isa. 65:17-25		
Psalm 98 or Isaiah 12	Psalm 98 or 98:5-10	Ps. 98:5-6, 7-8, 9
2 Thess. 3:6-13	2 Thess. 3:6-13	2 Thess. 3:7-12
Luke 21:5-19	Luke 21:5-19	Luke 21:5-19

Hollywood loves to speculate about Armageddon and the eschaton. There are as many different scenarios for the end as there are movies. Some envision a future that will look much like the distant past—a return to an almost caveman-like existence. Others foresee a future that is dark and violent, where human beings are held hostage to the technology they developed to set them free, such as *Bladerunner*. As the church year draws to a close, the Gospel readings that have previously focused on the ministry and preaching of Jesus turn their attention to his teachings concerning the end time. This serves as a transition into Advent, helping us to understand the continuity between the our past, present, and future in Christ. We not only look back to remember what Jesus said and did, but we also look ahead to his coming again.

AS THE CHURCH YEAR DRAWS TO A CLOSE, THE GOSPEL READINGS THAT HAVE PREVIOUSLY FOCUSED ON THE MINISTRY AND PREACHING OF JESUS TURN THEIR ATTENTION TO HIS TEACHINGS CONCERNING THE END TIME.

FIRST READING
MALACHI 4:1-2a (RCL);
MALACHI 3:13—4:2a, 5-6 (BCP);
MALACHI 3:19-20a (RC)

The first reading introduces the theme of the final time. Nothing is known about the prophet identified as Malachi. In fact, while it could be a name, it is in fact a title—"my messenger" (3:1). This messenger seems to have been writing about 515 to 400 B.C.E., the time that the people of Israel were returning from their captivity in Babylon. All lectionaries include his description of the day of judgment. (Note: Following the Hebrew text, the *New American Bible* has only three chapters; therefore, Mal. 3:19-20 [RC] is the same as 4:1-2a in the NRSV.)

Although the people had been released from their captivity and had returned to reclaim and rebuild, they had not reformed their hearts. It is not difficult to understand why the writer of this diatribe did not want his identity revealed. He chastises the priests and temple officials for their failure to present their finest to God. They have kept their best, which should have been their offering, for themselves, and God lashes out in anger, "If you will not listen . . . I will send the curse upon you and I will curse your blessings" (2:2).

Employing the metaphor of marriage, the writer charges that in the time of their exile the people of Israel had been unfaithful to the God who created them, and that they "married the daughter of a foreign god" (2:11). God may have remained faithful and kept the covenant, but they did not. Making extensive use of rhetorical questions (implying that the reader/listener knows the correct answer), the writer, perhaps sarcastically, reminds them that they already know the answer to their questions—"How have we wearied him [God]?" by saying, "All who do evil are good in the sight of the LORD, and he delights in them" (2:17). Clearly, the prophet implies, God does not delight in those who do evil, and doing evil will bring down God's wrath upon them.

A messenger is coming, writes Malachi. Whether that is the prophet himself or a divine messenger is not clear. The messenger will come to prepare the way by purging and purifying those who have fallen away. The messenger will be like a woman who washes clothes until they are clean, or like the silver or goldsmith who burns metal with fire to rid it of impurities. He also identifies those who will be caught up in this cleaning frenzy: liars, adulterers, and those who cheat and oppress the vulnerable and the weak. This is a message of judgment, but it is also a message of hope.

If they would do what they already know they should be doing, that is, pay their full tithes, give their finest offerings to God, care for the widows and orphans, then God will "open the windows of heaven for you and pour down for you an overflowing blessing" (3:10). God is ready to forgive them and return to them their former glory. They would no longer be a forgotten people in exile, and then "all nations will call you blessed" (3:12).

Verse 13 of the third chapter initiates a conversation between those who have turned their backs on God and feel that they have escaped judgment and punishment, and those who wish to return to the Lord. The evildoers may think that they have eluded God's anger, but the messenger has come to tell them otherwise. The day of wrath is coming, but God will spare the faithful. "I will spare them as parents spare their children who serve them" (3:18). Likewise, the passage chosen for today (4:1-2a, NRSV = 3:19-20a, NAB) gives us a vision of that day of wrath. Again there is the image of burning, purifying flame. But there is also the assurance that God will protect the faithful.

While the preacher will link this to Jesus' description of the end time in Luke 21:10-11, there is nothing in this passage that indicates this is an eschatological vision. Rather, Malachi seems to view this as the near future with the understanding that, if they do this, their lives—here, today, now—will be much better. But, if they don't, God will "come and strike the land with a curse" (4:6, not in the NAB). The closing lines of the prophecy are repeated in the opening of Luke (1:17) to apply to John the Baptizer with a significant change. Malachi reports that God "will send you Elijah . . . before the great and terrible day of the LORD comes" (4:5 or 3:24). But Luke, who believes that

> THERE IS THE IMAGE OF BURNING, PURIFYING FLAME. BUT THERE IS ALSO THE ASSURANCE THAT GOD WILL PROTECT THE FAITHFUL.

in Jesus the day of the Lord has come, John is standing in the place of Elijah. So, Luke 1:17 reads, "He [John] will go before him [Jesus] in the spirit and power of Elijah." John is not Elijah, and neither is Jesus (Luke 16:16).

ISAIAH 65:17-25 (RCL, alt.)

What is your idea of paradise? What would make the perfect life? In Albert Brooks's movie *Defending Your Life,* his character arrives at "Judgment City" after his new BMW rear-ends a bus. As the judges consider whether he should go on to heaven or be sent back to earth so he can get it right, Brooks is given a foretaste of the heavenly life. For example, one can eat all one wants and never gain weight. That sounds heavenly. Unfortunately, Brooks is not able to let go of his humanly way of viewing things, so he still watches what he eats and avoids all of the rich desserts placed before him. (Too bad for him.)

In Isaiah 65, Third Isaiah, echoing the vision of an earlier Isaiah (11:6-9), offers his own description of God's holy mountain. Like Malachi, this Isaiah is writing to a people who have returned from exile to discover that their lives are far from heavenly. This final section of Isaiah is a combination of chastisement and encouragement. On the one hand, Third Isaiah reminds the returning exiles that they must continue to follow the laws and maintain the covenant, while on the other, he gives them a portrait of what awaits them when "the former troubles are forgotten" (v. 16).

> ISAIAH DEMONSTRATES THAT WE CANNOT EVEN BEGIN TO IMAGINE WHAT GOD HAS IN MIND FOR US.

Notice that it is not only earth, but heaven as well, that will be made new. Verses 19 through 24 give us a picture that is entirely possible. But, in doing that,

Third Isaiah also gives us a picture of the lives the people were living. The vulnerable, the very young and the very old must have been dying prematurely. In the new earth, he says, all people will live their lives to the fullest. The people had been refugees, torn from their homes and land, unable to live in the homes they built and eat the crops that they had planted. In paradise, however, there are no refugees. And God's vision for all children is blessing and plenty, not sorrow and suffering.

In the final verse of this vision, Isaiah demonstrates that we cannot even begin to imagine what God has in mind for us. The final vision belies probability. Wolves and lambs do not live together, at least not for very long. But in God's plan, all creatures can live in harmony and respect.

RESPONSIVE READING
PSALM 98 (RCL);
PSALM 98:5-10 (BCP);
PSALM 98:5-6, 7-8, 9 (RC)

See the discussion of this psalm for November 7, Proper 27.

ISAIAH 12 (RCL, alt.)

Isaiah 12 includes two songs, a song of deliverance and a song of thanksgiving. The first, vv. 1b to 3, celebrates forgiveness. It is sung by a people who, aware of God's anger, are also aware that the anger was justified, and they now rejoice because God's anger has subsided. Rather than punishment, they have experienced the comfort offered by a God who is always faithful. The second song praises God and celebrates God's mighty works.

Both of these songs echo Miriam's song, Exod. 15:21, and the Song of Moses and the people of Israel, Exod. 15:1-18. These songs are celebrations of God who is acting in the lives of people released from oppression and slavery. The songs, both in Exodus and Isaiah, remind us that ours is not a distant God, indifferent and remote. No, ours is a God who has "seen the affliction of my people who are in Egypt, and have heard their cry because of their taskmasters; I know their sufferings, and I have come down to deliver them out of the hand of the Egyptians, and bring them up . . . to a good and broad land, a land flowing with milk and honey" (Exod. 3:7-8). While the theme of today's lections is the eschaton, the end time, Jesus urges us to live in the here and now, because we do not know when the final day will come. These songs from Isaiah invite us to reflect not upon a distant or unknowable future but on how and where God is acting today in our very midst.

SECOND READING

2 THESSALONIANS 3:6-13 (RCL, BCP);
2 THESSALONIANS 3:7-12 (RC)

With this reading we come to the end of Paul's letter to the church in Thessalonica. While at first it might seem to be a simple message about the importance of working, unrelated to today's lectionary theme (the last days), it is in fact directly related to that.

In the portion read today, Paul makes a simple, somewhat obvious point: If you don't work you won't be able to eat. Paul says that he has heard that "some of you are living in idleness, mere busybodies not doing any work" (v. 11). Were they just lazy? Perhaps not. If we back up and recall what Paul was discussing in last week's reading, cautioning them that the day of the Lord had not arrived, that he had not nor was not preaching that, then we might be lead to conclude that some within the Thessalonian community had begun living in "the day of the Lord." Why should we work if the end time has come? Why should we worry about putting money away for the future if the future is here and now, if the kingdom of God has already arrived? Why should we worry about the future at all if the future is in God's hands, not ours?

People live very differently when they don't think they have a future. As I was growing up, our family had close friends who had a son not much older than I was. Tom had cystic fibrosis and, although his case was very mild, it nonetheless consumed his life and that of his mother. He had to have daily treatments and took handfuls of pills at every meal. Fifty years later the treatments available are much better, but even with these advances, most people with cystic fibrosis have very shortened lives. When I was a child they called it the "Peter Pan" disease—because its sufferers never grew up. Tom received the best treatment available and, with a mild case, was able to live well into his thirties. But I remember how difficult it was for him to think about being an adult and about working and building for the future. Was he even going to have one? Tom ended up having a successful career in computers, but he was an unusual person who was able to live in and for the moment

Many people are not so lucky. Teens who grow up amid the poverty and violence of many American cities also live without a future. Many of them cannot even think about living past sixteen or seventeen because they have so many friends who are murdered during those years. Why, they argue, should they work hard in school or plan for a future? What most of them plan is their funerals—what music they want played and what clothes they want to wear in their coffins. The possibility of college and a career do not even enter their minds.

It is a gift to have a future and to know that one will be able to live in that future. That is what Isaiah celebrates—the people will build houses and live in them, plant crops and eat the fruit. And Paul assures the Christians in Thessalonica that they, too, have a future. The day of the Lord has not arrived; it will arrive but not yet. So they do have a future here and now, and they should live and plan for that future. They should not sit back and do nothing, waiting for the end to appear. Who knows how long they would be waiting. Paul lifts himself up as their model. Did they see him doing nothing, waiting for others to feed him, waiting for Christ to appear again? No, he did the work of the gospel, preaching the gospel Jesus commanded him to preach and working to put bread on the table and a roof over his head.

What is the Christian's relationship to the world to be? Are we to live fully in the world "eating, drinking, and making merry" as apparently many Thessalonians were doing? Are we, as Christians, supposed to retreat and avoid the sinful world, suffering patiently and quietly while we wait for our final, heavenly reward? Or are we to walk that fine, and often difficult line of being in the world but not of the world?

> IT IS A GIFT TO HAVE A FUTURE AND TO KNOW THAT ONE WILL BE ABLE TO LIVE IN THAT FUTURE.

These are difficult theological questions because they challenge us to think about how God is acting in and relating to our world. Their answer depends on our understanding of time, God's time, human time. Are we, as children of God, still citizens of the world, or do we now live in another world on a different plane? Jesus tells us that we are certainly very much a part of this world, but that God is with us every step of the way.

THE GOSPEL
LUKE 21:5-19 (RCL, BCP, RC)

What are the most permanent things in your life? What are those things that you count on to be there? No matter what we name—family, friends, home, trees, lakes, mountains—we know, whether or not we will admit it, that all of these can be gone in a minute. Many of us are able to recall when a volcanic erup-tion blew off the top of Mount St. Helens in a matter of seconds. And I can recall my reaction when someone told me that both towers of the World Trade Center had collapsed in seconds. It was beyond my comprehension. It couldn't be. How could 110-story buildings collapse, let alone in seconds? Today's Gospel is about the impermanence of our lives, our world, our human kingdoms, and the perma-nence of God's kingdom.

In Luke's Gospel, Jesus' teachings about the eschaton and its accompanying tribulations and the time when "the Son of Man [will be] coming in a cloud with power and great glory" (Luke 21:27) immediately precede and consequently prepare us for the passion. Following his triumphal entry into Jerusalem on the back of a colt, Jesus went into the temple both to teach and to observe all of the people who came to worship and perform their temple duties. After watching a poor widow put her contribution into the box, those sitting with Jesus seemed to ignore how he honored this poor woman for her contribution. Instead, they quickly changed the subject, remarking on the beauty and the glory of the temple. This was the center of their religious world. The temple and its beauty was the home of God and proved God's love for them and presence among them. How could one think that this temple that had taken hundreds of years to build wouldn't continue to stand for hundreds, perhaps thousands of years more? But this was not so.

Jesus quickly told them that their trust in human structures was misplaced. Very soon, he told them, the entire structure would be torn down and "there shall not be left here one stone upon another" (v. 6). In the other two Synoptic Gospels (although, interestingly enough, not here in Luke) this remark about the destruction of the temple becomes one of the cornerstones of his prosecution: "'We heard him say, "I will destroy this temple that is made with hands, and in three days I will build another, not made with hands"' (Mark 14:58). By the time Luke wrote his Gospel, probably in the mid-eighties, the temple had already been destroyed. Luke's listeners knew that Jesus was a prescient prophet who had foretold the destruction of the Temple. Nothing is permanent, nothing is lasting—nothing except God. And although they asked for a sign, as they had done earlier (11:16; 11:29), Jesus would not give them one. It is not that the followers of Jesus had difficulty accepting the possibility of the Temple's destruction (they, like we, lived in violent times). They wanted to know the signs that would enable them to be in control and avoid the turmoil.

Earlier in the Gospel, Jesus had told his followers that there would be only one sign, the sign of Jonah. Unlike Matthew, who saw this as a sign pointing to Jesus' death and resurrection and who equated Jonah's time in the whale to Jesus' time in the tomb (Matt. 12:39-40), Luke sees Jonah as the sign—specifically Jonah's preaching. He is finally answering God's call to announce to the people of Nineveh, "Yet forty days, and Nineveh shall be overthrown" (Jonah 3:4). That is the sign we have—that unless we repent, we will be destroyed. Look also at Luke 7, when the followers of John come to Jesus asking if he is the one who "is to come, or shall we look for another?" (7:19). The sign Jesus offers them is his preaching, teaching, and healing. "Tell John what you have seen and heard: the blind receive their sight, the lame walk" (7:22).

We think about the end time and we too want a sign. While Jesus assures us that we will see wars, earthquakes, famines, pestilence, it is not the end. As I write this, these words have never been more vivid. The United States is at war in Iraq, and hundreds of people are dying from a new illness, SARS. Yet Jesus is telling me that I should not give up and stop preaching. No, these are the times when we must be like Jesus, like Jonah. "This will be a time for you to bear testimony" (v. 13). We are not to run away as Jonah did. We are not to cease working as did the Thessalonians. We are to stand firm in the knowledge that all of life, all of time, our present and future are all in the hands of a loving God who will "give [us] a mouth and wisdom . . . but not a hair of your head will perish" (vv. 15, 18).

We can dream and speculate what the end time will be like. But as we come to the end of the church year and prepare once again to enter into Advent and the feast of the Incarnation, we are to remember that we believe in the God who was and is and is to come; it is this God who controls not only our beginning, but our end as well.

> WE BELIEVE IN THE GOD WHO WAS AND IS AND IS TO COME; IT IS THIS GOD WHO CONTROLS NOT ONLY OUR BEGINNING, BUT OUR END AS WELL.

Can we even begin to see the possibilities that God places before us? Or are we so caught up in the world of violence and death that we can see nothing else? While Jesus will not tell us when the end will come, he does not disabuse us of the knowledge that there will be a time when time and life as we know it here will come to an end. We are invited to meditate on what that will be like, but we are also encouraged to live in the here and the now.

LAST SUNDAY AFTER PENTECOST, CHRIST THE KING

Thirty-fourth Sunday in Ordinary Time / Proper 29
November 21, 2004

Revised Common	Episcopal (BCP)	Roman Catholic
Jer. 23:1-6	Jer. 23:1-6	2 Sam. 5:1-3
Psalm 46	Psalm 46	Ps. 122:1-2, 3-4, 4-5
or Luke 1:68-79		
Col. 1:11-20	Col. 1:11-20	Col. 1:12-20
Luke 23:33-43	Luke 23:35-43	Luke 23:35-43
	or 19:29-38	

Each year Christmas preparations seem to begin earlier and earlier (not to mention those Christmas stores that are open year around). It is difficult for those in the church not to rush into thinking about mangers, shepherds, and wise men. Yet, as we reach the end of the church year, the lessons are not about the baby Jesus, but rather about Christ crucified, risen, and ascended to the right hand of God. As we prepare to celebrate Advent, during which we reflect upon both the first and second comings of Christ and the feast of the Incarnation (God with us in the flesh), we are called to proclaim Christ the King.

THE LECTIONS TODAY EXPLORE ANSWERS TO AN IMPORTANT QUESTION JESUS ASKED OF HIS DISCIPLES, A QUESTION WE ALL MUST ANSWER: "WHO DO YOU SAY THAT I AM?"

We recall that Jesus the Christ is ruler of all—yesterday, today, and tomorrow. He is inviting our total and complete allegiance and devotion. The lections today explore answers to an important question Jesus asked of his disciples, a question we all must answer: "Who do you say that I am?"

FIRST READING

JEREMIAH 23:1-6 (RCL, BCP)

One of the first images of Jesus is a mosaic depicting him as a young man with a lamb draped tenderly over his shoulders. While the title of this day may be Christ the King, drawing on both the Davidic understanding of the king as shepherd as well as Jeremiah's understanding of loving prophet, the Good Shepherd was one of the first titles used by and given to Jesus Christ.

Jeremiah saw the prophets sent by God as shepherds of the people, but they were far from good. They had neglected their duties at best. At worst, they had led them into worshiping other gods. Verses 1 and 2 serve as a chastisement of the wicked, evil prophets, describing what they have and have not done. If the flocks have been scattered, that is, sent into exile in other lands, the fault lies on the heads of those who had been entrusted with their care.

Sheep have a tendency to focus only on the task at hand—eating. When they are so focused, they do not pay attention to where they are or where they are going; consequently they tend to get lost unless they have someone watching over them. Knowing this, God sent prophets to the people who would watch over and bring them back when they strayed. But "you have scattered my flock, and have driven them away, and you have not attended to them" (v. 2).

Not only will God "attend" to (read "punish") these prophets, but God will step in and personally care for these neglected sheep, first by finding them and bringing them home. Then God will give them a good shepherd who will love them, care for them, rule over them, and "reign as king and deal wisely" (v. 5). This brief passage from Jeremiah provides us with a list of kingly characteristics. The king whom God will put in place will be caring, righteous, wise, and just. Furthermore, this king will unite and rule over both kingdoms, Judah and Israel.

While it is important to honor Jeremiah's messianic prophecy as just that, a future hope, it has always been difficult for the Christian not to read this as applying to Jesus, seeing him as the fulfillment of that hope, the one risen up "for David a righteous Branch" (v. 5). It has given us both the titles of shepherd and king.

2 SAMUEL 5:1-3 (RC)

While Jeremiah was drawing on an earlier understanding of kingship, that of the king as shepherd, this reading from 2 Samuel goes directly to the source. David had been anointed by Samuel to be king of Israel when he was still a youth tending his father's sheep—and when Saul was still king but displeasing to God. Needless to say, Saul was not pleased with David and sought to destroy him. Throughout the books of 1 and 2 Samuel, we wrestle with the question: How does one come to rule over the people of God? Is it because God appoints and anoints, is strong and victorious in battle, has good looks and charm, or slays one's contenders? Who is our ruler? Who can or should demand our allegiance? What does God's ruler look like?

284

THE SEASON
OF PENTECOST
────────
LUCY
LIND HOGAN

In 2 Samuel 5, Saul is now dead and David is king of Judah. David has just triumphed over the remnants of the house of Saul when the people of Israel come to David demanding that he become their king as well, just as Samuel had told him. They remind him that he is one of them, "we are your bone and flesh" (v. 1), an interesting connection to the upcoming feast of the Incarnation. But not only is he of their lineage, he is a successful warrior—"it was you that led out and brought in Israel" (v. 2). Does one get to be king by blood or battle? David has both. But it could not have happened without divine approval, and the people knew that David had that: "The LORD said to you, 'You shall be shepherd of my people Israel'" (v. 2). Only then could they make covenant with David and anoint him as king.

RESPONSIVE READING
PSALM 46 (RCL, BCP)

How easily we sing God's praises and join with the psalmist in declaring that God and God alone "is our refuge and strength." But while those words may be on our lips and tongue, are they also in our heart and mind? Do we live as though we believe it? We may say that God is our "present help in trouble," but we also make sure that we have bank accounts, insurance, and a security system on our homes and cars. In whom do we trust?

The psalm invites us to declare that God, our God, who has been the God of all those who went before us, has command over everything that we see—the natural world, the political world, etc. It is God, not human leaders and warriors, who builds up and destroys. It is God, not kings and queens, presidents, and prime ministers, who ends wars and demands our allegiance.

The people of God have always had difficulty living into this reality. No sooner had Israelites been freed from their Egyptian slavery by God's almighty hand than they began complaining and demanding a god they could see and touch—a golden calf. No sooner were they given the land promised them by God, and guided by God's own judges and prophets than they began to demand a king: "Appoint for us a king to govern us like all the nations" (1 Sam. 8:5). We are all too willing to put our trust in earthly things. But, as the psalm reminds us, the earth will change, the mountains will shake, and the waters cover us; then we will know that it is only God who saves us.

> IT IS GOD, NOT HUMAN LEADERS AND WARRIORS, WHO BUILDS UP AND DESTROYS. IT IS GOD, NOT KINGS AND QUEENS, PRESIDENTS, AND PRIME MINISTERS, WHO ENDS WARS AND DEMANDS OUR ALLEGIANCE.

PSALM 122:1-2, 3-4, 4-5 (RC)

Jerusalem and the Temple within its walls was an outward and visible sign of God's love and faithfulness. As long as pilgrims could travel to the city and worship within the walls, they knew that peace and prosperity prevailed. This was a song that the pilgrims sang as they arrived at their destination. It was at the same time a song declaring the beauty they saw and the security they experienced, but also a prayer that this peace and prosperity would continue.

The psalm also makes reference to the thrones, both of David and of judgment, that were found in the holy city. This makes an interesting contrast for the preacher. How was Jesus enthroned in Jerusalem? How was his kingship received? While David sat on a throne, Jesus was lifted on a cross that bore the title King of the Jews.

LUKE 1:68-79 (RCL, alt.)

The Song of Zechariah, the *Benedictus,* accomplishes many things. It is the song that Zechariah, the father of John the Baptizer, sings after the birth and circumcision of his son, when his voice returns. Both his name and the form of this hymn connects Zechariah, his son John, and Jesus with their Jewish antecedents. This is not something entirely new. It is firmly grounded in all God has been doing. The song praises God for all the great things that God has done in the past, is doing now, and will continue to do. It also weaves together the lives and ministry of John and Jesus.

As we move into the first weeks of Advent, much of the focus will be on John and his call to "go before the Lord to prepare his ways" (v. 76). But when we are focusing on Christ the King, this song reminds us that Jesus is the anointed one of God who "raised up a horn of salvation for us" (v. 69). And, echoing Isaiah, Zechariah announces that this only one will be he whom the great prophet foretold. Jesus is the one who has come to bring light to "those who sit in darkness" (v. 79).

Second Reading
COLOSSIANS 1:11-20 (RCL, BCP);
COLOSSIANS 1:12-20 (RC)

Paul was quite clear that at the center of his preaching there was one message, and one message only: "We preach Christ crucified, a stumbling block to Jews and folly to Gentiles" (1 Cor. 1:23). On this Sunday when we lift up the one whom God lifted up, Christ the King, Paul urges us through this letter to the Christians in Colossae toward clarity of knowledge and understanding about the one who has won for us eternal life.

Colossae was a small town in Asia Minor (it is now Honaz, Turkey). Paul had heard from his colleague there, Epaphras, that a number of people in the church had been listening to teachers who were promoting what Paul considered to be a less than adequate Christology as well as an overly aesthetic, legalistic spiritual life. In this letter, written while he was in prison and apparently at the same time he wrote his letter to the church in Ephesus, Paul hopes to correct these misunderstandings and set these new Christians back on the path so that they will know that they already "share in the inheritance of the saints in light" (v. 12).

While it is frustrating that we do not have the content of that unorthodox preaching, we are able to surmise that it promoted a Christ who was not God, but rather was a part of the angelic, heavenly court. These preachers also seemed to have Gnostic tendencies in that they were promoting a secret knowledge that only they had. Paul assures his friends in Christ that while there was a time when the "mystery was hidden," now it has been "made manifest to his saints" (1:26). It is secret no longer, and Paul prays that "no one may delude you with beguiling speech" (2:4).

PAUL URGES US THROUGH THIS LETTER TO THE CHRISTIANS IN COLOSSAE TOWARD CLARITY OF KNOWLEDGE AND UNDERSTANDING ABOUT THE ONE WHO HAS WON FOR US ETERNAL LIFE.

After his customary greetings, salutations, praises, and prayers, Paul immediately sets about proclaiming the true nature of the Son in whose kingdom we dwell. To do this Paul uses a christological hymn that may have been well known to the community and one they may have sung frequently. Likewise, it becomes an important hymn for us, the descendants of these mothers and fathers in the faith, as we contemplate the nature and identity of the one who "has qualified us to share in the inheritance of the saints of light" (v. 12).

In the preface to the hymn, Paul is eager to remind that Christ is God's "beloved Son" (v. 13), and only in him do "we have redemption, the forgiveness of sins" (v. 14). Paul then turns to the hymn, which opens by declaring that Christ is the very image of God. To know Christ is to know God. As we read in the Gospel of John, "He who has seen me has seen the Father" (John 14:9). In fact, the entire hymn has a very Johannine feel. It would be incorrect to cast Christ within the ranks of the angels, because he is not only the "firstborn of all creation," but all that we see and know was "created through him" (v. 16). Christ is above all things, before all things, and "in him all things hold together" (v. 17)—our lives, the church, the world.

This deeply theological text presents preachers with great riches but also with great challenges. The tendency of recent preaching has been to tell the stories either of Jesus' life or the stories Jesus told. Consequently, we are more comfortable teaching the tales than preaching the teacher. How can we proclaim to a contemporary congregation that Jesus "is the image of the invisible God, the firstborn of all creation; for in him all things were created, in heaven and on earth" (v. 15)? It is difficult for people to absorb abstract, philosophical, theological constructs. But perhaps Paul offers us a suggestion in that he also knows that these were difficult for people to understand. As a solution he turned to hymns. Perhaps we should be singing our Christology. We should make certain that the hymns we use in our worship together are not only orthodox, but have a deep profundity, able to carry this important, crucial message. We all need to be reminded weekly that Christ was able "to reconcile to himself all things, whether on earth or in heaven, making peace by the blood of his cross" (v. 20).

We need to be reminded because we have a tendency to shrink our understanding of Christ. We seem to be more comfortable with one who is gentle and nonconfrontational. We want to see Jesus as our friend, not the one who is above all things. Paul calls us to "think big." We follow a Christ who is bigger, grander, more loving, more powerful, more forgiving than we can ever imagine.

THE GOSPEL
LUKE 23:33-43 (RCL);
LUKE 23:35-43 (BCP, RC)

For churches that follow the lectionary, there is perhaps no other Sunday that seems as out of sync with the secular culture as this. Stores are decorated for Christmas and everyone is beginning to think about gifts, cards, Christmas trees, and parties. As cookies are being baked and lights are strung on houses, the church turns its attention not to the manger but to the cross.

> WHEN WE ARE CELEBRATING CHRIST AS RULER OF ALL, WE READ ONCE AGAIN ABOUT HIS MOMENT OF PAIN, TORTURE, AND DEATH. WE REMIND OURSELVES THAT WE FOLLOW A KING WHO WAS HUMILIATED BY DYING THE DEATH OF A CRIMINAL.

The Gospel appointed for Christ the King Sunday would seem to be in the eyes of the world, as Paul observes in 1 Corinthians 1-2, folly. When we are celebrating Christ as ruler of all, we read once again about his moment of pain, torture, and death. We remind ourselves that we follow a king who was humiliated by dying the death of a criminal. This folly, this stumbling block, this reversal of temporal success, directs our attention from earthly to heavenly things (John 3:12).

Earlier in Luke's Gospel, Jesus asked his disciples a crucial question. After learning that the people were speculating that Jesus was perhaps John the Baptist,

Elijah, or one of the prophets, Jesus brushed away those answers and asked them directly, "But who do you say that I am?" (9:20). It didn't matter how others answered the question; what was important was what they had come to understand and believe and how this knowledge was going to change how they lived their lives. In that moment, Peter quickly answered that Jesus was "The Christ [anointed] of God" (9:20). Yet this same Peter would later deny Jesus over and over again: "I do not know him" (22:57). Who do you say that I am?

The passion narrative was the earliest story about Jesus that was told, yet each Gospel chooses to tell it with its own twist. Throughout Luke's account of the passion, the correct answers to the question "Who do you say?" are given by those seeking to kill Jesus. The chief priests and elders ask whether he is the Christ or the Son of God. Pilate asks if he is the King of the Jews, and Herod clothes Jesus in a robe befitting a king. In the portion of the narrative read today, note how many times Jesus is called Christ or king.

Luke's telling of the crucifixion is actually quite succinct: "And when they came to the place which is called The Skull, there they crucified him" (v. 33). After Jesus prays that God will forgive them (us) for what they do, a series of taunts begin which are in reality announcements of the true nature of the one hanging on the cross. First, the rulers declare, "He saved others; let him save himself, if he is the Messiah of God, his chosen one!" (v. 35). We now know he is the chosen one. Next, the soldiers shout, "If you are the King of the Jews, save yourself!" (v. 37). There is also the silent but powerful witness of the title that has been placed upon his cross, "This is the King of the Jews" (v. 38). And finally, one of the criminals (*kakourgos*, "evil worker") ridicules Jesus, "Are you not the Messiah? Save yourself and us!" (v. 39). In as many verses, we hear Jesus' titles five times, and we know that he is the Christ, the chosen one, the King of the Jews. We also know that it is in *not* saving himself that he does, in fact, save us.

LUKE 19:29-38 (BCP, alt.)

The alternate Gospel in BCP chooses to avoid the horror of the cross, turning rather to Jesus' ironically triumphal entry into Jerusalem.

Jesus is the prophet who is able to see what is to happen. He tells the disciples to go into a town where they will find a colt. They are to take it and bring it back to him. And even if someone challenges this, the mere fact that they tell that person, "The Lord has need of it," will be enough to smooth over the difficulty.

The fact that Jesus chooses to ride into Jerusalem on a colt both connects this action with the prophecy of Zechariah, "Lo, your king comes to you; triumphant and victorious . . . riding on a donkey, on a colt, the foal of a donkey" (Zech. 9:9), and also declares a new kind of kingship. He is not a warrior who will drive out the occupying Roman forces, as the people hoped ("We had hoped that he was the one to redeem Israel," Luke 24:21). No, he is coming as a prince of peace: "The battle bow shall be cut off, and he shall command peace to the nations; his dominion shall be from sea to sea, and from the River to the ends of the earth" (Zech. 9:10).

In Luke's Gospel, it is only the followers of Jesus, "the whole multitude of the disciples," who "praise God joyfully with a loud voice for all the deeds of power that they had seen" (v. 37). They spread their garments along the road as a sign that they acclaim him their king (2 Kings 9:13), but then they don't stay with their king in the moment of crisis.

The portion read today ends with the joyous acclamation, "Blessed is the King who comes in the name of the Lord! Peace in heaven and glory in the highest heaven!" (v. 38). We are invited to join the whole multitude of the disciples and declare our allegiance to the King of Peace.

While we would rather turn from and avoid the true nature of the passion, we must nevertheless look at it so that we fully understand God's gracious gift and see that the kingship of Christ looks nothing like that of human rulers. God's ways are not our ways, but God's way, through death to life, is the way to eternal life. God's anointed one "was despised and rejected by others; a man of suffering, and acquainted with infirmity" (Isa. 53:3a). The chosen one of God is the "one from whom others hide their faces; he was despised, and we held him of no account" (Isa. 53:3b).

The question is asked of us, "Who do you say I am?"

THANKSGIVING DAY

November 25, 2004 (U.S.A)
October 11, 2004 (Canada)

Revised Common	Episcopal (BCP)
Deut. 26:1-11	Deut. 8:1-3, 6-10, (17-20)
Psalm 100	Psalm 65 or Ps. 65:9-14
Phil. 4:4-9	James 1:17-18, 21-27
John 6:25-35	Matt. 6:25-33

Even though the roots of Thanksgiving may be biblical, the day that is now overwhelmingly secular and civil presents preachers with an interesting challenge. How does one move through the political back to the biblical roots? How do we praise and thank God for the good gifts that have been given to us as God's people without also equating a particular nation as the "chosen people"? We do have much for which to give thanks; how do we help people to adopt a posture of gratitude?

> HOW DO WE PRAISE AND THANK GOD FOR THE GOOD GIFTS THAT HAVE BEEN GIVEN TO US AS GOD'S PEOPLE WITHOUT ALSO EQUATING A PARTICULAR NATION AS THE "CHOSEN PEOPLE"?

FIRST READING

DEUTERONOMY 26:1-11 (RCL)

Although cast as an address and instruction by Moses, Deuteronomy—the "second law"—was the attempt by the now firmly settled Israelites to reinterpret that law during a period of religious reform. How were they to praise and thank God? How were they to remember what God had done for them, keeping God as the center of their lives? How were they to remember that the food they ate came from God's all-gracious hands and not theirs alone? These were important questions for them and are equally important questions for us.

This portion of the address first describes the liturgical action. Placing it in the future, "when you come into the land which the Lord your God gives you" (v. 1), which in reality they are already living, they were to take some of the firstfruits and place them in a basket. Then they were to present it to the priest who would, in turn, place it on the altar of God. It should be remembered that a significant goal of Deuteronomy was to affirm that the Temple in Jerusalem was the central place of worship:

You shall seek the place that the LORD your God will choose out of all your tribes as his habitation to put his name there. You shall go there, bringing there your burnt offerings and your sacrifices, your tithes and your donations . . . And you shall eat there in the presence of the LORD your God, you and your households together, rejoicing in all the undertakings in which the LORD your God has blessed you. (Deut. 12:5-7)

Through this liturgical action they would be reminded that God had given them the land, these fruits, and their very lives. The liturgical prescriptions identify the responsibilities of the people (the farmers), the liturgical officers, the priests (the only ones who may appear before God), and the place where this is to occur, "the place that the LORD your God will choose as a dwelling for his name" (v. 2).

Second, the address describes not only what must be done, but also why. The second portion of today's passage reminds the people why they are doing this—by rehearsing their own salvation history. As the priest places their basket on the altar, their liturgical response is "A wandering Aramean was my father" (v. 5, RSV), perhaps one of the oldest passages in scripture. That Aramean, Jacob, is spoken of as their father, not as their "ancestor." They recall how *they* were in Egypt, *they* were in slavery, *they* were brought out and into this wonderful promised land. It is not the distant, dim, anonymous past; it is their own personal history.

> THROUGH THIS LITURGICAL ACTION THEY WOULD BE REMINDED THAT GOD HAD GIVEN THEM THE LAND, THESE FRUITS, THEIR VERY LIVES.

Are we able to remember what God has done for us and be thankful? Those who celebrated the first Thanksgivings did so to place themselves firmly in the lineage of those people who presented baskets of firstfruits on the altars at the places of God's choosing. They understood themselves as being led out of slavery and oppression and into this promised land.

What are your firstfruits? That is an easier question to answer when you are part of an agricultural community, or a farmer, or even someone who has a small garden. I usually try to plant a few tomato plants so that, at the end of the summer, I can eat a tomato that really tastes like a tomato (rather than a red tennis ball). When you are involved in planting, tending, and harvesting crops, you know when the firstfruits come in. But it is not so easy to identify for those of us who work in jobs or professions that have nothing to do with the land, where we earn a salary not a crop, and where we do the same job year round. How, then, do we know what is ours and what is God's? How do we honor and "give back" to the Lord that which is the Lord's? Turkeys, mashed potatoes, and pumpkin pie are wonderful symbols once a year, but what about the other 364 days?

DEUTERONOMY 8:1-3,6-10,(17-20)(BCP)

It may be difficult to preach about not "living by bread alone" on a day devoted to eating too much. But Thanksgiving is actually a wonderful opportunity to invite people to reflect on our relationship with God and the ways that God meets our needs and how we are to respond to such gracious love.

This portion of Moses' address begins with the admonition that if the people of Israel are going to possess the land God has promised, there are certain things that they must do to complete their part of the bargain/covenant. Many chapters in Deuteronomy lay out the instructions by which the people will be able to fulfill their commitment to God. They are not to associate with people of other religions and they are to destroy religious idols. Sitting down at a Thanksgiving table with another nation is not one of the instructions. Nevertheless, we are encouraged by this passage to reflect on the great things that God has already done for us, with the assumption that God will continue to do these things for us in the future. The focus is not on creation and the natural order; rather, it is on the release from captivity and slavery in Egypt and the trip through the desert.

A particular focus is on manna and the way that God fed the people while they were on their journey toward the promised land. Lest pride overtake them, those traveling in the wilderness were allowed to go hungry so that "he might humble you, testing you to know what was in your heart, whether you would keep his commandments" (v. 2). The knowledge that hunger and privation were the testings of God rather than failure might have proved rather comforting to those living in a new land. If they thought that hunger was a testing, and they knew that they would prove worthy, that would have been a sign of hope. The passage ends in a wonderful message of hope and plenty. Manna may have been the food in the time of testing, but that was to be replaced quickly with wheat, barley, fig trees, pomegranates, olive trees, and honey. Manna may have lasted only a day, spoiling if saved, but if they proved worthy, they would soon find themselves in a land "where you may eat bread without scarcity, where you will lack nothing" (v. 9). That would have been good news to those early settlers, and it continues to be good news to us. An important question, however, is what we, today, would interpret as a life in which we lack nothing. Is that a life in which there is a roof over our head, clothing on our backs, and food on the table? Or does that mean a mansion, designer clothes, and gourmet food?

PSALM 100 (RCL)

The Deuteronomic law instructed the people of God to bring their first-fruits to the temple and there present them to the priests who would lay their offerings on the altar of God. What a joyous celebration and feast that meant. The food was not left on the altar to spoil; rather, it was then prepared and eaten by those in attendance. As one author observed, it was a "religious barbecue"!

I must confess that I am glad we don't have to eat all of our Thanksgiving meal in one day. Half of the fun is the leftovers. Turkey sandwiches and cold stuffing the next day allow us to continue the feast long after everyone has gone home. But there was a sense that manna and sacrificial offerings could not remain as "leftovers." We pray, "Give us this day our daily bread" to help us appreciate that, daily, our lives are in God's hands, and that God will provide for those daily needs. We do not store up God's grace; rather, we turn to God daily to sustain us.

> THIS PSALM WAS SUNG AS PEOPLE APPROACHED THE ALTAR TO PRESENT THEIR OFFERINGS, GIVING THANKS FOR ALL THAT GOD HAD DONE FOR THEM AND INVITING ALL TO JOIN IN THE CELEBRATION.

This psalm was sung as people approached the altar to present their offerings, giving thanks for all that God had done for them and inviting all to join in the celebration.

PSALM 65 or 65:9-14 (BCP)

See the discussion of this psalm for October 24, Proper 25.

Although we have beautiful churches that enliven and enrich our worship together, it is difficult for us to appreciate the meaning that the Jerusalem Temple had for those Israelites who worshiped there. The Temple was not only the nexus of their worship; it was the very dwelling place of God.

God was not far off in some distant heaven peering down, however lovingly, on the created world. When the people spoke of the temple as God's heavenly courts and house, they meant that God was right there in their midst. The psalm celebrates all of the things that this very present God has done for them. God has watered their crops and provided the wonderful bounty that will feed them. The psalm provides a portrait of a God who provides not just enough, but more than enough, full to overflowing.

SECOND READING
PHILIPPIANS 4:4-9 (RCL)

Paul may encourage us to rejoice, but does Paul know what kind of week, month, year, decade that we have had? He reminds us that we should not be anxious, but how can we not be anxious when we live in such a world as ours? I might suggest that we have every reason to be anxious.

My son is graduating from high school in a few weeks, and we have been thinking about all of the crises that he and his classmates have experienced in their four years of high school. They have lived through the panic and sorrow after September 11, 2001. Their high school is only a few miles from the Pentagon. They heard the low-flying plane when it went right over their high school and the crash as it smashed into the Pentagon. My son then had to walk through deserted streets, past armed National Guard soldiers, to get home that day. The high school is also just a few short blocks from the postal facility that is still closed because it is contaminated by anthrax. Many of the soccer and football games of last fall were canceled out of fear that the Beltway sniper might target them as they played. And the spring of this year was marked by war in Iraq and SARS. What does Paul mean that we should not be anxious but thankful? How can we do that? In his book *Listening to Your Life,* Frederick Buechner observes that "anxiety and fear are what we know best."[4] And, he notes, we are much more comfortable hearing bad news than good.

Paul knew suffering and grief. He also knew that the message of the cross and tomb and the message that Christ is risen are the messages that allow us to "rejoice in the Lord, always." And if we keep our eyes on that hope, that message that death is not the end, that God always has the last word, then we are able to lay aside the anxiety that can so easily hold us captive.

Paul's concluding doxology opens with the admonition to keep one's eyes fixed on the things of God. These are things that are true, honorable, just, pure, lovely, gracious, excellent, and worthy. This, again, is a difficult challenge for a world that is scarred by so much ugliness and hate. Still, we are able to recognize those moments of grace that shine through the difficulties of life that seek to cloud our vision of God's reign.

We don't know fully what the first Thanksgiving meal was like. I suspect it didn't look like the Thanksgiving posters or greeting cards of today. The settlers probably looked pretty bedraggled and worn. They had been, and would continue to be, living day to day, trusting that the food would hold out longer than the bad weather. But I imagine there was a moment of grace and hope when they realized they were able to sit down at the table and share a meal with those who had helped them learn how to live in this new place. This was a moment when they were able to direct their attention to the gracious and excellent God who had brought them this far. Remembering them invites us to do the same. Paul encouraged the Philippians to think of him and what they had seen him do; Thanksgiving invites us to do the same with our fathers and mothers, whomever they were and whenever they built a new life.

JAMES 1:17-18, 21-27 (BCP)

As Christians we walk a fine line between grace and works-righteousness. Paul saw how destructive and impossible it is when we try to live a life dependent on ourselves rather than on God. Likewise, James saw how misdirected it would be if we only listened to the good news but did not live it out in our daily lives.

When we present the firstfruits of our labors, we recall just that, our labors. Whether that labor involves tilling, planting, and tending fruit of the earth, or teaching, constructing, healing, or manufacturing, we work long and hard. Yet, in the midst of that, James encourages us to remember that it is only by the gifts and graces of God that we are able to bring forth those fruits.

I remember the first day I came home from a real, 7:00 A.M. to 3:30 P.M., job. I was working as a housekeeper in a hospital and had spent the day making beds, cleaning bathrooms, and washing floors. I could not believe how hard I had worked, and as I sat at the kitchen table talking to my mother who was making dinner, I fell asleep right there in the chair. Work is all-consuming, and we can all too easily think that we are responsible and in charge of what happens to us. Isn't that, after all, what the workplace encourages us to do? But James challenges us to rethink that image. We are coworkers with God. We need to work, but the gifts, the fruit of what we are doing, come because God has sent them.

THE GOSPEL
JOHN 6:25-35 (RCL)

Mark, Luke, and John tell us that five thousand men were fed. Matthew tells us that not only were there five thousand men but also women and children. They all mention the five loaves and two fish. John further qualifies it by noting they were barley loaves, reminiscent of the time that the prophet Elisha fed one hundred men with only twenty loaves of barley and fresh ears of grain that a man from Baal-shalishah had brought as his firstfruits offering (2 Kings 4:42-44). The evangelists also note that, as in the day of Elisha, there was more than enough food so that they gathered up what remained, and it "filled twelve baskets" (John 6:13).

But each of the Gospel writers wants us to know that there was a time when Jesus—out in a lonely place, a wilderness—fed a great throng of people, turning next to nothing into plenty.

Why do we follow God? Do we follow because our stomachs are full and our needs are met? Do we believe because no great calamities befall us or "because we ate our fill of the loaves?" (John 6:26). Following the account of the feeding of the five thousand, John inserts a lengthy discourse by Jesus that cautions against misinterpretation. Jesus performed this miracle so that they might have a sign that he is the true bread that comes down from heaven. But they are so short-sighted that they see only the physical bread that has slaked their hunger.

This wonderful miracle had occurred, and a great multitude had been fed. Jesus should not have been surprised, then, that people came looking for him, hoping to see more, hear more, and be fed. When they found him, he did not feed them with food that would perish. This time he fed them only with his word and with the knowledge that he alone had "come down from heaven, and gives life to the world" (v. 33).

> JESUS PERFORMED THIS MIRACLE SO THAT THEY MIGHT HAVE A SIGN THAT HE IS THE TRUE BREAD THAT COMES DOWN FROM HEAVEN.

If there was truly a first Thanksgiving feast, it was a meal of thanksgiving to God for all of the great gifts that had come the pilgrims' way—the gift of life, of food, of perseverance and endurance. The pilgrims were grateful for God's presence among them and God's continued support. All too often today our Thanksgiving meals focus more on the food that perishes than on "the food which endures to eternal life" (v. 27). How do we turn the attention of our people away from the transient and back to the imperishable? Too many of us have come to think of this day as a celebration of those brave people who came to a new land. Just as the children in the wilderness saw Moses as the source of their daily manna, we focus on the deeds of our pilgrim ancestors rather than on the God who gives all.

Where do we experience that eternal bread in our lives? When we are seated around our Thanksgiving feast, we may look up from the food and into the eyes of our family and friends. There we will see one way that God continues to feed and support us. It is not with turkey and mashed potatoes, but through the friendship and fellowship of others.

MATTHEW 6:25-33 (BCP)

Although this Gospel reading is yoked with the lection from James, the theme of anxiety is discussed above in the RCL second reading, from Paul's letter to the Philippians. The preacher may wish to refer back to that discussion.

In the Sermon on the Mount, Jesus proclaims what it means to live in God's realm. In this section he explores our attitude toward the material world and material things. He challenges our human tendency to worry and fret about every little thing because that betrays our trust in God and reveals our dependence upon ourselves. This section also reminds us that ours is a God of abundance who is always showering grace and love upon us.

This Gospel passage goes right to my heart. I must have been born with the worrying gene. I wish that it was only about the big things, but I worry about everything, big and little. Yes, I worry if my children will be successful, but I also worry whether I locked the car or turned off the stove. And while I am worrying, I also know that Jesus is correct, my worrying does not "add one cubit to [my] span of life" (v. 27). Only God can add one cubit to our lives. So Jesus is inviting us to live into God's gracious love, recognizing that just as God takes care of the plants of the field and birds of the air, so too will God take care of us.

> ONLY GOD CAN ADD ONE CUBIT TO OUR LIVES. SO JESUS IS INVITING US TO LIVE INTO GOD'S GRACIOUS LOVE, RECOGNIZING THAT JUST AS GOD TAKES CARE OF THE PLANTS OF THE FIELD AND BIRDS OF THE AIR, SO TOO WILL GOD TAKE CARE OF US.

This is also a lesson about priorities. It is not necessarily telling us that we have to give up our homes and our clothes, and live out in the fields. Rather, Jesus is reminding us that if we keep our hearts and minds firmly fixed on God's reign in our lives, things will fall into place. Instead of trying to keep up with our neighbors, watching what they wear, drive, or eat, we are to be keeping up with God. Thanksgiving is the moment to reset our priorities and think about God's abundance, not our own.

Thanksgiving can be a wonderful opportunity for our congregations to reflect upon the ways that they live out God's word. How does my church, my congregation, make the word come alive today in our community? How does it celebrate God's abundance? How does it celebrate and give thanks for the new life that it has received by reaching out to those who continue to sit in darkness? God has given us the gift of life. For that we should be always thankful, everyday, not just today.

Notes

1. Madeleine L'Engle, *The Irrational Season* (New York: Seabury Press, 1977) 108.

2. Kathleen Norris, *Amazing Grace: A Vocabulary of Faith* (New York: Riverhead Books, 1998), 367.

3. Rowan Williams, *Resurrection: Interpreting the Easter Gospel* (Harrisburg, Pa.: Morehouse, 1982) vii.

4. Frederick Buechner, *Listening to Your Life: Daily Meditations with Frederick Buechner,* complied by George Connor (San Francisco: Harper, 1992).

APRIL 2004

Sunday	Monday	Tuesday	Wednesday	Thursday	Friday	Saturday
				1	2	3
4	5	6	7	8	9	10
					Good Friday	
11 Easter Day	12 Easter Monday	13	14	15	16	17
18 2 Easter	19	20	21	22	23	24
25 3 Easter	26	27	28	29	30	

MAY 2004

Sunday	Monday	Tuesday	Wednesday	Thursday	Friday	Saturday
						1
2 4 Easter	3	4	5	6	7	8
9 Mother's Day 5 Easter	10	11	12	13	14	15
16 6 Easter	17	18	19	20	21	22
23 7 Easter	24	25	26	27 Ascension Day	28	29
30 Pentecost	31 Memorial Day					

JUNE 2004

Sunday	Monday	Tuesday	Wednesday	Thursday	Friday	Saturday
		1	2	3	4	5
6 Trinity Sunday 1 Pentecost	7	8	9	10	11	12
13 2 Pentecost	14	15	16	17	18	19
20 3 Pentecost Father's Day	21	22	23	24	25	26
27 4 Pentecost	28	29	30			

JULY 2004

Sunday	Monday	Tuesday	Wednesday	Thursday	Friday	Saturday
				1	2	3
4 Independence Day 5 Pentecost	5	6	7	8	9	10
11 6 Pentecost	12	13	14	15	16	17
18 7 Pentecost	19	20	21	22	23	24
25 8 Pentecost	26	27	28	29	30	31

AUGUST 2004

Sunday	Monday	Tuesday	Wednesday	Thursday	Friday	Saturday
1	2	3	4	5	6	7
8 9 Pentecost	9	10	11	12	13	14
15 Mary, Mother of Our Lord 10 Pentecost	16	17	18	19	20	21
22 11 Pentecost	23	24	25	26	27	28
29 12 Pentecost	30	31				
 13 Pentecost						

SEPTEMBER 2004

Sunday	Monday	Tuesday	Wednesday	Thursday	Friday	Saturday
			1	2	3	4
5	6 Labor Day	7	8	9	10	11
12	13	14	15	16	17	18
19	20	21	22	23	24	25
26	27	28	29	30		

14 Pentecost

15 Pentecost

16 Pentecost

17 Pentecost

OCTOBER 2004

Sunday	Monday	Tuesday	Wednesday	Thursday	Friday	Saturday
					1	2
3 18 Pentecost	4	5	6	7	8	9
10 19 Pentecost	11	12	13	14	15	16
17 20 Pentecost	18	19	20	21	22	23
24 21 Pentecost	25	26	27	28	29	30
31 Reformation Day Halloween 22 Pentecost						

NOVEMBER 2004

Sunday	Monday	Tuesday	Wednesday	Thursday	Friday	Saturday
	1 All Saints Day	2	3	4	5	6
7 23 Pentecost	8	9	10	11 Veteran's Day	12	13
14 24 Pentecost	15	16	17	18	19	20
21 Christ the King 25 Pentecost	22	23	24	25 Thanksgiving Day	26	27
28 Last Pentecost	29	30				